REDCOATED
PLOUGHBOYS

REDCOATED PLOUGHBOYS

THE
VOLUNTEER BATTALION OF INCORPORATED MILITIA
OF UPPER CANADA
1813–1815

RICHARD FELTOE

DUNDURN
TORONTO

Editor: Jane Gibson
Copy Editor: Allison Hirst
Design: Jesse Hooper
Printer: Marquis

Library and Archives Canada Cataloguing in Publication

Feltoe, Richard, 1954-
    Redcoated ploughboys : the Volunteer Battalion of Incorporated Militia of Upper Canada, 1813-1815 / by Richard Feltoe.

Includes bibliographical references and index.
Issued also in electronic formats.
ISBN 978-1-55488-998-3

    1. Canada--History--War of 1812--Regimental histories. 2. Upper Canada. Volunteer Battalion of Incorporated Militia. I. Title.

FC442.F45 2012   971.03'4   C2011-903782-3

1   2   3   4   5   16   15   14   13   12

We acknowledge the support of the **Canada Council for the Arts** and the **Ontario Arts Council** for our publishing program. We also acknowledge the financial support of the **Government of Canada** through the **Canada Book Fund** and **Livres Canada Books**, and the **Government of Ontario** through the **Ontario Book Publishing Tax Credit** and the **Ontario Media Development Corporation**.

Care has been taken to trace the ownership of copyright material used in this book. The author and the publisher welcome any information enabling them to rectify any references or credits in subsequent editions.

J. Kirk Howard, President

Unless otherwise attributed, images are courtesy of the author. All maps were created by the author. The author holds the copyright to both the images and the maps.

Printed and bound in Canada.
www.dundurn.com

Dundurn
3 Church Street, Suite 500
Toronto, Ontario, Canada
M5E 1M2

Gazelle Book Services Limited
White Cross Mills
High Town, Lancaster, England
LA1 4XS

Dundurn
2250 Military Road
Tonawanda, NY
U.S.A. 14150

This work is offered as a salute to the memory of those men of the original regiment of the Incorporated Militia of Upper Canada and their families, who helped defend and preserve our fledgling nation when it was in peril; as well as the troops from both sides of the lines who served, sacrificed, and died as they loyally obeyed their country's call-to-arms in the North American War of 1812–1815.
It is also dedicated to the men and women of Canada's modern-day military services, who honourably and bravely continue that legacy as they serve our country around the world today.

Contents

ACKNOWLEDGEMENTS

THE COMPLETION OF THIS WORK WOULD HAVE been impossible to achieve without the support, dedication, and selfless efforts of more people than it is possible to properly credit within this space. Therefore, I must restrict myself to naming but a few, whilst saluting the many.

To Diane, my long-suffering, understanding, and lonely wife, who supported me as I "hermitted" myself away over the course of the years it took to research and write this book: "Sorry pet, I promise the next ones won't be so bad."

Next, to the many dedicated staff members of the museums, archives, and libraries that I visited to undertake the research for this work and who cheerfully assisted my searches to fruition and sometimes revealed previously unknown nuggets of history that I could include.

Penultimately, to the guidance and support provided by Barry Penhale and Jane Gibson, and to my copy editor Allison Hirst and director of design Jennifer Gallinger, the creative team at Dundurn, for turning this idea into a reality.

Finally, to the memory of Karen, the one who taught me to appreciate Canada's heritage legacy. Always my harshest editorial and literary critic, she was at the same time my staunchest supporter and fiercest proponent of the value of my writings. She may not have lived to see this work completed, but her spirit and love of our history and heritage lives on within it.

INTRODUCTION

For over thirty years, my wife and I have had the unusual experience of simultaneously living in two distinct eras of Canadian history. The first being the present day, with all of the advantages provided by its modern conveniences and comforts — but also a place where technological development seems intent on reshaping our world with no regard for the people in it, while reports of ecological, social, political, and economic threats dominate the "news" media.

The second is the early part of the nineteenth century, where dates and events are comfortably fixed in place by the details of history. As living history re-enactors, we "step back in time" to recreate and interpret aspects of our nation's heritage and history.

To an outsider, this living history activity may be dismissed as "dressing up and playing at soldiers," or more charitably as a simple matter of escapism and nostalgia for a simpler or slower-paced way of life. For it is true that in re-enacting we make and wear period-style clothing; we live at historic sites in tents or in the historic buildings; we cook our food over open fires, engage in mock battles, and hold social "teas" and dances where period music fills the air. But our research has led us to recognize that, far from being an idyllic alternative to the stresses and pressures of the modern era, the world of 1800–1815 was rife with change and conflict.

Technology and industrialisation was changing the world at an ever faster rate and many people had deep concerns and fears about this rapid technological development creating a catalogue of social and economic disruptions. These included: commercial bankruptcies and worker unemployment in older, "obsolete" industries; banking failures through over-extended debts and investment "bubbles"; international economic slumps and inflation ruining national economies; and climate and weather changes leading to droughts and crop failures. They also had to contend with growing government monitoring of and interference in daily life. Not to mention political corruption undermining the confidence of the electorate in its representatives — all issues that we in the twenty-first century can easily identify with.

Consequently, far from simply viewing re-enacting as some form of escape, I and others within the living history community have come to hold a deep-seated appreciation and respect for these earlier people and the challenges they faced and overcame — without any of the "essential" technologies that we rely on today.

As if this was not enough, all the issues identified above were complicated by what may be considered the first real worldwide military conflict, known then as the Long War, and today collectively as the Napoleonic Wars. One part of that conflict was the North American War of 1812–1815, commonly referred to as the War of 1812. Within that smaller war, the region of Upper Canada (now Ontario) suffered at least a dozen full-scale invasions and countless raids and sorties by American military forces. In fact, more fighting took place in Upper Canada than anywhere else on the North American continent.

To defend their colony, all men of eligible age were required to serve as part of Upper Canada's part-time militia regiments. Others went a step farther, and volunteered to enlist in a full-time military force known as the Battalion of Incorporated Militia of Upper Canada. While this regiment only existed for two years, and was officially disbanded at the end of the conflict, its participation in and contribution to the events of the war was significant. Furthermore, many of its officers and men became prominent and influential members of their postwar communities and, in some cases, helped to mould the future destiny of the province of Ontario and of Canada.

As a museum curator, academic research has always been a natural part of my interests and activities. However, as a living history re-enactor, in-depth, detailed historical research became essential to ensure that our subsequent historical presentations might be rendered as accurately as possible. As a result, I eventually built up a significant dossier of information on a wide range of topics that became a reference source that other re-enactors, heritage organizations, museums, and historic sites found valuable. This, in turn, led to my being requested to provide answers on various questions of historical authenticity or information, to undertake public speaking engagements, and produce reference articles and research papers. Throughout these activities, numerous people suggested that I should write a book about this "stuff" for the bicentennial. So I did!

BACKGROUND

MEASUREMENT AND PRICING SYSTEMS IN EARLY NINETEENTH-CENTURY CANADA

To the younger generation, the metric system has become the standard for almost all calculations.

Writing an historical book that contains many references in the earlier Imperial system requires some form of conversion method for today's readers in Canada. There are a host of web-based sites that will provide mathematical calculations and conversions for those wishing to undertake the exercise, but for simplicity's sake, the following tabulations should be useful.

Distance:
1 inch (in.): 2.54 centimetres
12 inches (ins.) equals 1 foot (ft.): 0.30 metres
3 feet (ft.) equals 1 yard (yd.): 0.91 metres
1,760 yards (yds.) equal 1 mile: 1.60 kilometres

Weight:
1 ounce (oz.): 28.35 grams
16 ounces equal 1 pound (lb.): 0.45 kilograms
14 pounds (lbs.) equal 1 stone (st.): 6.35 kilograms
112 pounds equal 1 hundredweight (cwt.): 50.8 kilograms
20 hundredweight / 2,240 pounds equals 1 ton: 1.01 tonne

Volume:
1 pint (pt.): 0.57 millilitres
2 pints (pts.) equal 1 quart (qt.): 1.14 litres
4 quarts (qts.) equal 1 gallon (gal.): 4.55 litres

In the matter of money and pricing, however, things become somewhat more complicated. One has to not only understand the system of British currency used at the time (outlined below), but also the additional fact that the apparent pricing and monetary values given do not equate to "real" or modern purchase values. Although no absolute can be given, due to the number of variables involved, a multiplication factor of around 50 will come close to assessing 1812 values in terms of their modern equivalents in 2012.

Currency Denominations:
1 farthing (¼ d)
half-penny or ha'pny (½ d) pronounced "hay-p-nee"
penny or pence (d) "punse"
shilling (s)
pound (£)
guinea (G)

Values:
4 farthings to the penny
2 half-pennies to the penny
12 pence to the shilling
20 shillings or 240 pence to the pound
1 pound and 1 shilling to the guinea

Writing monetary values was done in a linear form, with the smallest denomination on the right and progressively moving up through the scale of values to the left:

Two pence: 2d
Four pence and a half-penny: 4½d
One shilling and no pence: 1/-
One shilling and eight pence: 1/8
Fifteen shillings, six pence, and a half-penny: 15/6½d
One pound: £1/-/-

One pound, three shillings, eleven pence and a half-
    penny: £1/3/11½d
Eighteen pounds and four pence: £18/-/4

To further confuse matters, there was also a separate North American financial system based on the
decimalized dollar. In British North America this
was calculated on values established at Halifax, Nova
Scotia. Thus, in 1812, the standard exchange rate
stood at four "Halifax" dollars to the pound. An item
costing £1/-/- in 1812 would convert to $4:00 Halifax
or approximately $200.00 in purchase values for today.

THE 1812 BATTLEFIELD

To readers unfamiliar with the details of the military
uniforms, weapons, and systems of drill and manoeuvre referred to in this work, the facts presented
may not always make sense. This is not surprising, for
according to the current methods of waging war, the
concept of having your soldiers stand out in the open
in long straight lines, dressed in brightly coloured
uniforms and polished brass may be appropriate for
a parade square or a military tattoo. But to do it in
on a battlefield, only a short distance from a similar
line of enemy troops who are shooting at you, seems
contradictory to the survival of the individual fighting
man — suicidal, in fact! What must be understood,
however, is that the battlefield tactics of the early
nineteenth century were entirely different from that
of today and were based on technologies then available for weapons production.

Today, armies can sit miles apart and use radar,
satellite, and aerial reconnaissance, long-range
artillery, missiles, and air support to destroy entire
military formations in a matter of minutes. Under
these circumstances, battlefield camouflage and con-
cealment is an essential element of tactical deployment. By contrast, in 1812 there were no long-range
weapons of rapid-fire or mass destruction. Instead,
the heavy weaponry of the day consisted of cumbersome pieces of muzzle-loading cannon. Military
commanders had to rely on hauling their artillery
within clear visual range of the enemy to pound
them into submission, flight, or destruction — one
shot at a time.

In the same vein, combat troops of today carry a
lightweight personal firearm that usually incorporates
a rifled barrel, automatic loading and firing mechan-
isms, multiple-shot magazines, and other high-tech
gadgets that produce devastating rates of fire and
effective killing ranges covering hundreds of yards. In
contrast, apart from units equipped with the slightly
more accurate and longer-range, but significantly
slower-to-load rifled weapons of the day, the standard
infantry weapon for most armies in 1812 was a heavy,
muzzle-loading, smoothbore flintlock musket. This
weapon had an extreme killing range of less than 250
yards, was basically inaccurate beyond 150 yards, and
had a single-shot capability that even under ideal conditions took at least fifteen seconds to reload. Climatic
variables, such as wind and rain, or mechanical problems such as dull flint, powder residues fouling the
ignition system, or a dozen other factors could also
reduce the firing rate for a musket from a satisfactory
eight successful ignitions out of ten times of pulling
the trigger to a frustrating one in ten. If one was lucky!

Because of these technological limitations, the only effective way to use an infantry force was to form the men into long lines that allowed the maximum number of muskets to be pointed at the enemy. This formation would then be marched to an effective firing range and, upon the word of command, fire a massed volley of soft lead musket balls toward the enemy, before going through the complicated process of reloading and firing again. The enemy, using virtually the same technologies and weaponry, was obliged to use the same tactics and formations in its attempt to achieve victory.

This produced the classic Napoleonic battlefield, with lines and columns of troops moving as unified formations, firing at fairly close range and generally ignoring the self-preserving method of lying down or sheltering behind a solid object to fire.

That is not to say that these latter tactics were not used. In fact, the terrain and dense forests of Upper Canada encouraged the use of smaller and more manoeuvrable formations of soldiers, referred to as "light" troops. These men were trained to fight as both line infantry and as independent detachments, moving and fighting as circumstances and opportunity dictated. This style of fighting was also used extensively by the Native allies, who perhaps had a more modern concept of how fighting an enemy should be conducted, using hit-and-run tactics. The fact remains that, except in specific instances, the traditional linear and column formations prevailed as the principal functional units for large-scale military engagements throughout the War of 1812–1815.

Under these conditions — with contending armies standing in the open, less than five hundred yards apart — the use of camouflage or low-visibility uniforms becomes irrelevant. Instead, it was the function of the uniform to make the wearer look taller, broader, and more imposing to the enemy. As well, the repeated firing of the weapons produced a dense cloud of grey-white smoke that, in the absence of a breeze, could thicken to the point where visibility was reduced to a few yards, creating the oft-referred-to "fog of war" that bedeviled many commanders during the course of an engagement.

Without the support of radio or electronic communication, it was vital for senior officers to be able to correctly identify distant troop movements and maintain control of their own formations as a battle progressed. Thus, the use of distinct national styles and highly visible uniform colours provided a means of identification and control in the chaos of a battlefield. Likewise, the addition of highly visible regimental "colours" (flags) served on the one hand as a valuable rallying point for soldiers and an indication of where a regiment's commander and senior officers would generally be located, while on the other as a perfect point-of-aim for enemy fire!

STYLE CONSIDERATIONS

Writing a military history and using quotes from original documents from another era often presents challenges. One is dealing with historical personalities, each with varied levels of education and skills of writing and spelling, much of which does not correspond to our own modern forms. The references to official military formations, regimental affiliations, ranks and appointments, battlefield tactics and manoeuvres, and so on, may appear alien to readers not familiar with the subject, and place names may have changed.

Directly quoted material has been checked repeatedly to ensure its accuracy and is presented as found in the original documents, without drawing attention to variant spellings. Generally recognized military terms are presented "as is" in the quotes; some of the more archaic words or jargon in the text are either followed by a modern equivalent word or referenced in a separate glossary of terms.

With the two principal combatant nations both using a system of numbers to designate their regiments, many modern-day writers have had to develop a system to maintain a clear identity for their readers, a convention that I have adopted. Here, British regimental numbers are shown as numerals (41st Regiment, 89th Regiment) and where required, with their subsidiary titles (1st [Royal Scots] Regiment, 8th [King's] Regiment). The American regiments are expressed as words (First Regiment, Twenty-Fifth Regiment).

Where place names often appear with a number of variants (e.g. Sackett's Harbour, Sacket's Harbour, Sackets Harbor, or Sacket's Harbor), one version was chosen based on a judgment of what was felt to be the predominant version used at the time, in this case Sackets Harbor. Where names have changed entirely, or would cause needless confusion (Newark became Niagara, and is now Niagara-on-the-Lake), the name that would clarify the location and simplify identification overall or a reference to the modern name (Crossroads becoming Virgil) is used.

On the maps, the formations of the units involved are shown graphically as follows:

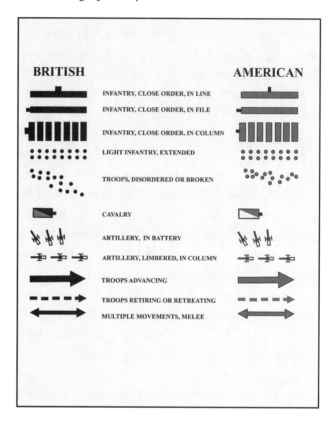

LIST OF MAPS

PART I:

THE WAR BEGINS

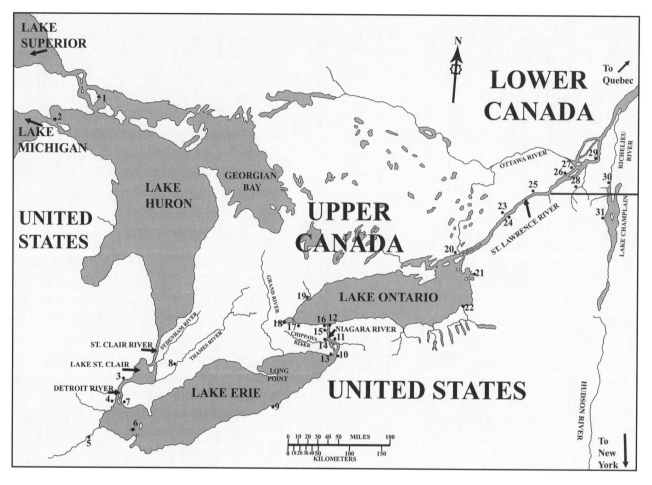

The "Northern Frontier" of the War of 1812–1815.

1. St. Joseph Island
2. Mackinac Island
3. Detroit
4. Brownstown
5. Perrysburg
6. Put-in-Bay
7. Amherstburg
8. Moravianstown

9. Presque Isle/Erie
10. Buffalo/Black Rock
11. Fort Schlosser
12. Fort Niagara
13. Fort Erie
14. Chippawa
15. Queenston
16. Newark

17. Stoney Creek
18. Burlington Heights
19. York
20. Kingston
21. Sackets Harbor
22. Oswego
23. Prescott
24. Ogdensburg

25. Crysler's Farm
26. Coteau-du-Lac
27. Cedars
28. Chateauguay
29. Montreal
30. Isle au Noix
31. Plattsburg

1

THE ROAD TO WAR

IN THE AFTERMATH OF THE AMERICAN COLONIAL rebellion, or as the victors preferred to call it, the American Revolution, the map of North America was completely redrawn, with a new border created between the United States of America and the still-loyal colonies of British North America. Though technically at peace, these new neighbours were more than a little wary of each other's intents and ambitions, and for several years after, a succession of political and military issues maintained a state of tension between them.

Foremost among these issues was that of the Loyalist colonials who had fought for the King during the war. The persecution heaped upon them by the victorious rebels made their continued stay in the United States virtually impossible. As a result, they were forced to abandon their homes and property and flee the country. While many went to Great Britain, others moved north to the relative safety of British North America, taking with them long memories of the injustices and persecution suffered at the hands of their former neighbours or even family members who had sided with the "rebels."

In recompense, the British government assigned these Loyalist families large tracts of land within the undeveloped regions of its Canadian colonies, including Upper Canada, thus establishing the core of what they hoped would become an entirely patriotic population.

However, during the first few years of the nineteenth century, increasing numbers of Americans also settled within Upper Canada, bringing with them their Republican sentiments. This new influx generated resentment within the community of Loyalist families and their descendants, splitting the population into rival camps. This had tragic consequences when war finally arrived. It also created security problems for the thinly stretched British military forces detailed to defend the border against any potential American aggression. Successive lieutenant-governors frequently recorded their unease at the increasing influence and pervasive opinions of these members of the Upper Canada population who held that their allegiance was to the United States, not the King, and who openly saw the annexation of Upper Canada by the American republic as merely a matter of time or opportunity.

Nor was this opportunity wanting, for Great Britain had been at war with France since February 1793 (apart from a short period of peace in 1802–03). This Long War, as it was called, had brought the nation to the brink of bankruptcy as it sought to pay for its ongoing military policies and campaigns. Britain's domestic economy was also in a state of crisis, the result of the combined effects of a severe economic depression and a succession of crop failures. Thus, already fully occupied, the British government failed to appreciate issues developing in North America — in particular, its relationship with the government of the United States.

Within that country, the westward expansion of white settlement into the previously off-limits treaty lands held by the Native populations of the Ohio, Michigan, and Kentucky regions was being met with armed resistance. Sending in the military had not helped, as these units frequently found themselves outnumbered and outfought. The U.S. military excused their inability to suppress the "savages" by claiming that the British were abetting them. Politicians from these western territories, wishing to accommodate future expansionist pressures, loudly advocated the invasion of British North America to isolate the Natives, thus causing them to be more vulnerable and more amenable to relinquishing their claims on the land and its resources. For other American politicians and hard-line nationalists, any British colonial presence on the continent of North America was seen as a stain on American pride, preventing the dream of creating a single continent-wide country, and blocking America's right to take its place as an equal on the world political and military stage.

At a more mundane level, there were also economic reasons to drive the British from North America. Cut off from its vital timber resources in the Baltic by the armies of Napoleon Bonaparte, the British government had turned to the vast forests of its North American colonies, including Upper Canada, to supply timber to the Royal Navy and to British industry. This development threatened the existing mercantile monopolies on the American east coast, who consequently pressured their government to bring those valuable economic resources under direct American control.

Another point of conflict arose from the fact that, while Napoleon's armies dominated the landmass of Europe, the British navy "ruled the waves," thereby controlling the world's ocean trade routes. As neither side could achieve a decisive military victory, both combatants resorted to economic warfare. France sought to exclude Great Britain from trading with any of the countries in Europe, while Britain effectively swept the French merchant marine from the seas. To circumvent these actions, both sides used intermediary and neutral shipping, a situation the Americans were quick to exploit; the United States soon gained control of most of the transatlantic shipping trade and reaped huge profits from both sides of the European conflict.

Over time, however, this lucrative income was threatened as the warring parties sought to inflict additional economic damage on the other. Through the implementation of the terms contained in Napoleon's Berlin Decree of 1806 and Milan Decree of 1807, France and all subject nations under Napoleon's jurisdiction were banned from trading with Great Britain. Britain responded to these decrees by imposing a total naval blockade on all ports under French control.

Pressure to maintain their new economic advantage, coupled with a determination not to bow to foreign decrees, led the Americans into direct confrontation with both countries. Interestingly, while the policies of both nations had a severe economic impact for American interests, it was those involving British actions that were repeatedly highlighted by anti-British American newspapers, resulting in an inevitable rise in public demand for retribution.

The rapid growth in American mercantile traffic had also created a shortage of experienced sailors and a corresponding rise in pay rates. This led to an increase in the already serious rate of British sailors deserting from the brutality of the Royal Navy in favour of the relatively more lenient American trading vessels. Determined to recover these deserters, and rejecting the concept that any British citizen had the right to

relinquish or change his nationality, the Royal Navy flouted international convention and strained maritime legalities to the breaking point by stopping and boarding American vessels to search for British nationals. This activity culminated in the international incident of the British warship HMS *Leopard* firing broadsides into the USS *Chesapeake* (June 22, 1807), compelling her to heave-to and submit to being boarded for the purpose of searching for British deserters.

By 1807, the fact that the legitimate grievances of the American government (citing that these searches also netted U.S. citizens) were met with blunt indifference from the British government brought the two countries to the brink of war. President Thomas Jefferson, faced with the difficult choice of declaring war or submitting to the economic pressures of both France and Great Britain, retaliated by introducing a succession of increasingly draconian and economically catastrophic *Embargo Acts*. These measures effectively quarantined the United States from all international trade and cut off all revenue derived from shipping and export industries. Faced with economic ruin, the American populace across the northeastern seaboard reacted with anger, resulting in a huge increase in organized smuggling and political unrest that threatened to topple the government.

The colonial authorities of British North America reacted to these incidents and the rising clamour for war being heard south of the border by implementing a series of new laws to formally establish a colonial militia army. This force would supplement the limited number of regular troops stationed in the colonies in the event of an American invasion.

In Upper Canada, the enactment became the *Militia Act* of 1808, and was passed by the fourth session of the fourth Parliament of the Upper Canada Legislature. This important document, written to establish the foundation of an entire system of military defence for the growing colony, contains a wealth of documentary details, all written in the expansive legal language common to the official governmental directives and documentation of any era. For the purposes of this work, however, the following synopsis of some of the clauses within it should suffice to clarify its intent:

- Every male between the age of sixteen and sixty and capable of bearing arms was to enrol for periodic training and subsequent militia duty within a new county-based regimental system that would see individual companies or regiments called out or "embodied" for varying periods of time as the individual circumstances required. These corps would be individually referred to according to their county name and collectively as regiments of "embodied militia." Those persons not enrolling would be fined 10/- (ten shillings) (Clause III).

- No man over the age of fifty was to be called upon for active service except in time of war. (Clause III)

- Commanding officers of regiments were to muster their men on June 4 of each year (unless that fell on a Sunday, whereupon it would occur on June 5) for a day-long course of military inspections and unit training, followed by a regimental parade and review. Fines were defined for failure to comply: officers refusing to attend, two pounds; fines for NCOs and privates, ten shillings. (Clause V)

- Regiments or individual companies were to be called out for additional training and inspections as necessary or required, subject to their annual inspection report. (Clause V)

- Because of the geographic dispersion of regimental companies across each county, captains of these companies were to subsequently call out their individual detachments between two and four additional times per year to inspect the men's firearms and to undergo separate military drill training. Fines for officers refusing to attend were set at two pounds; fines for NCOs and privates, ten shillings. (Clause VII)

- In case of war, the embodied militia was to be called out for duty and could be marched anywhere within the geographic boundary of the province for service. Fines for officers refusing to serve were set at fifty pounds and the loss of their commission; fines for NCOs and privates, twenty pounds, or jail for between six to twelve months. (Clause VII)

- No militiaman was to be embodied for active service for a period exceeding six months. (Clause VIII)

- The embodied militia was not to be called upon to serve outside of the boundary of Upper Canada except under the specific circumstances of:
  - going into Lower Canada in case of an invasion to repel the invader.
  - being in hot pursuit of an enemy invader.
  - destruction of enemy vessels or buildings that could be used for mounting an invasion.
  - pre-empting an enemy attack. (Clause VII)

- The local senior colonel would be authorized to call out detachments of the embodied militia without additional authorization in an emergency involving his immediate jurisdiction. He could commandeer carriages, wagons, and horses as the circumstances required, with compensation being given to their owners at a later date by the army. (Clause IX)

- Individuals called out for duty would be permitted to provide a volunteer substitute, subject to their passing the required medical approval. (Clause IX)

- Each regiment of the embodied militia was to be formed of between eight to ten companies, and each company of between twenty to fifty privates. (Clause X)

- Each regiment was to be commanded by two field officers, holding the respective ranks of colonel and major. Each company to be commanded by one captain, one lieutenant, and one ensign. (Clause X)

- Each regiment was to have an administrative staff of one adjutant and one quartermaster. Sergeants for each company were to be nominated by their respective captain. (Clause XI)

- Where there was insufficient manpower to form a complete regiment, "independent companies" were to be established, composed of between twenty and fifty men, and led by a captain, lieutenant, and ensign. (Clause XII)

- Where required, independent companies could be amalgamated to form ad hoc battalions or be attached as additional companies to existing formations of troops. (Clause XII)

- Each militiaman was to provide his own musket, rifle, or other type of firearm, plus a minimum of six rounds of ammunition — "powder and ball" — at each annual review, unless excused by the regimental commanding officer. Fines for failure to comply: five shillings at a review; two pounds in time of war. (Clause XIV)

- No embodied militia unit on active service was to serve continuously for more than six months. (Clause XXXII)

- Where no replacement unit was available to relieve the active unit, ballot lots were to be drawn from the remaining segments of the inactive (unembodied) militia force to match and replace the detachment then on service. (Clause XXXIII)

While sounding dramatic and martial in theory, the establishment of these part-time embodied militia regiments for the defence of Upper Canada turned out to be something entirely different in reality. The concept that a single yearly drill, followed by a series of small-scale practices could produce a military force capable of even resisting, never mind defeating, an enemy (read *American*) invasion force would be laughable if it were not so pitiable. Despite the intents and efforts of the local authorities, these annual reviews took on the aspect of not so much a military training exercise but more of a community holiday and social picnic. On the appointed day, the entire community would gather at a designated location to watch the men go through the motions of marching and arms drill — and laugh at the results. A communal meal would follow, with dancing, drinking, and usually a good old-fashioned brawl or two.

Meanwhile, in the United States, the continued westward expansion by white settlers into previously guaranteed Native territories provoked the formation of a confederation of tribes under the leadership of a charismatic Shawnee chief, Tecumseh (Leaping Panther) and his brother Lolawauchika (Loud Mouth), otherwise known as "The Prophet." In response, Governor William H. Harrison of the Indiana Territory began a series of military moves that culminated in the defeat of the Native alliance at the Battle of Tippecanoe on November 7, 1811. The surviving Native nations became firmly opposed to the Americans and saw any potential enemy of the American Republic as an ally to be secured.

During this period, the American congressional elections of 1810 resulted in the election of several vehemently anti-British representatives (later styled "War Hawks"), who were determined to precipitate a war against Great Britain. Gaining prominent positions on vital administrative committees, they formulated a succession of policies aimed at creating an atmosphere of crisis that would lead to war. Ostensibly using the claim of "Free Trade and Sailors Rights" as the basis for complaint, they swayed public opinion by making inflammatory speeches in the national legislature, publishing letters and editorials in the nation's press, and stigmatizing anyone who voiced an opposing opinion as being suspect or even traitorous. Ultimately, they effectively marginalized the issues with France and characterized Britain as a villainous bully that needed to be taught a lesson.

With this level of aggressive rhetoric thundering south of the border, it's not surprising that the British military authorities took a very serious look at what resources they could place in the way of any invading enemy force. The adoption of a single policy, or even a series of policies, however, was complicated by the fact that, instead of being a single unified country, British North America was rather a collection of individual colonies, each with its own governmental body and differing attitudes toward the prospect of engaging in a war with the United States.

In the event of war, official military documents claimed that the available complement of full-time regular British army troops, backed by its full-time colonial army equivalents, known as "fencible" regiments, amounted to some ten thousand men. In reality, such was the dominance of the policy of maintaining a defensive posture that the garrisons at Halifax, Quebec, and Montreal were manned by nearly 80 percent of these available troops and were supplied with a proportionate amount of the artillery, ammunition, and supplies. In contrast, Upper Canada was defended by little more than 1,200 men, scattered along a defensive frontier of over a thousand miles. Repeated pleas for additional manpower and supplies for the defence of Upper Canada, sent by Major General Isaac Brock, were repeatedly refused or excused away by his superior, Sir George Prevost, as being impossible to accomplish or a threat to the security of the lower colonies.

Left to his own devices, General Brock, being not only the senior military commander in Upper Canada but also the president of the civil administration of the province, implemented an amendment to the 1808 *Militia Act* to create a cadre of superior quality militia units called "flank" companies. These sub-units would be better trained and armed than their embodied equivalents. In case of war or invasion, they could be called out first and serve alongside the regular troops as a buffer force to delay the enemy until reinforcements from other parts of the province could arrive. The following points were included in the Repeal of the 1808 Militia Laws, passed at the first session, sixth Parliament of the Upper Canada Legislature, March 1812:

- In districts where embodied militia regiments had between five to ten companies, two of those companies would now be titled as flank companies, with a complement of between twenty to one hundred privates per company. (Clause IV)

- The two flank companies within each regiment were not to consist of more than one-third of the listed strength of the full embodied regiment. The men to serve as "flankers" were to be selected from those aged between eighteen and fifty and any deficiency in numbers was to be made up by the use of a ballot system from the remainder of men between the age of eighteen and sixty-five, excluding men with dependents who were the sole support for their families. (Clause VIII)

- Flank company captains were to initially call out their companies for a course of detailed training at least six times per month until the unit was deemed fully trained. Following which, successive training sessions were to be held at least once a month. During the continuance of peace, the remaining embodied "battalion" companies were to be called out for their training at least once a quarter. In case of war, this was then to be increased to once a month. (Clause XI)

- Whipping or flogging was prohibited as a form of punishment for infractions of duty.

Major General Sir Isaac Brock KB, J.W.L. Forster, artist, circa *1900. In 1812, Isaac Brock held the cumulative titles of senior military commander for Upper Canada, lieutenant-governor of Upper Canada and president of the Upper Canada Executive Council. News of his knighthood only arrived in Canada following his death.*

Sir George Prevost, S.W. Reynolds, artist, date not known. Appointed governor-in-chief and commander-in chief of the British forces in British North America in 1811, Sir George proved to be an able civil and political administrator. Unfortunately, his on-field military command capabilities were not as strong. Following flawed decisions made during the Plattsburg campaign of 1814, he was recalled to England at the end of the war to face a court martial inquiry. He died a month before the inquiry began.

Fortunately for General Brock, the increasing tension and rumours of impending war had raised the level of patriotic feeling within the embodied regiments to a point that, with the passing of this bill, it was not long before the rolls of the flank companies were filled and they began their appointed training.

On the other hand, the creation of a new elite grade of militia undermined the entrenched cliques of militia officers, who had previously dominated some of the embodied regiments and considered these units as their own private fiefdoms. As the new flank company system continued to be implemented, news of heated confrontations and letters of complaint from both the "new" flank officers and the "old" embodied officers arrived on Brock's desk.

Almost without exception, individuals who were later to serve in the Incorporated Militia fell into the "new" camp. For example, Abraham Rapelje (2nd Norfolk Militia), later captain of Company No. 2 of the Incorporated Militia, found himself embroiled in a conflict of words that led to him and his fellow reform officers being subjected to a smear campaign. Considering himself under attack, the regiment's lieutenant colonel, Robert Nichol, submitted a strongly worded letter on April 14, 1812, to Major General Aeneas Shaw on behalf of himself and his supporters, which read in part:

> While … I am using my utmost exertions and discretion to carry into full effect the intentions of His Honor Major General Brock, I feel that I shall require the countenance and support of the Executive Government to enable me to check those habits of insubordination which I am sorry to say have been but too prevalent in this part of the Province — I do not mean to attach the smallest blame to the men — on the contrary, I must say that they are exceedingly well disposed — but some of the ancient officers have conducted themselves in such a manner as to render it imperative on me to exhibit charges against them … and which will, I trust , appear … of sufficient consequence … to order a Court of Enquiry to investigate [and clear] the conduct of Lt. Colonel Ryerson, Captain Rapelje and myself.[1]

Nor was this the only incident of its kind. Brock's inspecting field officer of militia, Colonel Robert Lethbridge, during an official inspection tour of the militia regiments along the St. Lawrence Valley, wrote:

> Of the Militias of the Counties of Grenville, Dundas, Stormont, and Glengarry, I feel immense satisfaction in noting their uniform zeal to exert their best endeavours for the defence of their Country. Tho' in yet almost the infancy of discipline with

the exception of the Manual and Platoon exercise owing to the general want of instruction … The Dundas Militia are unhappily in a state of schism at least between the two Field Officers, Col. McDonnel and Major Merkley. The former certainly much advanced in years. The latter very shrew'd and I believe extremely able & zealous — Tho inflexibly stern. I beg leave to propose by way of healing the breach the substitution of Colonel Thomas Fraser to the command of the Dundas Militia.[2]

In response to these reports, Brock and the authorities moved quickly to remove the "ancient officers" from any positions where they could interfere with the establishment and training of the new flank companies across Upper Canada. This was just as well, for things were rapidly coming to a head in the United States, where the War Hawks' demands were reaching a fever pitch.

When the matter finally came to a vote on June 4, 1812, the United States was anything but united in its position, despite the efforts of the War Hawks. Party politics and strong regional opinions for and against a war created sharp divisions. The northern seaboard states (Massachusetts, Maine, Rhode Island, Connecticut, New York, and Delaware), supposedly where maritime issues mattered most, rejected the congressional vote and sent formal petitions of objection to the president. On the other hand, the inland states of Kentucky, Tennessee, and Ohio were strongly in favour of war, backed by the votes of New Hampshire, Vermont, Pennsylvania, Maryland, Virginia, North Carolina, South Carolina, and Georgia. Likewise, the U.S. Senate was divided in its vote of June 17, 1812.

Faced with these divisions and without an overwhelming majority vote in favour of war, President Madison initially hesitated to sign the declaration. However, circumstances changed quickly when urgent dispatches arrived from England reporting that the British prime minister, Spencer Perceval, had been assassinated by a lone gunman in the House of Commons on May 11. The British government was in a state of turmoil. Recognizing the advantage of the moment, Madison signed a declaration of war on June 18, 1812.

Although the Incorporated Militia was not officially formed as a regiment until 1813, many of its future officers, as well as more than one hundred men from the ranks, had already seen action during the early part of the war as part of the flank companies distributed across the province. These engagements ranged from small-scale skirmishes between patrols and detachments, through the larger actions at Detroit, Matilda, and Frenchman's Creek, to the first real battle of the war at Queenston Heights. These initial engagements were the first real opportunity for the flank company system to be tested in battle and subsequently provided the foundation of the decision to expand the still part-time flanker system into the full-time Incorporated Militia.

For the most part, it is not possible to isolate any particular actions made by individuals subsequently linked to the Incorporated Militia into the larger scheme of events, since they were generally serving in junior positions and did not rate a mention in official accounts and dispatches. However, their units were involved, and these men were there, gaining experience that would serve them in their future duties in the Incorporated Militia. To trace the later course of the war and the contribution made by the regiment, it is necessary to outline some of these early actions.

2

THE OPENING ROUND:
JUNE–OCTOBER 1812

IN UPPER CANADA, GENERAL BROCK EXPECTED that a declaration of war would result in the immediate transfer of regular troops to the likely points of invasion. Instead, following directives from England on the need to maintain a defensive posture and minimize the need for troops and supplies in the Canadian colonies, Prevost withheld these vital resources from Upper Canada.

If Brock could not rely on Prevost for substantial aid, neither could he expect any significant assistance from the Upper Canada Legislature, which was salted with several actively pro-American sympathizers who took every opportunity to block any legislation or expenditure designed to improve the defences of the colony. Similarly, the Upper Canada militias, who officially listed some 11,000 men of eligible age for

military duty in the event of war, were deemed to be of such dubious loyalty that Prevost stated: "it might not be prudent to arm more than 4,000."[1] In fact, it was recognized that the future security of British North America might depend on the tenuous alliance of the Native allies loyal to the British cause.

Following the official declaration of war in Washington on June 19, 1812, events began to occur at an increasing pace as notices were dispatched to the frontiers by a series of messengers. Although editorials on the imminence of war had filled the pages of American newspapers for months, once war had been officially declared, the British communications system proved to be more efficient. Consequently, detachments of British regulars and Canadian militia were able to capture a number of American vessels in the

St. Lawrence, Niagara, and Detroit Rivers. Similarly, farther north, the garrison at St. Joseph Island made a pre-emptive strike against the American base of Fort Michilimackinac (also referred to at the time and known today as Fort Mackinac). Totally unprepared, the Americans capitulated without a shot being fired.

According to local folklore, when the declaration of war was delivered to Fort George on the Niagara frontier, the officers of the British garrison were hosting American counterparts from Fort Niagara at a dinner in the officers' mess. In a show of courtesy, the British commander did not intern the now enemy officers. Instead, the dinner continued, with respective toasts being made and expressions of hope that a similar dinner could be held following the termination of hostilities. Following the meal, the American officers were permitted to return to Fort Niagara, there to prepare for war to commence the following day.

Despite these minor successes, the fact remained that the British position in Upper Canada was precarious in the extreme. Britain was attempting to wage war in Europe on a vastly greater scale, leaving little in the way of material resources or funds to be spared for North America. Nor could the local economies of the colonies provide the necessary agricultural or industrial resources to sustain any significant war effort on their own. As a result, virtually every item, from cannons to quill pens, uniforms to medical supplies, ammunition to thread, had to be diverted from the European theatre of war. Always under the constant threat of attack and capture, these goods had to be transported over a tenuous network of tortuous routes before being distributed to a series of remote bases, all without the availability of any effective road system.

In view of these obstacles, securing and defending the single lifeline of the St. Lawrence River and the Niagara corridor became a prime factor in the military planning of successive British commanders in Upper Canada. Unfortunately, each in his turn had to deal with Sir George Prevost's determination to retain the bulk of his manpower and supplies in Lower Canada, leaving Upper Canada to fend for itself.

THE DETROIT CAMPAIGN, JULY–AUGUST 1812

When hostilities finally commenced, the first invasion of the Canadas occurred far from the well-defended citadels of Montreal, Quebec, or Halifax. Instead, it happened on the Detroit frontier when the governor of the Michigan Territory, Brigadier General William Hull, with a combined force of some 1,500 regulars and militia, crossed from Detroit into Upper Canada on July 12, 1812. In contrast, the local British commander, Lieutenant Colonel St. George, had no more than three hundred regulars and a mixed body of half-hearted militia to defend the entire frontier area. Forced to conserve his limited resources and allow the invasion to commence unopposed, St. George sent an urgent message to General Brock for support.

The way was now open for a dynamic thrust by the Americans to secure the entire western end of the province and provide Washington with its demanded victory. Instead, apart from sending out detachments to strip the countryside of all available foodstuffs, General Hull ordered the rest of his army into a defensive enclave at Sandwich (modern-day Windsor), still within sight of Detroit. He also had printed and distributed a bombastic proclamation that condemned British "tyranny and oppression,"[2] and promised support to those of the local populace seeking to throw off their metaphoric shackles. He also sternly warned of the extreme consequences awaiting any who took up arms on behalf of the Crown, or were found fighting alongside the Native warriors, who were to be particularly targeted for imminent destruction.

After engaging in some minor skirmishing with the invaders, the British and their Native allies undertook a bold counteroffensive on the American side of the Detroit River, cutting off Hull's lines of communication at the small engagements at Brownstown and Maguaga. After receiving news of the loss of Michilimackinac and rumours that Brock was concentrating his forces on the Niagara, Hull abandoned his invasion and withdrew to Detroit on August 7, under a storm of protest from his more aggressively minded regimental commanders.

Meanwhile, General Brock had been preparing to meet Hull's army with force. Ignoring Prevost's orders to act with circumspection, his initial plan was to mobilize a corps of regulars, militia, and Natives, and march them to Amherstburg. However, the Six Nations on the Grand River declared their determination to remain neutral, while several units of the militia likewise refused to come forward as ordered. With a disturbingly sparse reserve of regular troops and only half-hearted support from the provincial legislature, Brock was left with no choice but to create a strike force composed of some forty regulars (41st Regiment) and 260 militiamen from the York and Niagara areas. (A comparison of existing militia records indicate this included around sixty men and at least three officers who later joined the Incorporated Militia.)

Brock left York (Toronto) and set out for Detroit on August 5. Marching across the Niagara Peninsula to Lake Erie, Brock personally addressed a gathering of over five hundred militiamen at Port Dover with such dynamism that, contrary to their earlier reluctance, the men volunteered en masse to follow him into battle. With only sufficient vessels to transport four hundred, Brock's small force climbed into barely seaworthy boats on August 8, while the remainder began the long march along the Talbot Road. The small flotilla of boats had to contend with atrocious weather, rough waters, and dangerous rock shoals, but eventually landed at Amherstburg on August 12, 1812.

After being briefed by Lieutenant Colonel St. George about widespread disaffection existing within the American army, Brock negotiated a pact with the Shawnee war chief Tecumseh for a counterattack on the American position at Detroit. Thus reinforced, on August 15, Brock began his offensive with an artillery bombardment of the American fort at Detroit from across the river at Sandwich (Windsor).

At dawn the next day, Brock's force of some three hundred regulars, four hundred militia, six hundred Natives, and five cannon crossed the Detroit River and marched on Fort Detroit. There, 2,200 American troops awaited them, entrenched behind a line of defences bristling with no less than thirty-three cannon. In a deft example of bravado and sleight of hand, Brock paraded his forces in front of the walls of the fort, spreading out his units to make them appear more numerous. As well, he made extensive use of Tecumseh's warriors to engage in psychological warfare by threatening attacks on the American flanks and notifying Hull that in the event of an onset of fighting he could not guarantee to control the bloodlust of his Native allies. Brock's ruses so demoralized General Hull that he soon entered into negotiations and, before noon, had surrendered the fort and his army. To cap off this singular victory, two sizable detached American forces returned to Detroit voluntarily and surrendered to Brock.

The American western army was now effectively eliminated. The biggest problem facing Brock was what to do with this overwhelming number of prisoners. Ultimately, most of the officers and regular troops, plus a select number of militia officers, were transported to Lower Canada, to remain there as prisoners of war or to be repatriated to the United States on parole until regularly exchanged for their British and Canadian equivalents. The remaining rank and file of the various state militias were freed, but only after agreeing not to engage in further offensive activities until formally released from their parole by a mutually agreed and signed written declaration by the two warring governments.

Despite this victory, Brock made a speedy return to the Niagara frontier in response to intelligence reports indicating a significant buildup of American forces at either end of the Niagara River. After arriving at Fort Erie, General Brock ordered that his prisoners be marched along the riverbank road, in plain sight of the gathering American forces on the east bank, possibly as a warning of their potential fate if they, too, attempted an invasion. It was a message that definitely carried some weight in the days to come.

THE BATTLE OF THE MATILDA, SEPTEMBER 16, 1812

While the action at Detroit was unfolding, the eastern portion of the province also saw action as detachments and units of regulars and militia from both sides engaged in small-scale probes and raids across the St. Lawrence River. However, on September 16, a larger engagement took place when a pair of American gunboats and an onshore force of around five hundred American militia attacked a convoy of British bateaux off Toussaint Island, near present-day Cardinal, Ontario. After running the cumbersome boats ashore on the adjacent Presqu'ile Island, the covering escort, composed of men from the flank company of the Dundas Militia, prepared to defend their cargo. Among these men were Ensign Duncan Clark (later lieutenant, Company No. 7) and seven men who later joined the Incorporated Militia. Witnessing the American gunboats, laden with troops and manoeuvring toward the far side of the island, Ensign Clark and his men crossed over the small island and "immediately fired on them with such effect that they retreated to Tusaut's island, a distance of about 100 yards, where they landed and took shelter in the woods, with the loss of one of their boats … which was taken possession of after drifting down the river by a party of the [Dundas] militia."[3]

Neither side could effectively outmanoeuvre or attack the other, thus the two groups remained in stalemate on the two islands, exchanging shots as targets of opportunity occurred. Meanwhile, the alerted Canadian militia on the north bank of the river was mobilizing to come to the convoy's aid:

> Captain Ault and Lieutenant Dorin were soon on the field of action with the remainder of the Company, as well as Captain Shaw with the men of the neighbourhood, and in a short time, the people of Matilda and many from Williamsburg assembled on Presq'uile Island with Colonel MacDonell commanding the Dundas Militia at the time. Such was the anxiety of the people to meet their old enemy, the Rebels of "76" that aged … veterans who had served under Sir William and Sir Johnson were foremost in the fight.[4]

The force was subsequently enhanced by the arrival of two companies of the Grenville Militia as well as a 9-pounder cannon, "under Lieutenant R.D. Fraser, whose well-directed shots, together with the fire of musketry kept up by the Dundas Militia, compelled the Americans to retire from their position on Tusaits Island and make a precipitate retreat to their own side of the St. Lawrence."[5]

After this action, Ensign Duncan Clark, Lieutenant John Fraser (1st Grenville Militia), plus thirty-eight other ranks subsequently joined the Incorporated Militia.

THE BATTLE OF QUEENSTON HEIGHTS, OCTOBER 13, 1812

Although the incident at Matilda was relatively insignificant and could be ignored, the debacle of General Hull at Detroit effectively derailed the 1812 American war effort. Desperate to create some kind of military success, the administration pressured General Henry Dearborn to produce positive results on the Niagara front to counter their failures elsewhere. Although it had only been a month since war had been declared, the American troops assembled on the Niagara frontier had already had already been led by two generals, William Wadsworth and Amos Hall.

On July 13, they gained their third new commander in the person of General Stephen Van Rensselaer. In taking up his command, Van Rensselaer discovered that, under his predecessors, an incompetent and corrupt supply system had left his troops without adequate food, clothing, or shelter. In addition, several of his militia regiments had balked at being ordered to go beyond their legal obligation to serve only within the geographic borders of the United States.

More serious, however, were the internal politics that saw a number of Van Rensselaer's subordinate officers consistently undermining his authority. Foremost amongst these culprits was Brigadier General

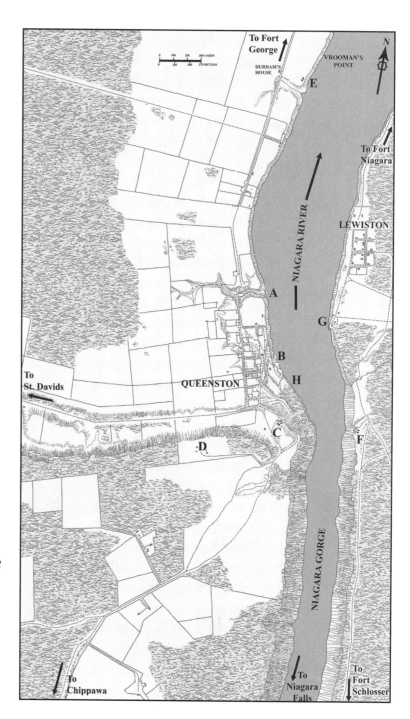

Site of the Battle of Queenston Heights, October 1812

A. Hamilton Dock
B. Government Dock
C. Redan Battery
D. Government Hospital and Warehouses
E. Vrooman's Point Battery
F. Fort Gray
G. U.S. Invasion, embarkation point
H. U.S. Invasion, initial landing point

Alexander Smyth, who had arrived at Buffalo in late September with over 1,600 regular troops. Technically, Smyth was under the command of Van Rensselaer and should have reported his arrival in person to his commanding officer. Instead, Smyth's ego refused to acknowledge the authority of a militiaman over a regular soldier and he defiantly set up a rival command headquarters of his own at Buffalo.

When preparing his plan of invasion, Van Rensselaer's original intention was for the attack to take place at Queenston on the night of October 11–12. However, this effort collapsed when, after marching from Fort Niagara in freezing rain, gale-force winds, and hail, the troops arrived at the embarkation point at Lewiston only to learn that the officer in charge of the boats had disappeared, taking with him a boat and all of the flotilla's available oars. Left with no means of propelling themselves across the river, the men were forced to endure a gruelling march back to their encampments before attempting

A postwar view from the escarpment of the lower reaches of the Niagara River as it flowed north toward Lake Ontario. T. Smith, artist, 1821.

Clement Library, University of Michigan.

to dry off and awaiting further orders. Despite this debacle, and fearing that further delays would result in the complete disintegration of his military force, Van Rensselaer ordered that the attack take place the following night — once some oars had been found.

Meanwhile, on the British side of the river it was expected that the American landing would take place at the mouth of the river, under the cover of the guns at Fort Niagara. News of the impending attack at Queenston was uncovered by Major Thomas Evans (8th [King's] Regiment) while he was delivering a message from Brock under a flag of truce. When he reported sighting a number of American boats hidden near Queenston to General Brock, Evans was at first considered as an alarmist. However, his persistence in repeating his warning persuaded Brock to order the various positions around Queenston to be on full alert for an imminent attack.

View at Queens Town of West Landing, Upper Canada, *Sempronius Stretton, artist, 1805. Hamilton House is prominent in this early view of Queenston, as are the "Heights" and Portage Road, winding its way up the escarpment. The Redan Battery would later be built just below the right-hand sweeping curve of the road.*

From the outset, the American plan of invasion began to fall apart. Not having an adequate number of boats to transport all the troops simultaneously, Van Rensselaer had to plan a shuttle service, using the available thirteen boats. After a chaotic embarkation, the heavily laden boats set out, but found themselves hard-pressed to maintain formation against the strong current. Attempting to avoid the known positions of the enemy in the village of Queenston, the convoy aimed for a landing upstream, directly below the escarpment and in a dead zone that could not be covered by the Redan artillery battery on the hillside overlooking the village.

Despite every precaution being taken to maintain absolute silence and surprise, the American flotilla was detected and the riverbank sentries fired a warning, alerting the prepared defenders. Once the element of surprise was lost, the American support batteries at Lewiston and Fort Gray also opened up, firing on the British positions. Rowing through a hail of crossfire, the boats reached the Canadian shore and those troops not already wounded piled out into the cold water before scrambling up onto the slippery embankment. They reached the main landing dock, which was occupied by the British regular and Canadian militia troops. There was nowhere to go but forward. After a brief but intense firefight, the defenders were forced to retreat into the village. But they soon returned with additional reinforcements and a small artillery piece. After another round of fierce gunfire, hand-to-hand combat, and significant casualties that reduced the ranks of both forces, the combatants mutually retired to regroup and look for additional reinforcements.

By that time it was apparent that several boats from the first wave of attackers had not returned to the American shore, either having been swept downriver by the strong current during the initial crossing, sunk by British gunfire, or, having suffered casualties, been rowed back the American side of the river and abandoned by their crews. Nonetheless, under heavy fire from the British artillery, elements of the second American wave made the dangerous crossing. Some joined Van Rensselaer's troops trapped on the shore, but others were pulled downstream by the current, where they came under heavy fire from additional defenders stationed near Hamilton House. Two of these boats, both containing a high proportion of officers, suffered so many casualties that they floated ashore and, after a brief fight, fell into the hands of the waiting Canadian flank company militia.

For the Americans, the situation now had all the makings of a disaster of the first magnitude. Back on the embattled beach, Lieutenant Colonel Solomon Van Rensselaer, the landing commander and cousin to General Stephen Van Rensselaer, initially considered a frontal attack on the troops massing before him. Instead, he and Captain John Wool determined that their only hope was to attempt a flanking movement toward the angle of the escarpment where it entered the gorge of the Niagara River. They had information that there was a rough path that would allow them to gain the high ground behind the hillside Redan artillery battery. With nothing to lose, the troops slipped off into the darkness in search of the path.

On the other side of the battlefield, General Brock considered things to be reasonably under control.

Having been awakened by the distant thunder of gun-fire, the commander had ridden post-haste from Fort George without waiting for either his troops or his aides. According to a later account, he was

met by Lieut. Jarvis [later lieuten-ant, Company No. 2] of Captain Cameron's Flank Company of York Militia, which … was stationed there. This officer had been on guard at what was called the half-moon battery, about mid-way between Queenstown and Niagara [when] an officer … arrived from Queenstown with intelligence that the Americans were crossing in force…. Lieut. Jarvis, who happened to be the only person mounted, was ordered [to contact General Brock] … and he had gal-loped about half way to Fort George, when he met General Brock, wholly unattended, cantering his charger up the Queenstown road…. Without in the slightest degree abating his speed even for an instant, the General lis-tened and then gave his orders. These were that Lieutenant Jarvis should go with all speed to Fort George, and order up General Sheaffe with the whole of the reserve…. Scarcely had Lieut. Jarvis lost sight of the General … when he was met by Col. Macdonell, who was following after his Chief, and who in his hurry … had left Fort George without … his sword … he begged Lieut. Jarvis to supply the deficiency, stating at the same time where he would find his own sabre in his quarters at Fort George, and desiring him to appropriate it to his use for the day.[6]

Continuing his ride to Queenston, Brock ordered each detachment of troops he passed to march to the sound of the guns. Arriving at Vrooman's Point, just downriver from Queenston, Brock paused to assess the situation at the battery commanded by Lieutenant Archibald McLean (3rd York Militia). This officer had already participated in the action at Detroit and would later become the captain of the Incorporated Militia's No. 6 Company. Moving on to Queenston, Brock saw that his greatly outnumbered regulars were holding the Americans in check, while the local flankers from the militias were proving their loyalty by turning out in numbers greater than he had predicted. Despite this, and certain that further waves of Americans would cross over, Brock was forced to order the Light Company of the 49th to join the troops below, instead of covering the hilltop and rear of the Redan battery on the escarpment.

With this augmented force, Brock's men inflicted severe casualties among the Americans on the water-front. However, by then the American force had suc-ceeded in scaling the heights and emerged on the higher ground immediately behind the unguarded Redan battery. Attacking from the rear, the Americans drove the gun crews out, but not before they were able to "spike" their guns, rendering them inoperable until repairs could be made to bring them back into action.

With the increasing light of day, the American gun batteries at Lewiston and Fort Gray were able to locate and target any British points of resistance. In short order, a number of the British guns, which had so devastated the earlier waves of American boats, were either disabled or forced to withdraw. In a similar fashion, the infantry came under increased fire and seemed likely to break unless matters improved. Recognizing that a crisis had arisen, Brock determined to regain the dominant heights to create a stronghold for further resistance until reinforcements arrived. Gathering together a small force of men from the scattered detachments of the 49th Regiment, the 2nd York, and 5th Lincoln Militias, the general led his troops against the American left flank.

Coming under a brisk musket fire from the front line of American skirmishers covering the hillside and the captured gun position, Brock's line was brought to a halt. Seeking to maintain the initiative, Brock rallied his men and moved out in front of his troops. Isolated in front of the line and wearing the highly distinctive uniform of a British senior officer, he quickly attracted the attention of the enemy and suffered the consequences when an American soldier took aim and shot the general through the chest.

Shocked by the sight of their commander falling mortally wounded, the British troops pressed forward, but made no headway against the secure positions of the Americans. Under a heavy fire, they collected the general's body and withdrew down the slope. Shortly afterward, Brock's aide, Lieutenant Colonel John Macdonell, attempted to avenge the death of his commander and succeed where his leader had failed by organizing a second assault on the hill. The remnants of the 49th Regiment and a composite company of the York Militia, including Lieutenant Archibald McLean, were involved in this attack.

Initially, the assault succeeded in pressing the Americans back up the slope to the earthworks of the Redan Battery, causing the Americans inside to re-spike one of the guns that they had only just cleared. But just as his commander had suffered for his bravery, so too did Macdonell. Hearing Macdonell call for assistance as he fell, McLean ran forward but he, in turn, was shot through the thigh and knocked off his feet. Within moments, the British offensive collapsed and a counterattack by the Americans threw the weakened and disheartened British-Canadian troops back down the hill, dragging Macdonell and McLean with them. With effective resistance to the invasion now all but collapsed, individual units withdrew from the village and attempted to regroup downriver at Vrooman's Point.

Seeing the British withdraw, the Americans began to solidify their perimeter position at the outskirts of Queenston to establish a secure zone for further troops to land. However, with less than a half-dozen boats remaining to ferry the waiting regiments to the Canadian shore, the reinforcement of the American bridgehead slowed to a crawl. Nevertheless, it appeared that despite all their earlier blunders, the Americans had carried the day and the battle was won.

As the morning progressed, additional detachments augmented the American force on the Heights. They even gained some artillery support in the form of a 6-pounder cannon and ammunition limber (cart). These heavy pieces had been laboriously transported across the river, dragged to the top of the escarpment, and sited astride the main Portage Road that led from Queenston to Chippawa. Desperate for additional reinforcements, the senior American officers at Queenston were frustrated that there were still a significant number of militiamen who were refusing to cross the Niagara and enter the battle. They sent an urgent message to General Stephen Van Rensselaer, impressing upon him the urgency of getting these recalcitrant troops onto the battlefield.

Meanwhile, the remnants of the defenders at Vrooman's Point were joined by the first of the reinforcements from Fort George — a band of nearly two hundred Native allies, led by their warrior chief John Norton (Teyoninhokarawen). Having encountered some of the retreating militia, and hearing of Brock's death, many of Norton's warriors took this retreat as a signal for their own withdrawal and melted into the woods. Norton, still determined to advance, led his remaining band of about eighty men in a flanking movement to the right that allowed them to pass around the American perimeter unperceived. After reaching the top of the escarpment and sending a messenger to the British garrison at Chippawa for assistance, Norton and his warriors dispersed under cover of the trees and began sniping at the Americans.

Startled by the sudden war cries and firing from the woods on their flank and rear, Lieutenant Colonel Winfield Scott (Second U.S. Artillery), who had left his own assigned post on the American side of the river to join in on the attack and was now the senior officer on the field, thought he was being attacked by forces coming from Chippawa. He therefore took it upon himself to establish a line of defence facing south from behind a fence that separated the open farm fields from the partially wooded military reservation lands that followed the line of the escarpment. Unable to drive off the Natives or fortify their dominating position while under fire, Scott and his troops were forced to retire back toward the edge of the escarpment to put more open ground between themselves and the repeated probes of the warriors.

By that time, General Roger Hale Sheaffe had arrived at Vrooman's Point with the remaining reinforcements from Fort George and was preparing to advance on the American lines. To support this attack, fix the American force below the escarpment in place, and further throttle the passage of reinforcements across the river, Sheaffe had his artillery, covered by a small detachment of troops, move forward along the riverbank and begin firing — with deadly results for those exposed in the open or on the river.

Hearing the renewed firing from the heights across the river, General Van Rensselaer made repeated attempts to pressure the remaining American militia units at Lewiston to join the troops on the Canadian shore, only to be soundly rebuffed. Humiliated by their refusal, he was finally forced to notify his frontline commanders of his inability to support their position with additional troops and of the fact that if they were unable to retreat to the riverbank their capture might become inevitable. By this time, the British reinforcements had also been seen by the troops stationed along the American defensive perimeter. Faced with this new threat and continuing artillery fire, an increasing number of men deserted their posts and began to filter back to the riverbank, where they endeavoured to recross the Niagara by any means possible.

Library and Archives Canada, C-128832.

Major General R.H. Sheaffe in later life. He was forty-nine years old at the time of the Battle of Queenston Heights. Following his removal by Sir George Prevost as lieutenant governor of Upper Canada (June 1813), Sheaffe was appointed as the military commander of the Montreal garrison. Because of further criticism from Sir George, he was recalled to England in August 1813, where he saw out the end of the war.

After having studied the American positions, Sheaffe decided that repeating Brock's method of a direct frontal assault would bring needless casualties and probable failure. Instead, he elected to follow Norton's example — reach the heights by a circuitous route and attack downhill, while a smaller detachment of infantry, supported by artillery, would hold the Americans' attention from the front. After a long, gruelling climb, Sheaffe's force arrived at the Portage Road above the escarpment and formed their line of attack. At this point, the detachments from Chippawa arrived and immediately wheeled into position on the right flank, extending the British line in a wide arc, composed of regulars, militia, and Native allies, all moving forward on a narrowing front and targeting the American centre.

Despite being outnumbered and isolated, the American line initially stood and opened fire on the advancing enemy. However, after trading several volleys, they heard the command for the line to retreat to the landing boats by companies. As each unit sought to break off and retire, the American command structure collapsed, the American line folded, and it became a matter of every man for himself. Some of the more dynamic officers attempted to stem the rout, but eventually they, too, were forced to join their fellows in scrambling down the steep slopes of the escarpment. Numerous Americans were injured or killed in their precipitous descent to the village of Queenston and the riverbank. Once there, and finding there were no available boats, some desperate individuals threw away their weapons and equipment and attempted to swim across the river.

Few, if any, made it safely ashore on the American side. Contemporary accounts record the spectacle of flailing bodies being swept downstream toward Lake Ontario, caught in the grip of the cold river current. For the majority, however, surrender was the only realistic option.

No accurate account of American losses in this affair are available, which is understandable considering the disorganized and broken nature of the units landing on the Canadian shore, and the confused mixture of regiments engaged in the various portions of the battle. Add to this the high level of desertions,

Brock's Monument, the second one to be built, as it looks today, marking the epicentre of the fighting at the climax of the Battle of Queenston Heights. The area, which was once covered with farmer's fields, military buildings, and dense forest, is now a manicured park that attracts tourists from around the globe.

both during and after the battle, and the unknown number of individuals who were swept away by the river during the initial assault or during the chaos of the rout at the end of the battle. However, more than nine hundred ended up as prisoners of war. In addition, a substantial quantity of equipment and ammunition fell into British hands — a valuable resource that would later be issued to the Canadian militia for use against its original owners.

On the British side, official accounts record a casualty roll that totalled less than a hundred dead, wounded, and missing, of all ranks. This disparity would normally stand as a glorious victory for the British, but the death of General Brock was credited as such a grievous loss that some contemporary accounts make more of this event than of the subsequent success of General Sheaffe in winning the battle.

THE FRENCHMAN'S CREEK FIASCO, NOVEMBER 29, 1812

Following the debacle of Queenston, General Stephen Van Rensselaer was forced to resign his position, and General Alexander Smyth was appointed as commander of the "Army of the Centre." No court martial or inquiry was ever held over the mutinous behaviour of Smyth, the shambles of the invasion, or the wholesale failure of a militia regimental system that legally permitted troops to refuse their officers' orders.

For his part, General Sheaffe took the victory of Queenston and the subsequent armistice he negotiated with the Americans as an opportunity to call out additional regiments of militia for patrol and garrison duties along the Niagara frontier and Grand River Valley. Away from the front, Sheaffe also issued a proclamation directing all citizens of the United States living in the province to leave by the end of the year, unless they were prepared to forswear their former country and take an oath of allegiance to the Crown.

Convinced that Smyth would attempt to outflank his defences with an invasion at either Fort George or Fort Erie, Sheaffe was forced to subdivide his army into individual detachments, each guarding extended lengths of the riverbank. Thus, when the Americans made a strong two-pronged attack on Saturday November 28, 1812, prior to making an all-out invasion, the American force of around 420 were opposed by a substantially smaller detachment of men manning, in the first case, a set of British battery positions opposite Black Rock, and, in the second, the bridge at Frenchman's Creek, located some two miles downriver.

The first flotilla of American boats, co-commanded by Captain William King (Fourteenth Infantry) and Lieutenant Samuel Angus (U.S. Navy), which were to assault the British artillery positions downriver from Fort Erie, became separated by the darkness and the swift current of the Niagara River. When the leading boats, crewed by the naval detachment, were detected while still in the process of pulling ashore, they came under heavy fire and suffered significant casualties. Upon landing, the naval party attempted to charge the closest "Red House" battery but were driven off.

Meanwhile, the boats under Captain King landed undetected farther downstream and immediately attacked another nearby artillery position. This pair of field guns were manned by several men who would

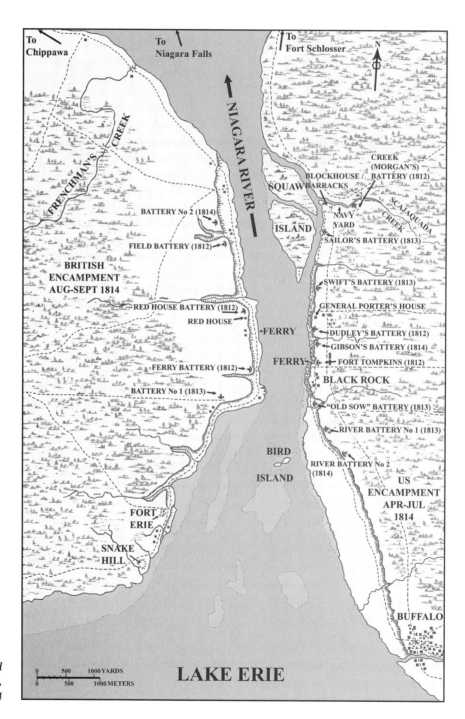

Military Positions Constructed Around
Fort Erie, Buffalo, and Black Rock,
1812–1814

later join the Incorporated Militia, including Captain Abraham Rapelje (2nd Norfolk Militia), later captain of Company No. 3, and Lieutenant George Ryerson (1st Norfolk Militia), later lieutenant in Company No. 3. Despite a strong resistance by the defenders, the Americans captured the position and then moved back upriver, attacking the Red House battery from the rear. After some vicious hand-to-hand fighting, this position was overrun, leaving only the southernmost battery, which was found already spiked and abandoned by its crew when King's force arrived shortly thereafter.

At the same time, the second American flotilla, under the command of Lieutenant Colonel Charles Boerstler, was also detected before they landed and came under heavy fire from the small British detachment guarding the Frenchman's Creek bridge. Consequently, many boats turned away, leaving only part of the American force to complete their mission and drive off the defenders.

With both positions in American control, the way was open for a larger invasion force to land. Fortunately for the British, no such force appeared to support the initial landing parties. As a result, the small garrison at Fort Erie, commanded by Major Ormsby (49th Regiment), was able to move north around King's bridgehead and easily retake the Frenchman's Creek bridge, thus securing the line of communications with the main British force at Chippawa. They also saw the bulk of Boerstler's force retreating into the darkness of the river without firing a shot in defence of their position and abandoning their own picket guards on the shore.

Coincidently, Captain King's detachment also found themselves stranded. When they returned to their landing craft after securing the third battery, they discovered that their naval comrades had taken the available seaworthy boats and rowed away, leaving behind their own vessels, which had been too badly damaged in the initial landing to remain afloat. Scouring the riverbank for any watercraft they could use to return to their own side of the river, King's men finally came across two small boats pulled up on shore. Recognizing there was no way his mission could succeed, King ordered his wounded, the British prisoners, and as many men as possible to fill the boats and cross to the American side. He remained behind with the rest to hold on to the beachhead from a nearby house until the boats could return for them.

At dawn, Ormsby's force at the Frenchman's Creek bridge was augmented by a relief column from Chippawa that included Captain James Kerby (2nd Lincoln Militia Artillery), the future captain of Company No. 1 of the Incorporated Militia, along with twelve future rank and file. Together, the combined units, under the overall command of Lieutenant Colonel Cecil Bisshopp, captured Boerstler's abandoned Americans and secured the riverbank at Frenchman's Creek before moving toward Fort Erie and the remaining scattered remnants of King's troops. Seeing the overwhelming number of enemy troops before them, Captain King and his party were left with no option but to surrender.

With their communication lines secure, Bisshopp's column, augmented by Native warriors, advanced on Fort Erie. Together the combined force easily retook the batteries from their American captors, only to see a fresh wave of boats approaching the Canadian shore. This new force, taken from General William Winder's command, was belatedly attempting a crossing in support of King and Boerstler's landings. A few volleys from a quickly formed British line-of-battle and Kerby's artillery pieces soon persuaded the Americans to come about and pull out of range, but not before losing between six to ten killed and twenty-two wounded. Upon inspection, all of the guns in the British batteries were found to have been dismounted and spiked but were otherwise undamaged. Without delay, Bisshopp ordered Captain Kerby to oversee the restoration of the barrels to firing condition and the manning of the guns in case the Americans made another assault.

On the American side of the river, Smyth watched the remnants of his scheme filter back into camp. Despite this military humiliation and the fact that the enemy was now fully alerted and ready, Smyth had a large force of men embarked in boats in full view of the enemy. He then sent across a repeat of his previous demand, this time addressed to Lieutenant Colonel Bisshopp, that Fort Erie and the troops defending it should surrender immediately "to spare further effusion of blood."[7] On the other side of the river, with his batteries once more in action and with a sizable force of defenders, Bisshopp ignored Smyth's bombastic demands. After an hour or so of waiting, the British force had the satisfaction of watching the Americans unload their troops and march away from the boats, without a shot being fired.

The following day, Smyth ordered another assault for the night of November 30–December 1, 1812. However, by now Smyth's credibility had totally evaporated and, once again, units of the militia refused to participate in any actions beyond their border. Even the regular troops procrastinated in the loading of the boats. By the time the supposed invasion force was embarked, the sun had risen and the fleet would have been an easy target for every musket and cannon on the Canadian side of the river. Totally frustrated, Smyth abandoned the assault, blaming everyone but himself for the debacle.

Discipline in the American Army of the Centre had now disintegrated and entire companies of men simply deserted in disgust. Within a week, Smyth was forced to decamp from his own army in fear of his life as unhappy soldiers took potshots in his general direction. He was subsequently "disbanded" from the army (a face-saving term used by the army to cover up the otherwise embarrassing need to hold a court martial or official inquiry) whereupon he retired to his home in Virginia, where he sat out the remainder of the war, writing his self-justifying memoirs for posterity.

Politically, the ramifications of the litany of military failures in 1812 shook the American political administration. President Madison held on to his office in the autumn elections, but was forced to remove Dr. William Eustis as secretary of war on December 3. In his place, Madison offered the post to several senior politicians, but none of them would touch the job. Eventually, a former senator and brigadier general of militia, John Armstrong, was appointed.

On the other side of the border, the New Year's loyal toasts given by the residents of Upper Canada were made with additional fervour that season, considering that they had been forced into a war for which they were unprepared and under-supplied in military manpower and equipment, then dismissed as potentially treasonous and expendable by their own governor. The fact that they were not living under an American flag was considered by some of the more devout of the Upper Canada civilian population to be little less than divine intervention. Problems remained, however, as it was recognized that the war was only just beginning and was likely to be a long one, with new and additional sacrifices to come.

PART II:

A NEW LEVEL OF WAR: THE 1813 CAMPAIGNS

3

FORMING THE INCORPORATED MILITIA

FOLLOWING THE DEATH OF ISAAC BROCK AT Queenston, General Sheaffe became the senior military commander and governor of Upper Canada. Unfortunately, he proved incapable of maintaining the delicate balance of alliances and providing the kind of charismatic leadership that Brock had. His brusque treatment of the political and social leadership of the province and his inadequate maintenance of positive relations with the proud Native allies, led to a crisis of political confidence in the early part of 1813.

This crisis coincided with the arrival of intelligence reports indicating a buildup of American forces around their new naval base of Sackets Harbor, only thirty-eight miles south of the vital transportation nexus of Kingston. Unable to procure additional regular troops from Sir George Prevost for the defence of Upper Canada, General Sheaffe was forced to look to the Upper Canada militia system for an infusion of military reinforcements. Earlier, his predecessor, General Brock, had undertaken a revision of the 1808 *Militia Act* to establish the flank companies. This, however, would not be sufficient if the Americans were to make any serious invasion attempts once the winter snows and ice melted and the navigation season opened on the lakes.

Fortunately, this issue had already been alluded to by one of Sheaffe's veteran senior officers, Lieutenant Colonel Thomas Pearson, who, in January, had prepared and submitted his own memorandum for the solution to Sheaffe's problem:

I have no hesitation in asserting that this force [the embodied militia] will never be brought to meet the expectations of the country. In the first place from the constant and numerous desertions of the militia, it is next to an impossibility ever to calculate on the force you can bring into action. This I principally attribute to the incapability of the generality of the officers who have been for the most part selected from family connections, without reference to capacity or respectability…. [Instead] two battalions of 500 R[ank] and F[ile], each from the flankers of the district [should be formed]…. These Corps I propose being commanded by militia Lt. Colonels with a Captain of the Line appointed as a Major, with two Lieutenants of the regulars as Captains to each of the Batt's. The remaining officers to be militia and to be selected by the Lt. Colonels subject to the approval of the Inspecting Field Officer. Their pay and allowances as at present, but the men to be clothed at the expense of the Government and to be embodied for the continuance of the American war…. These measures are the only ones by which the force of this country can ever be brought to be of real utility to the Province.[1]

Applying many of the elements of Lieutenant Colonel Thomas Pearson's recommendations, Sheaffe proposed the establishment of a number of full-time provincial militia units to be known as the Incorporated Militia. This corps would be established under the legislative authority of the Upper Canada Parliament and, therefore, not technically part of the British army, as in the case of the already established Glengarry Light Infantry Fencible, Nova Scotia Fencible, and Canadian Fencible regiments. Once recruited, this new corps would be instructed according to the regular army system of drill and manoeuvre, so that when its training was complete, the Incorporated Militia could be deployed in action as the near-equivalent of the fencible units. On January 21, 1813, Sir George Prevost replied:

I consider the suggestion for raising two or three battalions in the province of Upper Canada with the encouragement of a promise of land which might be recommended by myself to the Secretary of State, to be confirmed by His Royal Highness the Prince Regent to such as engage under those expectations, as a judicious measure. These corps would be literally incorporated militia, serving under the militia law and not to serve out of the province except as provided for by that act. As an inducement to promote the formation of such Corps, the legislature would no doubt accede to a certain sum being allowed each man as an outfit to provide some articles of necessaries not to exceed £5/0/0 currency. It has been proposed that a sum not exceeding £3/0/0 shall be given in this province [Lower Canada] for the outfit of each militiaman required for service in the next summer. It is very desirable these corps should not be encumbered with field officers from the militia but that intelligent and active Captains from the line, possessing discretion and skill should fill these situations. I am aware the execution of such a plan may be attended with great difficulty, notwithstanding the incontrovertible benefit arising from it to the service. Therefore, I only suggest the measure trusting to your judgment for the execution of the whole or a part of it, according to the disposition of the people you have to deal with.[2]

What is particularly noteworthy in this letter is Prevost's agreement with Pearson's proposal that, while the rank and file of the regimental ranks should be filled by the enlistment of local militiamen, both the senior officers of the companies and senior command staff should be drawn from the regular army regiments.

Unfortunately for General Sheaffe, while this idea had merit, the reality was to prove impractical. In the first place, there was already a shortage of experienced and competent field officers within the regular regiments and no regimental colonel would willingly lose his best and experienced officers to the militia. Second, any regular officer being seconded to the militia, while automatically getting a brevet promotion in rank, would effectively jeopardize his seniority of rank placement within his own regimental structure. Such a move could threaten his long-term military career, something no competent regular officer would consider as equitable to the distinction of having a temporary rise in rank.

Unable to implement the plan as originally conceived, Sheaffe was forced to adopt a new formula. Under this, the new Incorporated Militia regiments would have their "other ranks" component made up of volunteers drawn from the flank companies and their associated embodied militia regiments. These men would then be commanded, at the company level, by volunteer Canadian militia officers. However, the senior commander and regimental staff for the regiment would remain as originally proposed, and be drawn from officers transferred from the regular forces with a brevet promotion to empower their authority over the militiamen. With these terms established, a new *Militia Act* was drawn up and introduced to the Upper Canada Legislature in March 1813. By its provisions, the following changes were enacted:

- The 1812 *Flank Company Act* was revised, thereby entirely eliminating the official stratum of militia flank companies from the county regimental system. That being said, however, the use of the term "flank companies" continued to be used during the remainder of the war in numerous embodied regimental pay lists, as well as the postwar pension and land grant accounts. (Article V)

- The existing embodied militia regiments were to be reorganized into units consisting of eight to ten companies, each having between twenty to fifty privates, commanded by one colonel, one lieutenant colonel, and one major. Any regiment with less than ten companies was to be commanded by a lieutenant colonel and one major. Each company therein was to be officered by one captain, one lieutenant, and one ensign. (Article VI)

- A number of new full-time militia regiments were to be established under the designation of being "Incorporated Militia." These regiments were then to be deemed on active service for the duration of the war with the United States of America. The terms of service within the Incorporated Militia were to be based upon the voluntary enlistment of individuals. Officers to the companies were to qualify for their ranks within the Incorporated Militia regiments according to a yet-to-be-established quota of men they were able to persuade to enlist as rank and file. Appointed officers were then to be empowered to establish internal regulations and rules applicable to their regiments. No officer of the regular forces was to sit in judgment at any courts martial involving any member of the Incorporated Militia. No private was to be subject to the corporal punishment of being whipped for infractions of regulations. No militia officer currently within the embodied militia that subsequently served with the Incorporated Militia in a rank lower than that he held within his original regiment, would lose his seniority standing within his original unit. (Article X)

- During the course of the war, no NCO or private serving with the Incorporated Militia was to be liable to be sued or arrested for any outstanding debt of less than fifty pounds. Neither could any of that individual's goods, chattels, lands, or tenements be served upon, seized or sold. (Article XI)

- During their term of service within the Incorporated Militia, no NCO or private was to be required to pay taxes, rates, or assessments upon their property. Nor were they required to undertake manual labour upon any stretch of the King's highway adjoining or crossing their property. Nor do duty as a town or parish officer. The Incorporated Militia was not to be required to serve outside or leave the province of Upper Canada, except as provided under the statutes of the Militia Laws. (Article XIII)

Even before the above legislation had been officially passed into law, news of the proposed raising of a full-time militia force had circulated among the officers of the various embodied regiments and flank companies (which principally consisted of the younger, energetic, and enthusiastic members of the militia cadres).

This news prompted many to put their names forward for positions in the new regiment. Knowing in advance that they would be required to recruit a quota of men to qualify for their new ranks, some of the more enterprising individuals even commenced recruiting men to fill their quotas. As a result, as early as March 4, 1813, Major Titus G. Simons (2nd York Militia) was able to submit a list of officers within his own regiment who had already completed their qualifying quota. This was despite the fact that the official printed version of these regulations was not released until March 10.

When the new official regulations were issued, they confirmed that those officers of the embodied militias seeking positions within the Incorporated Militia were not required to follow the established British regular army procedure of purchasing their rank. Instead, they were expected to use their abilities to persuade and influence specific numbers of men to enlist into the Incorporated Militia regiments under their potential future direct command. This surprisingly "modern" attitude established a direct association or bond between the rank and file of the regiment and their officers — a distinct difference from the rigidly segregated social structure prevalent in the regular forces.

The required quotas were drawn up as follows:

For the rank of:	Required	Total
Lieutenant Colonel (1 position per regiment)	40 recruits	40 men
Major (1 position per regiment)	30 recruits	30 men
Captain (10 positions per regiment)	20 recruits	200 men
Lieutenant (10 positions per regiment)	10 recruits	100 men
Ensign (10 positions per regiment)	5 recruits	50 men

The result was to be a regimental ideal complement of 420 other ranks and thirty-two officers. Each company could then be added to, up to a maximum of fifty privates per company. Ideally, the end result was to establish ten companies per regiment, in accordance with standard British army practice for regiments of the line. Each company was to consist of one captain, one lieutenant, one ensign, three sergeants, three corporals, one drummer, and fifty privates — being "men between 16 to 45 years of age, if strong and healthy."[3]

This Canadian contingent would be supplemented by an experienced regimental staff and support team: "An Adjutant, Quartermaster, Quartermaster Sergeant, and Sergeant major to be obtained from the line if practicable or otherwise fit persons to be selected."[4]

Financial incentives were to be offered to encourage enlistment. Each volunteer was to be granted $8.00 (Halifax currency) from the coffers of the Upper Canada Legislature and $10.00 from the military funds of Major General Sheaffe to cover the costs of providing each man with the necessities of uniforms and equipment. There was also an unspecified assurance that there would be a future grant of Crown lands to each and that "the officers and men will have the usual pay and allowances of regiments of the line…. No man is to be enlisted but as a private, though it may be intended to raise him to the rank of corporal or sergeant."[5]

Despite this seemingly strong show of support by General Sheaffe, however, the financial state of the Upper Canada coffers had already been so drained by the expenditures related to the war that it soon became clear that they would be unable to "cough up" the required funds for the establishment of their own first full-time military regiment. Seeking to remedy the shortfall, Sheaffe penned an urgent appeal to Sir George Prevost:

> York, 13 March 1813 … An Incorporated Militia is to be formed of volunteers to serve during the war with the United States with a "bounty" of eight dollars, this bounty is granted in compliance with my suggestion of an "outfit." The House was restrained, I believe, from granting a larger sum by the consciousness of its limited means. The Speaker told me that he wished they could have raised the sum to twenty dollars, all the unapportioned funds of the province are however placed at my disposal, but there will be so many other demands on them that I shall not be enabled to add to the bounty, which I think too small for the purpose. May I therefore hope for your Excellency's aid and authority for making an addition to it of ten or twelve dollars, or of such other sum as you may deem sufficient.[6]

Without waiting for the official reply, Sheaffe took it upon himself to approve the specified $10.00 bounty only two days later, and sought to promote the regiment by issuing a public commentary on the new legislation:

> In place of flank coy's of militia established by virtue of a provincial statute passed the 5th Aug. 1812, the Governor … is now invested with authority to accept of voluntary services of militia men and to nominate and appoint officers and to embody and regulate one or more Regiments, to be styled regiments of Incorporated

Militia, to serve during the war with the United States of America. By which means it is hoped that the troops so raised may prove more efficient in all respects than ordinary militia.… The Legislature has paid particular attention to the raising of that body of men by holding out privileges and exemptions, as well as pecuniary encouragement to such volunteers as may enter that service.[7]

Having now publically committed himself, he also attempted to cover his own "position" from criticism by sending a separate letter directly to the attention of the British secretary of war, Earl Bathurst, in London, which was dated March 18, 1813:

The means at its [the Provincial Legislature] disposal being inadequate to the paying of so large a bounty to volunteers for the Incorporated Militia as would be necessary to answer every purpose, there were only eight dollars voted for each man … it being my own decided opinion that the sum granted was insufficient either to operate as an inducement for engaging in the Incorporated Militia during the war, or even to provide the necessary articles for an outfit. I

addressed a letter to His Excellency applying for further aid … written under the impression which I had received from … Sir George Prevost that but little of any hope could be entertained of a re-inforcement from Europe and that a most urgent necessity existed for forming, without delay, a force more efficient than the ordinary militia of the province and an additional aid for their purpose. I have announced it to be my intention to recommend the services of the Incorporated Militia to the favourable considerations of His Royal Highness, the Prince Regent, for a grant of land for each man.[8]

Fortunately, on April 8, Sheaffe's financial gamble appeared to have paid off, as he subsequently wrote to Prevost:

I have, this evening, had the honour of receiving from Your Excellency's letter of the 29th of March, in which it is significant to me that you have been pleased, in previous letters, to authorize me to give to volunteers of the Incorporated Militia, an additional sum of ten dollars, according to my desire … these letters have not yet arrived … they are probably in the possession of Lt. Col. Hughes, who is yet on the route from Kingston. I have directed a copy of the army bill reference to be prepared to be transmitted to Your Excellency by Major Bouchette.[9]

During the latter part of March, the military bureaucracy began to establish the proposed three regiments of Incorporated Militia. The first would recruit in the area bounded by the border with Lower Canada in the east and Kingston in the west; the second from the communities in and around York and the Head-of-the-Lake (Hamilton/Ancaster); the third, from the Niagara frontier region and settlements bordering the Grand River. Letters of authorization were issued to the officers of the embodied and flank companies who had already put their names forward as being keen to recruit men into the new companies.

There were also numerous bureaucratic details requiring attention, such as how to transfer men from their county-based militia affiliation into the new regiments from the point of view of maintaining the proper records of payrolls, attendance rolls, ration allowances, accommodation allowances, and associated deductions. As well, there was the matter of dealing with the conflicting claims of regimental ownership for the valuable and scarce supplies of firearms, accoutrements and uniforms already issued to those men in the embodied militias that would be transferring to the Incorporated Militia.

As the recruiting continued, the potential new officers became more occupied with raising their quotas and establishing their companies than filling out reams of bureaucratic paperwork. Consequently, the surviving records covering the York and Niagara Districts are relatively simplistic and cursory. For the Eastern and Johnstown Districts, however, authority for the region fell under the jurisdiction of Lieutenant Colonel Thomas Pearson. Working under his eagle eye and stern demands for exactitude, the officers of those detachments recruiting in the Prescott area found that no quarter or latitude was to be given in the execution of their official duties. As a result of his supervision, this segment of the regiment became operationally ready to take on the responsibilities of duty at an earlier point than their fellow detachments. However, operationally ready or not, it was the detachments at York and then Niagara who were to first receive their baptism of fire within the coming weeks.

4

THE AMERICAN INVASION, SPRING 1813

As PART OF HIS EFFORT TO PUT THE AMERICAN war "back on track" and to secure political electoral benefits in the upcoming elections, the newly appointed secretary of war, John Armstrong, implemented a massive capital investment and shipbuilding programme at the small New York State village of Sackets Harbor, with the goal of creating a fleet of vessels that would ensure control of Lake Ontario and thus sever the British military's supply lines. He also proposed a spring campaign that would see a two-pronged attack made against Upper Canada through the Kingston and Niagara corridors. His immediate objective was to have a combined naval and land force of over four thousand men eliminate the British fleet at Kingston and take control of Lake Ontario. This invasion force would then move on York (now Toronto) to seize the official capital of Upper Canada.

At the same time, a second force would be collected at Buffalo with orders to subdue the defences at Fort George before pressing westward to cut off General Proctor and his Native allies now controlling the Michigan territory along the Detroit River. With these locations in hand, he believed the combined victorious American forces could move at will across Upper Canada, supported and supplied by their fleet from its enlarged base at Sackets Harbor.

As preparations were underway to implement the new strategy, the newly appointed American naval commander at Sackets Harbor, Commodore Isaac Chauncey, proposed a change of campaign. Believing Kingston to be too heavily defended to be attacked without heavy cost, he persuaded his superiors in Washington to make York the first site for attack. This would be followed by an all-out invasion on the Niagara frontier. Chauncey's proposal was accepted, but a combination of poor weather conditions, difficulty assembling the necessary supplies, weapons, and troops, as well as a late spring thaw combined to delay this planned attack until mid-April.

An artist's impression of the Sir Isaac Brock *on the stocks at the small shipyard at York in 1813, Owen Staples, artist. The ship, never completed, was burned by the British as they retreated, to prevent it from falling into American hands.*

Aggravated by the continued delays, the overall mission commander, Major General Dearborn, finally pressured Commodore Chauncey into approving the embarkation of the waiting troops for the invasion of Upper Canada on April 20. After three days of intensive effort, and against the weather advice of his ship captains, Dearborn ordered the heavily overburdened American fleet to immediately set sail, only to have it run headlong into a severe storm system that forced the fleet to come about and run for shelter. Back in harbour, the troops were required to endure either being locked below decks and tossed around in cramped unsanitary conditions, or sit exposed on the open decks for a further two days of drenching rain and below normal temperatures.

It was not until April 25 that the American invasion of Upper Canada actually began. Major General Dearborn held overall command, while under him, Commodore Isaac Chauncey led the naval squadron and Brigadier General Zebulon Pike commanded the landing force. As Chauncey had proposed, their destination was not Kingston, but rather the town of York, capital of Upper Canada and the site of a small dockyard where a new vessel, the *Sir Isaac Brock*, was being built for the British flotilla.

Under changing winds and choppy swells that did nothing to improve the queasiness of many of the troops, the American fleet arrived within sight of the town on the evening of Monday, April 26. In response, the alarm guns at Fort York signalled to the citizens of York that war was descending on their quiet bayside community.

PART III:

THE SERVICE RECORD OF THE SEPARATE DIVISIONS OF THE INCORPORATED MILITIA, MARCH 1813–MARCH 1814

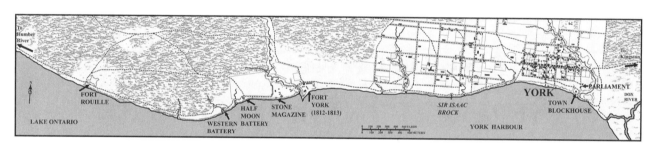

The Town of York in 1813.

5

THE YORK DIVISION

WITH THE ANNOUNCEMENT OF THE FORM-
ing of the Incorporated Militia, Captain
William Jarvie, accompanied by his subalterns, Lieutenant Thomas Humberstone and Ensign
Daniel Brooke, all of the 3rd York Embodied Militia
Regiment, soon succeeded in recruiting some twenty-
three men to the regimental rolls. At the same time, a
separate detachment of twenty-two men, subsequently
referred to as the Incorporated Militia Artillery,
was also formed at York under the command of a
Lieutenant William Jarvis. While these two units were
technically separate and composed of infantry and
artillery, both required training in the foundational
aspects of field drill and manoeuvres. Records indicate
that both units regularly paraded and trained together
during the first weeks after their establishment.

Because the bulk of the available supplies of
uniforms, arms, accoutrements, and other military
equipment were being diverted to the front-line
troops stationed on the Niagara frontier, the men at
York found themselves without many of the items due
to them as part of the "necessaries" promised by the
authorities at the time of their enlistment. To rectify
this shortage, on April 21 Jarvie and men from his
detachment received orders to man three longboats
and row east along the shore of Lake Ontario to a
pre-assigned location where a cache of weapons and
uniforms had been deposited and hidden by a similar
set of longboats secretly dispatched from Kingston.

Secrecy was required since once the navigation season had opened in March, American warships were prowling the Lake Ontario shipping

lanes between Kingston and York and the Niagara frontier. Their goal was to intercept and capture or sink any British vessel venturing out onto the lake, cut the main British supply lines, and thus weaken the ability of the military garrisons in Upper Canada to resist a future American attack. Under this threat, all military and civilian supplies being sent beyond Kingston had to either be hauled over the inferior and often impassable roads along Lake Ontario's north shore or broken up into smaller cargoes and loaded onto canoes and longboats that could hug the shoreline to avoid detection by the prowling American vessels. Understandably, only the most desperately needed supplies were being sent this way. The fact that Jarvie's men were to be provided with supplies is ample testimony to the urgency of the situation that the British command felt it was facing in late April 1813.

The Town of York in 1804, *Elizabeth Hale, artist,* circa 1804. *The Upper Canada parliament buildings and town blockhouse are visible in the distance, to the right.*

Library and Archives Canada, C-34334.

BAPTISM OF FIRE

Having recovered the cache, Jarvie and his men began their journey back to York only to have to take cover in a tree-lined creek when a large number of vessels, sailing from the direction of Sackets Harbor, appeared on the horizon. The American invasion had obviously begun, and their target was either Niagara or York. Forced to remain in hiding until the vessels passed to the west, Jarvie and his men redoubled their efforts to reach the relative safety of York. Unfortunately, time and circumstance were against them. Two days later, on the morning of April 27, as the boats passed below the tall bluffs at what is today Scarborough, their crews heard the distant sound of cannon firing from the direction of York.

Determined to avoid having their supplies fall into the hands of the enemy, yet still get into the fight that had already begun, Jarvie and his detachment beached the boats and moved the supplies under the cover of nearby trees. Taking whatever they could carry in the form of weapons and ammunition, they then set out on foot toward York. As Jarvie and his men marched through the small community, they could see the fleet of American boats moving west under the stiff morning breeze, away from the fort and toward the Humber River, some three miles beyond. Once at Fort York, Jarvie immediately collected the remainder of his company, sought out General Sheaffe, and reported himself and his men ready for action.

Since dawn on April 27, General Sheaffe had watched the American fleet approach the entrance to the town's sheltered harbour. Fort York had unfortunately remained a weak spot in the British line of communication and supply from the time the war began. Never designed to be a strongpoint of defensive fortification, it could be better described as a small supply depot, defended by mediocre blockhouses, loop-holed barracks, dilapidated gun batteries, and antiquated artillery pieces. So out of date was one of these cannon that it dated back to the period of Oliver Cromwell, some 150 years earlier! These derelict antiques had previously been condemned and had had their trunnions (elevating swivels) cut off to make them unworkable. However, at the onset of war, these substandard weapons had been resurrected for active use and mounted on makeshift carriages, using heavy-duty clamps and straps

Library and Archives Canada,
C-14822 and C-18803.

Fort York in 1803, *a panoramic black and white sketch, Sempronius Stretton, artist, 1803. The early fort (1793) with the Government House lies inside the low fence (centre left), while the 1813 fort (that the Americans attacked) lies to the right of the flagstaff. The stone magazine (not shown) was set into the lakeside embankment about where the low fence ends (far left).*

to hold the barrels in place. The only question was: Who would be the first to be killed by these guns, the enemy or their crew?

Although some work had been done during the course of the winter to construct additional defensive earthworks and a small battery position to protect the official governmental residence located to the west of the main garrison, none of these earthworks were completed or fully armed. Expecting that the Americans would make separate landings on both flanks of the fort, Sheaffe had divided his limited force and placed a strong force of regulars and militia on his eastern flank, closer to the town, with orders to cover his line of communications with Kingston. The remainder he held at the fort to determine where the enemy would land.

Pressed by the strengthening wind, the American fleet was forced west of its planned landing site below

This Cromwellian-era cannon used at the Battle of York is now on display at Historic Fort York in Toronto.

the fort, around a slight headland and into the wide bay beyond. This placed them well beyond the range of any of the fort's guns or detached batteries, leaving General Sheaffe with no option but to recall his eastern detachments and reconsider his entire plan of defence. Unfortunately, in the pressure of the moment, the general failed to make any coordinated plan of defence for the fort. Instead, he relied on a series of piecemeal orders that sent individual detachments of regulars, militia, and Native allies off toward the projected American landing site, with

no goal other than to attempt to stop the invasion by whatever means possible. As the leading units advanced along the main lakefront road, they came under the direct fire of the enemy fleet's cannon, and many following detachments opted to use the smaller inland trackways. While this diversion protected them from being fired upon, it also slowed their advance and delayed their involvement in the battle that was about to begin.

As the American longboats approached the shore to the west of the ruins of the old French trading post,

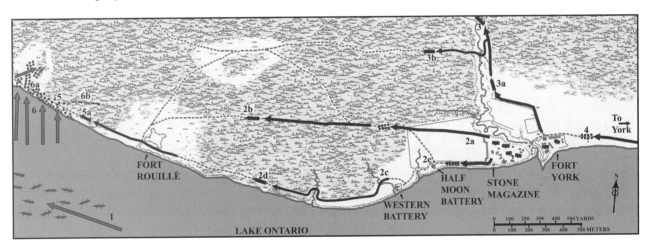

The Battle of York. The Initial American Landings at York and British Countermoves, April 27, 1813 (circa 5:30–8:00 a.m.)

1. The American flotilla (1) arrives off York, but strong winds push them past the entrance to the shelter of York Bay and into the open waters of Humber Bay, beyond the range of the defending batteries at Fort York, the Half-Moon Battery, and Western Battery.
2. General Sheaffe gathers his troops at Fort York (2) but fails to establish any coordinated response to the American attack. Units move out independently from Fort York toward the American landing by either taking one of the inland trails (to avoid being fired on by the American ships) (2a, 2b) or using the lakefront trail (2c, 2d). Lieutenant Jarvis's Incorporated Militia artillery detachment man guns in the Western Battery (2e).
3. Canadian embodied militia units (3) move north of the town to secure the main communication road leading west and await orders, followed shortly afterward by the Glengarry Light Infantry (3a). En route, the Glengarry Light Infantry break off and march toward the sounds of gunfire (3b).
4. Captain Jarvie and his men (4) arrive at York and march to the fort to join the action.
5. Native allied warriors (5) lead the advance of the units sent to oppose the American landing, followed by a company of the 8th (King's) Regiment (5a).
6. The American advance force (6) lands under fire from the Natives and 8th (King's) and engage in fierce close-quarter fighting. With the support of additional troops landing on the British-Native flank (6a), the Americans overwhelm the defenders and consolidate a bridgehead, while the scattered defenders retreat toward Fort Rouillé (6b).

Fort Rouillé, their only opposition came from the Native contingent in place under the cover of the treeline. Firing on the boats, they inflicted casualties among the tightly packed Americans until increasing numbers of U.S. riflemen landed on their flank and forced them to retreat. At this point, a single company of grenadiers from the 8th (King's) Regiment finally arrived. Although greatly outnumbered, they opened up on the landing troops. In the severe firefight that followed, the small King's detachment suffered heavy casualties and were eventually forced to retreat. This allowed the Americans to consolidate their bridgehead and land successive waves of troops before advancing toward the British garrison. At Fort Rouillé, the American advance was halted by fire from a hastily assembled force of defenders, including elements of the Glengarry Light Infantry, the Royal Newfoundland Regiment, and Jarvie's detachment of the Incorporated Militia.

Taking their place in the line-of-battle, Jarvie's men initially stood their ground beside the British army's colonial regiments. Shortly thereafter, another company of the 8th (King's) Regiment arrived to bolster the line and Jarvie's company was sent to the British right flank to skirmish alongside the remnants of the Native allies against the advancing American riflemen. For a time, this combined force beat off the encroaching infantry units, though at an ever-increasing cost of casualties, including the wounding of Captain Jarvie and four of his men. Despite putting up a fierce resistance, the British right wing was eventually outflanked by an overwhelming number of U.S. troops and forced to withdraw east.

In a similar manner, the British left wing, already suffering casualties from the American infantry and artillery fire, became the target for a deadly bombardment of cannon fire from the naval vessels moving east a short distance offshore. The British position was now untenable, and orders were issued for units to withdraw and make a fighting retreat to the detached battery positions located to the west of Fort York. Here, it was hoped, a further stand could be made with the support of the battery's artillery. It was also expected that additional reinforcements would be available in the form of several detachments of embodied militia that had initially mustered at Fort York when the alarm guns sounded. The embattled defenders at the lakefront were to be entirely disappointed, however, since these troops had previously been dispatched inland to secure that quadrant and now remained isolated and unused throughout the remainder of the action.

As the American formations approached the Western Battery position, the conflict resumed with a new round of fierce volleys and exchanges of artillery. However, moments later, disaster struck when an accidental ignition of some exposed artillery ammunition in the battery wrecked the guns and killed or injured over thirty individuals. Included in the subsequent roll of wounded from this incident were four men from the Incorporated Militia Artillery Company and their commander, Lieutenant William Jarvis, who was struck in the eye by some explosion debris. Despite immediate efforts to repair and bring the Western Battery back into action, the explosion made any further defence of this position impractical. Consequently, orders were given for the spiking of the remaining guns and the independent retreat of all

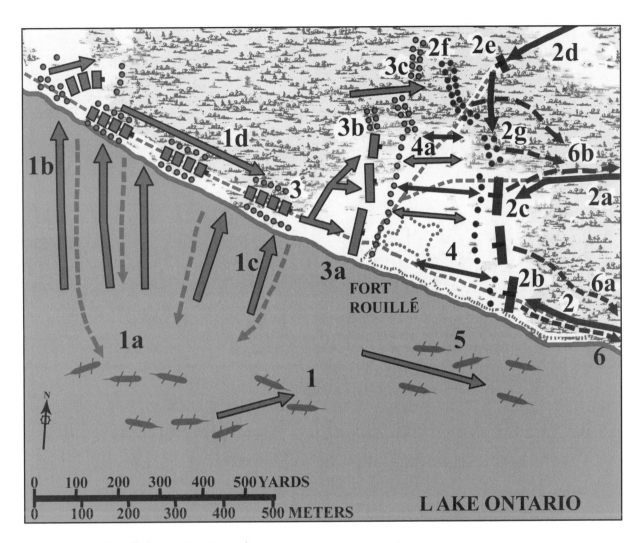

The Battle at Fort Rouillé (circa 8:00–9:30 a.m.)

1. In support of their landings, part of the U.S. flotilla (1) begins to sail east, firing onshore at any target of opportunity, while the remainder (1a), continue to land troops along a wide front (1b, 1c). Onshore, American units press forward along the lakefront trail (1d).
2. British units advance toward the clearing near Fort Rouillé (2, 2a) and upon arrival establish a rough line of defence (2b, 2c). Captain Jarvie's company of Incorporated Militia arrives (2d) and is initially placed in-line on the right flank (2e) in support of the Glengarry Light Infantry (2f). Subsequently the company is redeployed into an open skirmish order to act as light troops (2g).
3. Reaching the Fort Rouillé clearing and seeing the British line, the American units (3) form line-of-battle (3a, 3b) with the rifle units and militia on their left flank (3c).
4. Close-quarter fighting fluctuates across the open clearing (4, 4a).
5. U.S. vessels (5) move alongside the British-Canadian position and fire into their flank, causing significant casualties.
6. Overwhelmed by U.S. numbers and firepower, the British-Canadian units begin a fighting withdrawal toward the Western Battery and Fort York (6, 6a, 6b).

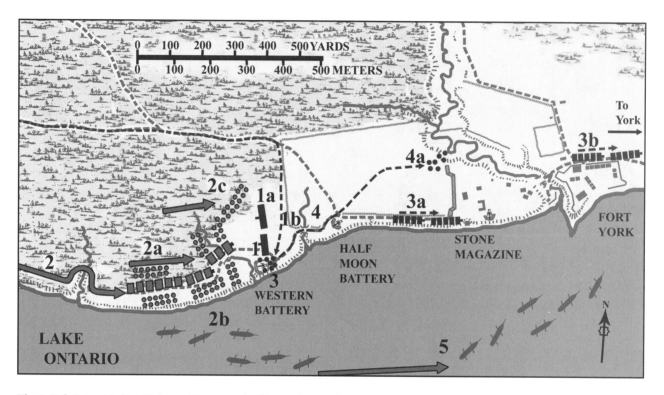

The British Retreat to Fort York and Disaster at the Western Battery (circa 9:30–11:30 a.m.)

1. British forces, having retreated to the Western Battery, establish a new line of defence (1, 1a). Captain Jarvie's company arrives and enters the battery (1b).

2. The main American force (2) advances along the lakefront trail (2a), supported by the firepower of their fleet on their right (2b) and riflemen on their left (2c).

3. Fire from the British line and Western Battery (3) halts the American advance until an accidental explosion inside the battery causes serious casualties among the defenders and makes the position untenable. Following the explosion, some defending units retreat toward Fort York (3a), while other detachments begin an evacuation toward York (3b).

4. Captain Jarvie's and Lieutenant Jarvis's companies (4) evacuate the Western Battery and move into the shelter of the creek bed lying north of Government House and the stone magazine (4a).

5. American fleet vessels (5) move into the York harbour and begin a bombardment of the Fort York defences, as well as firing on any targets of opportunity.

units toward Fort York. All that now remained as a line of defence to oppose the American advance was the incomplete earthen wall and dilapidated wooden stockade surrounding the land face of Fort York.

To counter any further defensive opposition, the American fleet moved to a position directly south of the stockade and began firing into the fort, systematically demolishing everything in sight and making any exposed movement by the defenders highly dangerous. After evacuating his unit from the Western Battery, the badly wounded Captain Jarvie led his remaining men in a wide detour away from the lake to avoid any further cannonading from the enemy boats and possible capture by the American troops to the west. Reaching the relative cover of the shallow streambed located on the north side of the Government House grounds, Jarvie halted his men. Prior to the attack, this position had been designated in the garrison's general orders as the place of assembly for the militia and served as a known point to which further orders should come. Shortly thereafter, they were joined by the remnants of Lieutenant Jarvis's artillerymen as well as other militiamen who had become separated from their units. Still without any firm orders, Jarvie decided to continue to remain where he was to await directions or developments.

By this point, General Sheaffe had conceded that the day was lost. Seeking to preserve what remained of his forces, he ordered his remaining regular troops to begin a general retreat east toward the town. Not wanting to leave anything behind that might be of value or use to the enemy, he gave orders to destroy the fort's sturdy stone ammunition magazine that had been built into the bank of the waterfront, directly below Government House. This magazine held, by one estimate, over 30,000 pounds of powder and explosive shells. Unfortunately, he neglected to notify the detachments of militia at the streambed assembly point, thus leaving them behind and unaware of the pending detonation.

Meanwhile, considering the day as won, General Pike marshalled his troops on the open ground to the southwest of the fort. He was expecting to receive notice of a ceremony of formal surrender, since the Royal Standard still flew over Government House. Suddenly, a huge smoky fireball erupted into the afternoon air. Within seconds, the debris of the magazine and fragments of bedrock crashed to earth among the exposed American troops, causing havoc in the regimented columns. Over 250 men were instantly killed or badly injured, including General Pike, who was struck by a large stone fragment and died shortly thereafter. Even aboard the American ships offshore, the explosion caused damage and casualties as shards of stone, wood, and metal flew over five hundred yards from the point of detonation.

At the streambed, the sound of the explosion, only two hundred yards away, was deafening and the concussion wave shook the ground beneath the feet of Jarvie's detachment and their fellow militiaman. Although significantly closer to the source of the explosion than the Americans, they were initially partially protected from the worst effects of the direct blast by the raised bank of the stream and embankment of the fort's defences. However, only seconds later they were subjected to the impact of a torrent

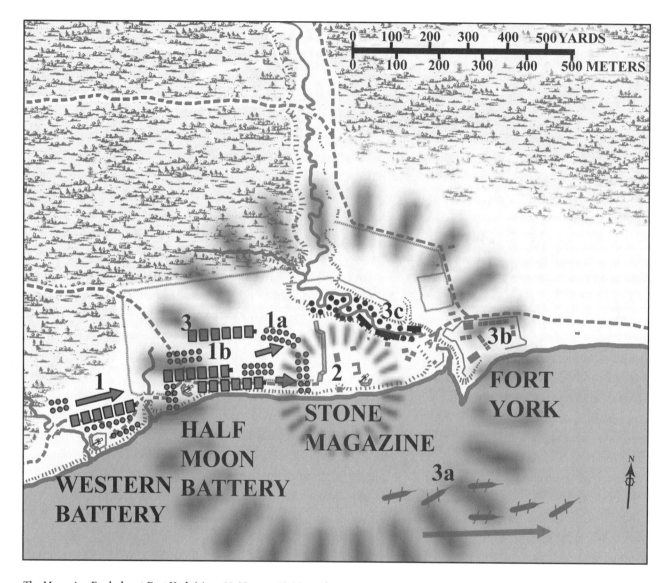

The Magazine Explodes at Fort York (circa 11:30 a.m.–12:30 p.m.)

1. The American force (1), considering the day won, advances to the west of Fort York and after sending pickets forward to cover their front (1a) begin to form units in preparation for an expected formal surrender of the fort and town (1b).
2. A detachment of British troops rig and detonate the main stone magazine to deny it to the Americans (2).
3. The resultant blast and explosion debris causes significant casualties within the assembled American columns (3). Lesser degrees of damage and injury are also inflicted aboard vessels of the American fleet (3a), within Fort York (3b), and among the ranks of Jarvie's and Jarvis's forgotten units of Canadian militia in the Garrison Creek bed on the north side of the Government House (3c).

of soil, stone, and building debris, which resulted in numerous injuries.

Believing the explosion to be the precursor to an immediate British counterattack, the deputy American commander, Colonel Cromwell Pearce, had great difficulty rallying his shocked and disorganized troops. Sheaffe, however, failed to take advantage of the moment and continued his retreat toward the town. En route, he ordered the burning of the nearly completed *Sir Isaac Brock* on the stocks, as well as a quantity of valuable naval supplies, to prevent their falling into American hands. He then abandoned his militia and continued his march east, straight through the town and out onto the road (today's King Street) leading to Kingston. Thus, it was left to Lieutenant Colonel Chewett and Major Allen (3rd York Militia), accompanied by the local firebrand clergyman, the Reverend John Strachan, to treat with the Americans for the terms of surrender. Frustrated in their attempts to lay hands on the *Sir Isaac Brock*, and having suffered severely from the explosion, the Americans dealt harshly with the Canadian negotiators and imposed severe terms for the surrender of the town.

During the next few days, the Americans, abetted by disaffected members of the local population and pro-American sympathizers, emptied the military storehouses and major private warehouses around the town, transferring most of their spoils to the awaiting fleet for transport back to Sackets Harbor. Despite previous official American assurances to the contrary, several incidents of personal intimidation and the looting of private homes took place. Eventually, on May 2, the American forces began to board the waiting ships.

Later that day, Commodore Chauncey and General Dearborn sailed for Fort Niagara to begin preparations for the next phase of the campaign. The remainder of the fleet, however, became trapped in the harbour by foul weather conditions until the 8th, when they finally set sail for the Niagara frontier. Behind them, the traumatized citizens of York began to pick up the pieces of their lives, while the paroled militia and entire civilian citizenry of the town condemned Sheaffe for abandoning them at their time of greatest need. So loud did this subsequent criticism become that it precipitated a crisis of confidence in the continued leadership of the Upper Canada governor. As a result, Sir George Prevost was eventually forced to relieve General Sheaffe of his command and replace him with a new commander — General Baron Francis De Rottenburg.

During the period of American occupation, most of Jarvie's and Jarvis's men had unwillingly become part of the militia forced to submit their paroles to the Americans. However, Jarvie and a few men sought to remain free and went "on the run," hiding in the woods or sheltering with sympathetic residents of the town. In fact, despite being severely wounded, Captain Jarvie was reported to have remained at large for two days in the woods before being forced to surrender and receive medical treatment. This, however, was at the cost of his submitting to a parole not to engage in any active or combat activities against any American force until officially exchanged for an equivalent ranking American officer on his parole or otherwise released from his obligation by the signed mutual agreement of representatives of the warring nations.

Another officer who had put his name forward for the new regiment, Captain Archibald McLean, had similarly volunteered himself to General Sheaffe at the start of the battle. Previously, McLean had been serving on the general's staff as the acting quartermaster general of militia while he recuperated from the severe wound he had received at the Battle of Queenston Heights the previous October. Now, although still only partially recovered, he took on the job of ensuring ammunition was forwarded to the troops during the early part of the battle and supervised the removal of supplies from the military stores once the retreat was ordered. With this duty completed when the British forces abandoned York, instead of surrendering, Captain McLean took it upon himself to carry away the regimental colours of his former regiment, the 3rd York Militia, to prevent their being captured as trophies of war by the Americans. These two flags had only recently been formally presented to the regiment, and were the pride of the corps, having been sewn by the wives and ladies of the town and not issued from Britain. Removing the colours from their poles, he took them to a house on the northern edge of the town. However, when informed that parties of Americans were approaching and searching nearby buildings, he made a hasty exit with the colours and buried them in a nearby wooded lot before making his way east to rejoin the British force retreating toward Kingston.

The American occupation of York lasted until May 8, 1813, when the fleet sailed south toward the Niagara River. With its garrison buildings and other military structures burnt to the ground, and

virtually all of its local militia restricted by their paroles, the town of York was left with no capability to mount any kind of defence against any future attack. Moreover, there was no immediate sign of the British military making a rapid return to start the rebuilding process. Using the excuse of being on parole, many of the men connected with the embodied militia units took the opportunity to return to their homes and farms. Captain Jarvie, however, took a more serious view of the situation. Despite his wounds, he established his company as an effective garrison police force until the end of the month, when the first units from Kingston arrived to begin the reconstruction of the British military garrison at York.

GARRISON DUTIES

During June and July, Jarvie's paroled company were fully occupied in a combination of non-combat duties. On the west side of Garrison Creek they cleared away the debris of the old government buildings that had been destroyed by the explosion of the magazine, and on the same ground laid out the lines of a new fortification, which would become the new Fort York. As well as working on the construction of the new barracks and fortifications, they acted as garrison guards and provided crews for small boats used to courier dispatches between the forces fighting on the Niagara frontier and the main British headquarters at Kingston.

Toward the end of July, a new threat to the partially reconstructed position at Fort York arose when

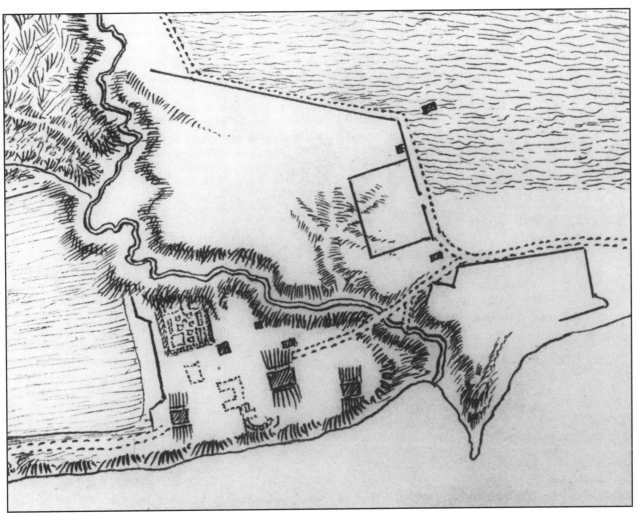

Library and Archives Canada, NMC - C-38847.

A map of the new 1814 Fort York site during reconstruction after the earlier 1813 fort had been destroyed by the Americans. The empty waterfront enclosure to the right of the Garrison Creek marks the location of the earlier fort. The original Government House, also ruined, is marked by the three-sided dotted outline. Curiously, the highly distinctive crater left by the explosion of the magazine (located to the left of the half-moon battery emplacement and seen in all other versions of maps from this period), is omitted.

an American flotilla, loaded with nearly five hundred infantry and marines, sailed into the bay and proceeded to land a new invading army, unopposed and virtually without firing a shot. This American force had previously made an amphibious attempt to attack and destroy the vital British supply depot and communications hub at the Head-of-the-Lake, but had been thwarted by the British having rapidly concentrated all of their available forces, scattered across the region, for the defence of that post. Included in that redeployment were almost all of the garrison of troops stationed at Fort York, thus leaving the post virtually empty, except for the on-parole men from the Incorporated Militia.

Although this affair at the Head-of-the-Lake rated as a victory for the British, it had an unfortunate consequence, as the American naval force was then able to move up to York far more quickly than the fort's garrison could march back along the shore, thus allowing the Americans to easily capture the fort and town. Even had their paroles not prevented them from actively opposing the American landing, the small number of men forming this division of the Incorporated Militia could never have mounted any credible defence against the overwhelming force held by the enemy. Instead, they used what little time they had to spirit off and hide as many military supplies as possible in secret caches in the woodlands north of the town. Once the enemy landed, however, the men from the Incorporated Militia were forced to watch impotently while the invaders sought to destroy all of the military and public structures that had been rebuilt during the previous two months. To the militiamen's added dismay, the Americans, by using threats,

intimidation, and the connivance of sympathetic local civilians, were able to locate and seize much of what had been hidden.

The most irksome aspect was that this raid was commanded by Colonel Winfield Scott. Scott had been captured the previous year at Queenston Heights, and, in exactly the same manner as Jarvie's and Jarvis's men, had been released on his parole of honour not to engage in any hostile activities until he was officially exchanged for a British officer of equal or a quota of other ranks. To the men of the Incorporated Militia, Scott's active involvement in the attack was a flagrant breach of his parole and a stain upon his honour as a gentleman — a matter that far outranked the immediate military issues.

Considering Scott's behaviour as releasing them from their own paroles, a number of men from the two companies perpetrated a few minor acts of sabotage upon the occupiers by way of retaliation. Unable to accurately identify the specific culprits, the Americans resorted to randomly arresting men of the Incorporated Militia, including: Lieutenant Thomas Humberstone, Private John Murphy, Private John Deetsman, Private John Drake, and Private William Starkey. These men were subsequently charged with breaching their paroles, a crime that rendered them liable to being punished with sentences of imprisonment or execution. Fortunately, the Americans only chose to reclassify these men as prisoners of war and took them into captivity in the United States when they left York a few days later.

Jarvie's men, now reduced to being commanded by Ensign Daniel Brooke, once again constituted the bulk of York's military garrison and remained on active duty until the return of British forces the following week. During this interval, they maintained a steadying presence amongst the distressed citizenry, who had now suffered two invasions in less than six months and, in a number of cases, had seen their homes and properties looted. They also took those persons who had actively aided the enemy into custody and held them for subsequent interrogation and action by the appropriate authorities.

Once the British troops returned to York, work recommenced on the refortification of Fort York, with the marking of ground lines for the construction of barracks, blockhouses, and batteries. However, because the previous cycles of building and destruction had used up most of the readily available stocks of building materials, the rate of new construction slowed to a crawl.

During the succeeding months of August and September, the military situation on the Niagara frontier took precedence in the minds of the British military commanders. All available supplies of men and *matériel* were ordered to be forwarded there with the utmost speed. This left the garrison at York relegated to being a low-priority post for receiving new supplies. However, because the American naval fleet was effectively blockading the direct naval shipment of British military supplies from Kingston to Niagara, everything had to be routed through York. Consequently, while Jarvis's company served in the fort's artillery batteries, Jarvie's company was regularly seconded to the Commissariat and Transport Departments for extra duties, including the collection of stockpiles of supplies from Kingston

and transporting them up to York in small boats that could hug the shoreline to avoid detection. They would then transfer the stores to the military warehouses in York and maintain them before finally loading the supplies once more and manning the boats assigned to move the *matériel* on to Niagara.

By the end of this transportation work, although they had lost all of their own equipment and baggage during the April attack and then witnessed what little was resupplied to them confiscated in the second American landing at York, Jarvie's company was the only one from the entire corps not sending urgent letters to their superiors for requisitions of clothing, uniforms, and other "necessaries." One can only presume this was purely by coincidence.

By October 1813, as far as the British command was concerned, the military situation in Upper Canada had changed considerably, and for the worse. Sickness was ravaging the ranks of the regiments fighting on the Niagara frontier. The British flotilla on Lake Erie had been decisively beaten and captured by its American counterpart on September 10. The entire western end of the province was now in the hands of the Americans, following the chaotic forced retreat of the British army from the Detroit frontier and its subsequent humiliating rout at the Battle of Moravianstown on October 5. Their principal Native ally, Tecumseh, had been killed at Moravianstown, leaving the future of an effective British-Native alliance in serious jeopardy. And the American military leadership had shifted their attention from the Niagara and Detroit corridors and were planning to attack the vital St. Lawrence supply route and its strategic strongholds of Kingston and Montreal.

For this campaign, large numbers of American troops had been withdrawn from the Niagara frontier to Sackets Harbor to prepare for an amphibious assault on Kingston, after which, a two-pronged pincer movement was contemplated for the reduction of Montreal and the severing of the lifeline of supplies to the British garrisons in Upper Canada. To counter this offensive, General De Rottenburg ordered a repositioning of his own troops away from the Niagara frontier toward Kingston. As a result, large numbers of men and huge volumes of supplies now had to be sent back the way they had come only weeks before. For the men of the Incorporated Militia garrisoned at York, this reversal of flow meant that once again they were pressed into service as transport troops, working extended hours transferring military supplies "downlake" to Kingston aboard whatever bateaux or other small boats were available.

During the course of these duties, one detachment of Jarvie's men had a narrow escape. On October 6, as they rowed along the Lake Ontario shoreline, they spotted ahead of them an additional flotilla of boats filled with two companies of troops from the DeWatteville Regiment. These troops had just completed the arduous journey up from Lower Canada to join the British forces on the Niagara front when the changing military situation demanded their return to Kingston. Although they were hugging the shoreline to evade the prowling ships of the dominant American fleet, the British convoy was unlucky enough to be sighted. As enemy naval vessels began to close in from the south, Jarvie's men ran their boats ashore at a small creek and took up a defensive position under the cover of the heavy treeline blanketing the shore and prepared to defend their cargo.

The boats carrying the troops, however, unwisely attempted to make a run for it. Unwilling to engage in a ship-to-shore contest, and with the easier target of open boats available to them, the Americans swept down on the hapless British force, forced it to surrender, and made all onboard prisoners of war. Once the Americans and their prisoners left the area, Jarvie's detachment completed its journey to Kingston and reported the incident to the authorities, precipitating a major exchange of recriminations between the Sir George Prevost and Sir James Yeo, over Yeo's failure to provide a proper escort for the ill-fated convoy.

Returning to York, Jarvie's company served within the garrison during the next four months. No accounts have been located to provide details of this time; however, the monthly roll call accounts show that detachments of men served at several different locations and worked on a variety of projects. These assignments included construction work at the new Fort York, cutting wood for fuel and construction, and burning lime to create an ingredient that was then used in the production of mortar to be used in building projects. At other times they served in the Commissariat Department, tended cattle, served at the Humber River telegraph station, or acted as garrison and picket guards at outlying posts such as Gibraltar Point, the Yonge Street blockhouse, and the Don River blockhouse. They continued to crew boats and sleighs ferrying supplies from Kingston to York and Burlington Heights, as well as to act as transfer guards to parties of American prisoners of war being sent to Kingston and Montreal after the actions at Fort Niagara and Buffalo.

In February 1814, orders were posted for the consolidation of the several detachments of Incorporated Militia at York. Since Captain Jarvie was still not capable of resuming his duties and had been on an extended leave of absence to receive medical treatment, his and Jarvis's companies were merged into a single infantry unit, which subsequently became Company No. 2 of the new regimental line under the command of Lieutenant Jarvis.

6

THE NIAGARA DIVISION

Having already seen service during the latter part of 1812 as part of the flank companies of their respective embodied militia regiments in the actions at Detroit, Queenston, and Frenchman's Creek, the men who volunteered to serve in the Niagara companies of the Incorporated Militia were already relatively well trained when they came to their new regiment. Nevertheless, an intensive round of company-level drill instruction was immediately commenced by the company commanders, Major Titus G. Simons (2nd York Militia), Captain James Kerby (2nd Lincoln Militia), and Captain Abraham A. Rapelje (2nd Norfolk Militia). At least three other officers from the flank companies, S. Cook (1st Lincoln), A. Cameron (1st Lincoln), and J. McKenny (regimental association not known), were unsuccessful in attaining the quotas needed to attain their desired ranks.

The three established companies continued to recruit additional volunteers from within the communities bounded by the area of the Grand River (Long Point to Port Dover), Head-of-the-Lake (Ancaster to Hamilton), and the Niagara frontier (Newark to Fort Erie), and with the issue of several items of military clothing, including shirts, trousers, gaiters, boots, and forage caps, they gradually took on a more regimental appearance. Regimental "red" coats, on the other hand, were in desperately short supply.

While some well-worn and damaged regular army regimental coats were issued to Rapelje's company during early April, the other two companies had to make do with an issue of part of the newly authorized

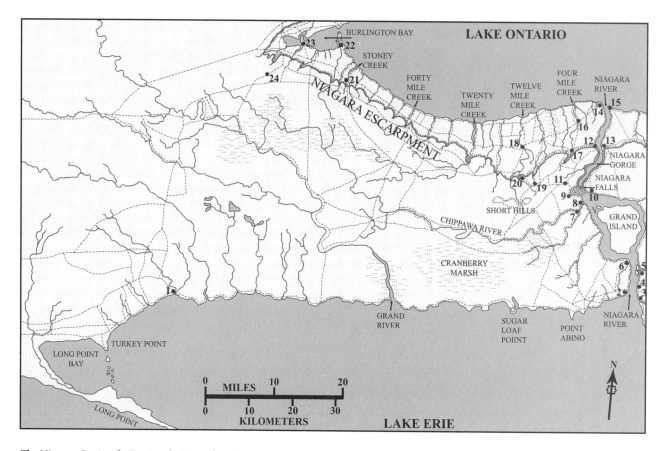

The Niagara Peninsula During the War of 1812–1815

1. Port Dover
2. Fort Erie
3. Buffalo
4. Black Rock
5. U.S. Naval Yard on Scajaquada Creek
6. Frenchman's Creek
7. Weishoun's
8. Chippawa
9. Bridgewater Mills
10. Fort Schlosser
11. Lundy's Lane Hilltop
12. Queenston
13. Lewiston
14. Newark
15. Fort Niagara
16. Crossroads (Virgil)
17. St. Davids
18. Shipman's Corners
19. Beaver Dams
20. De Cou Mill
21. Stoney Creek
22. King's Head Inn
23. Burlington Heights
24. Ancaster

interim "green with red facings" uniforms that had been approved for issue to the Canadian militia in early 1813. This alternative uniform was forced upon the British military authorities due to a breakdown in supply of ready-made coats from Great Britain, coupled with a scarcity of the heavy red wool coating material being available locally to produce sufficient regimental coats as per the regulation "red with green facings." (For more detail on uniforms, see Appendix B.)

FIRE AND RETIRE

By early May 1813, the three Niagara companies of Incorporated Militia were actively engaged in patrol and garrison duties, with Major Simons's company being stationed at Burlington Heights, Captain Kerby's at Chippawa, and Captain Rapelje's at Fort George. For the men of Captain Rapelje's detachment, the news of the British defeat at York was followed closely by the arrival of the American fleet, transporting their victorious army to the Niagara frontier. During the succeeding weeks, this enemy force was strengthened by

additional detachments arriving from Sackets Harbor. It was obvious that a major attack was imminent, but exactly where it would fall was not known. Faced with a limited supply of defending troops and conflicting reports of enemy troop concentrations at several widely dispersed points, the local senior British commander, General John Vincent, was placed in a difficult position. To cover most of the potential invasion points, he was forced to disperse his force into undermanned "penny-packet" detachments, sometimes stationed at wide intervals that left undefended gaps in the line. Anticipating that any American attack would occur in the darkness of the pre-dawn, Vincent ordered that the defenders were to be roused at 2:00 a.m. and remain on full alert until dawn.

This stressful situation continued for over a week until the night of May 24–25, when one detachment, stationed downriver from Queenston, heard the sounds of boats being launched from the opposite bank. In response, they fired into the darkness with every weapon they had. This alarm cascaded down the Canadian side of the riverbank with successive

Sketches from Nature Made in Upper Canada in the Years 1803, 1804, and 1805, E. Walsh, M.D., 49th Regiment, artist, 1805. Part of the view shows the Canadian bank of the Niagara River at Newark (Niagara-on-the-Lake) in 1805. Fort George and Navy Hall lie to the left, while Newark is to the right.

Clement Library, University of Michigan.

posts opening fire until dawn revealed a small flotilla of lightly manned boats skirting the American shore just upriver from the town of Newark. As the boats came in range of the British batteries at and alongside Fort George, their militia gunners, including volunteers from Rapelje's company, began to open fire with an estimated five pieces of artillery. The American battery positions on the opposite shore retaliated with no less than twenty-five cannon and mortars, either firing explosive shells, or "hot shot" cannonballs. By noon, almost every building inside Fort George, as well as the surrounding wooden stockade, was burning fiercely. The militia artillery crews, although initially attempting to maintain the unequal contest with the American batteries, were eventually forced to abandon their posts.

The modern reconstruction of Fort George, as seen from the American side of the Niagara River. Photo taken in 2009.

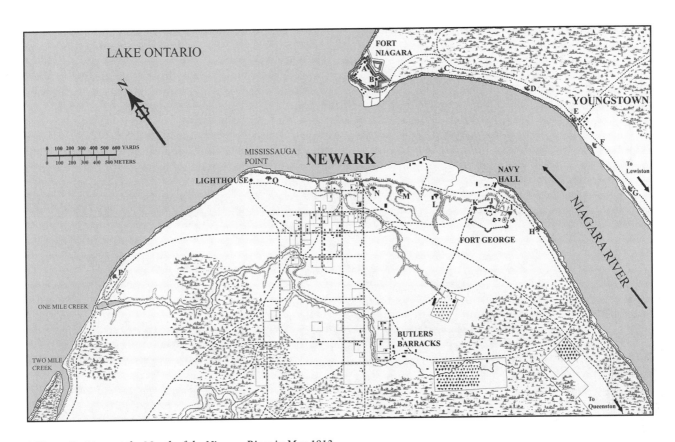

Military Positions at the Mouth of the Niagara River in May 1813

A.B.   U.S. battery positions at Fort Niagara
C to G.   U.S. detached riverside batteries
H.   British detached upper riverside battery
I to K.   British battery positions at Fort George
L to O.   British detached lower riverside "Newark" batteries
P.   British detached lakeside battery

Throughout the afternoon, sentries watched impotently as ships from the American fleet edged along the Lake Ontario shoreline, making soundings and placing buoys. Their movements clearly indicated that the American fleet would place itself in the rear of the British positions to provide fire support for any landings in that quarter. By nightfall, the British fully expected an assault on the morrow, but where the blow would fall was still unclear. Fort George had been reduced to a gutted wreck and the troops manning the various posts at the river mouth were by now thoroughly exhausted. Taking the chance that the anticipated American attack at Fort George would preclude any simultaneous action above the Falls, Vincent ordered Kerby's detachment at Chippawa, as well as several of the embodied militia units, to march to Fort George to bolster the British position there.

Under the cover of a thick fog and in the still air of the predawn on May 27, some sixteen American warships and over 130 landing craft rowed, or were towed, out into Lake Ontario. They moved westward until they reached a position directly behind the British left flank. With daylight came a slight breeze, which rolled away the thick curtain of fog to reveal the American

The Invasion at Fort George, *adapted from an original sketch made by an American surgeon (A. Trowbridge) onboard the American fleet during the troop landing on May 27, 1813. Fort Niagara is the flagged fortification on the left bank of the river and Fort George the flagged fortification on the right bank. The town of Newark and Mississauga Point Lighthouse are shown in the centre. The American vanguard of boats is pulling toward the British Two Mile Creek Battery, the small, flagged fortification at the right.*

Library and Archives Canada, C-23675.

intentions. At a signal from the flagship, the entire fleet began to move toward the shore. The larger ships began a systematic pounding of the shore batteries, while the smaller armed vessels edged inshore to cover the proposed landings. Between them, the first wave of boats pulled for the shore, packed with troops, and led, once again, by Colonel Winfield Scott.

On the Canadian shore, while Vincent ordered an immediate redeployment toward the lakefront, the first defenders destined to face the Americans were detachments from the Glengarry Light Infantry, the Royal Newfoundland Regiment, Runchey's Company of Coloured Men, the Lincoln Militia, and a party of Norton's warriors, in all no more than 220 men.

Seeing the enemy boats aiming for a landing adjacent to Two Mile Creek, the composite force moved up and began firing into the packed boats from the dominant waterfront bluffs that overlooked the beach. However, after engaging in a round of attacks and counterattacks, the small force was eventually driven away from the shoreline by the firepower of the supporting American ships and the threat of additional formations of enemy troops landing on their flanks. Reforming farther inland at the far end of some open fields, they were reinforced, and renewed the conflict with the advancing Americans. Once again, the overwhelming firepower of the American formations proved too much, and, after suffering significant numbers of casualties, the defenders began to give way and retired toward Newark.

During this time, a further composite force of troops had been assembled at Fort George under the direction of Lieutenant Colonel John Harvey.

This formation was composed of companies of the 49th Regiment, Kerby's and Rapelje's companies of Incorporated Militia, and scratch units of men assembled from the local embodied militia regiments, unassigned artillery crews, and hospital invalids. Leading this motley formation to a position in front of the town, Harvey formed a new defensive line near the Presbyterian churchyard and along the bank of the adjacent Gordon's Ravine. There, he also rallied several sizable bodies of men retreating from the lakefront and prepared to re-engage the enemy.

Having beaten the initial formations of defenders and seeing them retreat through the woods bordering One Mile Creek, the American attackers paused while they awaited further reinforcement, then formed their regiments into columns. Once in position, these columns advanced across the open ground following the shoreline, ensuring they remained under the cover of the guns aboard their fleet. Despite facing an overwhelming force, Harvey's composite line opened fire on the American columns, and for nearly half an hour held back the repeated attacks made by the American centre. But once Scott's light troops outflanked the British left wing, there was no alternative for Harvey but to retreat through the town to the garrison common behind Fort George.

Fortunately for the British, the Americans once again did not immediately press their advantage, allowing General Vincent to begin regrouping his remaining units behind the shelter of the partially destroyed earthworks of Fort George. In this "dead zone" they were hidden from the fire of the U.S. batteries on the other side of the river and had direct

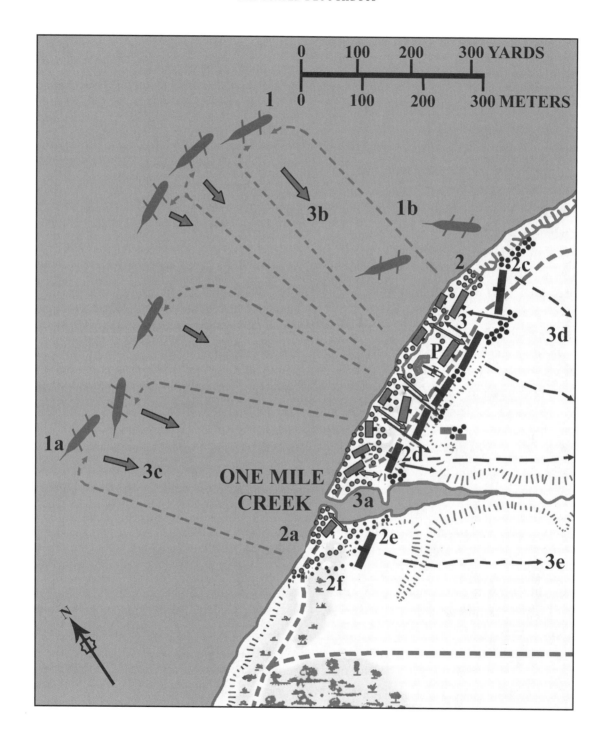

ONE MILE
CREEK

The Battle of Fort George, the Fight for the Landing Ground (circa 8:00–9:00 a.m.)

1. The main American flotilla (1, 1a) takes up station opposite One Mile Creek to cover the amphibious landing, while other vessels move inshore (1b) and bombard the covering shore battery (P).
2. U.S. advance forces (2, 2a) land under fire from a composite force of British regulars, Canadian militia (2c, 2d, 2e), and Native allies (2f), and are initially contained on the beach.
3. U.S. forces (3, 3a) make a number of unsuccessful attempts to push off the beach, resulting in a succession of close-quarter engagements that fluctuate across the open ground above the landing ground. With the landing of an increasing number of American troops (3b, 3c), supported by artillery fire from the fleet, the defenders suffer enough casualties that they are forced to retire to a new position away from the waterfront (3d, 3e).

P. Detached gun battery at One Mile Creek

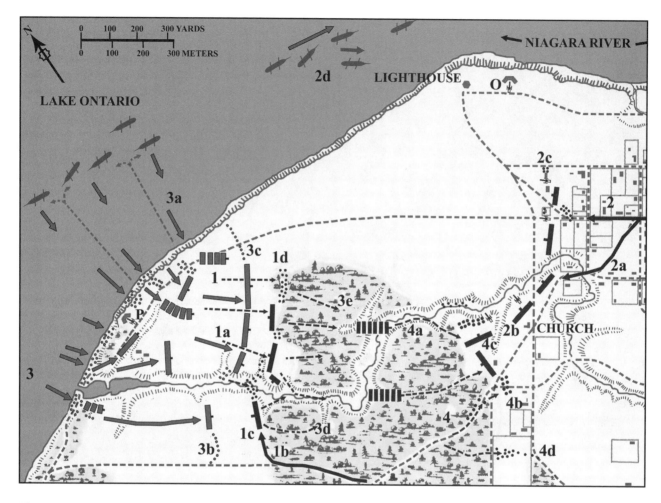

The Americans Overwhelm the Initial Defenders' Positions (circa 9:00–10:30 a.m.)

1. British forces retreating from the beach (1, 1a) are reinforced (1b) and establish a new line of battle (1c, 1d).
2. A composite British force (2, 2a), including Captain Kerby and Captain Rapelje's companies, move up from Fort George and establish a defensive position near to the Presbyterian church (2b, 2c), but far enough away from the waterfront to avoid gunfire from elements of the American flotilla that are moving up into the river mouth (2d).
3. Backed by additional waves of reinforcements (3, 3a), U.S. forces move off the beach and advance on the British line (3b, 3c). While heavy, close-quarter firing results in significant casualties on both sides, overwhelming American firepower decimates the British line. Consequently, the British break off and begin to retreat (3d, 3e).
4. Remnants of the British force (4, 4a) retreat through the woods and gully of One Mile Creek. Reaching the secondary British position, some units re-form on the left flank of the British force (4b, 4c), while others leave the area or rejoin units at Fort George (4d).

O. Lighthouse gun battery
P. Detached gun battery at One Mile Creek

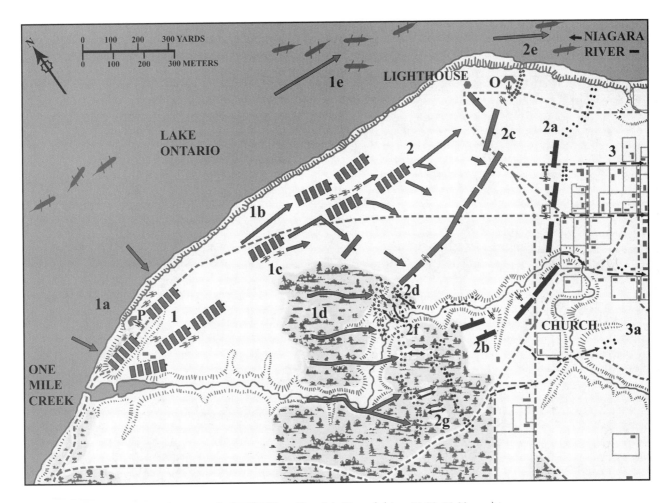

The Main Engagement Takes Place Near the Presbyterian Church in Newark (circa 10:30–11:30 a.m.)

1. After seeing the British disengage and retire, the main American force (1) forms into columns and waits for additional reinforcements (1a). They then advance along the shoreline in two main columns (1b, 1c), protected on the right by their light troops in the woods (1d) and their fleet on the left (1e).

2. Approaching the lighthouse at Mississauga Point, the U.S. columns (2) are confronted by the British force on their flank (2a, 2b). The Americans wheel into line and engage (2c, 2d), backed by gunfire from the American flotilla (2e). At the same time, U.S. light troops, advancing through the woods on the American right flank are engaged by re-formed British and Canadian units (2f, 2g).

3. Following fierce fighting and after suffering additional heavy losses, depleted British and Canadian units (3, 3a) begin to retreat toward Fort George, spiking and abandoning the riverside batteries as they go.

O. Lighthouse gun battery
P. Detached gun battery at One Mile Creek

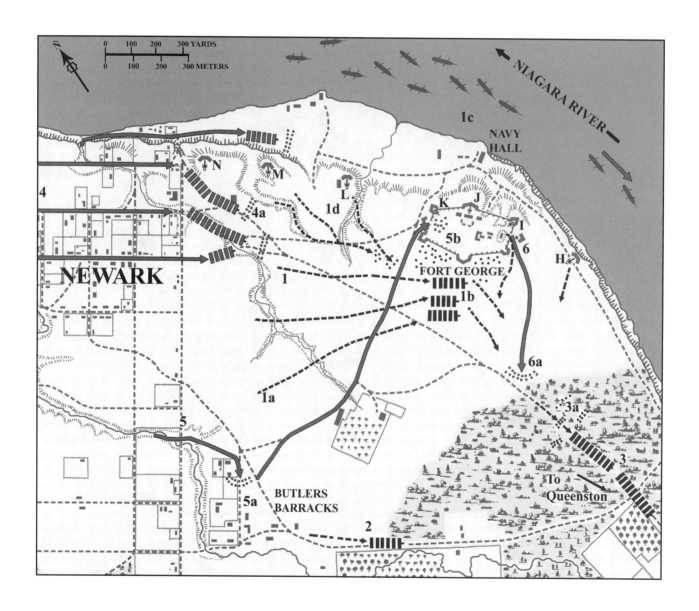

The British Retreat from Fort George and Newark (circa 11:30 a.m.–1:00 p.m.)

1. Depleted British units (1, 1a) retreat through Newark, and attempt to re-form behind Fort George (1b). However, Chauncey's flotilla outflanks the exposed British right flank (1c), forcing a general evacuation from all the remaining British battery positions (1d), Fort George and Butler's Barracks.
2. Remaining elements of the militias and Native allies at Butler's Barracks march to join in the retreat toward Queenston (2).
3. Surviving British-Canadian and Native allied units begin a full-scale retreat toward Queenston (3), covered in part by Captain Kerby's company of Incorporated Militia (3a).
4. After seeing the British disengage and retire, Major General Lewis orders the main American force to wait until all American reinforcements have arrived before cautiously advancing on Fort George (4, 4a).
5. U.S. light forces and detachments of militia (5) press forward upon the American right flank to secure Butler's Barracks (5a), then advance on Fort George but only capture some British wounded, stragglers, and women (5b).
6. Against orders, Winfield Scott commands his light troops to pursue the British (6, 6a).

H.L.M.N.　British detached riverside gun batteries
I.J.K.　British battery positions at Fort George

access to the main road leading to Queenston for communication, reinforcement, or retreat. However, once the ships from Chauncey's flotilla moved up the Niagara River, the Americans were able to fire across this previously sheltered position and the road.

Deprived of any position to base further resistance, and fronted by a force vastly outnumbering his own, this new threat to his line of retreat convinced Vincent the day was lost, and he ordered the evacuation of the ruined fort and the withdrawal of all units to Queenston. For the duty of rearguard, Vincent assigned the remnants of the Native allies and Kerby's company of militia. Having fought in the battle, both Kerby's and Rapelje's companies were fortunate not to have suffered any wounded or killed. However, as the retreat began to degenerate into a flight, they had to abandon most of their regimental supplies and baggage. As well, while skirmishing with the leading elements of the American pursuers in the thick woods to the south of the fort, a number of men from Kerby's rearguard became separated from their unit, and in two cases were made prisoners of war.

Although Vincent had initially planned to move south to Fort Erie, his subordinate commanders warned that this would expose his army to the possibility of being cut off and surrounded. He accepted their recommendations that the army march west toward the strategic crossroads at Beaver Dams, thus maintaining a secure line of retreat. He also sent dispatches ordering the garrisons at Chippawa and Fort Erie to destroy their posts and march to join his force at Beaver Dams. Despite having suffered severe losses of manpower and supplies, most of Vincent's surviving troops, especially the militia and Native allies, expected that their commander would concentrate his forces at Beaver Dams, then make a counteroffensive on the American invaders once troops from Chippawa, Fort Erie, Burlington Heights and additional parties of Native warriors from the Grand River joined them. Instead, and to their grave concern, new orders were posted the following day that ordered the continuation of the retreat to a new position at Forty Mile Creek. After a disorganized march and remaining only two days at this eminently defensible position, yet another retreat was ordered — this time, all the way back to the Head-of-the-Lake and the British supply depot at Burlington Heights.

Rather than being encouraged to stay with the regulars and continue to fight the invaders, most of the embodied militia units were officially disbanded and told to return to their homes. Once there, they would be vulnerable, awaiting the advancing Americans and submitting to certain capture and possible imprisonment or parole. Not surprisingly, morale within the army plummeted. The Natives reacted by leaving en masse to see to the protection of their families and homes along the Grand River, and even the most ardent Crown supporters wondered if this was the end of Upper Canada as a province. Everything now hinged on the actions of the Americans.

Reaching Burlington Heights on the evening of May 31, General Vincent's forces began to dig in on the dominant promontory of land that marked the Head-of-the-Lake, the lynchpin of British control of Upper Canada. Outnumbered by the

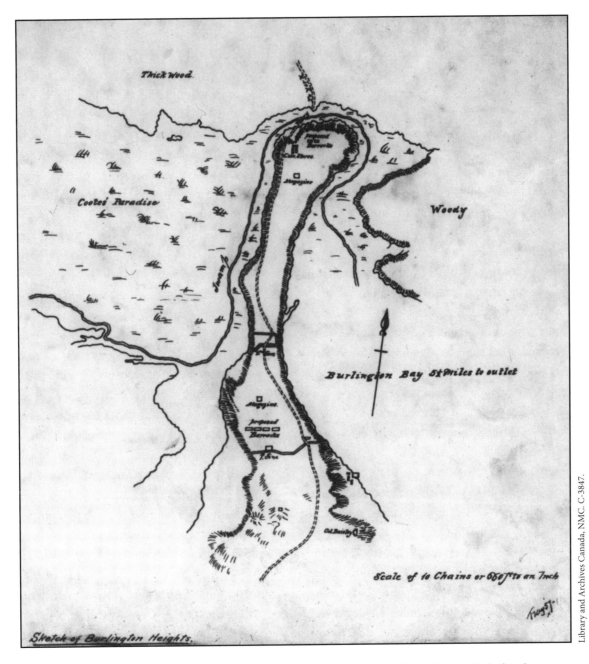

A contemporary British map of the defences established at the strategic transportation and supply hub of Burlington Heights (Hamilton), circa 1816.

enemy at least three to one, Vincent knew he had a vital decision to make regarding his further movements. His position at Burlington Heights allowed him to continue to supply Brigadier General Proctor and the Lake Erie fleet. Any further retreat would cut that lifeline and effectively hand Upper Canada to the United States. On the other hand, Vincent also recognized that if he were to remain in position, the Americans could use their naval superiority to cross Lake Ontario, land troops in his rear, and cut off any retreat to York and Kingston. The Americans, however, remained at the Niagara River, enabling Vincent to hold his position and call for reinforcements and supplies to be dispatched from Kingston.

With this change in circumstances, the embodied militia units were once again called out for active duty and placed under the supervision of the Incorporated Militia's senior officer, Major Titus B. Simons. Shortly thereafter, Captain Rapelje's company joined this force, after having been part of the rearguard, with orders to collect any supplies of food and abandoned equipment that could be found, thus denying them to the enemy. Kerby's company, on the other hand, remained with the rearguard, serving alongside detachments of Native allies and provincial dragoons. Together they watched for the Americans' next move.

On June 1, 1813, an American force of some 1,400 men finally advanced from Fort George under the command of General William H. Winder. Marching out at dawn, Winder's column failed to make any serious reconnaissance to ascertain the position or strength of the British forces opposing them, or even to determine the best route for the army to follow toward the Head-of-the-Lake. Moving along the lakeshore road, and staying on the plain below the escarpment, the column kept in close contact with its small flotilla of longboats packed with heavy supplies. Taking this route meant that the American advance was under constant observation from Kerby's troops stationed on the commanding heights to the south. Nor did the weather assist the Americans, as a succession of rainstorms reduced the main road to a mud-choked quagmire.

That same day, the American plan of campaign was disrupted when news arrived that on May 29 the British had made a determined but failed attempt to destroy the American naval base at Sackets Harbor. Fearful for the security of his main shipyard and base of operations, Commodore Chauncey unilaterally withdrew his squadron and sailed east. Without this naval support, any plan to cut off Vincent's line of retreat was rendered void. Dearborn was left with no alternative but to reinforce his land attack. For this duty, Dearborn ordered General John Chandler to advance with an additional 1,600 troops, assume the command of the combined force, and press on to make a frontal attack on Burlington Heights. Expecting to find the army approaching Burlington and preparing to attack the British garrison there, Chandler instead found Winder's troops camped at Forty Mile Creek, far short of their objective. Uniting the forces and taking command, Chandler ordered the advance to continue.

After engaging in a succession of skirmishes with elements of the British rearguard (including Kerby's detachment) during the afternoon of June 5, the American advance was almost in sight of

Burlington Heights. Some miles behind, the main American army of well over three thousand troops was now less than a day's march from the British base at the Head-of-the-Lake. With night drawing on, the army was ordered to encamp in the area now defined as Stoney Creek. Despite the known proximity of the British base, the American troops were positioned along an extended line that stretched from the escarpment to the lake, a front of around two miles. Inevitably, gaps and weak spots in the defensive perimeter developed as the regimental troop placements were left primarily to the discretion of individual commanding officers.

During the course of his earlier retreat to Burlington Heights, General Vincent had been facing the dilemma of either abandoning Burlington Heights — his main supply base and hub of land communications with Proctor — or taking the offensive against a significantly numerically superior enemy and risking annihilation. Looking for local expertise on how best to bolster his position, Vincent sent orders on June 3 for Major Simons to leave his newly formed militia detachments and report immediately for other duties:

> My Dear Sir, General Vincent desires me to say that you must come to headquarters. Your local knowledge and other qualities not necessary to enumerate render you particularly valuable to him at the present moment. Some other officer must take charge of the militia going to Stoney Creek and you must give us the benefit of your advice and assistance here.[1]

On the afternoon of June 5, General Vincent consulted with his senior staff and came to the decision that an attempt should be made to stall the American advance by making a night attack upon the encampment. However, certain that this could only delay, not prevent, a further American advance, Vincent limited the attack force to a total of five companies of regular troops from the 8th (King's) and the 49th Regiments under Lieutenant Colonel Harvey, while Kerby's company and detachments of Natives were sent up onto the escarpment to watch over that flank.

Later that night, the British made their surprise assault. Unfortunately, once the initial fighting began, a breakdown in regimental discipline within the British line allowed the Americans to recover and establish a defensive perimeter. In the darkness, the battle quickly degenerated into a confusing maelstrom of smaller actions between individual detachments of troops scattered across the fields and adjacent woodland. As part of this confusion, both senior American generals, several senior field officers, and almost one hundred rank and file became British prisoners of war. After over an hour of fighting, and having suffered more than two hundred casualties — nearly 30 percent of his disposable force — Lieutenant Colonel Harvey was concerned about revealing his numerical inferiority in the light of the approaching dawn. For this reason, he ordered a withdrawal to Burlington Heights, convinced he had suffered a tactical defeat.

For the Americans, the loss of their commanding generals left the now senior officer Colonel James Burn (Second Light Dragoons) uncertain as to how to proceed. Following an acrimonious and accusatory exchange of views among the surviving command officers, Burn later recorded: "A majority coincided in opinion with me that we ought to retire to our former position at the Forty Mile Creek, where we could be supplied with ammunition and provisions and either advance or remain until further orders."[2]

During the course of the following day, both forces regrouped and planned their next move. For Harvey at Burlington Heights, the night's action had not only inflicted heavy casualty figures, but also resulted in the temporary disappearance of his senior officer, General Vincent. According to subsequent accounts, Vincent had become separated from the attacking force and had wandered around in the darkness until located (according to different versions) by either a party of Natives or Kerby's militiamen. In assessing the British position, Vincent considered that, while the Americans had been halted, they had not been defeated, and still posed a significant threat to the British position at Burlington Heights. He would, therefore, wait for Yeo to arrive with vital reinforcements before commencing any kind of offensive move. In the interim, he dispatched his Native allies and Kerby and Rapelje's companies of Incorporated Militia to shadow and report on the actions taken by the Americans regrouping at Forty Mile Creek.

Watching from the vantage point of the top of the escarpment during the course of June 6, Kerby and Rapelje's force, supported by a small detachment of Natives, could clearly see and make detailed counts of the American force spread out along the Forty Mile Creek on the plain below. Beyond, out on Lake Ontario, there was also the welcome sight of Yeo's flotilla sailing west toward the Head-of-the-Lake with the expected reinforcements. And what had previously only been a small band of dedicated Native allies had become substantially enlarged with the appearance of numerous additional warriors. These new arrivals had heard of the British victory and now offered their services to fight the Americans, whereas only two days before they had been as adamantly determined to remain neutral.

Shortly before sunset, the movement of a strong column was seen on the plain below, not coming from the west, as hoped, but rather from the direction of Fort George in the east. An American force under General Lewis had arrived to bolster the American position. For the men of the Incorporated Militia, it appeared the opportunity for the British to achieve a quick victory had been lost. After sending messengers to Vincent with this developing news, Kerby, Rapelje, and their men could only watch and wait for Vincent's orders.

On the morning of June 8, Yeo's ships appeared once again and anchored opposite the American positions before opening fire. Replying in kind, the Americans began an artillery duel with the British ships. Frustrated at having been inactive for over twenty-four hours, the Native troops clamoured for descending the escarpment and making an attack on the enemy's camp from the rear while their focus was on the ongoing action at the lake. Under orders to maintain his reconnaissance duties and not hazard his men unnecessarily, Kerby opposed the Natives' reckless plan. However, once it was evident that nothing would stop their foray, he detached Rapelje's company to descend to the foot of the escarpment as a reserve to support the attack if it succeeded, or as a rearguard if it failed.

As expected, the initial Native assault caught the Americans by surprise and succeeded in penetrating the southern fringe of the camp. However, almost as quickly, the Americans counterattacked under the leadership of Lieutenant Joseph Eldridge (Thirteenth Regiment), routing the Native force. Seeing the warriors falling back in disorder, Rapelje and his company made a slow fighting retreat back to the crest of the escarpment and rejoined Kerby's waiting line. Behind them, Eldridge's men, disorganized and blown following their steep climb, scrambled up onto the upper ground, fully expecting to see the Natives and Canadians fleeing in panic. Instead, they were brought to a sudden halt by the disciplined volleys of the two companies of militiamen. After firing back a few shots, the Americans rapidly retired back down the slopes to their camp, leaving the militiamen to resume their vigil. In the aftermath of this minor skirmish, General Lewis chose to represent the events with a certain degree of licence in his subsequent report to the secretary of war, John Armstrong.

> A party of savages … made their appearance on the Brow of the mountain (which being perfectly bald, exhibited them to view) approached … and commenced a fire on our Camp.

> I ordered Col. Christie [Chrystie] to dislodge them … but found himself anticipated by Lieut. Eldridge … who … had already gained the summit of the mountain and with a party of volunteers … routed some militia and the Barbarian allies of the defender of the Christian faith.[3]

Far from being routed, the two companies of militiamen, accompanied by a small number of returning Native allies, watched and reported as the Americans broke camp on July 9 and began marching east toward Newark and Fort George. In making this retreat, General Lewis was obeying the directives of his senior commander, General Dearborn. However, he was also concerned that the British vessels offshore could land troops to cut off his direct line of retreat and force him to fight a disadvantageous battle on two fronts if Vincent also arrived with his forces from Burlington Heights. He, therefore, chose not to follow the direct and shortest line of march back to Fort George. Instead, he diverted his army into making a wide detour away from the lake and along the foot of the escarpment, directly below the eyes and guns of the men of the Incorporated Militia, who had now been significantly reinforced.

This new contingent consisted of detachments of regular troops under the command of Lieutenant James FitzGibbon (49th Regiment) and over three hundred volunteer Native warriors from Lower Canada. Taking over command from Kerby, FitzGibbon pursued an aggressive course of action against the retreating

Americans over the next few days. Using his composite force to advantage, FitzGibbon succeeded in harassing the enemy into hastening their retreat, thus capturing a substantial quantity of supplies and more than eighty prisoners. At the same time, Yeo's naval contingent on the lake overtook and captured the bulk of Lewis's heavy baggage being transported back to Fort George aboard a number of American boats. Despite these serious losses, General Lewis again chose to represent the course of events to Armstrong in his own way:

> Between 7 and 8 o'clock the few wagons we had were loaded, first with sick and next with ammunition etc. The residue of Camp Equipage & Baggage was put in the Boats…. When they had progressed about 3 miles, a Breeze Sprang up and an armed Schooner overhauled them; those who were enterprising kept on and escaped. Others ran to the Shore and deserted their Boats. We lost twelve of the numbers, principally containing the Baggage of the Officers and Men. At Ten I put the Army in motion on our return to this place [Fort George], The Savages, and Incorporated Militia hung on our flanks and rear throughout the march and picked up a few stragglers.[4]

Upon reaching the commanding heights above Queenston, FitzGibbon detached Kerby's company and a number of Natives to press south along the Portage Road and report on any American presence at Chippawa and Fort Erie, while the remainder of the force, including Rapelje's company, moved north in their continued pursuit of General Lewis and his now demoralized army. Within the week, the arrival of General Vincent with the bulk of his regulars from Burlington Heights completely reversed the balance of power on the Niagara frontier. The previously victorious and dominant American army was forced to abandon its positions at Fort Erie and Chippawa and had been reduced to occupying a narrow enclave of land centred around Fort George and Newark, closely blockaded by an increasingly aggressive force of British regulars, Canadian militia, and Native allied warriors.

CONTAINING THE ENEMY: THE SIEGE OF FORT GEORGE

Over the next two months, the companies commanded by Captains Kerby and Rapelje were occupied as part of the British forces maintaining a confining blockade around the Americans in and around Newark and Fort George. As light troops with Native parties, they repeatedly skirmished with their American counterparts within the surrounding woodlands and farms, as well as serving as a rotating cadre of garrison troops at the Chippawa fortifications. Although no official records credit these companies as participating in specific firefights, there are strong indirect references to their participation through other military and personal accounts of the day.

One such reference comes through a comparison of the official records that credit Captain Kerby's company for taking a number of prisoners in a skirmish at the Crossroads (present-day Virgil) on July 8, with other accounts of an event occurring on that day and at that location, which coincidently involved Captain Kerby's wife. According to the captain's later account, his wife was attending a small social gathering at the farm of Mr. Peter Ball, located a short distance to the front of the crossroads and therefore in the "no man's land" between the two opposing lines. Suddenly, polite conversation was interrupted by the sound of gunfire coming from the adjacent farm of Castle Corus. Fighting had broken out when a small combined force of British regulars, militia, and Natives had been attacked by a body of Americans during an operation to recover a large chest of medicines and surgical tools hidden at the farm during the British retreat in May. Witnessing the battle taking place outside their window, the guests watched with alarm as stray shots struck the house:

> Among them was Mrs. Law, niece of Mr. Daniel Servos and wife of Captain John Law of the 1st Lincoln Militia…. Captain Law was mortally wounded and his eldest son William Law … killed at the taking of Niagara by the Americans [on the] 27 May, 1813. Their youngest son John Law,

then a boy of 13, in order to revenge the deaths of his father and brother, got a musket and ammunition and ran down to the front line of the skirmishers, among the Indians and fired some time at the enemy. His mother … fearing … her young son might also be killed, ran down into the very thick of the battle, among the wild and yelling Indians, and inspite of the balls flying all over the field, she found her boy, who was too full of the fright to leave when she called him. When Mrs. Law took hold of him by force and carried him in her arms out of the field to the house, uninjured.[5]

Similarly, Rapelje's men are credited as participating in a skirmish on July 17, which is referred to in the journal of another militia officer, Lieutenant T.G. Ridout (3rd York Militia):

> On Saturday, 17th, Henry Nelles and I rode down to the Cross Roads, three miles from Niagara, where the Royals, King's, and 600 or 700 Indians are posted. I understood the Americans were advancing into Ball's Fields. Immediately the yell was given and Blackbird and Norton set out with their followers to meet

them. Nelles and I rode along, and in a few minutes the skirmish begun by the Western Indians getting upon the left flank and the Five Nations upon the other. The enemy consisted of 500 men. They soon retired, firing heavy volleys upon Blackbird's party, which was the nearest. The road was so straight I could see into town and Nelles and I rode on with the Indians to within one and a quarter miles of Niagara, when we perceived a large re-inforcement from them, with a piece of artillery, and they advanced … firing grape shot. The Indians scattered into the woods, but we were obliged to keep to the road. By this time, three companies of the Royals, one of militia and a brass six-pounder came up and were posted on this side of Ball's field. The Yankees came up and were posted on the other side. We fired for some time, when the Americans thought fit to retreat. At one time, from the farther end of Ball's field a mile and a half this way, the road was covered with Indians, officers, soldiers and horses…. A good many Yankees were killed.[6]

There are also indications that several men from Simons's company served as volunteers in a surprise attack the British made on the American base at Black Rock on July 11, 1813. The attack was so successful that the American detachments manning the various artillery positions were routed without the attackers suffering a single casualty. After stripping the nearby warehouses of their valuable supplies, most of the militia were assigned the task of bringing their "prizes" back to the Canadian shore, where they arrived unscathed. On the other side of the river, however, the Americans had regrouped and launched a counterattack on the last of the British troops as they were in the process of embarking their final detachments. Forced to make a fighting retreat, the British suffered a number of casualties. These included: killed: 1 officer, 13 rank and file (including the mission commander, Lieutenant Colonel Bisshopp); wounded: 5 officers, 1 sergeant, 20 rank and file; missing/prisoner: 1 officer, 6 rank and file. In comparison, the company muster rolls for the Niagara division of the Incorporated Militia list one man lost as a prisoner on that date. Similarly, the regimental accounts for this period credit a total of five officers, six NCOs and eighteen privates, as being eligible to receive "prize money" from the subsequent sale of captured American goods.

While these events were occurring to the other elements of the Incorporated Militia stationed within Niagara, Major Simons had been required to remain at the army headquarters, where he continued to serve as a staff officer for General Vincent. Seeking to resume the active command of his own company, Simons was instead given the additional duties of supervising the embodied militia units periodically called out for service: "Militia General Order; 14 July 1813, Major

Simons will remain at headquarters and take charge of all militia. J. Harvey, Lt. Colonel. D.A.G."[7]

Fortuitously, his wish for action was granted only a fortnight later when the Americans initiated an amphibious operation aimed at transporting over five hundred infantry, marines, and sailors around the British positions and landing them directly at Burlington Heights. Although this fleet set sail from the Niagara River on July 27, strong winds blowing east and periods of violent weather forced the ships to tack into the wind, slowing their advance and allowing the British time to react. On July 29, Major Simons received an urgent communication from Lieutenant Colonel Harvey:

Dear Major

… proceed immediately with your militia to the Head-of-the-Lake, collecting and taking under your command all the regular troops you may find between Shipman's and Burlington and using your utmost endeavour to forward them whole by wagons if possible. There are strong reasons to apprehend that the enemy means to attack our depot at Burlington, which we must not lose.… It is far too valuable to this army to be lost.[8]

Collecting together a detachment composed of the men of his own company, as well as some available embodied militia, Simons immediately began a thirty-mile forced march, since there were not enough wagons to complete the mission as proposed. On the way, he enlarged his contingent by co-opting men from the 104th Regiment (Major Moodie) at Forty Mile Creek. Marching through the night, the force arrived at Burlington in time to see the American vessels approaching the low sandbar that marked the end of Lake Ontario and separated it from the excellent harbour of Burlington Bay.

Without delay, Simons took charge of the local units of embodied militia already mustered in response to the emergency. Shortly thereafter, they were further reinforced by a body of Native warriors from the Grand River settlements and two companies of the Glengarry Light Infantry who had just made a similar forced march from York. Stationing his Native forces in an arc covering the southern flank and the Glengarries to the north, Simons's remaining units established a strong defensive position across the dominant high ground and awaited the Americans' next move.

At the lakefront, after disembarking his forces from the ships and preparing them for their march on the Heights, the American commander, Colonel Winfield Scott, was not a happy man. He had been assured by his superiors that he was going to attack an unprepared and lightly defended supply depot. Instead, he was facing a well-prepared and entrenched body of regular and militia infantry, manned artillery batteries, Native warriors, and a British naval gunboat

The sandbar dividing the western end of Lake Ontario (right) from the harbour of Burlington Bay (left), Owen Staples, artist, 1910. This is where the Americans landed to attack Burlington Heights on July 29, 1813. The building (centre) is the King's Head Tavern, which the Americans had burned in May.

moored directly below the depot. Recognizing that his force was not sufficient to guarantee a military success, and that if the enemy advanced on his flanks they could cut him off, Scott decided not to attack (a sensibility he declined to repeat almost exactly a year later, when he faced these same soldiers at Lundy's Lane). Instead, he re-embarked his troops aboard their waiting vessels. A bloodless victory had been gained by the Allies, but, as noted earlier, in his frustration at not being able to destroy Burlington Heights, Scott took his troops north to ransack York, where they encountered Jarvie's and Jarvis's companies.

Toward the latter part of August, the senior British commander, Sir George Prevost, arrived on the Niagara frontier to assess the military situation. In a report to Earl Bathurst in England on August 25, he recorded:

> I found 2,000 British soldiers, on an extended line, cooping up in Fort George, an American force exceeding 4,000 men; Feeling desirous of ascertaining in person the enemy's works

and of viewing the means he possessed for defending the position, I ordered a general demonstration to be made on Fort George.[9]

The attack, which took place on August 24, began with four columns of infantry moving toward the American positions at Newark. On the far left flank, the column commanded by Major Robert Moodie (104th Regiment) was spearheaded by an advance party composed of Native warriors, Kerby's company of the Incorporated Militia, and a small detachment of newly arrived cavalry from the 19th Light Dragoons. Aided by the reduced visibility caused by a heavy fog, the initial attack quickly overwhelmed the outlying American pickets. Pressing forward into the town, the British found that resistance stiffened as the U.S. troops used the community's buildings and fences as cover and strongpoints for defence. By moving around

The Presbyterian church, in Newark (Niagara-on-the-Lake), used as an observation post by the Incorporated Militia and subsequently burned in retaliation by the Americans sometime between August and December 1813.

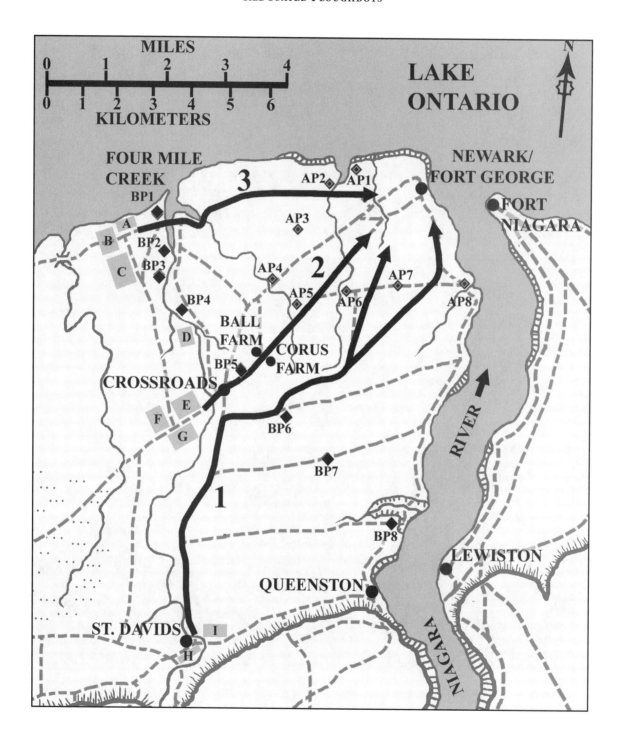

Military Positions and Picket Posts Occupied by Both Armies During the Siege of Fort George, July–September 1813, and the British Probing Attack of August 24, 1813

A to C: British military encampments at the Lake Ontario/Lakeshore Road
D: Native allies' encampment
E to G: British military encampments at the Crossroads (Virgil)
H, I: British military encampments at St. Davids

BP1 to BP8. British picket positions
AP1 to AP8. American picket positions

Prevost's Probe of the American Positions on August 24, 1813
1.   British "St. Davids" column (1)
2.   British "Crossroads" column (2)
3.   British "Lakeshore" column (including the Incorporated Militia Niagara Division) (3)

and flanking these positions, Moodie's column soon forced the defenders to abandon the town and retreat to Fort George and its adjacent defensive lines.

As he had already captured fifty prisoners and was seeing the enemy retreat with speed, Major Moodie was convinced that, if supported by the advance of the other columns, a further immediate assault on the main American position by his column would break the back of the American resistance and result in a major victory. He sent word to Prevost, asking for approval to launch his attack and for the other columns to move up in reinforcement. While waiting for a reply, Moodie assigned some of Kerby's militiamen to escort the prisoners to the rear, while others were detailed to climb up the steeple of the nearby Presbyterian church and establish an observation post that could see into the American entrenchments.

Prevost's reply arrived shortly afterward, but instead of authorizing Moodie's plan, it ordered him to abandon his gains and retreat, even though there

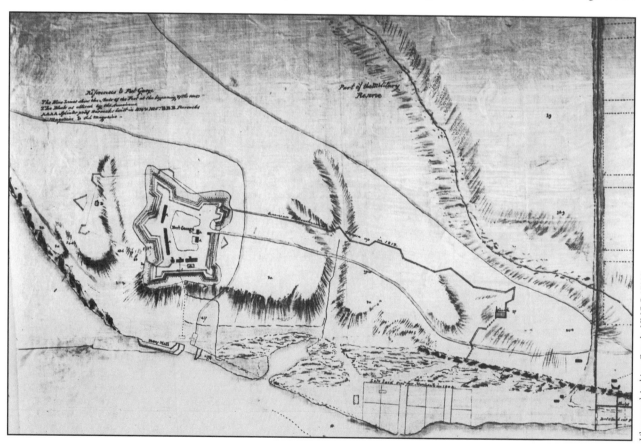

A map from 1816 showing the altered state of Fort George and the adjacent American siege lines in 1813.

Library and Archives Canada, NMC.C-17883.

was no threat of a counterattack from the enemy lines. When subsequent criticism arose regarding Prevost's overcautious command of this action and the loss of such an opportunity to eliminate the American threat to Upper Canada, Prevost excused his failure by claiming that he had ordered the retreat as a deliberate stratagem to entice the Americans to leave their defence lines and contest the ground in the open. Naturally, the Americans declined to expose themselves and Prevost was reduced to reporting to his superiors in London:

I found myself close to the camp which is formed on the right of that work [Fort George], both of them crowded with men, bristled with cannon, and supported by the fire from Fort Niagara…. I am now satisfied that Fort George is not to be reduced, strengthened and supplied as it is by Fort Niagara, without more troops and the co-operation of the fleet and a battery train. To accomplish this object, a double operation becomes necessary, Fort Niagara must be invested, and both places be attacked at the same moment, but my resources and means do not allow me to contemplate so glorious a termination to the campaign in Upper Canada.[10]

For the respective commanders of both contending armies, the campaign on the Niagara had stalled and was now in a state of stalemate. During the weeks that followed, neither side felt strong enough to initiate a major offensive campaign. Instead, both armies returned to a state of inactive warfare around Fort George and along the rest of the Niagara River. The engagements that did occur were often between small detachments of foragers and individual pickets. As such, they scarcely warranted being recorded in the letters and journals of the day, let alone the official daily reports. As a result, the only combat information applicable to the Incorporated Militia during this period is that Captain Kerby's company recorded two men wounded and Captain Rapelje's one wounded and one missing.

Casualties did not always come from combat, however, and a review of the company rolls indicate that the list of sick rose significantly in August. Although fatigue undoubtedly played a part in this situation, strategic circumstances also had a role to play. For weeks at a time, the men of the blockading British force had been on active campaign, living most of the time in the open or under whatever cover could be scrounged or otherwise "acquired." Because the main strongpoints and encampments had to be sited according to security and strategic considerations, this sometimes placed them in close proximity to swampy, insect-ridden tracts of land. Inevitably, sickness and disease began to deplete the ranks of the British and Canadian regiments alike.

By the end of August, the Incorporated Militia companies on the Niagara could only muster forty men as fit for duty from a total of eighty-two rank and file. Reduced in strength, the companies were eventually pulled back from the front lines and sent to the rear to convalesce, with Kerby's company being stationed at St. Davids, and Simons's and Rapelje's at Twelve Mile Creek.

SEE-SAW ON THE NIAGARA

While military matters on the Niagara remained at an impasse and the British seemed to have the upper hand, events unfolding elsewhere within the wider course of the war were combining to alter the pendulum of war once again. Having failed to conquer the Niagara frontier, the American administration decided to switch its future campaign strategies to the St. Lawrence River corridor and Lower Canada, with the aim of severing the British lifeline of supplies into Upper Canada. On August 26, 1813, General Wilkinson held a council-of-war with his senior commanders at Sackets Harbor, where, after considering several alternative strategies, he finally decided

> to rendevous the whole of the troops on the lake in this vicinity, and in cooperation with the squadron, make a bold feint at Kingston, slip down the St. Lawrence, lock up the enemy in our rear, to starve and surrender, or oblige him to follow us without artillery, baggage, or provisions, and eventually to lay down his arms; to sweep the St. Lawrence of armed vessels and in concert with the division under Major General Hampton, to take possession of Montreal.[11]

To personally oversee the planning for this campaign, Secretary of War Armstrong and a substantial staff moved to Sackets Harbor in early September. At the same time, General Wilkinson went to the Niagara frontier to make preparations to withdraw the bulk of the forces there and transfer them to the St. Lawrence offensive. After many delays and difficulties, these troops finally set sail on October 1, followed a day later by their commander. A small force of regulars, artillery, and militia were left behind at Fort George to maintain the American presence in Upper Canada.

Receiving reports of the enemy's buildup at Sackets Harbor, General De Rottenburg reacted by withdrawing most of his own regular regiments on the Niagara to bolster the garrison at Kingston. This redeployment, however, was interpreted by most of the Upper Canadian populace, and, more importantly, by the British Native allies as an abandonment of General Vincent and a precursor to a British withdrawal from Upper Canada entirely. This perception was compounded when the entire southwestern end of the province was lost to American control following two British military disasters: the decisive U.S. naval victory at the Battle of Lake Erie (September 10), and the subsequent disastrous and humiliating retreat and eventual rout of General Proctor's land forces at the battle of Moravianstown on October 5.

Faced with these significant defeats, General De Rottenburg believed that the only logical recourse was to abandon Upper Canada as far as Kingston and make preparations to withdraw down the St. Lawrence to Montreal if conditions worsened. Despite his own personal misgivings and the fact that his troops were still in total control of the Niagara frontier, Vincent recognized that American control of the western end of the province now gave them the opportunity to advance from that direction and capture Burlington Heights from the rear. This would then cut off any retreat and place his forces between two enemy armies.

In response, Vincent ordered an immediate withdrawal of all British forces on the Niagara to Burlington Heights and the fortification of that vital post. Regrettably, the subsequent retreat was not conducted in an orderly fashion and soon degenerated into a virtual rout. Large stockpiles of clothing, weapons, ammunition, and food, all brought up during the summer at enormous cost and effort, were now either abandoned or destroyed. By the end of October, the British army found itself back in the same position it had occupied the previous May, while the abandoned Niagara frontier was again vulnerable for attack and occupation by American troops.

As part of this retreat, the convalescent companies of the Incorporated Militia were assigned as part of the rearguard to the army, with orders to destroy all bridges and block the roads to impede any enemy advance. They were also detailed to retrieve any lost or abandoned items found after the British columns had passed. With so much *matériel* being abandoned it proved impossible to salvage everything. Once their company wagons were filled to capacity and detachments of men had hauled away the highest priority items, the remaining stockpiles were deliberately burned.

After retreating to Stoney Creek and Burlington Heights, the three companies joined the remainder of the British army. There, they awaited further orders from their generals, who, in turn, were awaiting the next move of the Americans. Life in camp became a matter of survival as food supplies ran short, causing incidents of petty theft to become rampant around the Head-of-the-Lake, as recorded in the letter of Thomas Ridout, a captain in the Lincoln Embodied Militia Regiment:

> We collect balm from the garden for tea … there is an extensive robbery of peas, onions, corn, carrots etc, for we can get nothing but by stealing except milk. Bread and butter is out of the question. We have an iron pot which serves for teapot, roaster and boiler and two window shutters … for a table.[12]

With the precipitant retreat of the British, the Americans now had the opportunity to advance across the Niagara Peninsula to evict Vincent's forces from Burlington Heights, eliminate the British Native allies as a military threat, and possibly secure Upper

Canada for the Americans. Instead, they only made a half-hearted advance from Fort George. Finding that the bridges had been demolished and felled trees blocked the roads, the U.S. force, commanded by General George McClure, gave up their pursuit of the British and, instead, went on a rampage of looting through the communities and farmsteads at Beaver Dams, Lundy's Lane, Chippawa, St. Davids, and Queenston. They wantonly killed any animals that could not be carried off and rendered buildings uninhabitable by destroying their doors and windows. They then returned to Fort George, and remained in place until mid November, when further orders arrived, stripping yet more troops away for inclusion in the St. Lawrence offensive.

Ordered to move with the bulk of his forces to Sackets Harbor and with no sign of the British making any offensive moves on the Niagara, the senior American commander, General William H. Harrison transferred his command to General McClure. He also made a recommendation that subsequently proved highly embarrassing to himself and the United States army. He advocated that McClure make use of a small unit of renegade Canadian turncoats, serving in the U.S. army under the ironic title of Canadian Volunteers, as a force to police the local population. He also stipulated that this measure was only to be undertaken under the condition that they would in turn be properly supervised and restrained in their activities by McClure. Led by a former Upper Canada politician and journalist/newspaper publisher, Joseph Willcocks, these disaffected Canadian Volunteers held many personal grudges against their former neighbours and were already infamous for their depredations and looting.

Ignoring Wilkinson's call for supervision, McClure gave Willcocks and his men a free hand. Without fear of being brought up on charges for excessive activities, the Canadian Volunteers began a new round of reprisals and intimidation, paying particular attention to the families of men serving with the British at Burlington Heights, including those with the Incorporated Militia. As this reign of force grew, so did the retaliation of the remaining men from the local populace. The result was an escalation of violence being meted out by both sides in this miniature local "civil war."

With most of the regular troops having been withdrawn from the Niagara, General McClure sought to call out additional militia troops to mount another attempt to attack Burlington Heights. Not only was he unsuccessful in this attempt, but there were increasing signs that his current troops would refuse to undertake any further offensive operations once their term of enlistment ended. By the end of the month, the American garrison at Fort George had withered away to less than six hundred men as individuals, detachments, and whole companies unilaterally crossed the river back to the United States as their militia enlistment periods expired.

At the other end of the peninsula, the troops at Burlington Heights were buoyed by the collapse of any effective American offensive action on their position. As well, news arrived from the Lower Canada that the American invasion down the St. Lawrence had been completely defeated. Previous British plans for the abandonment of Upper Canada were now to be reversed. New orders arrived from General De Rottenburg for the improvement of defensive positions and the construction of barracks and food storehouses at Burlington Heights and York. There was also the prospect of the British mounting a new offensive to recapture the Niagara frontier. In preparation for this, the companies of Incorporated Militia saw an increase in their duties, acting as both advanced pickets and reconnaissance units.

REVENGE IS A DISH BEST SERVED COLD

On November 29, 1813, one outpost of the Incorporated Militia stationed at Stoney Creek, received word that Willcocks and his men were pillaging near Forty Mile Creek. Having previously received news of the ills perpetrated upon their families, a determined detachment of Major Simons's company, supported by men from the embodied militia and some regulars mounted an impromptu sortie to intercept and capture the renegades. They failed to do so, but following a brief skirmish, the escaping Willcocks and his men fled back to the American positions, bearing tales of having faced and fought a wholesale British advance. Within hours, McClure had ordered the withdrawal of his entire force toward the Niagara River. This, in turn finally encouraged General Vincent to approve a general advance, spearheaded by units that included the three companies of Incorporated Militia.

Advancing across the snow-covered ground in a fleet of sleighs, Kerby's company, accompanied by a force of Native warriors, pushed forward to Twenty Mile Creek, arriving there on December 10. There, they again encountered the Canadian Volunteers and immediately attacked them. After a brief firefight, Willcocks's men were again routed with a loss of one killed and four taken prisoner. The survivors fled to Fort George, where their reports spread panic among the remaining troops in the garrison. Desertions now increased to the point where the American Native allies outnumbered the men of the army detailed to guard the post.

McClure now faced the prospect of either trying to hold his position or retreating back across the river after destroying the reconstructed Fort George along with large stockpiles of supplies and tents left behind by the regular army. Instead, he sent notice that the town of Newark was to be razed by Willcocks and his Canadian Volunteers. In the teeth of a strong winter storm, the remaining citizens of Newark, composed principally of the old, the sick, women, and children, were herded into the streets and forced to watch their homes being reduced to ashes. Fortunately, a few outlying barns and sheds in the surrounding fields remained unscathed. While most of the refugees huddled in what little shelter there was and tried to keep warm as the snows piled higher around them, others sought refuge with the advancing British forces.

When the first of the homeless civilians reached the outposts of Murray's advance guard, word of the atrocity spread like wildfire among the troops, who had halted some miles short of the town to await reinforcements before approaching the fort.

Desperate for news of their families, the men of the Incorporated Militia, as well as the embodied militia detachments from the area, called for an immediate advance. Without any formal orders, and regardless of the threat of attack from the American garrison, the leading element of the British advance descended on Newark to find it still burning and the militiamen's families destitute, but still alive. As they moved on to the fort, it initially appeared intact and fully ready for defence. On closer inspection, however, the gates were found open and the garrison gone. After taking over the fort without opposition, they sent word for the main column to come up as quickly as possible to secure the position, while measures were taken to ensure the defence of the perimeter in the event of an American counterattack.

Next day, Captain Kerby and his company were sent out in sleighs to scour the frontier and apprehend any American stragglers. Accompanied once again by a party of Native allies, they reached Queenston, only to see the village being bombarded by the American battery positions at Lewiston. Several buildings were on fire due to the enemy's use of "hot shot," clearly indicating an American determination to lay waste to everything on the west bank. Continuing south in their sleighs, the detachment reached Fort Erie just in time to catch the last of the fort's American garrison abandoning their positions and retreating to boats on the riverbank.

Taking advantage of the enemy's vulnerability at that moment, Kerby's militiamen and their Native companions fired their muskets, then immediately charged, attacking with bayonet, knife, and war hatchet. Without

suffering any casualties on their own part, they inflicted heavy losses upon the hapless Americans, killing or wounding several and capturing over twenty men. Even those already in the boats and afloat found they were not entirely safe, for they soon came under fire and suffered additional casualties before they were able to pull out of range. The Canadian side of the Niagara River was now firmly back in the hands of the British.

Following their return to Fort George with news of the American bombardment of Queenston, Kerby's company joined in the general call to take the war to the far bank, to give the Americans a taste of their own medicine. This time someone was prepared to listen and act on these demands. Once again, changes had taken place in the senior British command structure — the result of the British victories that had taken place at Chateauguay (October 26) and Crysler's Farm (November 11) on the St. Lawrence frontier.

General Vincent was now placed in command at Kingston, while General De Rottenburg took up a new post at Montreal. As their replacements, Prevost chose to install what was hoped would be two more dynamic and aggressive officers, General Gordon Drummond and General Phineas Riall. En route, General Drummond paused briefly at York to officially assume command as administrator of Upper Canada and commander of the troops on December 13, 1813, then immediately pressed on to personally assess the state of defences and troop deployments along the Niagara frontier. Learning of the American depredations at Newark and Queenston, Drummond immediately ordered a retaliatory strike on the centre of American operations — Fort Niagara.

While Colonel Murray had commenced preparations for undertaking such an assault on Fort Niagara immediately after occupying Fort George, the necessity of placing his troops and the destitute refugees under adequate cover during the bitterly cold weather had preoccupied his attention. Besides, with the retreating Americans having taken or destroyed every boat on the west bank of the river, there was no means of transport immediately available. Determined to exact revenge on the enemy for the mistreatment of their families and friends, the men of the Lincoln and Incorporated Militias volunteered to collect and transport sufficient boats from the depot at Burlington Heights to allow the attack to take place.

Despite bad weather and freezing temperatures, parties from the two militias, under the supervision of Captain Kerby, navigated the boats along the Lake Ontario shore to Four Mile Creek. To avoid detection by the Fort Niagara garrison, the men then hauled the boats, each weighing upwards of two tons, up on the shore and manhandled them across nearly five miles of frozen countryside before secretly relaunching them on the Niagara River, well above the fort and its outlying batteries. The stage was now set for the war to move to the other side of the river.

The night of December 17–18 was initially fixed for the attack, but continuing storms and logistical delays caused a postponement to the following night. In spite of having taken every possible precaution to preserve the secrecy of the mission, word of an impending attack became known to the garrison commander at Fort Niagara, Captain Nathaniel Leonard. After placing his garrison on full alert and under arms for two consecutive nights, Leonard inexplicably relaxed his guard and placed the garrison on a lower footing of readiness, while he rode out to visit his family at a farmhouse a few miles from the fort.

Lieutenant General Sir Gordon Drummond GCB, *G.T. Berthon, artist, circa 1882–83. Having served in Canada before the war, Drummond was stationed in England when he was appointed to his command in Upper Canada. Following the end of the war, the newly knighted Drummond was appointed to replace Sir George Prevost, and served as the administrative and military commander-in-chief of both Upper and Lower Canada until he returned to England in May 1816.*

Archives of Ontario, Acc. 693127.

— 125 —

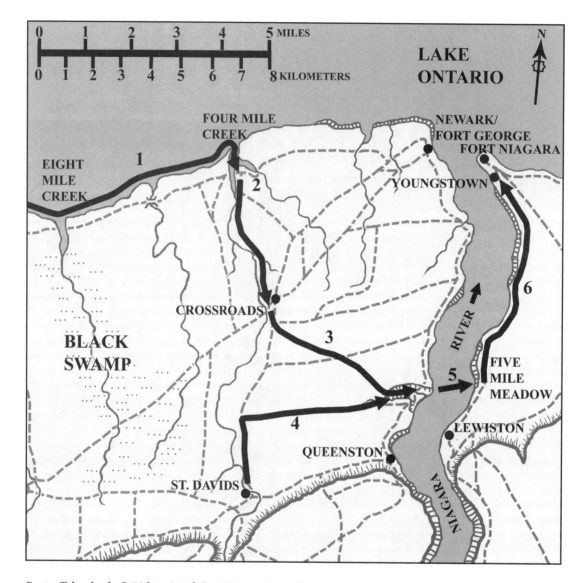

Routes Taken by the British to Attack Fort Niagara, December 17–19, 1813

1. The boats are sailed up from Burlington Heights (1).
2. The boats are hauled on shore at Four Mile Creek (2).
3. The boats are hauled overland to the Niagara River (3).
4. The British attack force marches from St. Davids (4) to rendezvous with the boats.
5. The crossing of the Niagara River (5).
6. The British column advances on Youngstown and Fort Niagara (6).

Library and Archives Canada, C-99561.

Fort Niagara, as seen from alongside a Canadian battery position located at Newark, J.E. Woolford, artist, 1821.

On the other side of the river, the men of the Incorporated and Lincoln Militias, although not officially detailed to take part in the assault, were determined to play their part, and volunteered to act as boat crews to transfer the troops across the Niagara. Around midnight, the first part of the assault force embarked and the boats pushed out into the frigid water. Manoeuvring to avoid large chunks of ice floating downstream, the boats made an undetected landing in a meadow about three miles above the fort. As the advance party moved off into the darkness to reconnoitre the road leading to the fort, the remainder of the first wave secured the landing ground and the boats returned to the Canadian shore to collect the next two waves of troops. Once all of the attacking force had crossed, they formed into columns. Guided by Captain Kerby and a number of his men who were familiar with the American side of the river, they marched in silence toward Fort Niagara. Reaching the small village of Youngstown, only a mile from the fort, the British advance guard eliminated the outlying picket guard. Not expecting any attack and suffering from the intense cold, these men had gone inside to warm themselves, and suffered the consequences. After extorting the night's password from the picket, the British continued their advance, and by 4:00 a.m. were within sight of the fortifications. Here the column divided into three separate formations, each with its own designated point of attack. Captain Kerby and men from his company were again recorded as being unofficial participants in this assault. According to one later account, Kerby was the first officer in the attacking column to land on the American shore and the first to actually enter the fort.

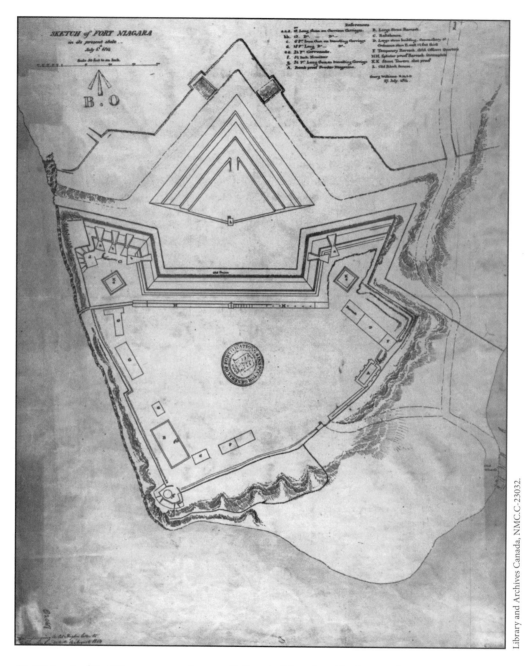

An 1814 map of Fort Niagara, appearing essentially as it did on the night the British attacked. The path to the main gate is seen in the bottom right of the image.

Taking advantage of lax American security and catching the American guards in the act of changing sentries, one column of attackers seized the small riverside gate and stormed through into the fort's compound. The other two columns used scaling ladders to mount the walls. Elated by their easy success, the men raised a loud cheer, which had the unfortunate result of alerting the garrison that an attack was underway.

With the British already inside the fort's compound, the defenders sought to use the barracks, storehouses, and stone redoubts (blockhouses) as strongpoints. Several clashes of hand-to-hand fighting in the buildings' narrow internal rooms and staircases ensued. Despite meeting some strong resistance, the British overwhelmed the defences and secured the fort in less than an hour. Although a few members of the garrison escaped by dropping from the walls into the snow-filled ditches and crawling away into the darkness, the bulk of the captured troops were herded into the parade square, searched for weapons, and then secured under guard until the following morning.

Fort Niagara today (2011), clearly showing the chilling isolation of this exposed location in winter.

In the light of day, and with the fort securely in British hands, the American prisoners were allowed to gather their personal belongings before being transferred to the Canadian side of the river and marched to York, all under the guard of a detachment from Captain Kerby's company. At York, these prisoners were transferred first to the custody of Jarvie's company for movement to Kingston, and then through the hands of the Kingston and Prescott divisions of the Incorporated Militia to their eventual destination at the prison hulks at Quebec.

THE ASSAULT ON BUFFALO

With the lower reaches of the Niagara River under British control, Generals Drummond and Riall decided to press their advantage by launching an attack on the other main American base of operations at Buffalo and Black Rock. Without access to sufficient transport to take an assault force across the river, however, Drummond issued new orders to Major Titus G. Simon. Under these directives, the men of Simon's and Rapelje's companies of Incorporated Militia, plus the attached volunteers from the Lincoln Militia, were to collect the large bateaux used in the Fort Niagara crossing on December 19 and transport them to Fort Erie for the proposed attack.

While this command may sound simple, it meant that the vessels had to be moved a total of more than thirty miles in total secrecy. The first stage involved navigating the boats upriver to Queenston — rowing all the way against a strong current and avoiding ice floes. At Queenston, the already heavy boats had to be hauled out of the water and placed on large wooden

A modern winter view of the Niagara River at Queenston (right bank below the bridge). The challenge of hauling the heavy boats up the height and slope of the escarpment was only the first obstacle facing the boat crews.

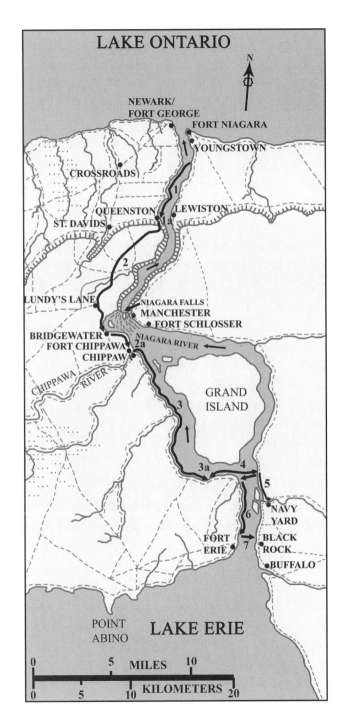

Transferring the Boats and the Attack on Buffalo,
December 26–30, 1813

1. The boats are sailed up the Niagara River to Queenston (1) and hauled out of the water (1a).
2. The boats are hauled overland (2) to the Chippawa River and relaunched (2a).
3. The boats are sailed up to the first embarkation point (3-3a).
4. The first crossings and infantry landings are made below the U.S. Navy Yard (4).
5. The infantry advance to attack Black Rock (5).
6. The boats are moved up to the second embarkation point (6).
7. The second crossings and infantry landings are made at Black Rock (6).

frameworks mounted on sleds, all without alerting the enemy sentries on the opposite bank. Once on the sleds, the cumbersome loads had to be dragged up the escarpment before being hauled another nine miles cross-country to the Chippawa River. There the boats would need to be relaunched and remain hidden until just before the intended attack, when they would have to complete the final eighteen-mile journey upriver to the intended place of embarkation.

After encountering considerable difficulties during every part of the passage, the boats were brought forward from Chippawa on the evening of the December 28, and plans were made for the foray later that night. However, the appearance of American troops at the proposed landing site at Black Rock, plus the arrival of more than 250 exhausted British reinforcements, persuaded Riall to defer the crossing for twenty-four hours.

The British plan of attack was to make a two-pronged assault, with the first phase requiring an undetected crossing of the Niagara River and unopposed landing some distance above Black Rock. This would require two additional waves of embarkation and crossing to deliver the total required number of troops to the American shore. Once assembled, the assault force would then march south and attack the American positions from the rear, in the same manner as Bisshopp's raid had done earlier in the year. Once this part of their task was completed, the assault boats would need to be brought back to the Canadian side and navigated upriver to Fort Erie, again without being detected, to embark the fourth wave of troops for a direct frontal assault on Black Rock.

Once again, Major Simons was required to assume crucial responsibilities in the attack. He was put in charge of overseeing the embarkation of each successive wave of troops, the speedy completion of the first phase of the attack, and the relocation of the boats upriver. All of which was to be conducted in the dark, in complete silence, and directly under the guns of the enemy at Black Rock. Volunteers from both Simons's and Rapelje's companies acted as crews for the boats, and guides for the initial land-based assault column.

On the evening of December 29, the boats were moved up from the Chippawa to a point about two miles below Black Rock. Around midnight, the initial embarkation and crossing took place without incident or detection. After surprising the picket at the bridge over Scajaquada Creek and overrunning the nearby Navy Yard and "Sailor's" Battery (so called because it was crewed by men taken from vessels trapped in port for the winter), the advance element of the column was forced to halt to await reinforcement, since the ice floes on the river had delayed the transportation of the remaining troops.

The delay allowed units of the now-alerted American militia to arrive from Buffalo, block the road leading north from Black Rock, and execute a feeble attempt to drive back the growing body of enemy troops.

Once the remainder of their reinforcements arrived, the British advanced once again to attack the American militias from the front. At the same time, detachments of British Native allies moved through the adjacent woodland and around the flank of the defenders to make their own attack from the rear.

Outnumbered and attacked on two flanks, the U.S. militia force, already weakened by casualties and extensive desertions, was only able to sustain their position for a matter of a few volleys before they broke and fled toward Buffalo — chased and harassed by the Native warriors. Apart from small detachments of men who rallied around any officer who stood his ground, nothing in the way of an organized defence was left to hold back the British land assault.

Meanwhile, things were not proceeding as smoothly as planned for the second phase of the British attack. The initial landings had taken longer than anticipated, delaying the movement of the boats upriver to Fort Erie. Once underway to the secondary embarkation point, many ran aground due to unusually low water levels in the partially ice-clogged river. Militia crews had to climb out and wade waist-deep in frigid water to manhandle the boats past the shoals and into deeper water, all the while maintaining the strictest silence as they were "under the point blank fire of the enemy's heaviest batteries."[13]

By the time these problems had been overcome and the boats loaded with troops, the cover of darkness had gone. Nonetheless, the final assault waves began their crossing as the enemy's positions, lining the bank of the river, opened fire, first with artillery and then, as the boats closed into range, with volleys of musket fire. Suffering an increasing number of casualties, the men of the 1st (Royal Scots), Incorporated Militia, Lincoln Militia, and Natives were only able to reply with an intermittent fire from the crowded vessels. They soon found themselves stranded when the boats began to run aground well short of the riverbank, due to the low water levels. As a result, the troops were left with no alternative but to wade ashore, through the freezing water, to begin their attack.

With both elements of the assault force ashore, the British were able to link up and soon overwhelmed the remaining pockets of American resistance at Black Rock. Seeing the American forces in full retreat, they pressed on to Buffalo and accepted the surrender of the village before noon. The military magazines, warehouses, barracks, dockyards, and defences at Buffalo and Black Rock were ransacked during the next two days and their contents transferred to the Canadian side of the river. The structures were then set on fire or otherwise destroyed. While these measures were deemed legitimate for military facilities, the desire for revenge for the events at Newark, which had taken place only two weeks earlier, unfortunately overtook some of the attacking troops. They initiated a retaliatory round of looting and burning that left the community of Buffalo a wasteland of ashes when the British withdrew to their own side of the river.

As in the earlier case of Captain Kerby after Fort Niagara, Major Simons's and Captain Rapelje's companies were subsequently detailed to act as guards and escorts for some 279 prisoners of war taken during the course of the day's fighting. They marched their charges to York before returning back to the Niagara frontier. For his part in this action, Major Simons was mentioned in dispatches as being "useful and indefatigable in embarking the troops,"[14] while twenty-six men of the Incorporated Militia's Niagara Division were subsequently listed as being entitled to prize money shares from the government coffers.

With the frontier secure for the present, the army on the Niagara was withdrawn from the field and went into winter quarters. As local residents, however, the companies of Incorporated Militia were more fortunate, being granted extended furloughs during the months of January and February. This leave allowed the men to return home to their families and enjoy a brief period of rest before the renewed trials of the spring campaigns began with the unification of the companies at York.

7

THE KINGSTON DIVISION: SOLDIER, BUILDER, OR SAILOR?

O F THE FOUR PRINCIPAL RECRUITING CENTRES for the Incorporated Militia in March 1813, the most populous location in Upper Canada was Kingston. So, it might be assumed that the companies formed at this location would have enjoyed the highest levels of recruitment. However, the facts tell a different story, as, unlike the other divisions, the rate of recruitment for the two Kingston companies being raised respectively by Henry Davy and Daniel Washburn proved extremely slow.

Despite being relatively well-populated, Kingston was also the hub of the British war effort in Upper Canada. As a result, the military commissariat, the naval dockyards, military and civilian warehouses, civilian manufacturers, victuallers, transportation and shipping contractors, hoteliers, storekeepers, and the city council all competed for the available labour force, making it a buyer's market. Labour was at a premium, and every kind of job had to pay well above the average to attract prospective workers. Against this kind of competition, the financial inducement offered to join the military for an indefinite period paled in comparison to the wages a fit labourer could demand and get, with no threat of injury or death as part of the package.

The following month, news of the American fleet leaving Sackets Harbor with a substantial landing force of troops sent an alarm throughout the Kingston area. With the two bases only thirty-eight miles apart, and with Kingston being the centre of the entire British transportation network, its value as a military target was obvious. Thus, the level of alert was raised.

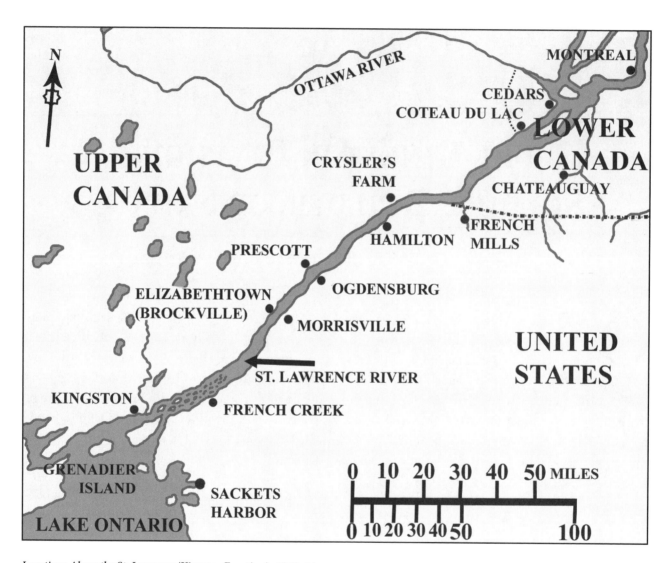

Locations Along the St. Lawrence/Kingston Frontier in 1813–14.

The embodied militias were called out and the naval yard made preparations for engaging the enemy as soon as their sails were sighted. Within days, the two companies of Incorporated Militia received numerous recruits. By April 24, 1813, the muster rolls listed Captain Daniel Washburn, Ensign Charles Short, and thirty-six other ranks in the first company, and Captain Henry Davy, Lieutenant Henry Ruttan, Ensign Henry Robins, and fifty other ranks in the second.

But their preparations were for naught, since no attack materialized at Kingston. Instead, the Americans attacked York, inflicting a significant defeat upon

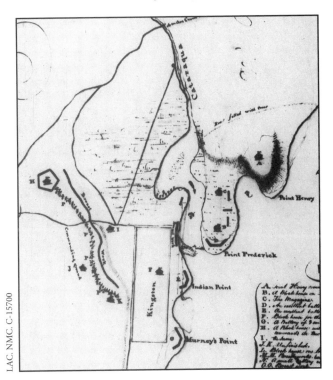

LAC. NMC. C-15700

A contemporary map of the defences constructed during the war to protect the vital supply depot and shipbuilding centre of Kingston.

General Sheaffe's small force, before moving across to the Niagara to commence operations against General Vincent's army. Recognizing the opportunity of the moment, Sir George Prevost rapidly cobbled together a major amphibious operation against what was believed would be a lightly defended Sackets Harbor. Sailing from Kingston on May 27, the expedition took the greater part of the town's garrison with it. Left without its normal force of regular and fencible troops, the defence of Kingston now rested on the newly formed Incorporated Militia contingent. Despite having been formed only a few weeks before, the two companies were considered significant enough to be placed on the garrison roster for guard duties.

The return of the fleet brought with it the news that the attack on Sackets Harbor had been turned from a hard-won victory into a humiliating defeat by Prevost's timid military leadership. According to circulating accounts, the general had ordered the retreat of his army at the very moment the Americans were abandoning their defences and setting fire to their own warehouses.

This was immediately followed by news from the Niagara frontier that the Americans had crushed General Vincent's force in a battle at Fort George, forcing him to abandon his fortifications guarding the Niagara area and to retreat toward Burlington Heights.

The British position in Upper Canada now appeared precarious in the extreme. Thus, while officially troops were being readied to reinforce the British at Burlington Heights, secret plans were being made for the complete evacuation of Kingston, to be followed by a projected retreat toward Montreal.

A view of the shipyards at Point Frederick (centre) and the town of Kingston (right distant), as it looked at the end of the war from the hillside alongside Fort Henry (left). Sir E.W. Grier, artist, circa 1896 *(after Admiral Henry Bayfield R.N.)*

Fortunately for the British, the action at Stoney Creek (June 6–7) halted the American advance in its tracks and led, within a week, to a British advance back toward the Niagara River. As troops and supplies were forwarded from Kingston to Niagara during the remainder of June, Washburn's and Davy's companies were, once again, used as garrison and guard troops. They also undertook extensive fatigue duties at the military garrison warehouses and naval yard, transporting military supplies and food from the depots to the waiting vessels.

Two interesting incidents occurred within the Kingston detachment during this time. In the first instance, on June 8, Captain Davy, despite his experience as a Revolutionary War veteran and the commander of the single largest company detachment in the entire corps, was taken away from his recently formed company. Instead, he was assigned new duties as the commander of a newly launched gunboat, with orders to patrol the waters off Kingston and through the Thousand Islands.

Davy's boat, the *Thunder(er)* (there are discrepancies in the records as to her correct name), was technically referred to as a "lugger," measuring some forty feet long and eight feet in the beam. Her sailing rig consisted of two masts with square sails rigged in the fashion of a schooner (fore and aft), supplemented by twenty-two long oars (sweeps) that could be used to propel the vessel in narrow waterways or windless conditions. She also carried an armament of a single 6-pounder artillery piece, mounted forward of the front mast, giving a clear arc of fire across her bow.

After collecting men who had experience of sailing or working in a maritime environment, Captain Davy and a detachment of a dozen men

A watercolour (artist not known) depicting a gunboat similar in design to the Thunder(er), *showing how the combination of both sail and oar were required for manoeuvering through the narrow channels and swift currents of the St. Lawrence River near Kingston and the Thousand Islands region.*

from the Incorporated Militia took command of the *Thunder(er)*. Along with an equal number of embodied militiamen and two gunners from the Royal Artillery, they engaged in working-up drills in the Kingston harbour before going on active duty early in July.

With the departure of their commander, Davy's subordinate officer, Lieutenant Henry Ruttan, initially took up the duties of commanding the Kingston company. In conjunction with Captain Washburn's company, the depleted company provided duty guards at the garrison and fatigue parties for the Engineers Department to work upon the construction of additional defensive positions along the Kingston waterfront.

The second incident occurred on June 16, when one Edward Walker received a commission as a captain in charge of a new company of the regiment within the Kingston detachment. The only problem was that, unlike all the other officers in the corps, there are no records or lists that show him as having served as an officer in either the embodied or flank companies. In fact, the only previous reference to an Edward Walker is as a private in the 1st Frontenac Embodied Militia. Nor are there any accounts that show that he recruited anyone to qualify him for the rank of captain. Instead, the men forming this new company were taken directly from both Captain Washburn's and Captain Davy's company. Since this forced transfer also included Lieutenant Henry Ruttan, it deprived the lieutenant of his command and left the remaining men of his company under the inexperienced Ensign Robins. As far as current research shows, there are no official documents to explain these two incidents or any solid evidence to prove that they might be in some way connected. However, the timing of Captain Davy's transfer and Captain Walker's elevation to command a new company without having recruited anyone to qualify him for the rank is perhaps unusually convenient and deserving of further investigation.

GARRISON ORDERS, MAY 7, 1813

"In the event of an alarm … the detachment of the Kings … will form the Left Wing, which will extend from Murney's Point in the direction of Number One blockhouse. The Incorporated Militia to form on the right of the Kings, the Embodied on the right of the Incorporated and the Canadian Voltigeurs on the right of the whole, the Indians will be divided on either flank to act as skirmishers…. The line will be formed in three Divisions, the left consisting of the Kings and the Incorporated Militia under the command of Lt. Col. Evans."[1]

MOVEMENT ORDERS, AUGUST 2, 1813

"Captain Washburn's company of Incorporated Militia to be attached to the Corps of Royal Engineers. To embark this evening at 6 o'clock for Point Haneray and will take a weakes provisions. The acting Quartermaster General will furnish a bateaux for that service."[2]

AUGUST 14, 1813

"A party of 1 Sergeant and 6 Rank and File of Captain Davy's Company to join the working party at Point Henry."[3]

With three companies of infantry ashore and a detachment afloat, the few surviving documents relating to this division indicate that they were placed under the titular administrative command of Lieutenant Colonel Allan McLean (1st Frontenac Embodied Militia). For the most part, they spent the next five months acting as part of the Kingston garrison, undertaking the regular and monotonous duty of guards and pickets. The only break from this routine came from participation in practice alerts in case of an American attack, joining in official parades, or being attached to fatigue and construction details for the building of the new citadel on Point Henry, opposite the main naval dockyard. This new fortification, named Fort Henry, was to become the lynchpin of the British military presence in the upper province for the next fifty years and a Canadian military base well beyond that, surviving to this day as a National Historic Site that still dominates the Kingston skyline.

Having enlisted to fight the enemy but instead being relegated to work as garrison and construction labour caused the men to lose morale. This led to several instances of men going AWOL for days before returning. Investigation showed that the men concerned were farmers who had left their families for the regiment, leaving their dependants to manage the land. Without any active danger confronting them, they were not deserting, but simply making an unofficial temporary departure to see the crops gathered before voluntarily returning, taking their punishment, and resuming their duties. Initially, they were simply placed in close confinement for a week on bread and water, until official channels came up with a surprisingly understanding answer, indicating perhaps that this was not an issue confined to the Incorporated Militia:

Royal Military College, Massey Library, Kingston, Ontario.

Kingston, 1815, *E.E. Vidal, artist, 1815. This image is a detail taken from a larger painting showing Fort Henry as the Americans would have seen it from their ships.*

[Garrison Orders, July 12, 1813]

His Excellency the Commander of the Forces, being desirous that the public service should be considered with as little inconvenience to individuals as possible, and being especially anxious that the crops of hay and grain should not suffer, has been pleased to authorize the Colonel [McLean] to grant leave of absence for one month to certain portions of the militia … as standing most in need of the indulgence…. They are however, to hold themselves in readiness to return at a moments warning and it is expected that they will not abuse the indulgence granted by overstaying their furlough.[4]

On the other hand, there were nearly twenty actual desertions, principally from Captain Washburn's company. Notations in the monthly rolls indicate that for the most part the miscreants were believed to have absconded to the Newcastle District, Montreal, or out of the country entirely. But in the cases of Private David Palmer and Private Peter Wyatt (both of Washburn's company), they received the infamous notation "deserted to the enemy" beside their names.

At the time, Captain Davy's marine detachment was serving on Lake Ontario and the St. Lawrence River aboard the *Thunder(er)*. Unfortunately, no accounts or log of their activities have, as yet, come to light. The only first-hand information that does appear is from the monthly roll call registers, which indicate that on July 31, Privates John McGinnis and John Stackhouse deserted from the boat; on August 21, Private Philip Wolfram drowned when he fell overboard while the boat was under sail; and on September 21, Private Jacob Mason deserted to the enemy.

There are indications from secondary sources, however, that Davy's boat was involved in a number of small skirmishes with American naval units during this time. These include an action that took place in late July at Goose Bay, just downriver from Kingston. There, American privateers had succeeded in capturing a flotilla of British bateaux loaded with supplies and ammunition. Seeking to recapture the boats, as well as the Americans, the leading boats of the British force entered the adjacent Cranberry Creek, where they were met with heavy fire from an American force stationed on both sides of the waterway. After suffering a number of casualties, the British retired and the Americans escaped with their prize. Davy's role in this affair is not known, but no casualties are recorded for his section during this period. On the other hand, the records for October 10 contain a reference to what can only have been a direct action with the enemy. Again no account of the event has come to light, only the fact that in the aftermath, nine privates of Davy's detachment are listed as becoming prisoners of war.

At the end of October, the alarm bells once again rang across Kingston as General Wilkinson's plan to pursue an attack on the St. Lawrence River was put into action with a buildup of United States troops on

Grenadier Island. Fully expecting the primary target of any projected attack to be Kingston, General De Rottenburg maintained a heightened state of alert, with troops on constant duty until reports arrived on October 30 stipulating that the Americans were bypassing Kingston and moving directly into the St. Lawrence River with the goal of attacking Montreal. A flotilla of gunboats and bateaux from Kingston, under the combined command of Captain William Mulcaster, sailed in pursuit. As part of this force, the *Thunder(er)*, manned by Captain Davy, his composite crew, and additional men taken from vessels remaining at Kingston, was subsequently engaged with the enemy at French Creek on November 3 and 4. The vessel was then withdrawn to Kingston to take additional troops on board before pursuing the Americans down the river.

Having left French Creek on November 4, the U.S. flotilla passed Prescott on the night of November 6–7. Behind them, the British "Corps of Observation" was simultaneously preparing to leave Kingston under the overall command of Lieutenant Colonel Morrison (89th Regiment), while the naval force, including the *Thunder(er)*, remained under Captain Mulcaster. Moving swiftly downriver, the British vessels reached Prescott on the evening of November 8, where a substantial portion of the Prescott garrison was added to Morrison's force. While the Prescott companies of Incorporated Militia were not officially included in this attachment, it being principally composed of regular troops, a significant number of volunteers from the companies with St. Lawrence River experience did join the expedition.

Next day, the *Thunder(er)*, piloted by Private Robert Thompson (from Captain McLean's company of Incorporated Militia), was part of the advance force of boats that engaged the U.S. rearguard near the American village of Hamilton, New York (present-day Waddington). After firing their artillery into the American formations on the shore, the boats closed on the riverbank and landed their complement of troops. After driving off any opposition, the landing party occupied the village, while the vessels moved farther downriver and covered the main riverbank road with their guns, preventing a counterattack. In a similar manner, on November 11, Davy's crew of the *Thunder(er)* are recorded as indirectly participating in the action at Crysler's Farm by firing on the American boats beached on shore and the nearby troop concentrations.

Following the battle of Crysler's Farm and its decisive British victory, the American invasion effectively collapsed. General Wilkinson's army retreated farther downriver and crossed to the American shore, where it remained for a short while before eventually withdrawing into winter quarters at French Mills. The British gunboats on the St. Lawrence initially remained on station to maintain pressure on the retreating Americans, and then were shot through a stretch of rough and dangerous rapids into Lake St. Francis. After patrolling there and ensuring that the enemy had fully retreated, the boats were steered to the British garrison at Coteau-du-Lac and moored there on November 22.

Having reached Coteau-du-Lac, the question for the gunboat crews, including Davy and his men from the Incorporated Militia, was *What happens now?* The navigational season on the St. Lawrence was definitely in its last days. Sudden winter storms and swollen river currents had made sailing conditions increasingly dangerous, and downpours of freezing rain and snow had coated the British gunboats in a thick layer of ice. Even if they were cleared of this encrustation, any further buildup of ice while under sail could cause the ships to capsize without warning. There was no realistic possibility of manhandling and towing the gunboats back up through the rapids in the face of increased currents, deteriorated weather, and riverside towpaths now virtually impassable because of knee-deep mud. Thus, the *Thunder(er)* and other British gunboats were hauled up on shore and stripped of their rigging and sails, which were put into storage for the winter. The crews were dismissed from their naval duties and ordered to return to their original regimental ship or depot postings.

After an exhausting march of 140 miles, Captain Davy and his crew finally arrived back at Kingston on December 2 and rejoined their company. Upon resuming his command, Davy sought to obtain the men who had previously been transferred to Captain Walker's command. However, his request was rejected.

On December 6, a far more sombre event took place when the courts martial of Privates Amos McIntyre and Joseph Seeley took place at the Kingston garrison. Both men had originally enlisted in April for duty in Captain Jonas Jones's company in Prescott, but had subsequently been transferred in June to Captain John McLean's company. Private McIntyre was arraigned on the charge of "deserting from Prescott to the enemy on or about the 4th day of July 1813 and not returning until brought back a prisoner from Ogdensburg on or about the 17th day of September 1813."[5]

McIntyre pled not guilty to this charge.

Private Seeley was arraigned on two charges. The first was "for deserting from Prescott to the enemy on or about the 28th day of August 1813 and not returning until brought back a prisoner on or about the 20th day of November following," and the second was "for aiding and assisting in piloting one of the enemies boats down the river St. Lawrence on or about the 20th day of November 1813."[6] He pled not guilty to both charges.

Summoned to act as witnesses, Captain John Kerr (Kerr's company), Lieutenant Duncan McDonell (McLean's company), and Corporal Leaky (McLean's company) had been ordered up to Kingston from Prescott at the end of the previous month and been billeted with the Kingston detachment while awaiting their turns to testify. A second order brought up four additional men from the ranks to also act as witnesses.

The initial arraignment did not last long, adjourning immediately after the pleas were heard. The court reconvened on December 11, and was almost as brief in finding Private McIntyre guilty as charged after only a single day of testimony. Whereupon, he was sentenced to be "Shot to Death! At such time and place as his Honor the President … may be pleased to direct."[7] In the case of Private Seeley, more time was taken, as the case proved more complicated than initially thought. The following day, the verdict came down that he was guilty of desertion but not guilty on the charge of aiding the enemy, due to lack of evidence. He was placed in prison pending transport to a penal colony, where he was to serve seven years of hard labour.

On December 20, at 8:00 a.m., Private Amos McIntyre was marched out in front of the full garrison parade at Kingston for execution. According to common British army practice of the day, the firing squad would have been made up of men from his own regiment, with one individual unknowingly being provided with a blank load. Following the execution, the entire force of troops in the garrison would have been marched past the corpse as a stern warning to others of their fate in similar circumstances. For the regular army troops, this scene would have been severe but

Scenes at la Prairie 1812.13.

Execution, Lower Canada, *black and white sketch, artist unknown, circa 1812. A military execution by firing squad in Lower Canada.*

probably familiar. For the men of the Incorporated Militia, however, it must have been a stark shock and dire warning. Whether it was this warning that was responsible or not, records indicate that while there were subsequent desertions from the corps as a whole during the following year, none were to the enemy.

For the remainder of the year, and during the months of January and February 1814, the detachments remained in winter quarters within the newly named Fort Henry, working on its surrounding fortifications. They also enjoyed a rotating system of furloughs that permitted those men whose families were not already with their men in the barracks to return home for a period of up to four weeks.

Finally, on February 21, 1814, the order arrived for the consolidation of the companies at York. At the end of the month, the entire detachment left in a convoy of sleighs that reached York on March 7.

8

THE PRESCOTT DIVISION

I F THE KINGSTON DIVISION OF THE REGIMENT could be seen as being spartan in its documentary records, then the papers relating to the division at Prescott could only be described as an embarrassment of riches. In studying this treasure trove of information, it would appear at first reading that the companies recruited at Prescott and its adjacent locations were composed entirely of shirkers, scoundrels, and misfits, whose officers neither obeyed orders nor cared anything about their regimental or patriotic duties.

Day after day, a litany of official complaint seems to have emanated from the office of the garrison's commander, and one must wonder why. If these men and their officers really were so bad and lazy, why did they volunteer for full-time active military duty when they did not have to? Why, when they are accused of repeatedly failing in their duties, did the officers not simply resign and rejoin their embodied regiments without penalty? The answer, it seems, lay not so much with the regiment, but more in the expectations of the garrison commander, Lieutenant Colonel Thomas Pearson. Some background pertaining to this man is essential to understand the subsequent references.

HARD LABOUR

Thomas Pearson was a seasoned military veteran, having served as an officer in the British army (23rd Regiment) since 1796, when he was seventeen years old. He had seen extensive action while on campaign in Holland (1799); Egypt (1801), where he was wounded; Denmark (1807); Martinique

(1809), where he was wounded a second time; and then Portugal and Spain (1811), where he was severely wounded in the leg. This injury failed to heal properly, leaving him with a permanent limp and in constant pain. During his time, Pearson had commanded both the 1st and 2nd Battalions of the 23rd Regiment, a brigade in the Copenhagen campaign, a light infantry division in Martinique, and an elite fusilier brigade in the Spanish Peninsula under Wellington. He had then been transferred to North

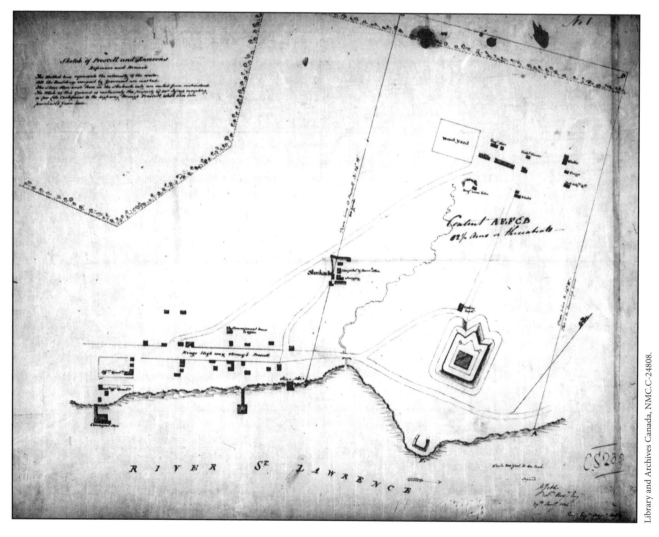

The British garrison post at Prescott presented a formidable obstacle to the passage of the American flotilla, which was forced to try to sneak past in the dead of night.

America in February 1812 with the senior military rank of inspecting field officer of militia for the whole of British North America.

In September, this role was changed to garrison commander of Montreal, which was still a prominent military position. After only a few weeks, however, this was then changed to garrison commander at Prescott, a backwater post on the St. Lawrence River, far from any prospect of action, with virtually no fortifications and defended by a skeleton force of worn-out regular troops and an untrained and undisciplined levee of embodied militia. Despite this obvious demotion in position, Pearson was determined to improve the military defensive capabilities of the garrison, the military condition of his regulars, and the standard of training of his militia flank companies. By January 1813, Prescott and its garrison had changed beyond all recognition, due to Pearson's impressive but iron hand of discipline and leadership.

As a dedicated professional soldier, with extensive experience of battles and campaigning, he had no time or patience for anyone who wore a uniform as a social statement or served in any military capacity without fulfilling their duties to less than the exacting standards Pearson would have demanded of himself. In Pearson's view, it did not matter whether that uniform sat on the shoulders of a private or colonel, regular or militiaman, labourer or prominent social citizen, yeoman or well-connected politician. Several accounts describe Pearson giving acidic tongue-lashings to relatively senior officers of the Canadian Militia for infractions of duty or failure to perform field commands properly with their companies of men.

As the commander of Prescott, Pearson also had to deal with the irritating raids the Americans had been making upon the Canadian shore in late 1812, spreading panic and seizing valuable military supplies. The obvious course of action was to remove this threat by attacking the American base of operations at Ogdensburg. He pressed Sir George Prevost for approval to attack throughout the winter of 1812–13, but was ordered to remain inactive.

However, in February 1813, he found himself transferred to command at Kingston with the expectation that he would improve performance there also. Taking up this post and immediately instituting yet another round of reforms aimed at achieving administrative and garrison improvements, Pearson was only in command for two months before suddenly being ordered back to Prescott. Although there is no direct evidence to connect it, this second transfer was not long after Pearson had administered a particularly acerbic and public parade-ground dressing-down to an embodied militia senior officer who had proved himself entirely incapable of giving the required commands for a particular parade-ground manoeuvre to his troops. Unfortunately, this militia officer was also one of the more politically influential and well-connected individuals in Kingston.

During that intermission, Pearson's former second-in-command, Lieutenant Colonel "Red" George Macdonell, had commanded the Prescott garrison. He had also effectively ignored Prevost's injunction against initiating any provocative acts against the Americans, and used all of Pearson's improvements to launch a successful surprise attack on Ogdensburg, thus garnering all the official kudos and credit. His command style, while being properly military, was not as rigid as Pearson's. He had openly attempted to encourage the militias by appealing to their sense of honour in defence of their country.

The announcement of the formation of the Incorporated Militia, a month after the raid on Ogdensburg, caused the more enthusiastic members of flank companies of the embodied militia within the district to begin a competitive recruitment for men to complete their quota to command companies. All was proceeding in a fashion comparable to that of the other regional detachments, and by the end of the month recruitment had reached a point where the Prescott division stood at six captains, seven lieutenants, six ensigns, thirteen sergeants, eight drummers, and 245 rank and file. Things were now in a presentable enough state that Colonel Macdonell issued the following regimental orders on April 26:

The Incorporated Militia to be immediately completed with arms and accoutrements and ammunition. Lieut. Colonel Macdonell will inspect all the militia in garrison by companies on Wednesday forenoon at Ten o'clock & every officer commanding to be prepared with correct states of his company and appointments.[1]

The next day, he followed this up with further details:

Lieutenant Colonel Fraser is to take command of all the Embodied Militia regiments, and Captain Walker for the present, for that of the Incorporated Militia. Their officers will give in a morning state of their Corps and be responsible in every respect for the complete equipment and regularity.

All men off duty fatigue to attend drill at 6 o'clock in the morning and at 2 o'clock in the afternoon … at sunset, all servants and fatigue men are to attend the evening parade. The troops of the Line and Incorporated Militia are to parade at their own quarters … the arms and ammunition of every man to be inspected at every parade. Every officer must exert himself in making his men active and attentive to their duty … having their appointments in order and be ready to get under arms night or day in a proper state to repel the enemy. Lieutenant Colonel Macdonell will not employ militia officers who do not use the greatest energy and activity in keeping their men together and promoting their discipline.[2]

The following week (May 3), Macdonell made his strongest appeal yet to his new militiamen:

> Commanding officers of Corps and detachments are to see personally that their men do receive every allowance of pay, provisions, etc. any neglect of this duty will expose those officers to the Commandant's extreme displeasure. No soldier to presume to say he has not received his pay nor provisions unless he has taken such proper means of applying for them in the established manner.... They must recollect that these are more serious times than what even a personal consideration must give way to their zeal for their King and Country. They must remember that trifling sacrifices will purchase permanent security for themselves and their properties and every man ought to glory in suffering privations in the service of his Country. The brave british soldiers come many thousand miles from their wives and families to shed their blood defending the farms and property of the militia of this Country — The militia therefore ought to blush with shame of the idea of not sustaining in equal sacrifices with their officers their attention to their duty.... Lieutenant Colonel Macdonell will feel the most lively pleasure in making the militia service which is due to their Sovereign and Country as light and easy to the militia as possible.... [The militiaman] must swallow up all idea of private profit or commerce ... and if compelled by the bad conduct of any militiaman he [Macdonell] will punish them with the severity that will be remembered to the last generation.[3]

Unfortunately, this appeal and warning had no time to take effect, since the very next day Macdonell was ordered to return to his regiment, and the garrison came, once again, under the command of Lieutenant Colonel Pearson. Upon his return to Prescott on May 12, Pearson found that while he had previously dealt with the militia as a part-time supplementary military force, many of those same individuals were now officering the companies of the newly formed, full-time Incorporated Militia. This new regiment was obviously formed in response to his recommendations promulgated in January. However, despite his strong injunction to have such units commanded by regular officers, they were, instead, not merely in the hands of colonial militia officers with little more experience than their men, but officers who had gained their rank by being persuasive or popular enough to encourage sufficient men to enlist to qualify them for their ranks. In Pearson's book, this smacked too much of a "Yankee" system of military thinking and had no place in a "British" regiment, even if it was a colonial militia!

During the next few days, a series of new orders were posted that clearly indicated the colonel was not going to waste any time or leniency in dealing with his new charges:

[Garrison Orders, May 13, 1813]

Colonel Pearson will inspect the Incorporated Militia and Flank companies of the Embodied Militia on Sunday next at 11 o'clock. It is expected they will have their arms and accoutrements and ammunition in <u>perfect</u> order.... Lt. Colonel Sherwood of the 1st Leeds Militia will repair to Prescott and take charge of the Incorporated Militia at this post.... All officers in Garrison to be properly dressed in their uniforms immediately, the commanding officers of Corps and detachments to be prepared to answer questions respecting their command of detachments. All men off-duty to be properly dressed.[4]

Regimental orders followed on May 14: "The Officer on fatigue to be uniformly dressed — A party to be given to the Barrackmaster to clean out the Barracks as the Governor will inspect them in an hour and a half."[5]

The next day's orders added: "At morning parade, all Regimental cooks and orderlies and all others not employed in the King's works to attend. The Town major will immediately parade camp colours and have the parade cleared of every kind of rubbish."[6]

Then, two days later:

<u>A Code of Orders and Instructions to be used by the Incorporated Militia of the Eastern and Johnstown Districts</u>.... Captains and officers appointed to divisions will immediately provide themselves with rolls of their respective divisions which will be drawn, the men of each division will be formed into messes and a non-commission officer appointed at the head of each mess.

• Regular hours will be established for these messes, viz ... Breakfast at eight o'clock in the morning and dinner precisely at one, when the roll of each division will be called by the orderly officer and all absences reported.

• The men to be formed every morning at 5 o'clock for drill and to continue until half past 7 when they are to be dismissed.

• The morning parade to be formed at 10 o'clock, when it is expected every person will be present with the exception of two orderlies from each division who will be left to clean the barracks and to cook for the whole.

- The Evening parade for drill to be formed at 3 o'clock.

- Men will be selected for Sergeants and Corporals according to their merits and the advancement and progress they make.

- In their several duties, the Captains and Subalterns of the day will regulate the cleanliness of the Barracks and the General room.

- The bedding will be neatly piled up every morning at sunrise and brought in front of the Barracks and placed in a line by divisions, preserving proper divisions between each division, as nothing so much contributes to the health of the soldiers.

Colonel Pearson calls on Lieutenant Colonel Sherwood, the Captains and Subalterns of the Incorporated Militia to the strictest attention to their most essential part of their duty and begs to inform them by their punctual discharge of the duties necessarily impressed on them. Their claims for commands and appointments of this Corps will be considered and the merit of each individual will be duly appreciated.[7]

A view from the 1813 earthen ramparts of Fort Wellington at Prescott. The existing central blockhouse is a postwar construction. The far bank, beyond the St. Lawrence River is the United States.

In a similar fashion, Lieutenant Colonel Pearson obviously felt that regimental discipline and appearance within the Incorporated Militia needed tightening up, and posted the following as part of the garrison orders for May 21, 1813:

> No Privates of the Incorporated Militia will in future be allowed to pass without leave from an Officer commanding the Division beyond or in rear of the public highways proceeding from the bridge above the barracks to the house of Philip Spencer below the … barracks. But every man will keep within the space between the highway and the river St Lawrence. This order however is not to prevent the men from resorting to the Inns and shops in Johnstown.[8]

On May 22, the militia order put the emphasis on cleanliness:

> As cleanliness is absolutely necessary for the health and comfort of all persons … the men's beds and blankets are to be frequently aired and to be shaken and folded up and the rooms swept. Men in tents are to lay out their blankets back of them and clean out the dust … the men to shave more frequently and not to come on parade with long dirty beards.[9]

By May 25, the successful officers of the seven new companies of Incorporated Militia were confirmed in their ranks, while those officers who had failed to achieve the required number of recruits were dropped from the rolls. In the case of the men already recruited by the failed officer candidates, they were assigned to companies to even out the total numbers in the ranks.

Interestingly, surviving military records for these companies reveal several personal details about the men who enlisted in the regiment, including their age and height. For the most part, they ranged across a wide spectrum of ages, from a drummer boy thirteen years old in Captain H. Walker's Company to a sixty-two-year-old private in Captain Fraser's Company, and in height from four feet five inches (the same drummer boy) to a six-foot private from Fraser's company. However, the company recruited by Captain Archibald McLean (after his arrival from York) does not fit the standard pattern seen in the other companies. In terms of age, his youngest consisted of a drummer boy of thirteen, while many of the privates were in their late teens and early twenties. No man of the company was over the age of forty-nine. In terms of height, there is an even more striking statistic, as the shortest man, the drummer, stood five feet nine inches and the tallest private six feet two inches, with the entire rest of the company measuring between five feet ten inches and six feet.

MUSTER ROLL FOR THE EASTERN AND JOHNSTOWN COMPANIES OF THE INCORPORATED MILITIA, MAY 25, 1813[10]

Captain Hamilton Walker
Lieutenant Henry Burritt
Ensign Ziba M. Phillips
3 Sergeants
2 Drummers
37 Privates (present)
4 Privates (present, sick)
1 Private (AWOL)
1 Private (discharged)

Captain Thomas Fraser
Lieutenant Duncan Clarke
Ensign John Kilborn
2 Sergeants
2 Drummers
31 Privates (present)
5 Privates (present, sick)
5 Privates (absent, sick)

Captain John McDonell
Lieutenant Alexander Rose
Ensign James McDonell
2 Sergeants
1 Drummer
31 Privates (present)
5 Privates (present, sick)
5 Privates (absent, sick)
4 Privates (AWOL)

Captain Jonas Jones
Lieutenant William Morris
Ensign John McDonell
2 Sergeants
1 Drummer
37 Privates (present)
2 Privates (present, sick)
2 Privates (AWOL)

Captain John Kerr
Lieutenant Philip VanKoughnet
Lieutenant John Fraser
Ensign John Fraser
2 Sergeants
1 Drummer
38 Privates (present)
2 Privates (present, sick)
2 Privates (AWOL)

Captain Archibald McLean
Lieutenant Daniel McDougall
Ensign Andrew Warffe
2 Sergeants
1 Drummer
39 Privates (present)
2 Privates (present, sick)
2 Privates (AWOL)

RETURN OF CLOTHING ISSUED TO THE ACTING QUARTERMASTER OF THE INCORPORATED MILITIA OF THE JOHNSTOWN AND EASTERN DISTRICT, MAY 28, 1813[11]

From Commissariat Stores at Quebec:

300 Jackets

299 Trousers (pairs)

300 Regimental Caps [shakos]

300 Bugles [cap badges]

From Prescott (part of the clothing captured at Ogdensburg):

7 Jackets

8 Trousers (pairs)

7 Caps

This cannot be considered a statistical anomaly and points to the fact that Captain McLean was determined to only have the biggest men serving in what he considered *his* company. Little wonder then that after a few parades, the men of this company appear to have acquired the unofficial nickname of being "grenadiers." (This term was used in the British army for the official company that was posted on the far right of the regiment on parade and generally composed of the tallest men, but a term that was not applied in any subsequent official document relating to the Incorporated Militia or this company.) Unfortunately, this nickname seems to have subsequently caused a problem for several later prominent historians, as they seemingly took this nickname as being an official designation, and

thus gave McLean's company a regimental title and line placement that it never actually enjoyed.

Finally, for May 1813, one other reference of note exists that hints at the relationship between the new regiment and Colonel Pearson. This relates to the issuance of new uniforms within the completed companies. Although those men who had been part of the flankers had brought their muskets and accoutrements with them, there was still the matter of clothing to be issued. A shipment of uniforms, which included the green-faced red uniform adopted earlier that year, had been ordered and shipped from the Quebec Commissariat. These items were now issued to the companies, but there were not quite enough to go round. Accordingly, it was decided to make temporary use of a small number of green uniforms already lying in storage at Prescott. The only problem was that these uniforms were those of the American First Rifle Regiment, and had been part of the spoils of war captured at Ogdensburg in February.

Seemingly, the officers of the Incorporated Militia had no problem making do with what came to hand, as long as they and their men were clothed. Thinking the captured uniforms were perhaps a little more dashing, the officers took them and wore them themselves. Colonel Pearson, on the other hand, had another opinion on the matter and, in the garrison orders of May 26, wrote: "Colonel Pearson is much surprised that any officer in the district should appear in the dress of an American rifleman, as some have lately presumed to do, and most positively forbids it in future."[12]

During the month of June, the companies were rotated between Prescott and Johnstown, a few miles downriver. With no action in the offing, their duties consisted principally of providing men for garrison duties, picket patrols, transportation crews for bateaux, and escorts for American prisoners of war being moved to Lower Canada. There was also the never-ending need to provide working parties for fatigue duties, a task the men of the Incorporated Militia seem to have been particularly suited for, considering the number of times it appears in the daily order schedule during that month. Even here, however, the men could not escape the eagle eye of the lieutenant colonel, who wrote in the regimental orders of June 20: "The men of the Incorporated Militia are particularly prohibited from wearing their jackets when on fatigues."[13]

The "Stockade Barracks" at Prescott. Built in 1810, this house was taken over by the military at the start of the war and was regularly occupied by the Incorporated Militia between March 1813 and March 1814. It saw service as a barracks, storehouse, and hospital during the war.

As with their Kingston brethren, monotony and boredom wore on both the men and the officers, and it is most likely that regimental discipline and attentiveness to duty would have suffered. The difference between the two divisions was that the Kingston companies did not have to contend with Lieutenant Colonel Pearson and his absolute judgment of the proper responsibilities and duties of any and all military personnel.

When Lieutenant Colonel Pearson issued the following, everyone was made well aware of what was expected:

[Garrison Orders, June 16, 1813]

As Major General DeRottenburgh will be in Prescott tomorrow morning, Lt. Colonel Pearson expects that all officers will carry attention to their duty and be regimentally dressed at all times…. The Incorporated militia under the command of Lieutenant Colonel Sherwood at Johnstown will march tomorrow morning at 6 o'clock from thence to Prescott and occupy the stone barracks vacant by the Royals. The detachments of the same Corps now occupying the Glengarry barracks will remove at 4 o'clock tomorrow morning to the same barracks.[14]

The events that took place during that visit are unknown, but no official censures were issued. However, in reviewing the daily logs for the remainder of the month, it appears that following this inspecting visit, the succession of night-picket duties, followed by daytimes of fatigues upon the earthworks seem to have been constantly filled with detachments of the Incorporated Militia. How these menial duties were perceived by the regimental men is not documented, but its impact on the willingness and attentiveness to duty of the officers is easy to assess:

[District Orders, July 5, 1813]

It having been reported to Lieutenant Colonel Pearson that guards and piquets of this garrison have been frequently kept on guard beyond the usual time by the irregular attendance of some of the officers doing field duty, it is the Commanding Officer's positive order that all officers who are for the future negligent in this point of duty be reported to him that he might ascertain from such officers the reason of their instructions to the existing order of the garrison.[15]

This generic censure was then immediately followed by a more targeted blast:

[District Militia Orders, July 5, 1813]

It is with severe regret that Lieutenant Colonel Pearson is under painful necessity of publicly exposing his displeasure at the conduct of the following officers of the Incorporated Militia: Captain J. McLean, Captain A. McLean, Captain Kerr, Ensign Warffe, Captain John McDonell, Lieutenant Rose, Ensign Campbell, Lieutenant Fraser, Ensigns McDonell, Fraser, Philips, and Lieutenant Van Koughnet … for not attending to their respective stations.[16]

Normally, this open official criticism would be sufficient to censure any recalcitrant individual and would be considered justified if the facts warranted it. But here it is used to broadly condemn more than half of the entire corps of officers, with representation from every company in the unit. However, this was not the end of the lieutenant colonel's critique.

It is but too obvious to the behaviour of many of the Militia Officers in the Garrison that the emoluments arising from their commissions are to be the only objects of their attentions…. If men whose properties, families, and connections are all dependant on these exertions will not cheerfully come forward and defend their own fireside, what can they expect from others, who have not these inducements towards them but are instigated solely by that impulse of honor, which is the proud characteristic of every British soldier…. How pleasing must then the satisfaction be to thinking men that by his present exertion he has contributed discomfiture of his countries enemy and salvation of his own property.[17]

To date, no documented response or record of the opinions of the officers named in this public rebuke has come to light, but it is unlikely it would have been met by any positive response. Fortunately, during the next two weeks, at least two of the companies were recorded as having been sent on detached duties away from Prescott to transport and guard a large contingent of American prisoners of war (captured on the Niagara in the action at Beaver Dams on June 24, 1813) being moved from Prescott to Montreal. As well, Captain Kerr and a sizable detachment from his company were assigned duties to command and man the gunboat *Brock*, with orders to patrol the St. Lawrence River and act as protection for convoys of bateaux conveying supplies upriver.

These assignments, however, still left a significant body of men at Prescott to continue the ongoing duties of guards and fatigues on the fortifications. Obviously,

Pearson's admonishment either had no effect or at least not enough to satisfy the commanding officer, for on July 23, he found another issue:

[Militia Orders]

Lieutenant Colonel Pearson dis-approves of any soldier of the Incorporated Militia being employed as servants [for their officers] unless their masters provide the men so employed with shoes, a coarse fatigue jacket and trousers as it is of the utmost importance that the clothing of the men should proceed with as much care as possible.[18]

Four days later he returned to his earlier com-plaint:

In consequence of the reluctance manifested by some of the officers, particularly of the Incorporated Militia, to perform the duties required of them as officers of His Majesty's service, Lieutenant Colonel Pearson directs that the Officers of the Incorporated and Embodied Militia will parade the men of their respective companies on the general parade for the full hours they are required for fatigue duty … the hours for Garrison fatigue will during the hot weather be as follows — The men to turn out at revalee beating in the morning and remain until 8 o'clock, they will recommence until twelve, at which time they will leave off until 3 o'clock, they will then fall in and work until sunset.[19]

Allowing for the one-hour difference created by the subsequent introduction of daylight saving time and the calling of reveille half an hour before sunrise, this would effectively make the men's daily workday as approximately 4:15 a.m. to 8:00 a.m. (with meal break of perhaps thirty minutes); 8:30 a.m. to noon (break); and 3:00 p.m. to 7:45 p.m., for a daily total of over twelve hours of actual labour, thirteen if one included evening twilight!

While this was taking place at Prescott, Captain Kerr's detachment, serving on the *Brock*, became involved in the same action with the enemy previously referred to in the Kingston section under Captain Davy's gunboat service. According to Kerr's account, however, this action took place in August and not July, and at Goose Creek and not Cranberry Creek. The date differential is inexplicable, but the location can easily be solved, as Cranberry Creek flows into Goose Bay on the St. Lawrence River.

According to Captain Kerr:

I do hereby certify that in the month of August 1813, I commanded one of the gun-boats sent from Prescott with a detachment of the 41st Rgt. (commanded by Major Frend) and a party of Incorporated Militia for the purpose of assisting in the retaking [of] a brigade of bateaux loaded with stores for His Majesty's services that had been captured by a party of the U.S. forces when passing through the Thousand Islands on their way to Kingston, and been conveyed up Goose Creek about four miles up from the entrance of that place, on the American shore. On our arrival at the entrance of that creek, in the dusk of the evening, we discovered gun-boats on shore, some officers of the navy, a body of sailors, and a detachment of his Majesty's 100th Rgt.... We found that their forces had followed up the reconnoitring boat of the enemy too late in the evening, when it was discovered they had shifted their post on farther up the creek, and therefore, made it too late to proceed and make an attack. Major Frend being the senior officer, assumed the command; and according to arrangement, our force rowed up the creek at night in time to arrive to make an attack at daylight. We then found they had barricaded the creek by felling trees across it, and fortified themselves within, at a turn of a point, covered by a thicket; from whence commenced a brisk firing from riflemen and a six-pounder, mounted on a flat-bottomed sloop, which was returned with rapid precision. The foremost gunboat was soon disabled by the loss of the gunner, and after by the overthrow of her guns. Mr. P. Grant, animating his men, passed the first boat, after a Midshipman was wounded in the arm, himself in the head, and his gunners felled by shots from the tops of trees. Captain Mills … was killed in the rear gunboat [Kerr's]. The flat-bottomed boats not having come up, the gallant Captain Fossett with his men of the 100th Rgt. Waded on shore, driving the enemy before them.[20]

What the captain fails to mention is that this attack failed to achieve any of its goals and was forced to withdraw with significant casualties and damage to the boats involved.

Back at Prescott, the expressions of Lieutenant Colonel Pearson's continued determination to whip the Incorporated Militia into a military force that would meet his exacting standards of regimental quality were still being issued. He also added a new item to his list of complaints against the unit:

[Garrison Orders, August 6, 1813]

The Commanding Officer has to desire that Lieut. Colonel Sherwood and the whole of the officers of the Incorporated Militia will make themselves acquainted with the daily Garrison and District Orders. He also desires that all the orders of the Garrison will be more strictly attended to by that Corps than heretofore, particularly in what relates to the attention to the cleanliness of their barracks and to the personal cleanliness of the respective companies…. The attention of the Commanding Officer is likewise called to some regimental arrangement in the accommodation of the Women and Children in obtaining or providing huts for them, as their remaining in barracks is positively prohibited.[21]

As the summer began to wane and winter's approach was in the offing, it is to the credit of Lieutenant Colonel Pearson that, irrespective of any other issues, he was not about to see the troops under his command deprived of proper supplies of clothing. As a result, official requisitions were sent to the lower province for the necessary items, including regimental coats, greatcoats, trousers, gaiters, forage caps, barrack jackets, regimental caps, shoes, stockings, knapsacks, and shirts. Everything was done by the book and according to the July regulations that now authorized the use of red coats with dark green facings to replace the green coats faced red.

By the end of September, at least a portion of these supplies had arrived at Prescott and were ready to be issued: "The new clothing will be issued to the troops on the first day of next month [October], as will the equipments immediately on their arrival from Montreal."[22]

In Montreal, Lieutenant Colonel Noah Freer acknowledged the receipt of Pearson's requisition, but also felt compelled to point out his error of address: "Your requisition for greatcoats for the Incorporated Militia and Cavalry should have been made upon Kingston, directions have however been sent to Major General DeRottenburg to send you the number required."[23]

The issue of new uniforms to the men of the regiment now placed them, in appearance at least, as comparable to the regulars alongside whom they paraded and drilled. Whether that would serve in a time of combat, however, was yet to be tested. And that time of testing would appear in short order, as increased reports of American campaign intentions toward the St. Lawrence corridor began to filter in and Pearson stepped up the state of alert at Prescott. Increased drills were supplemented by the allotment of duty stations in case of an alarm: "Officers commanding Divisions of the Incorporated Militia will immediately give into the Adjutant returns of what ammunition they have in their possession and they are deficient, and also the state of their arms."[24]

This was followed by additional orders issued on the first of October:

> In the event of any alarm during the night, the following will be the distribution of the troops in garrison.... One company DeWattevilles with the Incorporated Militia and Embodied Militia will be formed in column of Divisions at ¼ distance, Right in Front, under Lieutenant Colonel De May, this force will be considered as disposable and to act when the enemy might first make their attack.[25]

In other words, in case of an enemy attack, the Incorporated Militia would be among the first units to go into action! But did that mean Pearson had finally decided the men were good enough to serve in battle alongside the regulars, or that they were the most expendable as cannon fodder?

This state of alert remained in force throughout October and, as usual, Pearson was (quite justifiably) determined to ensure that all elements of his garrison were ready to oppose the enemy if the occasion arose: "The Incorporated Militia will be kept off duty tomorrow and will be inspected by Lieutenant Colonel Pearson at 2 o'clock in the afternoon. Every person of any description not having Lieutenant Colonel Pearson's leave to be present."[26]

On the other hand, he continued to find new infractions to lay against the Incorporated Militia, or rather, against their families:

> [Garrison Orders, October 15, 1813]
>
> In consequence of the number of children returned as belonging to the Incorporated Militia is much greater than the Commanding Officer supposed to be really the case, Department Assistant Commissary General Green is directed not to issue rations to such women and children unless the return is regularly certified by the Commanding Officer of the Corps particularising that such children so estimated are the children of the respective women so returned and that those women are the legal wives of the soldiers now serving in the garrison and belonging to the Incorporated Militia.[27]

In justice to Lieutenant Colonel Pearson, it must be recognized that, under regular army regulations, the number of wives and children accompanying the men of the regiment on foreign duty or campaign was strictly restricted and chosen by lot. The remainder were simply left behind on the dockside in the home country. In dealing with this militia regiment, however, Pearson had to contend with a regimental formation whose regulations and internal economies legitimately ignored everything his training and experience demanded was essential for the formation of an efficient fighting machine — no corporal punishment or flogging for infractions, officers in positions of authority by virtue of personality or contacts, and a horde of hangers-on and non-military encumbrances at a time when ration supplies were becoming harder to find and there was the increased likelihood of enemy action against the garrison. Little wonder that Pearson's disapproval spilled over on to the men.

Things could not have been easy for anyone in this situation — something had to give. Interestingly, it was not a man from the rank and file who was involved but one of the more experienced and senior officers of the corps. This incident seems to have taken place on October 18, for shortly thereafter the following documentation was submitted:

Charges against Captain Archibald McLean of the Incorporated Militia, who is now in arrest:

1. Neglect of duty and disobedience of orders, as Captain of the Day on the 18th of October in not obtaining instructions for duty nor going on rounds of posts.

2. Disobedience of orders, in not making returns on greatcoats wanting in his company and leaving the garrison without leave.

3. Neglect of duty and disobedience of orders in not making his men turn out for fatigues.

4. Insolent behaviour and disrespectful language to the Field Officer of the Day.[28]

What is surprising here is that this was an officer who had come from a prominent family, whose father had served as county sheriff, militia colonel, and judge — a man who had trained as a lawyer until he volunteered for militia duty when the war began. He had seen action at Detroit and York, and had been severely wounded while participating in the charges on the hill at Queenston. While still convalescent, he had served General Riall by undertaking interim positions as assistant adjutant general of militia and assistant quartermaster general of militia at York. He had personally saved the colours of the York Regiment during the American attack on York, and then made his way back alone to Kingston before going on to Prescott to raise a company of Incorporated Militia. This would not normally be the military record of an officer who was now being charged with dereliction of duty and insolence to a superior officer.

Interestingly, this entry is the one and only reference to the incident that is known to exist — no dismissal from the corps, no official letter of reprimand, no report of an inquiry, court martial, testimonies, or depositions. The matter simply ended here and the captain kept his company and clean record. And as to Pearson's reaction to this lack of action, nothing is documented.

PURSUING THE ENEMY

As continued reports of an American buildup of troops, supplies, and boats near Kingston came in during September, they were coupled with accounts of a major American probe in the Lake Champlain corridor and later on the Chateauguay River. Fortunately, this threat was neutralized by the successful defensive victory at Chateauguay (October 26, 1813). These incidents, however, left Lieutenant Colonel Pearson in no doubt that his post was not going to remain isolated from the action for much longer. His efforts to strengthen the fortifications had paid substantial dividends, and the position was now well-prepared for any potential American thrust. All that remained now was to see that his garrison was not caught unawares.

As early as October 13, the entire garrison was put on twenty-four-hour alert. No man was to undress at night, but instead, "as the enemy have made their appearance on the frontier … Lieutenant Colonel Pearson … orders that every man will sleep in his accoutrements, ready to turn out at a moments warning. The men to be outfitted with arms, flints and ammunition."[29]

This meant that each man would be attempting to sleep while wearing his full uniform, including boots and gaiters, as well as his fully-loaded leather cartridge box on its cross-belt and bayonet/cross-belt combination. With the news of the British/Canadian victory at Chateauguay, the American threat on that flank was eliminated. Lieutenant Colonel Pearson made preparations to take his regular troops into action, or at least to move at the shortest possible notice to support the garrison at Kingston should the threatened American attack from Sackets Harbor fall on that vital stronghold. On October 31, he ordered: "the detachments of the Canadian regiment, DeWattevilles and Incorporated Militia will form the immediate garrison of the Fort under Lieutenant Colonel DeMay."[30]

He also hedged his bets, assessing that instead of Kingston, the St. Lawrence transportation corridor itself and the main military supply centre at Montreal might be the ultimate target. Fortunately, countering this threat did not require the movement of large numbers of troops, since the garrison could simply wait for the enemy to come to them. What was required was sufficient early warning. Interestingly, Pearson personally chose one of the few officers from the Incorporated Militia who had not been on his blacklist for this responsible duty:

To Lieutenant Clark, Incorporated Militia, 1 November 1813

Sir,

You will immediately proceed to Elliot's where you will take up your station with a view of watching the navigation of the river and strictly ascertaining the nature of all crafts passing down with troops and scows containing horses, artillery, etc. or should anything else suffer to lead you to suppose the enemy is passing down to Prescott, or the neighbour-hood, or should they be seen in any situation, you will instantly take horse and repair to Prescott with all pos-sible diligence, alerting the country as you pass down.

T. Pearson
Lieutenant Colonel, Commanding[31]

After waiting at his designated post five miles upriver from Elizabethtown (present-day Brockville) for three days and nights without recording any significant activity on the river, Lieutenant Duncan Clark finally saw the leading elements of the American force moving downriver. According to a later published account, "at an early hour of the fornoon, an advance guard of vessels hove in sight. Lt. Clark promptly took possession of a farmer's horse and in a few minutes rode into Brockville on his foam covered steed and announced 'the enemy are at hand.' With only a moment's pause, he dashed away for Prescott with the report for his commanding officer."[32]

Immediately following the receipt of Clark's report, the garrison was put on full alert and every cannon was primed to engage the American fleet once it came within range. The troops were stationed on the defences or posted in the nearby forest, where they could move into action without becoming exposed to enemy gunboat fire. During the next forty-eight hours, nothing could be seen to move on the river except the current. The absence of the American flotilla was due to the fact that, having received detailed reports of the strength of Prescott's defences and manned readiness, General Wilkinson was not willing to hazard his army by making a direct assault on the post.

Instead, on the evening of November 6, the bulk of the American army disembarked on the American side of the river a few miles upriver from Ogdensburg. Under strict orders to maintain absolute silence, the army marched inland and around the community before returning to the riverbank at dawn to await the boats. At the same time, under cover of the fog-laden darkness, the empty American flotilla hugged the cover of the American shoreline in an attempt to float past Prescott undetected. However, due to the alertness of the Prescott garrison, the attempt failed.

Despite having to contend with the challenges of targeting a series of fast moving, low-in-the-water targets, at a range of over 1,800 yards, and in dark, foggy conditions, the Prescott garrison's artillery opened fire. This barrage continued for over three hours, but according to American accounts only caused minor damage to some vessels and inflicted few casualties. What it does not say is that the Ogdensburg warehouses were subsequently filled with military supplies, supposedly "left behind" as the army advanced. Why this was done, when the army needed the supplies and there a sufficient number of boats to transport the goods prior to arriving at Ogdensburg, but not afterward, is not explained. Perhaps the barrage had more effect than was revealed.

Having succeeded in bypassing Prescott, the American army re-boarded their transports and continued downriver, heading for Montreal.

With the enemy moving away, Pearson ordered the garrison to assemble and prepare to pursue the Americans, while immediately dispatching an advanced unit of light artillery and embodied militia to delay and harass the enemy on the river. He also sent notice to the citizens of Ogdensburg that, to avoid being attacked themselves, they were to make an immediate declaration of further neutrality and non-belligerence and to surrender any food supplies, ammunition, and arms left behind by Wilkinson's force. For this piece of bravado he garnered two siege mortars, a stash of ammunition, thirty barrels of salted pork, and twenty of whisky, all of which he intended to collect later, once he had returned from following Wilkinson.

However, plans changed the next day (November 8) when Lieutenant Colonel Morrison's flotilla of boats from Kingston arrived with its complement of around eight hundred regular troops. Determined to participate in the upcoming action, Pearson made a proposal Morrison could not refuse, by offering to provide a substantial part of his garrison's force, as well as bateaux and crews for the pursuit. The two separate forces were merged under the overall command of Morrison, and left Prescott early on the morning of November 9, taking with them Lieutenant Colonel Pearson and more

than four hundred of the Prescott garrison. Left behind, ostensibly to protect the fort at Prescott, was the main body of the companies from the Incorporated Militia.

That is not to say, however, that no one from the Prescott Division of the Incorporated Militia had any part to play in the unfolding events on the St. Lawrence River. In addition to the aforementioned Captain Davy and his crew of militiamen, Private Thompson from the Kingston garrison and Captain Kerr and his gunboat detachment were ordered to re-man their boat. A number of other experienced boatmen and those from the regiment who had crewed boats between Prescott and Montreal (and thus were familiar with the treacherous currents and rapids of this stretch of the river) were also included to assist in piloting the flotilla downriver after the Americans.

Over the next few days, this group of volunteers, as in the case of Captain Davy's unit, were involved in the raid on Hamilton, New York, and were engaged in firing on American forces on the banks of the St. Lawrence during the battle of Crysler's Farm. Following the end of the battle and the American retreat, Kerr's detachment was part of the force that shot the rapids and made harassing probes against the retiring rearguard at Grasse Creek. Here, they succeeded in attacking and capturing one of the American gunboats, which they towed back to Coteau-du-Lac as a prize, later assessed at being worth seventy-five pounds.

After being ordered to leave their boat at that post, Kerr and his men marched the eighty miles back to Prescott to find that the remainder of the companies had not been entirely idle. They had fulfilled Lieutenant Colonel Pearson's intention to collect the surrendered goods at Ogdensburg by rowing across the river in broad daylight and openly hauling off the *matériel* in question without firing a shot or in turn being fired upon. As well, a smaller detachment had been detailed to undergo some new and additional training to supplement the depleted artillery contingent at the fort:

[Garrison Orders, November 10, 1813]

The Canadian Regiment and Incorporated Militia will each select 12 and the Embodied Militia 6 active young men for the purpose of being instructed in the great gun exercise. The above men to be regularly paraded to their exercise by an orderly Non-Commissioned Officer at 10 o'clock in the morning and at 2 o'clock in the afternoon.[33]

Finally, after thirty-seven days of continuous implementation, the military alert at Prescott was finally downgraded somewhat, and the garrison order of November 17 stated that "the troops in the fort are permitted to undress themselves and go to bed, except one third of each regiment or detachment, who are to lie down with their accoutrements, and servants, tailors, pioneers and all other descriptions of persons are to do the night duty in their turn."[34]

KEEPING WARM

With the end of the immediate threat of enemy action against Prescott, the life of the garrison began to return to normal with daily drills and inspections. That is until November 25, when some completely unexpected news arrived. Lieutenant Colonel Pearson had been ordered to take up a new post at Cornwall, forty-five miles downriver, with a mandate to improve the alert status of that garrison and maintain a watchful eye on the Americans at French Mills. In one of the last orders he signed before leaving, Pearson directed Captain Kerr, Lieutenant McDonell, and Corporal Leaky to "proceed to Kingston by the first opportunity to give evidence before a General Court Martial for the trial of Amos McIntire, a deserter from that Corps."[35]

> ### GARRISON ORDERS, JANUARY 15, 1814[36]
>
> "A party of the following detail will hold themselves in readiness to escort Prisoners of war to Cornwall tomorrow morning ... 89th Rgt: 2 Subalterns, 2 Sergeants, 1 Corporal, 20 Privates Incorporated Militia: 1 Corporal, 15 Privates, 19th Light Dragoons: 2 Privates."

With the departure of Pearson, the garrison of Prescott came under the command of Lieutenant Colonel Clifford (89th Regiment) who, despite the winter weather, maintained a steady round of drills and garrison duties for the troops, as well as fatigues and transportation duties. But, interestingly, under this officer, the number of instances of official complaints levelled against the Incorporated Militia between the beginning of December and the end of January 1814 dropped to zero.

During this period, Lieutenant Colonel Levius P. Sherwood, the senior militia officer assigned to command the Incorporated Militia detachment at Prescott, had to deal with the fact that the delivery of the promised new clothing to see the companies through the winter had failed to materialize before Lieutenant Colonel Pearson was transferred. Initially, he wrote to Pearson on December 17, complaining that "neither fatigue jackets or forage caps have as yet been given to the men, both of which articles are much wanted. The clothing was inspected and with the exception of Great coats is in a bad shape. Another suit of clothing will be necessary at the end of the year or sooner if practicable."[37]

When no satisfactory answer was received from Pearson, Sherwood forwarded his complaint on to Major General Aeneas Shaw, the adjutant general at York. He then took steps to requisition anything that was already at hand in the garrison stores and in the December 22 regimental orders, stated: "The officers in command of companies will take immediate steps to provide their men with shoes with all possible dispatch, these are now in the Commissary's at this post."[38]

But there was another task. Despite the severity of the weather and extreme need of his men, Sherwood had to stamp out a thriving black market in clothing that had sprung up in the garrison between the better-supplied regular soldiers and their militia counterparts:

[Regimental Orders, January 15, 1813]

The Non-Commissioned Officers and men of the Incorporated Militia are strictly prohibited from buying any of the clothing, shoes, mitts, or other necessaries belonging to the Non-Commissioned Officers and men of the regular forces stationed at this post and the Officers of the Corps are called upon to confine any man who shall offend in this particular.[39]

Without official issues or acquisitions from the other regiments at the post, the men of the Prescott companies had to simply "bundle up" and hope that the winter would not be a long one. That is, except for one more enterprising detachment that took a different path toward supplying their needs.

This episode began on December 21, when a combined detachment of twelve men from the Incorporated Militia and eighteen from the 89th Regiment were assigned the task of escorting a number of prisoners of war from Prescott to Cornwall in a convoy of sleighs. The Incorporated Militia's part of the detail, commanded by Captain Kerr, arrived with their prisoners, and, like their regular counterparts, expected to return to Prescott forthwith. Instead, they were ordered by Lieutenant Colonel Pearson to remain at Cornwall to undertake duties in the quartermaster warehouses related to the ships' rigging and other sailing gear stored from the gunboats beached there the previous November.

While working on this duty, it would appear that a complaint about the lack of sufficient winter clothing came up in conversation between Kerr and an old associate of his, Captain Reuben Sherwood. Coincidently, Sherwood was the son of Kerr's commanding officer at Prescott, Lieutenant Colonel Sherwood, and one of the few militia officers given Lieutenant Colonel Pearson's full approval. In a letter to Prevost, Pearson rated the young Sherwood as "of all the men I have met within this country the best qualified for an appointment … for superintending and organizing the procuring of secret intelligence."[40]

Sherwood had indeed done some exceptional secret intelligence work on the American side of the St. Lawrence River, including reconnaissance of their storehouses and positions along the Grasse Creek all the way to the American main camp at French Mills. With this knowledge in hand, Sherwood informed Kerr about the existence of a large stash of clothing, blankets, accoutrements, food, and drink that had been captured from a British bateaux convoy during the previous summer. It was lying relatively unguarded at the village of Hamilton, New York.

The two officers quickly created a plan and approached Pearson with a proposal that would see Captain Sherwood lead Kerr's men in a raiding party across the river to "reclaim" the captured supplies. This was just the sort of dynamic military initiative Pearson had been trying to instill in the Canadian Militia. Not only did he approve the mission, but he added a detachment of one subaltern, two sergeants, and twenty privates from the Royal Marines detachment wintering at the post to Sherwood's party.

Although the St. Lawrence River was frozen over, there would be thin spots to avoid, and if the raid worked, the recaptured goods would need to be carried away. It took time to prepare a number of the beached bateaux for the cross-river journey and haul them to Point Iroquois, opposite Hamilton. But as soon as the sun had set and the darkness provided cover, they were ready.

The raiding party reached the American shore undetected and succeeded in surrounding the small village. After setting sentries to prevent anyone escaping to raise the alarm, they entered the main warehouse, only to find it empty of the desired goods. They questioned the community leaders and learned that the captured stores had only shortly before been transferred nearly fourteen miles farther inland to another storehouse in Madrid (present-day Columbia). Some rapid discussion among the leaders led to the decision, in the words of the old maxim, "In for a penny, in for a pound."

The raiders rounded up the frightened residents of Hamilton, put them under tight guard, then harnessed up every sleigh they could find and drove through the night, guided by Reuben Sherwood, who knew the route intimately. Reaching Madrid, they stripped the warehouse of much of the desired goods without any opposition from the alarmed residents of that village.

According to Captain Sherwood's later report, the sleighs were loaded by around 4:30 a.m. However, they found so much *matériel* that even when all the sleighs were fully loaded, enough to fill twenty more had to be left behind. The convoy of sleighs returned to Hamilton in full daylight but the goods were loaded into the waiting boats unmolested. Sherwood, however, referred to some of the local American militia at Madrid pursuing the raiders until they were dissuaded from continuing by being fired upon by the convoy's rearguard.

In another account later published in *A History of St. Lawrence and Franklin Counties*, a less military version of this incident comes to light:

> The party engaged in this incursion returned about daylight, decked out with ribbons and streamers of brilliant colours, which formed part of their capture, and re-crossed the St. Lawrence, without the loss of a man.... A party was hastily rallied to pursue and recover the goods, but when a quantity of Shrub, a very agreeable mixed liquor, was left in a conspicuous place ... [it] had its desired effect and the pursuing party were thus disarmed.[41]

Small as this raid was, its impact upon the United States citizens along this stretch of the river was not without consequence, as the county history also recorded:

This incursion, from the boldness with which it was conceived and executed, created a general feeling of insecurity among the inhabitants, and convinced them that the state of war was a reality; that they were at any moment liable to an unexpected and welcome visit from the enemy, and that their lives and property were alike at the mercy of the British. From this time forward, there was nothing attempted that might provoke retaliation or invite an unceremonious visit from Canada.[42]

Over the subsequent months, the captured goods were shipped to Montreal and auctioned off by the authorities as war prizes, netting Captain Kerr and his men £260 in prize money. The amount, however, had not been received by July 1819, as there is a letter of complaint from Captain Kerr to the government attesting to this fact. Once back at Cornwall, the raiding party received all the accolades of victors. However, one person was absent from this celebration — Lieutenant Colonel Pearson. He had received new orders to return to Prescott and take up command at that garrison once again!

On February 5, 1814, the gales of winter did not blow as cold as the wind of change that blew in with Lieutenant Colonel Pearson's return to the garrison at Prescott. Once again, it was the Incorporated Militia that received much of the colonel's attention. During the previous month, several changes had taken place within the companies due to the fact that a number of officers had decided to resign from the corps. The resignations included Captain Jonas Jones and Captain John McLean, and their respective subalterns; Lieutenant William Morris; and Ensign Alpheus Jones. Lieutenant Colonel Sherwood had also submitted his resignation to General Drummond, but once informed that there were plans in the works to amalgamate the various divisions into a single unit (see below for details), he agreed to remain technically in command of the Eastern and Johnstown division until the unification occurred. However, he could not remain with the companies at Prescott, as he had to journey to York to attend to his parliamentary duties in Drummond's new session of the legislature.

With these resignations, the men associated with the now vacant companies were in the process of being reassigned to other companies. Other men were being switched between companies to balance out the men into a more regimental, but still unofficial, affiliation of grenadier, battalion, and light companies. These changes, however, were not completed by February 5, and one of Pearson's first actions upon taking command of the Prescott garrison was to oversee this reassignment in short order. He also wanted to review the companies for a report he had been ordered to compile for General Drummond:

[Garrison Orders, February 8, 1814]

Lieutenant Colonel Pearson will inspect the Incorporated Militia on Thursday next at 11 o'clock. Their arms, clothing and state of discipline will be particularly attended to, for the information of his Honour Lieutenant General Drummond. Every person to be present — After the inspection, the Company books will be seen in the orderly room, any complaint which the men might have to exhibit are to be brought forward immediately after the inspection."[43]

This inspection, scheduled for February 10, was postponed for twenty-four hours due to a sudden winter storm. The results of this review are not documented, but if the following order from February 19 is any indication, it might not have been a particularly glowing report: "The garrison to be under arms tomorrow morning at 10 o'clock. Every person whatever to be present, the Commanding Officer of the Incorporated Militia is directed to pay more attention in gathering his men under arms at the appointed hour and is likewise requested to see every man of his Corps is present."[44]

However, any plans or further alterations that Pearson might have had in mind were circumvented when the order arrived from General Drummond ordering the companies at Prescott and Kingston to join those of the Niagara Division at York. During the final fortnight prior to their departure, Lieutenant Colonel Pearson attended to the administrative details of a transfer of command with scrupulous efficiency:

[Garrison Orders, February 24, 1814]

The Commanding Officer of the Incorporated Militia will immediately give in correct returns of the Corps to the Orderly room, specifying what men are absent and by whose permission. All men on furlough to be immediately called in.[45]

[Garrison Orders, March 1, 1814]

The Incorporated Militia of the Eastern and Johnstown districts to be in readiness to proceed to Kingston at the shortest notice. Every man to be warned and to be in garrison tomorrow at 12 o'clock. Lieutenant Colonel Pearson will inspect the Incorporated Militia tomorrow at 12 o'clock in marching order. Every man to be present without exception.

L. Pearson, Lieutenant Colonel, Commanding.[46]

It is also interesting to note that in this case, despite the rocky relationship that had existed between Lieutenant Colonel Pearson and the officers and men of the Incorporated Militia during their term of tenure under his command, he still had time to make some favourable comments about them in his official parting order and in a separate private submission to General Phineas Riall:

Lieutenant Colonel Pearson cannot allow the Incorporated Militia of the Eastern and Johnstown district to quit this post without expressing to them his greatest satisfaction at the orderly conduct which they have invariably practiced since their being first embodied and assures them he has already made a favourable report of the same to his Honor the President.[47]

The men generally speaking are a very effective and serviceable body, and capable of being made a most efficient corps.[48]

Finally, on March 3, the companies of Incorporated Militia at Prescott marched out on their way to York, leaving behind the last piece of paperwork they would do for Lieutenant Colonel Pearson for some time, but not forever!

**GENERAL RETURN OF THE INCORPORATED MILITIA,
EASTERN AND JOHNSTOWN DISTRICT FORT WELLINGTON[49]**

1 Lieutenant Colonel (On Command, Parliamentary duty at York)

5 Captains

5 Lieutenants (Present)

1 Lieutenant (On Command at Cornwall)

5 Ensigns (Present)

1 Ensign (On Command at the Cedars)

1 Adjutant

1 Quartermaster

12 Sergeants (Present)

2 Sergeants (Sick)

1 Sergeant (On Command)

11 Corporals (Present)

1 Corporal (Sick)

6 Drummers (Present)

1 Drummer (Sick)

1 Drummer (Absent with Leave)

130 Privates (Present)

13 Privates (Sick)

5 Privates (On Command)

4 Privates (Absent with Leave)

3 Privates (Absent without Leave)

23 Women

80 Children

PART IV:

THE UNITED BATTALION

9

UNITED WE STAND ON GUARD

By THE END OF 1813, THE IMMEDIATE THREAT of American invasion had, once again, been thwarted, thanks to the British military victories at Chateauguay, Crysler's Farm, Fort Niagara, and Buffalo; the British retaliation for the burning of Newark had left the American side of the Niagara River a devastated wilderness of smoking ruins.

Despite these successes, the military situation for the continued defence of Upper Canada was not a positive one as far as General Drummond was concerned. Battlefield losses and the extensive territory he was expected to defend necessitated not only replacement troops but substantial reinforcements if he was to maintain this temporary advantage and possibly recover the territory lost along the Detroit River at the western end of the province. He urgently requested General Prevost to dispatch additional troops from Lower Canada. Prevost's reply, however, did not contain good news. Despite retaining nearly 70 percent of all the military forces in North America in static positions between Halifax and Montreal positioned against the possible threat of an attack on the lower province, Prevost now proposed removing yet more troops from the upper province:

[January 5, 1814]

The demonstration which has been made [by Wilkinson toward Montreal] and continues to be perceived in directing their whole disposable force

… against Lower Canada must be as unequivocally done away with before I can feel myself qualified in making any alteration in the troops below Kingston…. You had recently so good an opportunity of observing [your concerns about] the limited removal of Regulars for the defence of Lower Canada (a consideration which must never be lost sight of and to which every other consideration, as of minor importance, must give way), that consideration must convince you of the impossibility of complying with your request for the 13th Rgt.[1]

Without the resources of the regular army to call upon, General Drummond was once again forced to look to his Upper Canada militias to fill the military void for the upcoming 1814 campaign season. Unfortunately, despite the best efforts of the previous year to recruit the men required to create three battalions of full-time Incorporated Militia, the reality was that the number who actually had enlisted did not even amount to enough to create a single full-time battalion of volunteers. Moreover, since the effective dissolution of the flankers system in March 1813, the level of training for the remaining embodied militia regiments had remained at an essentially subpar state. To solve both these problems, General Drummond introduced a number of amendments to the *Militia*

Act that were intended to eliminate anomalies and streamline procedures, while setting up a system whereby the overall training of the embodied militias could be enhanced.

For example, under this new system, every male inhabitant of Upper Canada between the age of sixteen and sixty and physically able to bear arms was automatically deemed a militiaman and was required to enlist for prospective service (Clause V). Having signed up, these men were subject to being called to active duty for periods up to three months by means of a ballot system that would designate a specific portion of the total body for immediate service and the remainder placed on reserve for subsequent call-up (Clause XLI). At the end of the three-month active service period, the first detachment would be replaced by the second balloted detachment, and so on (Clause XLIII). In the event of a man's death while on active duty, which left

a widow or child or children lawfully begotten … his said widow shall be entitled to receive during her widowhood, and in the case of the death of said widow, the eldest child or guardian for the use of the child or children of such Officer, Non Commissioned Officer or Private Militia man, until the youngest thereof shall have attained the age of sixteen years, an annuity of Twenty Pounds.[2]

He sent the details of his expectations for these alterations to his commander, Sir General Prevost, at Quebec:

[February 18, 1814]

Entertaining a reasonable hope that considerable alterations and improvement will be made during the present session of the Legislature in the existing Militia Law of the province, whereby I am led to expect that I shall be enabled to establish that body into a tolerably efficient force ... and being particularly desirous to form them in discipline and interior economy as much as possible like troops of the line I propose incorporating such as become at my disposal into battalions of about 600 men each.[3]

He also sent the following message to Earl Bathurst in England:

[March 20, 1814]

The law passed in the session of last year, authorising the incorporation of battalions of militia volunteers for service during the war, not having answered the expectation then formed of it, a small number only having engaged under its provisions. I therefore found it necessary to recommend at the late sessions some modification of it. Under the present statute, a fourteenth of the whole of the population fit to bear arms, who are to be selected by ballot, and to serve for a year at least, may be embodied. This proposition it is supposed will produce about six hundred men with which with those engaged [in the Incorporated Militia] under the former act will form a battalion of nine hundred men.[4]

The theory was that a rotation of balloted draftees from the embodied militias would be attached to the Incorporated Militia for a course of enhanced training. In reviewing the service of that same Incorporated Militia, Drummond noted that the individual company detachments had made worthy military contributions during the course of 1813, and had, in some cases, made dynamic individual forays against the enemy. It was clear to him that if three battalions could not be achieved, there was at least enough manpower already recruited to produce a nucleus for a single combined force. The embodied militia draftees could be attached to this single force once the various detachments were brought from their respective locations to a central assembly and training location.

Although these images were drawn prior to the War of 1812, they accurately depict the appearance of a British military formation on the march. W.H. Pyne, artist, circa 1804. From Microcosm; or, A Picturesque Delineation of the Arts, *1808.*

The first official indication of this intent appeared in a letter from General De Rottenburg in Montreal to General Drummond, dated January 26, 1814, informing him that Lieutenant Colonel Sherwood, the commanding officer of the division at Prescott, was intending to submit his resignation due to ill health. For a replacement, De Rottenburg was recommending Lieutenant Colonel Thomas Fraser (Dundas Militia). On the back of this note is an annotation made by Drummond referencing his reply to De Rottenburg: "As it is intended to make some alterations with respect to the Incorporated Militia, no officer will be appointed to succeed Lt. Colonel Sherwood."[5]

Logistically and geographically, Kingston would have been the logical central location for assembling the dispersed units. However, strategically, Drummond already had significant numbers of troops at Kingston, while York was relatively undermanned and was in a location where the unit could be easily dispatched to the Niagara, Long Point, Burlington Heights, or Grand River fronts as circumstances warranted. Consequently, orders for the amalgamation of the dispersed divisions into a single battalion were drawn up and issued at York on February 18, 1814.

Setting out from their separate locations, the companies were making their way to York at a time of the year when travel by boat on the Great lakes was still hazardous due to late winter storms, high winds, and ice floes. The detachments were instead forced to march or, in one lucky case, ride in sleighs along the meandering rough tracks that passed for roads in Upper Canada at the time. For the Niagara detachments, this constituted a distance of around eighty-five miles. For the Prescott detachments, however, it meant travelling some 225 miles, a distance that was covered in just fourteen days — an average daily march of approximately sixteen miles! What is also important to note is that this trek was not done simply by the men of the regiment, for unlike regular army regiments of the day, all the married men of the Incorporated Militia were permitted to take along their families when they changed station. Thus, not only were the individual columns composed of the officers and men, but also included the entire cadre of connected wives and children, baggage, tents, and camp furniture, regimental accounts and registers, spare equipment, and anything else that might have been deemed essential. The result was a series of motley cavalcades that arrived at York during the first two weeks of March.

Immediately upon arrival, the first order of business for the garrison commander at York was to find sufficient cover to accommodate the new influx of manpower (and their associated dependents). Since the fortifications and barracks at Fort York were still undergoing reconstruction after being razed by the Americans the previous summer, the various detachments were initially billeted in whatever space was available — in the partially rebuilt barracks, nearby barns or stables, or, for the lucky few, in nearby residences of the citizens of York.

There was also the issue of merging these disparate units into a single fighting force. For this duty, a captain from the regular army was appointed to command the "Volunteer Battalion of Incorporated Militia of Upper Canada." Detached from the 8th (King's)

Regiment of Foot, and given a temporary brevet promotion to the rank of major within his own regiment, Captain William Robinson took over command as the lieutenant colonel of the Incorporated Militia in York on March 5, 1814.

William Robinson's military career began in 1805 when he received his commission as a captain. He had served with his regiment during its service in Denmark in 1807 under Sir Arthur Wellesley (later the Duke of Wellington), in garrison duties at Halifax in 1808, on the expedition to Martinique in 1809, and again in garrison duties at Quebec City from 1810 to the commencement of the war.

Once in Upper Canada, Captain Robinson had seen action against the Americans in the engagements at Fort George, Stoney Creek, Black Rock, and Buffalo. As a result, he was seen as an experienced combat officer who had the knowledge of what it took

A contemporary view of life in camp "on the march." Note who is doing the cooking. Artist unknown, circa 1790–1803.

THE INCORPORATED MILITIA DIVISION ROLLS, YORK, MARCH 181[46]

NIAGARA DIVISION

1 Major
2 Captains
3 Lieutenants
3 Ensigns
7 Sergeants
40 Rank and File
19 Women
61 Children

YORK DIVISION

1 Lieutenant
1 Ensign
3 Sergeants
26 Rank and File
12 Women
46 Children

KINGSTON DIVISION

3 Captains
2 Lieutenants
1 Ensign
6 Sergeants
2 Drummers
79 Rank and File
29 Women
68 Children

PRESCOTT DIVISION

5 Captains
5 Lieutenants
5 Ensigns
14 Sergeants
7 Drummers
155 Rank and File
23 Women
80 Children

TOTAL

32 Officers
339 Other Ranks
83 Women
255 Children
7 Drummers
155 Rank and File
23 Women
80 Children

to train men to military duties. Fortunately, the military authorities did not leave him to carry the burden of command alone, since they also appointed a small group of other regular and non-commissioned officers to act as regimental staff. These included Ensign Dennis Fitzgerald as regimental adjutant, George Thrower as regimental quartermaster, and Sergeant Major William Robinson as drillmaster. Each of these individuals was taken from the 41st Regiment, a unit that had seen hard campaigning during the early part of the war on both the Niagara and Detroit frontiers and had suffered severe casualties in its rank and file at the defeat at Moravianstown the previous October. Because of these losses, the 41st had an effective surplus of officers who could now be assigned for duty with the Incorporated Militia.

Supported by this regular core of support, Lieutenant Colonel Robinson began the challenging task of creating a single battalion force out of a collection of highly individualistic detachments. Fortunately for the men of the Incorporated Militia, their new commander was not cut from the same cloth as Lieutenant Colonel Pearson at Prescott, and did not maintain the same rigid and restrictive opinion of what was required to mould this collection of men into an effective fighting force. According to a later account, written by physician William "Tiger" Dunlop:

> Billy R. of the King's who to all of the qualifications of a most accomplished soldier, added all the light-heartedness and wit of an Irishman … [was] of the Falstaff build [corpulent or large] … no sooner was he seated than a group of officers was established around him and to these he would tell funny stories and crack jokes by the hour together. He was appointed to the command of the Incorporated Militia, and a more judicious selection could not have been made, not only on account of his military talents and good humour, which endeared him to his men, and made them take a pleasure and a pride in obeying his orders and attending to his instructions. Some idea may be formed of his talents in this way, when I state that in the course of a very few months, he rendered a body of raw lads from the plough-tail as efficient a corps as any in the field.[7]

However, this glowing assessment of Robinson's abilities was written after the war and with the benefit of hindsight. At the time, things looked considerably different as he began his service as commander. For example, each of the company detachments had been recruited and commanded by officers from their own regions. They had already served together for almost a year and had naturally formed a bond within their own sections. Unfortunately, these companies also had widely varying numbers of men, and a redistribution of manpower was required to balance out the sizes of the individual companies within the collective whole. Naturally, neither the men nor the officers were happy about these forced transfers. As well, medical inspections revealed that around two dozen of the rank and file were not in any condition to undertake the rigours of an expected campaign. These men were recommended for discharge and dismissal to their homes — after having just marched for up to fourteen days to get to York in the first place!

In creating this single battalion from a series of independent sections, Robinson also had to contend with the fact that because these sections had served on different fronts, they had received differing amounts and standards of internal company discipline, weapons training, and formation drill — not to mention having differing qualities and quantities of supplies such as uniforms, accoutrements, and weapons. As well, there was the thorny question of regimental seniority among the officer corps. Within the regular army, such matters of seniority were established not only by rank but by centuries of military custom, and were well-respected and rigorously followed. Here, however, the scattered establishment of the regiment's sections led to ambiguities of internal regimental precedence now that they were unified into a single unit, a matter of no little importance to the honour and influence of those concerned.

Not surprisingly, Robinson's actions regarding these matters, especially those focused on the general tightening up of regimental discipline and adherence to military duties, led to an increase of dissatisfaction within the regiment. A spate of men began exhibiting increasing levels of insubordination and, in a few cases, individuals began going AWOL (absent without leave) before returning of their own accord to "face the music," instead of being labelled deserters and facing execution or transportation to a penal colony.

Determined to quash this dangerous trend, Lieutenant Colonel Robinson immediately convened a series of courts martial for the miscreants. However, while the standard punishment for crimes of this sort in the regular army was the application of the cat-o'-nine-tails, or lash (regularly into the hundreds of lashes that systematically shredded the man's skin and flesh), here, no such punishment was allowed under the men's original terms of enlistment. As court president, Robinson had to come up with some alternate forms of punishment that would act as a deterrent to others contemplating a similar absence, while not creating a reign of tyranny that could destroy any hope of regimenting this corps of otherwise willing volunteers. Perhaps remaining true to his recorded Irish sense of humour, he came up with a novel set of punishments, which, while doing no serious harm to the individual concerned, nonetheless firmly established his command over the men. (For further details, see Appendix H).

With all of the individual companies now assembled, the first full "regimental" parade of the Volunteer Battalion of Incorporated Militia of Upper Canada took place at Fort York at 2:00 p.m. on March 20, 1814. At the parade, orders were issued that, effective immediately, the unit would begin a rigorous round of "company" and "battalion" instructional drills at 9:00 a.m. and 4:00 p.m. each day.

For the next several weeks, the men of the regiment, including the officers, were marched from their individual company lodgings to the parade square assigned for their drill instruction by Sergeant Major Robinson. They also undertook weapons drills that would later see them firing their muskets in full section, company, and battalion volleys — an essential system of shooting that the men had to learn and practise until it became automatic if they expected to function properly on the battlefield alongside the regular British regiments.

During this same period, the first influx of those men of the embodied militia who had been chosen by ballot to attend training with the Incorporated Militia arrived. This consisted of fifty-five men from the 1st York, ten from the 2nd York, fifty-six from the 3rd York, and twenty-eight from the 1st Durham Militia, for a total of 149 men who could now be added to the Incorporated Militia's roster.[8]

While matters were proceeding apace to bring the regiment up to campaign standard internally, elsewhere other events were having an influence on the unit, sometimes with negative consequences.

First, General Drummond expected that the Americans would repeat their gambit of 1813 by opening the campaign season with an amphibious assault or invasion as soon as the unseasonably cold weather improved and the lakes cleared of ice. He was therefore forced to put his troops on alert from the middle of March, increasing the duties they had to perform and the dispersed locations they had to protect against the expected attack. For the Incorporated Militia, this meant having to increase the pace of training and the potential of involvement in action sooner than anticipated. They also had sections of men repeatedly detached from the regiment to perform fatigue or transport duties to assist in the larger war effort of improving

A British regimental "line," composed of about two hundred modern re-enactors, but appearing with variations in "company" uniforms very much like the original Incorporated Militia might have appeared once its dispersed detachments were amalgamated at Fort York.

the defences at York and shuttling supplies to the Niagara Frontier, as exampled by the following two sets of orders:

[General Order, March 30, 1814]

The Incorporated Militia will furnish a fatigue party of 18 Rank and File for the engineers until further orders.... The Deputy Quartermaster General will provide ... bateaus to proceed at daybreak tomorrow morning for Fort George with ordnance stores, the Incorporated Militia will furnish 1 Subaltern, 2 Sergeants and 20 Rank and File.[9]

[General Order, April 3, 1814]

In compliance with directions received from Major General Riall, the troops composing the garrison at York, as well as the Incorporated Militia ... will at all times be in a state to move at the shortest notice. Commanding officers will see that every man of these corps is provided with 60 rounds of ball cartridge and two good spare flints. The detachments now occupying the yellow house will return to the small barracks now occupied by the Incorporated Militia, who are to be quartered in the yellow house, this movement to take place tomorrow at one o'clock.[10]

So desperate did this latter situation become that, on April 8, Robinson wrote a letter of complaint to his superiors:

I have made but small progress in the training of the militia, and not withstanding your letter desiring that no men should be employed by the company of engineers, 46 Rank and File have been sent to the artillery and 22 in bateaux to Fort George: lacking off the York [drafted-in militia], paroled men with the company [Jarvie's company] and the daily guards, hardly men enough remain to allow of the instructions of the officers in Battalion exercise.[11]

Obviously, this appeal did have some effect, as a subsequent garrison order, issued on April 9 for an additional detachment of one officer, one sergeant, and twelve rank and file to assist in the bateaux transportation of artillery pieces to Fort George, was countermanded the following day.

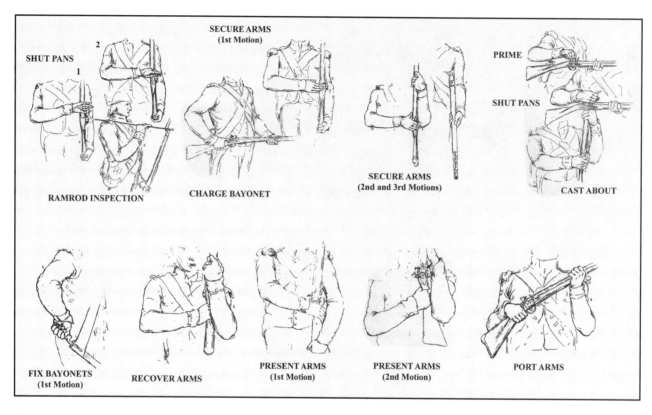

Illustrative details taken from pages in a contemporary regimental drill instruction manual, Lieutenant D. Roberts, adjutant 1st Foot Guard, artist. These moves form part of the training the men would have received and are taken from the Manual at Arms (handling the musket) and Platoon (loading and firing) exercises. In R.K. Porter, "Military Instructions … of the Manual and Platoon Exercises…," 1798.

The second, issue facing General Drummond was that, during the course of 1813, the active warfare along the Niagara and Detroit frontiers had not only seen widespread devastation inflicted upon the larger settlements such as Newark and York, but also on a myriad of farmsteads that produced much of the vital grain and other foodstuffs needed to feed the troops and Britain's Native allies in Upper Canada. The region's agricultural base of supply was effectively ruined and, after a particularly long and harsh winter, food supplies were running desperately short. Instead of taking the issue to his civilian council at the Upper Canada Legislature, General Drummond bypassed the civilian system and imposed martial law on the province. By these measures, civilians withholding grain from the military commissariat would be subject to severe punishment if they failed to deliver up any additional stocks in their possession when called upon to do so.

GENERAL ORDER, MARCH 25, 1814[12]

"There being every reason to expect a very active campaign, the Lieutenant General commanding refers officers commanding divisions and corps to the General Order of the 5th June 1813 which is now republished for their information. The above order with the modifications hereafter specified is to be enforced by Major General Riall, who will take the earliest opportunity of sending to Lower Canada all the women and children belonging to the Corps of the Right Division above three women per company and the General Officer commanding at Kingston will be responsible that no more than that proportion of women be permitted to accompany any regiment proceeding to join the Division."

In an interesting side note to this issue, this shortage of flour within the colony seems to have provided a window of economic opportunity to one enterprising, if less than honest, soldier from the Incorporated Militia. After what must have been at least a month or two of activity, Corporal George Huffman (No. 4, Captain Washburn's company) was arraigned on a charge of having taken advantage of his assignment within the garrison bakery to abscond with enough baked bread and stocks of flour to total the equivalent of 153 loaves of bread, each weighing the standard military four pounds. He then sold these on the black market to the hungry citizens of York. Pleading guilty to the crime, Corporal Huffman apparently wanted to make a clean breast of things and asked for a further seventy-seven loaves of bread to be taken into consideration in his charges, thus totalling 230 loaves of bread, or the equivalent of 920 pounds of flour. In handing down its sentence, the military court imposed an unusually humane punishment for the period; instead of receiving corporal punishment or imprisonment, Huffman was simply reduced to the rank of private and had a substantial portion of his pay docked until the requisite sum was repaid.

On a much more serious note, however, this shortage of food forced General Drummond to reimpose the General Order for the evacuation of the majority of military women, children, and other dependants from Upper Canada to Montreal in Lower Canada, a distance, in the case of travel from York, of over three hundred miles.

To the men of the Incorporated Militia, and especially those from the St. Lawrence and Niagara detachments, this news was catastrophic. Having only just got their families settled in at York after a long and gruelling journey, to now be expected to see them shipped off en masse, not merely back to their home settlements (where they could expect some form of support from family and friends), but out of the province entirely (where they would be at the mercy of the military authorities at Montreal), was more than could be tolerated. With the full compliance and support of their company officers, a desperate plea was made to their new commanding officer. He, in turn, made a personal visit to General Riall to explain the exceptional circumstances of the Incorporated Militia if this order was enforced upon them.

For once, the military machine seemed to exhibit signs of having a heart, and an exemption was made. The military authorities would not forcibly ship any of the men's families to Montreal but would permit any women and children wishing to do so to return to their homes instead. However, in doing so, they would then relinquish their right to draw upon the military system for food, as the garrison order of April 4 explained: "The women and children of the Incorporated Militia cannot draw rations unless with their husbands at some military post."[13]

Although the number of families listed at York declined somewhat, many women remained with their men and subsequently suffered the reduction of what was already a meagre ration of daily foodstuffs.

The third situation that would negatively influence the unit was the fact that, after having fought a series of hard military actions and campaigned across over a thousand miles of frontier during the course of 1813, the regiments serving in Upper Canada were left with uniforms, clothing, shoes, accoutrements, and other military equipment as close to being worn out as to leave the men wearing little more than rags. Nor were replacement supplies readily available, for although the direct threat of invasion had been beaten off at the battles of Chateauguay and Crysler's Farm, Drummond's long and tenuous supply line between Lower and Upper Canada, along the St. Lawrence River, continued to be throttled by the threat of further American action along that frontier.

It would not be until the demise of winter that the upper province's relative isolation would end with the reopening of navigation in the spring. This scenario, combined with the previous huge losses of military supplies during the disastrous retreat on the Niagara in October, the entire loss of General Proctor's army and its supplies at the battle of Moravianstown, the interception and capture of supply convoys on the St. Lawrence, and the double destruction of the York supply warehouses in April and June, had reduced the locally available stocks of replacement military supplies to nearly nothing.

Everything now depended upon opening the supply lines from Lower Canada as early as possible. In the meantime, repair and recycling became the watchword of the army. For the Incorporated Militia, already well down on the priority list for receiving military supplies and clothing, this shortage simply added to their current discomfort, as they, too, had seen their clothing worn to threadbare or worse during the course of the winter.

General Drummond had already written to Sir George Prevost on February 18 regarding this matter: "Being particularly desirous to assimilate their [the militia] appearance to the … troops of the line … I have to request Your Excellency will be pleased to assist me in this desirable object by ordering 2,000 suits of scarlet clothing, complete, to be forwarded to Kingston immediately … and for the use of the Incorporated Militia, whose clothing will become due in a very short time."[14]

In reply, the military secretary to Sir George Prevost assured General Drummond that orders had been issued to forward 1,500 scarlet jackets and trousers, plus a similar quantity of shoes, felt caps, half stockings and flannel waistcoats[15] as soon as the shipping season opened. However, when the time came, there was still no sign of the items. Even when uniforms or equipment were issued, the quantity and quality were often insufficient. Lieutenant Colonel Robinson, trying to clothe his men adequately for war, described his dilemma in a letter to Lieutenant Colonel Foster, the adjutant general of militia, on April 8:

> The red coats which were received for the militia from Burlington by the Lieutenant General's order are the old coats of the 103rd [regiment], which were bought from the men of that regiment at Quebec and given to the 1st Battalion of Militia in Lower Canada for slops before the arrival of the militia clothing from England. 160 coats were issued to the 41st last winter at Burlington, which number of coats Major Frend has ready to return if his Honor pleases; If I am to receive them, I suppose it will be necessary to alter the facings to that of the clothing which is now on its way for the use of the Incorporated Militia of Upper Canada.[16]

This extraordinary document reveals some interesting facts. The military commissariat system in Upper Canada was in such a desperate state that it was only capable of supplying the men of the Incorporated Militia with coats that had been issued to the troops of the 103rd Regiment no later than 1811, and used by them continuously until they were worn threadbare, or for two years, whichever came first. These coats had then been taken and issued to the 1st Lower Canada Militia Regiment at Montreal in 1812 or early 1813, not as proper uniforms but as clothing only fit for use in the performance of labouring, fatigues, and other dirty jobs. Following this extended and assumedly rough usage, the uniforms were then collected and shipped to Upper Canada to clothe the remnants of the 41st Regiment after its catastrophic defeat at the battle of Moravianstown in November 1813. After having been used for an additional five months of daily wear and tear by the men of the 41st, these uniform coats were then expected to be in a good enough condition (without any kind of laundering or cleaning having taken place during their previous service) to be re-tailored to outfit the men of the Incorporated Militia!

Fourth in this lengthy catalogue of problems was that of the status of the men who had been captured and then paroled the previous year. Specifically, those of Captain Jarvie's company at York and Captain Davy's men, who had been made prisoners of war the previous October, released on parole in January, and were now at Kingston.

The men at Kingston were being employed in the Commissariat Department and were considered essential to that service for the foreseeable future.

Jarvie's men at York were more than willing to serve but were precluded from doing so by the terms of their paroles. Furthermore, Captain Jarvie was not available to champion his men's cause as he was still incapacitated by his wounds. As a result, Lieutenant Jarvis took the matter to Lieutenant Colonel Robinson, who in turn made representation to General Drummond.

Taking up this case necessitated navigating a labyrinthine set of command connections that included General Prevost's headquarters, Whitehall in England, and the United States administration in Washington. Also complicating matters was an ongoing feud between London and Washington over the fate of twenty-three American soldiers captured by the British, who claimed they were British subjects and therefore classed as traitors and subject to the extreme penalty of death. In retaliation, the Americans had taken an equivalent number of British prisoners hostage to ensure the lives of their men. This led to an escalating series of tit-for-tat actions by both sides that effectively ground the process of prisoner exchanges and parole releases to a halt. When no movement on this issue had occurred by mid-March, General Drummond wrote a letter to General Prevost, referring him to the complaint of the men of the Incorporated Militia. Prevost responded:

[March 31, 1814]

I have not failed in giving every consideration to the claims of the militia of Upper Canada and I consider the imputation of a neglect of them as unfounded and unjust. The government of the United States replies reluctantly to any communication on the subject of an exchange of prisoners and always with evasion. This capricious conduct has rendered it almost impossible to carry on any exchange but you may assure the relatives of His Majesty's brave and faithful subjects of Upper Canada, who have unhappily fallen into the hands of the enemy, that it will give me the most cordial satisfaction to effect their exchange.[17]

Shortly afterward, the original issue was worked through sufficiently to allow for tri-national negotiations to recommence, and on April 17 a notice was issued that "the militia of Upper Canada who may have been made Prisoners of War and are on their parole may be released from their obligations on the 15th May 1814 and resume their military duties if required."[18]

Additional good news reached the regiment on April 18 that Private Joseph Seeley, previously sentenced to transportation to a penal colony, was instead being given an alternate opportunity to pay for his crime:

I hereby transmit to Joseph Seeley, late a Private in the Incorporated Militia of Upper Canada, but now a prisoner under sentence of transportation as a Felon for the term and space of seven years, my full and unlimited pardon upon the condition however, that he enlists as a soldier into the New Brunswick Regiment of Fencibles now raising. Be pleased to cause this communication to be made known to the prisoner and direct his release in consequence.

General Gordon Drummond.[19]

At the end of the month, several housekeeping concerns that had arisen during the period following the amalgamation were attended to in the regimental books and within the companies of the unit. Captain Henry Davy, veteran of the Revolutionary War and gunboat actions on the St. Lawrence the previous year, resigned his commission due to age, and the remaining thirty men of his company were redistributed to the other companies of the regiment where numbers were wanting. Similarly, Lieutenants William Chisholm and Peter McCullum, both from Major Titus G. Simons's company, and who had been continuously attached to the Commissariat since the previous December, were officially transferred and removed from the regimental roll. Captain Jarvie, whose wounds had still not healed sufficiently to allow him to take up his duties with his company, was also retired from the regiment.

On the plus side of the ledger, Doctor Grant Powell, acting surgeon with the regiment since March, was officially appointed to his duties and associated rank and Lieutenant Kemble of the Glengarry Light Infantry Regiment was attached for duty as paymaster. Finally, Major T.G. Simons, who had previously acted as both senior officer and a company officer during 1813 on the Niagara frontier, relinquished his direct company command in favour of becoming the Second in Command of the regiment, which resulted in his men being transferred into Captain Rapelje's company. As a result, the company designation and ranking of officers within the company structure of the Incorporated Militia was set for the remainder of the war.

COMPANY DESIGNATIONS[20]	
No. 1 Company:	Captain James Kerby
No. 2 Company:	Captain William Jarvie (Lieutenant Jarvis)
No. 3 Company:	Captain Abraham Rapelje
No. 4 Company:	Captain Daniel Washburn
No. 5 Company:	Captain Edward Walker
No. 6 Company:	Captain Archibald McLean
No. 7 Company:	Captain Thomas Fraser
No. 8 Company:	Captain John Kerr
No. 9 Company:	Captain John McDonell
No. 10 Company:	Captain Hamilton Walker

10

THE CALM BEFORE THE STORM, APRIL–JUNE 1814

THE ARRIVAL OF SPRING AND THE REOPENING of navigation on the St. Lawrence River and Lake Ontario allowed supplies to flow once again into Upper Canada. Once it was determined that the Americans were not preparing to move against Kingston or York from Sackets Harbor, the heightened state of alert implemented across Upper Canada in March was reduced for most regions, but not along the Niagara frontier. There, intelligence reports revealed that Generals Jacob Brown and Winfield Scott were amassing a sizable force of regular and militia troops in the vicinity of Buffalo. The British interpreted this buildup as preparation for a new invasion of Upper Canada across the Niagara River. These reports had also indicated that this assault would be supported by the American fleet from Sackets Harbor, which would sortie and rendezvous with Brown's army to supply it with additional troops, heavy artillery, and ammunition.

Accordingly, General Drummond proposed making a pre-emptive strike against Sackets Harbor, with the simultaneous goal of destroying the American fleet, the port's dockyard, and military warehouses, thus crippling American army plans for the Niagara frontier. As part of his proposal, the Incorporated Militia was expected to provide some 150 volunteers for the attack force. However, once again citing higher defensive priorities in Lower Canada, Prevost vetoed this dynamic thrust.

Without the authority or manpower to attack the main American base on Lake Ontario, Drummond was left with little option but to try to counter the increasingly alarming American buildup at Buffalo by launching a smaller-scale amphibious operation against the American supply depot at Oswego, but without the involvement of the Incorporated Militia.

Although the British fleet succeeded in reaching Oswego without notice or opposition on May 5, 1814, because of poor weather and an unusual degree of caution on the part of General Drummond, the landings were delayed for over twenty-four hours. The American garrison took advantage of this delay and was able to remove a substantial part of the depot's supplies before the base was finally assaulted and captured the following day. Nevertheless, more than a thousand vitally needed barrels of flour, pork, salt, and other supplies fell into the hands of the British.

Meanwhile, back at York, the round of garrison duties, training exercises, and transportation crews continued unabated. As the garrison order of April 19 clearly reveals:

> Lieutenant Colonel Robinson will select a Corporal and three men as bateaux crew from the Incorporated Militia…. The bateaux is to be kept at the battery, the crew quartered in the garrison. All guards and piquets will be under arms every morning at an hour before daybreak and remain so until it is clear daylight. The reveille

Library and Archives Canada, C-99558.

Fort York in 1821, *J.E. Woolford, artist, 1821. This view shows the Fort York of 1814, as seen from the site of the previous fort that was attacked and destroyed by the Americans in April 1813. Several of the buildings seen in this watercolour are the oldest surviving structures in the city of Toronto.*

will sound about an half-hour before sunrise.... A piquet consisting of one Subaltern, two Sergeants and eighteen Rank and File of the Incorporated Militia will mount every morning until further orders. They will fall in at retreat beating and march to the Don Bridge, where they are to be stationed all night, and to send out patrols under the direction of the Captain of the Day, to be dismissed at daylight.[1]

On the other hand, there was still no sign of the desperately needed replacement uniforms, associated clothing, or accoutrements to outfit the men properly. In addition, the overall shortage of ready-made ammunition and stockpiles of black powder forced the military authorities to conserve what supplies were available for use in case of an actual attack. As a result, although the men of the unit had practised the mechanics of loading and firing volleys in a variety of line and light infantry formations, no actual live firing had been done on the regimental range. On May 6, this unsatisfactory situation was referred to in a report submitted by Lieutenant Colonel Robinson to Colonel Foster, the adjutant general administering the Upper Canada militias: "The Militia and Officers are fairly well trained now, but we have not lately fired cartridge of any description, as it appears there is no spare ammunition either made-up or not, at this post [York] ... we are otherwise in want of canteens and haversacks."[2]

Shortly thereafter, on May 17, while reporting on the overall state of the regiment, Lieutenant Colonel Robinson referred to an order previously received on March 25 that read: "every Corps shall be provided with light felling axes in the proportion of one to every six men and a part of its field equipment which the Commissariat is directed to provide or if provided for by the Corps themselves to pay for."[3]

As these items had arrived, he used the opportunity to acknowledge their receipt, while at the same time dropping some heavy hints about other items that were on his requisition list:

Dear Sir,

I have the pleasure of yours of the 12th. The axes were rec'd and are in possession of the companies and I shall take care that they are kept compleat and in good order. We have no camp kettles, nor are there any kettles to be had for the use of the barracks. One for every ten men is, I believe, the allowance. I do not know of any article of equipment we stand in need of that can be had. I have written to the Glengarry Regiment for some Pickers and Brushes, which are not to be had except from that Corps. Even brass wire is not to be got. There is no such thing as Bugles in the country except in possession

MAJOR NOEL FREER TO W.H. ROBINSON, COMMISSARIAT GENERAL DESPATCH ORDER FOR SUPPLIES TO BE SENT TO THE UPPER CANADA MILITIA MAY 21, 1814[7]		
Coats:	40 (Sergeant's),	1,000 (Private's)
Trousers:	40 pairs (Sergeant's),	500 pairs (Private's)
Gaiters:	40 pairs (Sergeant's),	1,000 pairs (Private's)
Waistcoats (Flannel):	40 (Sergeant's),	1,000 (Private's)
Caps:	40 (Sergeant's),	1,000 (Private's)
Half Stockings:	1,040 pairs	
Stocks and Clasps:	1,040	
Serge Drawers:	1,040 pairs	

of the Ordnance. I have applied to Colonel Battersby, who will share some if he can.

We bake for ourselves and I am now building an oven for the barracks. We keep tolerably clean. The men are not in regular messes they have a great aversion to it and as no vegetables, peas or cabbages of any kind is to be purchaced, I conceive it is not of much consequence, especially as we generally get pork in the whole.

I think we get on tolerably well, the officers are very willing and the men, I understand, think themselves comfortable. Desertion is entirely stopped. The Court Martials sentence them to 4 months hard labour on the stocks with a 24 [lb.] cannon shot to their legs, which amusement they

don't much relish…. There are now 200 suits of militia clothing in our possession and 20 sergeants [coats], we have no sashes.[4]

Despite the desperate state of their own uniforms, the new suits referred to above were not, in fact, destined for the men of the Incorporated Militia. Instead, they were the old interim-issue militia coats (green with red facings) that had been previously withdrawn from use and stockpiled at Kingston and were now being issued to the men of the embodied militia draft serving with the regiment, according to the terms of an order issued earlier that month:

The Incorporated Militia is short 10 draftees, 300 were assigned for three months in the charge of an Officer and a Sergeant for each Corps. The Incorporated Militia is to clothe the men with jackets, arms and accoutrements, which are then to be re-used with the next batch of draftees. Sergeants sashes to be ordered from stores or to be made locally.[5]

Meanwhile, the military supply links in Kingston, Montreal, and Quebec were exchanging communications about the delays being encountered in receiving and forwarding the required shipment of proper uniforms (red coats with green facings), clothing, and accoutrements for the Upper Canada militia in general, and more specifically for the men of the Incorporated Militia. It appeared as though the military bureaucracy was finally moving to deal with this issue, as can be seen in a the following communication sent by Major Noah Freer, Sir George Prevost's military secretary, to Captain Foster, the military secretary in Kingston:

[May 16, 1814]

His Excellency has ordered 1,000 scarlet jackets of green facings, light and dark, with an equal proportion of the other articles mentioned in my letter of the 7th March (excepting trousers which are not yet arrived from Quebec,) to be forwarded from hence immediately for Kingston and as soon as the supply of clothing expected from England arrives, the additional 500 suits will be sent...[6]

The Western Brick Barracks, Fort York National Historic Site, built in 1815 to house the troops and their families. The buildings were without running water or toilet facilities or kitchens, and heated only by large, open fireplaces, but by the standards of the day, they would have been considered luxury accommodation for the rank and file soldiery and their dependents.

The Centre Blockhouse, Fort York National Historic Site, built in 1813, was constructed of heavy balks of timber to withstand artillery fire. Structures of this type were designed as multi-function buildings and sometimes served simultaneously as defensive strongpoints, artillery platforms, soldiers' barracks, warehouses, or hospitals, as required.

The Officer's Mess, Fort York National Historic Site, built in 1815. According to the social class separation of the day, this building was reserved for use by the officers of the regiment for accommodation, dining, social activities, and so on. It was administered by a staff of NCOs and men acting as servants and mess stewards for the officers.

With or without the proper uniforms, however, the training continued. Orders for company-level volley-firing practice with live ammunition commenced on May 23, and continued on a daily basis by a rotation of companies throughout the first two weeks of June.

This was not a moment too soon. American troops were making increasingly aggressive probes of the thin line of defensive positions marking the British western boundary along the Grand River and landing raiding parties on the exposed shores of Lake Erie. The largest of these incursions took place on May 14, when some eight hundred troops were transported by vessels from Erie, Pennsylvania, to the area around Long Point and Port Dover. During the next two days, the communities at Patterson's Creek,

Charlotteville (Turkey Point), Port Talbot, Dover Mills, Finch's Mills, Long Point, and Port Dover all suffered from attacks that saw the destruction of their public buildings. In particular, the region's grain mills, distilleries, and barns of the outlying farms, including some belonging to men from the regiment, were singled out for burning. Even cattle and crops in the fields were deliberately destroyed to reduce the region's ability to support the British army in the field.

Had the Americans pressed home their advantage, or been properly supported by additional reinforcements, there would have been nothing to stop them from marching overland, taking Burlington Heights, and cutting off the entire British army on the Niagara frontier. Instead, they completed their destructive campaign along the north shore of Lake Erie and retired from the region after only a couple of days. Nevertheless, the threat of further actions of this kind so alarmed General Riall that the entire region of the Upper Thames Valley was effectively abandoned to American control.

Additional orders were prepared to withdraw most of the troops from their forward positions along the Niagara River and concentrate them at Burlington Heights to counter any future American advance from the south, west, or east. As part of these preparations, the Incorporated Militia was put on immediate notice to be ready to march from York to defend Burlington Heights until the regulars could retreat from the Niagara frontier.

Once informed of Riall's intentions, General Drummond countermanded his directions, ordering Riall to maintain his current disposition of troops and to strengthen his positions along the Grand River boundary as much as possible. By adopting these measures, Drummond not only hoped to slow any possible American attack until reinforcements could be concentrated from their scattered positions elsewhere or brought up from York and Kingston, but also to protect those inhabitants still attempting to scratch out a living and grow crops that could feed his troops.

The American raids along Lake Erie had another repercussion that stretched beyond wanton destruction. They prompted the hardening of official attitudes toward those considered to be turncoats and traitors. In one particular case, a group of nineteen Upper Canada residents who had been captured while participating in earlier American raids were arraigned on charges of high treason, with a further fifty being charged *in absentia*. The trials for those in custody were held at Ancaster, and lasted for two weeks in June. While the regiment was not directly involved in the trials, an order issued on May 25 at Fort York suggests their indirect connection:

> A crew for two bateaus, consisting of 2 Non-Commissioned officers and 12 Privates from the Incorporated Militia will parade at the provision store tomorrow morning at 4 o'clock to row the guard [of the 41st Regiment] and fifteen prisoners to Burlington, from whence they will return to York without delay.[8]

Regarding those men placed on trial, one pled guilty and four were acquitted. The remaining fourteen were found guilty and sentenced to death. Of these, eight were executed on July 8, while the remainder were reprieved and received varying terms of imprisonment.

In returning to the clothing and supplies issue, it is recorded that on June 7, 1814, news reached the garrison at York that

> Colonel Stewart having received information that the schooner Penelope, laden with Commissariat stores and medical stores is run on shore near Smith's Creek [modern-day Port Hope, Ontario], directs that an Officer or clerk from the Commissary department proceed there forthwith to preserve and restore such stores as it may be found practicable. A party of 1 Subaltern, 1 Sergeant and 6 Privates from the Incorporated Militia … will parade at the Provision Store at 3 o'clock this afternoon to proceed to Smith's Creek in such bateau or craft as may be pointed out by the deputy Assistant Quartermaster General.[9]

It is likely that at least some of these stores were destined for the use of the regiment, for two days later, after the goods had been salvaged and brought to

York, another garrison order was received: "A board of survey, consisting of 1 Captain and 2 Subalterns of the Incorporated Militia will assemble at the provision store this morning at 10 o'clock to inspect and report on the Commissariat stores recovered."[10]

Finally, on June 10, good news came from Kingston:

My Dear Robinson,

I am happy to inform you that one thousand suits of clothing, <u>complete</u>, have at last been received at this post and it is intended to send forward without delay a sufficient quantity to equip your battalion completely … the clothing is of different facings but blue cloth is to be purchased to new the whole, which must be done by the regimental tailors … I suppose there are yet plenty of prize shoes remaining. Nothing new here.

Lt. Col. Nichol
P.S. There are plenty of half stockings and gaiters.[11]

Depending upon how he read his daily correspondence, this cryptic reference to blue cloth for facings might have come as something as a surprise to Lieutenant Colonel Robinson, since on the same day he received notice that the military authorities had decided to amend the regulation uniform code for the Incorporated Militia from a green-faced unit to one faced with blue. Thus, all of the uniforms that had been so long in their arrival were now to be received. But instead of being issued directly to the men, they were supposed to be immediately picked apart by the regimental tailors and then re-sewn to change the colour of the cuffs and collar to suit the new regulation!

11

PREPARING FOR ACTION

By June 1814, the accumulation of intelligence available to General Drummond indicated that the threat of an American invasion from Buffalo was becoming increasingly imminent. Additional regiments of American regular and militia infantry were seen arriving daily at the main American camp opposite Fort Erie. The nearby shoreline of Lake Erie was the centre of intense activity, as squadrons of longboats and scows were observed being repaired and fitted out for obvious use in the near future. On the Canadian side of the river, however, British forces along the frontier and rear echelons were strung out to an alarming degree, since all potential landing sites had to be guarded. Apart from attempting to speed up the pace of building additional defensive positions or repairing and upgrading those already in existence,

little else could be done physically to prepare for the impending attack.

On the other hand, preparing individual regiments for combat was something that could be addressed. Throughout the first weeks of June, the British military headquarters at Kingston issued a series of high-priority orders for additional stocks of weapons, ammunition, and food to be pushed forward to York, Burlington, and Niagara as quickly as possible. Implementation of the embodied militia draft for the second round of training was speeded up and all selected draftees were ordered to report to York by June 10.

For the men of the Incorporated Militia and their new draft of recruits, these orders meant undergoing an increased number of intensive field drills and firing

WEEKLY DISTRIBUTION OF THE "RIGHT" DIVISION
UNDER MAJOR GENERAL PHINEAS RIALL, JUNE 22, 1814[1]

Fort Niagara (Lieutenant Colonel Christopher Hamilton, 100th Regiment)

Royal Artillery: 1 Officer, 12 Gunners

Royal Marine Artillery: 2 Officers, 3 Sergeants, 30 Gunners

100th Rgt.: 23 Officers, 33 Sergeants, 21 Drummers, 535 Rank and File (fit), 25 Rank and File (sick)

Fort George & Dependencies (Lieutenant Colonel John Gordon, 1st (Royal Scots) Regiment

19th Light Dragoons: 2 Officers, 2 Sergeants, 16 Buglers, 28 Troopers (fit), 5 Troopers (sick)

Provincial Light Dragoons: 2 Officers, 3 Sergeants, 16 Troopers

Royal Engineers: 1 Officer

Royal Artillery: 2 Officers, 1 Sergeant, 2 Buglers, 18 Gunners (fit), 5 Gunners (sick)

Royal Marine Artillery: 3 Officers, 2 Sergeants, 1 Bugler, 32 Gunners

Militia Artillery: 2 Sergeants, 2 Gunners

Royal Artillery Drivers: 5 Drivers

1st (Royal Scots) Rgt.: 23 Officers, 44 Sergeants, 18 Drummers, 677 Rank and File (fit), 88 Rank and File (sick)

103rd Rgt.: 4 Officers, 6 Sergeants, 1 Drummer, 129 Rank and File

Coloured Corps: 1 Officer, 2 Sergeants, 20 Rank and File (fit), 4 Rank and File (sick)

Queenston and Dependencies (Major Thomas Deane, 1st (Royal Scots) Regiment)

19th Light Dragoons: 1 Sergeant, 18 Troopers

Royal Artillery: 40 Gunners

Royal Artillery Drivers: 3 Sergeants, 1 Bugler, 15 Drivers

1st (Royal Scots) Rgt.: 120 Officers, 13 Sergeants, 4 Drummers, 195 Rank and File (fit), 8 Rank and File (sick)

Chippawa and Dependencies (Colonel Robert Young, 1st (Royal Scots) Regiment.)

19th Light Dragoons: 1 Sergeant, 4 Troopers

Militia Artillery: 8 Gunners

Royal Artillery Drivers: 7 Drivers

8th (King's) Rgt.: 25 Officers, 28 Sergeants, 8 Drummers, 398 Rank and File (fit), 88 Rank and File (sick)

Fort Erie and Dependencies (Major Thomas Buck, 8th (King's) Regiment)

19th Light Dragoons: 1 Officer, 1 Sergeant, 23 Troopers

Royal Artillery: 12 Gunners

8th (King's) Rgt.: 8 Officers, 7 Sergeants, 1 Drummer, 111 Rank and File

Long Point and Dependencies (Lieutenant Colonel Parry J. Parry, 103rd Regiment)

19th Light Dragoons: 3 Officers, 6 Sergeants, 1 Bugler, 54 Troopers

Provincial Light Dragoons: 1 Officer, 1 Sergeant, 13 Troopers

103rd Rgt.: 11 Officers, 13 Sergeants, 2 Drummers, 187 Rank and File (fit), 4 Rank and File (sick)

Kent Volunteer Militia: 3 Officers, 3 Sergeants, 41 Rank and File

Burlington (Colonel Hercules Scott, 1st (Royal Scots) Regiment)

Provincial Light Dragoons: 3 Troopers

Royal Artillery: 1 Officer, 17 Gunners (fit) 1 Gunner (sick)

Royal Artillery Drivers: 1 Officer, 1 Sergeant, 15 Drivers

103rd Rgt.: 18 Officers, 29 Sergeants, 20 Drummers, 350 Rank and File (fit), 20 Rank and File (sick)

York (Colonel Archibald Stewart, 1st (Royal Scots) Regiment)

Royal Artillery: 1 Officer, 12 Gunners

Royal Artillery Drivers: 1 Officer, 1 Sergeant, 9 Drivers

Royal Engineers: 2 Officers, 1 Sergeant, 17 Rank and File

1st (Royal Scots) Rgt.: 2 Officers, 1 Sergeant, 3 Rank and File (fit), 9 Rank and File (sick)

8th (King's) Rgt.: 1 Sergeant, 3 Rank and File (fit), 4 Rank and File (sick)

41st Rgt.: 29 Officers, 33 Sergeants, 17 Drummers, 493 Rank and File (fit), 12 Rank and File (sick)

Incorporated Militia: 29 Officers, 27 Sergeants, 11 Drummers, 339 Rank and File (fit), 25 Rank and File (sick)

exercises, as well as performing additional guard duties, working in extra numbers of fatigue parties, and being detached for service within urgent transportation assignments. On the positive side, the arrival of the new uniforms and equipment at York raised spirits mightily, and since there was no supply of blue woollen material on hand to alter the facings, the clothing was issued to the men of the regiment. A few days later, on June 20, the entire Incorporated Militia regiment, plus its embodied volunteers, paraded for inspection in their new uniforms. Although the inclusion of the embodied militia draftees meant that the company lines were a visible composite of red-faced green and green-faced red uniforms, the uniformity of appearing as a properly dressed battalion would have certainly given rise to some swelled chests and bravado within the ranks at that parade.

Nor were the officers to remain immune from these improvements in appearance, for the next day a new order was posted applying to the uniform to be adopted by officers of the Upper Canada militias, including the Incorporated Militia:

> All officers on duty shall appear in a scarlet jacket, dark blue facings, yellow buttons, gold lace round collars and cuffs only, plain gold epaulettes according to their rank. Gray pantaloons or trousers etc. Cap according to regulations for regiments of the line. But where such cannot be provided, round hats will be permitted with a regulation feather cockade etc. on the left side. The jacket to be made according to the King's order for corps of the Line.[2]

That same day, at Kingston, General Drummond was reviewing the latest intelligence reports of the enemy's preparations for invasion. Under normal circumstances and in accordance with his previous plans, the weakened state of several of the regiments would have seen them withdrawn from the front lines on the Niagara frontier and replaced with stronger units. But the continued refusal of Sir George Prevost to dispatch additional regiments into Upper Canada and the imminent threat of the buildup of American forces combined to force him into some difficult decisions.

First, he suspended his previous orders for the rotation or relocation of units as a whole and ordered the retention of every able-bodied man with his regiment. Only those whose ill health made them unfit for service and a drain on the limited resources of their units were evacuated. Second, on June 21, he ordered that the 41st Regiment be immediately transferred across Lake Ontario from York to bolster his line, and to be followed as soon as possible by the Incorporated Militia: "I propose further strengthening the Right Division on the immediate frontier by the Battalion of Incorporated Militia under Lieutenant Colonel Robinson."[3]

Looking to obtain the service of every available man, he also made an appeal for men of the embodied militia detachments to volunteer for active service. Of the 178 draftees then serving with the Incorporated Militia, forty-nine subsequently volunteered and joined the regiment's ranks for the duration of the upcoming campaign.

Movement orders were prepared, and in a letter from Lieutenant Colonel Thomas Nichols to Lieutenant Colonel Robinson, dated June 21, all of the recent issues related to the regiment were addressed:

I have just been desired by the Lieutenant General & President [Drummond] to say that he has given an order for the 41st Rgt., marching to replace those of the King's that were ordered to York and that for the Incorporated Militia to move in the same direction. It is his wish that the troops should be as effective as possible and therefore he has directed me to say that to such of the Embodied Militia as shall volunteer to go on this service on the frontier you may issue clothing, those who do not volunteer are not to be compelled to leave York (I mean all the time the conscripts) and they are not to receive clothing. Blue cloth for your facings has been ordered and is not yet arrived, when it does it shall be forwarded. We have neither canteens, haversacks, or forage caps for you but they have been asked for. In the mean time, the General desires me to say that he will authorise his Commissary to pay for the stuff if it can be had and the men can get them made up themselves.[4]

General Drummond also made reference to this projected movement in his report to General Prevost early in July:

Major General Riall reports that the enemy broke up from Buffaloe … and has proceeded to Eleven Mile Creek. — From thence to the mouth of the Tonnewanto [Tonawanda Creek] it is only six miles on a good road; where it is thought they will collect their boats for the purpose of crossing over between Navy and Grand Islands…. Major General Riall has considered it advisable, in which I fully concur with him, to place the 100th Regt. at Chippawa and Fort Erie; the Incorporated Militia; now in an admirable state of discipline and efficiency under Captain Robinson of the King's Regiment, with the Light Companies of the Royals and 100th under the command of Lieutenant Colonel Pearson, between those places; Lieutenant Colonel Tucker with the 41st Regt. at Fort Niagara and Lieutenant Colonel Hamilton at Long Point with part of the 103rd.[5]

What is interesting to note in this reference is General Drummond's intended attachment of the Incorporated Militia with the light companies of regular regiments. His words make it possible to infer that, by this point, the level and type of training the men of the Incorporated Militia had acquired was sufficient to persuade a senior regular army commander that they could function and maintain the level of service expected of an elite light infantry formation. On the other hand, the Incorporated Militia's assignment to a point between Fort Erie and Chippawa would also see it placed directly at the expected American invasion point, thus posted where it would take the initial brunt of any attack occurring there.

After packing their regimental belongings, the married men of the Incorporated Militia prepared to say goodbye to their wives and children, who were to be left behind at Fort York with a small detachment of men deemed too sick to travel. The Volunteer Battalion of Incorporated Militia thus prepared for its first experience of war as a full military unit at the beginning of July 1814. However, it did so without the direction or participation of its senior field officer, Major Titus G. Simons.

12

THE AFFAIR OF THE MESS DINNER

THE ABSENCE OF MAJOR TITUS SIMONS WAS THE result of a singular set of events that had taken place during the course of the previous month; but first, a little background to stress the seriousness of what ensued.

The officer's mess and its social etiquette is a tradition well-established within the regular officer corps in the British army and one that the officers of the Incorporated Militia would have inevitably followed. In 1814, the establishment of the regimental officers' mess for the Incorporated Militia would have been integral to the regimental organization.

What should be made clear is that, as well as the official rank structure of the British army, there were also parallel social and economic strata that "placed" a man firmly in a category from which few were elevated, but many found themselves "demoted." As "Gentlemen," serving officers in regiments were expected to socialize and dine within their regiment in an officers' mess on a regular basis. The mess was presided over by a "president," who effectively acted as the host and held authority for assigning penalties for infractions of mess etiquette.

For example, it was forbidden to attend mess wearing one's regimental cap or sword, or to leave the table prior to the drinking of the Loyal Toast to the King, and thereafter without the express permission of the president. In reality, depending on the individual regimental regulations, circumstances of time and location, as well as those participating in the event, these mess dinners could be anything from solemn, dignified affairs to raucous "stags."

If the latter, the liberality with which spirits were drunk could also often determine the number of hangovers needing curing or affairs impinging on an officer's "Honour" that would need to be settled the following morning.

Major Titus Geer Simons, *artist unknown. Following his unexpected departure from the Incorporated Militia, Simons returned to the 2nd York Embodied Militia. At Lundy's Lane, he took over command of the regiment when its titular senior officer bolted to the rear. Simons then led his troops forward into action until he was seriously wounded and had to leave the field.*

Toronto Reference Library, JRR459.

Just such an occasion occurred on the night of June 4, 1814, in the officers' mess of the Incorporated Militia at Fort York. Located in the two-storey Commandant's Building, the Incorporated Militia's officers' mess consisted of a large room on the upper floor, with a withdrawing or vestibule room on the lower that connected, through a passage, to the parade square outside. On the evening in question, all parties subsequently examined by the Court of Enquiry agreed that the officers and some guests were dining in the upper room. Around 10:00 p.m. an argument developed between Lieutenant Duncan McDonell (of Hamilton Walker's 10th Company), who was acting as the mess president, and Ensign John Lampman (of Jarvie's 2nd Company). According to the testimony later given by Lieutenant Fraser of the 1st (Royal Scots) Regiment:

He [Fraser] was an invited guest at the mess of the Incorporated Militia, when he observed Lieutenant McDonell, President of the Mess begin to verbally abuse Ensign Lampman, who made no reply. Ensign Lampman left the mess [obviously without asking permission] and went downstairs to the room where caps and swords had been left. Lieutenant McDonell followed and drew a sword from a table and advanced towards Ensign Lampman. Captain Rapelje intervened, taking hold of the sword and after a short struggle wrested it from Lieutenant McDonell. Ensign Lampman then laid hold of Lieutenant McDonell and threw him to the ground in the corner.[1]

Similarly, Captain Rapelje's testimony stipulated that after Ensign Lampman had quit the mess without asking permission, "Lieutenant McDonell rose from the table and said he would flog Lampman for behaving in an ungentlemanly like manner.... Lieutenant McDonell followed Ensign Lampman downstairs … and began to violently abuse Lampman.... Lieutenant McDonell drew a sword and swore he would sacrifice Lampman."[2] Captain Rapelje then seized the sword and pried it loose, while a scuffle developed between McDonell and Lampman.

From this point on, testimonies vary according to the individual's personal bias. However, piecing together the constant threads, it appears that while this altercation was occurring, Major Simons and Ensign Charles Short both entered the room. According to Lieutenant Fraser's testimony, Major Simons then "begged them to desist, shamed them for their ungentleman like conduct and said that he felt much hurt that a quarrel should take place after so pleasant an evening,"[3] while Ensign Short, "who had not been of the party, stripped off his clothes [jacket] and proposed to be Lieutenant McDonells champion."[4]*

Major Simons then demanded Ensign Short stand back and desist, as in his view McDonell was at fault. Ensign Short refused and the matter between these two officers escalated into a heated exchange of verbal insults. According to Captain Rapelje's testimony, Ensign Short refused, claiming McDonell had been violently ill-used, "whereupon Major Simons called Short a Damned scoundrel and coward and challenged Short to go outside and fight. Ensign Short refused and said he would only respond as a gentleman."[5]

Following this, Major Simons left the room and taunted Short into following him to receive satisfaction, but, upon receiving no reply, waited outside in the darkness. When Ensign Short eventually left the building, Simons, in the presence of and witnessed by several men from the regimental ranks, struck the ensign without warning with either his fists or a piece of wood.

According to the second version of the testimony, Ensign Lampman stated:

> Major Simons said you may as well call me a liar, only a scoundrel would attempt to make gentlemen behave like blackguards and left the room. Ensign Short drew his sword, Major Simons, being warned by a yell, called Ensign Short a cowardly rascal and said no soldier would draw a sword

---

* In other testimonies, the term used is "friend," which implied his readiness to act as a "second" in any ensuing duel between McDonell and Lampman.

on an unarmed man. The sword was taken from Ensign Short in a scuffle [by Major Simons] and Major Simons went to his quarters."[6]

Irrespective of which version was the more accurate, the fact that two junior officers had engaged in an altercation within the privacy of the officer's mess was one thing, and a circumstance that could be dealt with internally. On the other hand, an altercation between

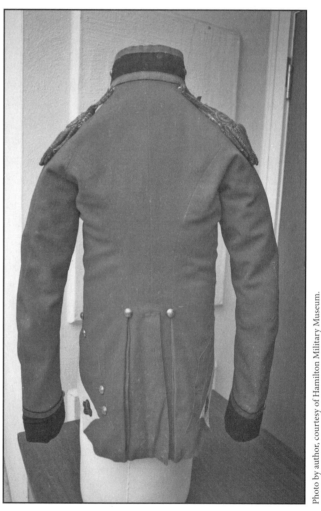

Photo by author, courtesy of Hamilton Military Museum.

The original dress uniform of Major Titus G. Simons as on display in the Hamilton Military Museum. Interestingly, in the regular army regiments, the officers' facings would match that of the regiment as a whole. For the Upper Canada Militia officers, however, dark blue was authorized, irrespective of the fact that the Incorporated Militia's facings at this time were green.

the most senior field officer of the regiment and one of its most junior ranks, in public and in front of the men of the regiment, was another matter entirely, and far more serious. Seeking to address the matter the following day, Lieutenant Colonel Robinson was disturbed to find that Major Simons was nowhere to be found within the confines of the garrison or at any nearby home or inn.

Investigation subsequently revealed that the major had ordered his regimental servant to saddle his horse at dawn and that he then left the post without orders or permission. Nor did he return during the course of the following week to explain his conduct or resume his duties. By June 16, the official axe finally fell as the regimental adjutant, Dennis Fitzgerald, wrote, "Sir, I am directed by Lieutenant Colonel Robinson to desire that you are to consider yourself in arrest for behaving in an improper manner on the evening of the 4th June. The circumstances attending which misconduct have been laid before his Honor the President, and his determination thereon will be transmitted to you."[7]

In accordance with the president's subsequent instructions, an official court of inquiry was convened on June 22, 1814, and took statements from both the officers and the rank and file who witnessed the various incidents. Major Simons, however, remained conspicuously absent. The following day a letter from Major Simons was delivered to the inquiry, complaining that the whole affair was an organized conspiracy and that he had only left the post on legitimate urgent business. Unimpressed by this claim, the adjutant general of militia, Lieutenant Colonel Foster, rejected Simons's reasoning and privately informed him that he faced only two alternatives. Either he could quietly submit his official resignation from the corps of the Incorporated Militia, return to his position within the 2nd York Embodied Militia, and retain his rank as major, or he could face a full court martial, with the expectation of being found guilty and reduced in rank or cashiered entirely.

On June 29, Major Titus Geer Simons's official letter of resignation from the Incorporated Militia was received at headquarters and entered upon the books for subsequent official approval on July 10 — a less than impressive end to a service that had been so highly valued by the army only months before.

And what of the original protagonists and the incident that sparked this controversy? The Lampman family maintained an oral tradition, later documented in a descendant's memoir. Allowing for the years that had passed (that distorted details of rank and so on) and the fact that this is only one side of the story, it nonetheless provides an interesting suggestion of how the matter began and the conclusion to this episode:

> The men of the barracks at Fort York were drawing their regular ration of rum in the tin service cups with which every man was supplied. [Later at dinner] Captain McDonald [McDonell] … charged Lt. Lampman … with being no soldier because he threw his rum over his shoulder instead of drinking it. Lampman denied the charge, the lie was passed,

the men clinched and McDonald was thrown into the fireplace. He rushed for his sword and returning with it drawn sought Lampman, who meantime had gone into another room and hid behind the door. When McDonald came through with drawn sword, Lampman seized the sword and wrenched it from McDonald's hand and had him at Lampman's mercy. A challenge was given by McDonald to fight a duel the next morning at sunrise on the beach of the lake. The challenge was accepted, Seconds chosen, the decision to be made with pistols at 20 paces. Lampman, the Seconds, and a doctor were at the beach next morning at sunrise, but McDonald failed to appear. His friends had induced him to drink enough to incapacitate him for his mad [and illegal] project of a duel and had him hopelessly drunk when sunrise came. The duel was declared off, the duelists made up friends. McDonald was said to have been an excellent soldier, but a bit hot tempered at times.[8]

PART V:

THE NIAGARA CAMPAIGN OF 1814

13

THE INVASION BEGINS

As the Incorporated Militia was preparing itself for possible relocation from York, a series of events began to unfold on the Niagara frontier that would propel the unit into combat earlier than planned. It is necessary to review these events before continuing the story of the regiment's involvement in this developing campaign.

Having prepared his army for invasion during the previous three months, the senior American commander, General Jacob Brown, issued his embarkation orders on July 2, 1814. Early the following morning, the American boats grounded on the Canadian shoreline just below Fort Erie. As the first wave of men rushed forward into the darkness to establish a perimeter for the bridgehead, the British picket guard, not able to hold back this vastly superior force, retired to the fort to notify the garrison's commander, Major Thomas Buck (8th [King's] Regiment), that the invasion had begun.

Placed at the end of the British defence perimeter, and with a garrison of only 137 regular troops and a detachment of local Lincoln Militia, Major Buck was facing hopeless odds, without any hope of relief for at least a day or two. Despite these unfavourable circumstances, some of the garrison's officers pressed Buck to adopt a "to the last man" defence of the post. The majority opinion was that as the loss of Fort Erie was certain in the event of an American assault; capitulation to the inevitable would avoid unnecessary casualties. Accordingly, Buck sent out a truce flag and entered into negotiations for the surrender of the garrison. Around 5:00 p.m., Buck's force marched out into captivity, while American musicians played "Yankee Doodle" and the new occupants raised the Stars and Stripes as a sign of ownership.

Having received word of this American invasion around 8:00 a.m. on July 3, General Riall sent off urgent orders to Burlington Heights and York for the immediate concentration of every available regiment and detachment on the Niagara frontier. By that evening, most of the American invasion force was on the west bank of the Niagara River and preparing to move north in the morning.

General Riall and Lieutenant Colonel Pearson, meanwhile, were busily engaged in improving their strong defensive position on the north bank of the Chippawa River. Additional earthworks were being constructed and manned by the various companies of troops that arrived as the day progressed. Although the Chippawa line gave General Riall his best hope of stopping the Americans, he realized he needed to slow down any American advance to complete his defences and allow enough time for his rear echelon forces to appear. He also believed, erroneously, that Fort Erie was still holding out and that most of the American force would be occupied in forcing its surrender, leaving him the possible opportunity of making a rapid counterattack should only a part of the American army advance on Chippawa. To gain time for the British concentration to develop, Lieutenant Colonel Pearson was ordered to march a strong detachment forward during the night and delay the Americans as much as possible should they advance from Fort Erie.

Chippawa, *Sempronius Stretton, artist,* circa *1804. Looking south across the Chippawa River bridge to the hamlet of Chippawa in 1804.*

By the following morning (July 4), the First Brigade of the American Army, commanded by General Winfield Scott, had advanced about four miles north from Fort Erie, only to encounter Pearson's force drawn up on the far bank of the turbulent Putnam's Creek, swollen by heavy rains that had fallen during the past several days. The only way to cross was over a small wooden bridge, but the British had torn up the wooden roadbed, partially demolishing it. Faced by what he considered an inferior force of infantry, artillery, and cavalry, Winfield Scott changed his brigade formation from column into line-of-battle.

On the other side of the creek, the vastly more experienced Pearson, instead of immediately engaging the enemy, patiently watched and waited as the Americans completed their manoeuvres. Before the Americans could open fire, Pearson had his men fire a single volley into the American line, then immediately march away — leaving Winfield Scott and his troops looking at an empty field!

Forced to wait while the bridge was repaired before advancing, Scott's force again moved north, only to have this sequence repeated at every creek between Fort Erie and the Chippawa.

The American force eventually reached main British defences at the Chippawa River, but Pearson's delaying tactics had done exactly what was required and used up the bulk of the day. Once the last of the British rearguard had crossed the Chippawa bridge, the centre spans of the roadbed were torn up, making the structure impassable. At a width of

Looking south across the Chippawa (Welland) River today (2011), from the perspective of the wartime British defensive positions.

over two hundred feet and some twenty feet deep at its mouth, the river was well chosen as the primary line of British defence.

As they approached the river, Winfield Scott's brigade was met with heavy fire from the British artillery batteries on the opposite shore. Recognizing that nothing more could be achieved that day, and knowing his men were exhausted and frustrated after their daylong encounters with Pearson's rearguard, Scott marched his troops back some two miles to a position along Street's Creek. Here, he established his camp and decided to await the arrival of General Brown with the remainder of the army before tackling the significant barrier of the Chippawa and its defences.

On the other side of the river, General Riall was confident in the strength of his defensive position and pleased with the delay tactics of Lieutenant Colonel Pearson. As well, the support of Native troops gave him an additional light force to harass the enemy flanks. By the morning of July 5, further units of regular and embodied militia infantry had arrived to bolster his line. His choice now was whether to remain on the defensive or to attack.

Having previously formed a low opinion of the quality of American troops after their dismal showing at Buffalo the previous December, General Riall was also under the mistaken impression that Fort Erie was detaining a sizeable part of the American force. He decided there was an opportunity to strike at the enemy while they were divided. He was unaware that, in addition to Ripley's Second Brigade, Porter's Third Brigade was also advancing north to create a force that far outnumbered his.

Prior to acting on this decision, Riall had sent his Native troops out during the night with orders to skirt the American encampment and scout out their dispositions, but not to engage the enemy. However, as the morning of July 5 passed, some Natives found the American sentries too much of a tempting target and began firing, inevitably drawing fire in return. Initially ignoring the harassing fire, Brown later decided to flush this opposition out from their cover in the woods by sending Porter's troops and American Native allies in after them.

Coincidently, this was taking place about the time General Riall ordered his troops to repair the Chippawa bridge and prepare for an attack. Because a wide band of trees blocked the line of sight between the open ground of the Chippawa riverbank and the fields in front of the American camp, neither general knew of the movements taking place in the camp of the enemy. With both sides advancing their light troops and Native allies through the woods to the west of the American camp, a collision of forces became inevitable.

Around 3:30 p.m., the Americans began to encounter small parties of British Native allies and embodied militia, and the battle began. For nearly an hour the fighting in the dense woodland surged back and forth. Eventually, after additional militia and regular troops were committed by the British, the American flanking force, under General Porter, was routed and put to flight.

Reacting to the sounds of fighting in the woods, General Brown ordered General Scott's First Brigade forward to engage the British until General Ripley's

Second Brigade could arrive in support. General Riall, meanwhile, had marched his main force of regulars along the riverside road and through the deep stand of trees that blocked his view of the American encampment. Leading the British force of some 1,200 rank and file onto the field, General Riall ordered his column to deploy into line across the open ground. Unfortunately, there was not enough clear ground to allow all units to deploy side-by-side, causing the units to overlap and a gap to develop in the British line.

At the same time, Winfield Scott pressed his First Brigade forward across the Street's Creek bridge and deployed his own line, supported by three artillery pieces. Having seen considerable battlefield service and having practised long and hard over the previous months, each of these regiments reacted to the situation with calm efficiency and discipline.

Watching from the other side of the field, General Riall realized that despite the grey coats worn by these troops (which had previously misled him into believing them to be relatively undisciplined militia troops, such as those he had routed at Buffalo only six months before) he was, in fact, facing regularly trained and fully disciplined regiments. He is reputed to have stated, "Why, these are Regulars by God!"[1]

After engaging in a period of counter-battery artillery fire, the British infantry line advanced, but in doing so they masked the firing of their own artillery, thus reducing the effectiveness of their firepower. As the lines closed to less than one hundred yards apart, the first American volleys tore into the redcoat formation. The battle stalled, becoming a brutal matter of face-to-face pounding and attrition, as neither side

could advance and neither was willing to retire. In this kind of competition, the advantage lay with the defenders, as the American static position had the full support of its artillery, which could pound the British flanks at point-blank range. A further American advantage lay in the fact that General Riall had no reinforcements whatsoever, while General Brown now had the entire Second Brigade on the move toward Street's Creek. As well, General Porter had succeeded in re-forming his Third Brigade, including those that had not previously joined his initial attack, and was preparing to re-engage from the American left flank.

The deciding factor in the battle came shortly afterward as fresh batteries of American artillery moved into a firing position and opened up, tearing unfillable gaps in the already depleted ranks of the British line. Under the cumulative slaughter of this remorseless and increasing assault, the British line began to recoil, beginning with the flanks, which had suffered most throughout the entire conflict. Seeing his force involuntarily beginning to lose ground, and perhaps noting the substantial American reinforcements of Ripley's Brigade entering the field, General Riall knew his gamble had failed and ordered a withdrawal. Defeated, but not beaten, the British force disengaged and retired their reduced line out of musket range before forming a relatively orderly column and marching toward the Chippawa River, followed shortly thereafter by the Americans.

In his subsequent report, General Riall referred to his attack as "not attended with the success that I had hoped for."[2] While crediting the Americans for their improved quality of battlefield effort, Riall deliberately overestimated the American force at over 6,000, while under-reporting his own at 1,800. Fortunately for Riall, General Drummond recognized the damaging effect on morale this defeat would create if it were admitted that a force of British regulars had been beaten by an equivalent number of American troops. So he publicly supported Riall's account of bravely fighting against overwhelming American numbers, as in his turn did Prevost. Privately, however, both senior commanders realized that the humiliating defeats the British had inflicted on the American army over the previous two years were now things of the past.

14

THE KING COMMANDS AND WE OBEY: OVER THE HILLS AND FAR AWAY

At York, news of the American landings arrived as the Incorporated Militia were already preparing to move out for the Niagara frontier. However, Riall's initial orders for immediate reinforcements only included the regular troops at the garrison. The Incorporated Militia were to remain as the principal garrison for the defence of Fort York and its adjacent positions: "The Incorporated Militia will give the whole of the [guard] duty tomorrow.... A fatigue party of 1 Subaltern, 4 Sergeants and 56 Rank and File will parade at 2:30 pm at the Provision Stores."[1]

Things changed once again on the morning of July 6, once news of the British defeat at Chippawa reached York via the morning courier boat, as recorded in the diary of Ensign Andrew Warffe (No. 6 Company): "A severe engagement took place near Chippaway, which lasted about two hours, the enemys force consisted of 7,500 and ours of about 1,500. Supposed we lost about 600 men killed and wounded and the enemy almost double that number."[2]

Although the removal of the Incorporated Militia would leave the town of York relatively undefended until additional troops could be forwarded from Kingston, orders were issued for the immediate transfer of the regiment to the Niagara frontier by boat that very day. No families were to be allowed to accompany the troops. Thus, that afternoon, 379 men of the regiment were crammed into "a brig of war and four schooners"[3] for the cross-lake journey, leaving behind only a small detachment consisting of one ensign, one sergeant, seventeen rank and file, and twelve sick to supplement the garrison's remaining guard. Also left behind were sixty-six women and 133 children, who lined the beach to wave goodbye to their men as the boats sailed away.

After a relatively quick crossing, the regiment landed at the dock alongside Fort George shortly before sunset. Under normal circumstances, the unit would then have encamped and awaited orders in the morning. However, such was the level of alarm about the state of defences at the Chippawa that it was decided to store all of the surplus equipment and baggage at the fort and make an immediate night march toward Niagara Falls, some sixteen miles south. For the companies recruited from this area it was no significant challenge to navigate their way, since the men were already intimately acquainted with all of the local roads. But as a precaution, men from Kerby's and Rapelje's companies were attached to the other companies to act as guides to prevent units from becoming separated in the darkness. The regiment arrived at Queenston around 10:00 p.m., and received instructions to halt and secure the position while awaiting further orders.

Occupying whatever shelter was available, the men sat out the following day: "A severe storm of hail and rain, thunder and lightning occurred where we were encamped and were out all day and night under a small tent. [The lightning] killed two horses at a short distance, which were hobbled together."[4]

There is also a small reference for this date that reveals the level of comforts that the men were able to take with them. For the rank and file, their only coverings would have been their greatcoats and a blanket. However, for the officers, a little more leeway

was permitted: "My clothes that I had at York when ordered away were two trunks and a bed. The bed and a quilt [I left] at Sedy Jarvis, One trunk at Squire Gilbert's. One trunk took to Niagara also 3 blankets and a quilt."[5]

Farther up the Niagara River at Chippawa, the campaign was continuing to evolve as both sides considered their next moves in the face of the Battle of Chippawa. A review of the 1814 Niagara campaign to place the subsequent service of the Incorporated Militia in its proper context follows.

THE WIDER CAMPAIGN

Following the defeat at Chippawa, many British officers believed that Riall had erred in going on the offensive before all of his available reinforcements had arrived. In addition, having suffered a severe number of casualties, virtually all of the surviving Natives quit the Chippawa position, as did many of the embodied militia, depriving Riall of most of his light troops, and weakening his position.

At the same time, in the American camp, General Brown recognized that this success had only been achieved at the cost of a substantial number of casualties from the force that had trained for so long that spring. Nor were there any equivalent troops that could take their place. Moreover, the British still blocked the only road that led to his planned rendezvous on July 10 with Chauncey's fleet at the mouth of the Niagara River. After evacuating the wounded and prisoners across the Niagara River and burying the dead of both sides in long common graves on the battlefield, General Brown decided to outflank the British defences by crossing the Chippawa River farther upstream at Weishoun's Point, at the junction of Lyon's Creek and the Chippawa River.

The following morning (July 8), General Brown ordered Ripley's (Second) and Porter's (Third) Brigades to march to Weishoun's Point, construct a bridge across to the north bank, and attack the British from the rear. However, upon their arrival at Weishoun's, the Americans found that their preparations had alerted the British, thus allowing General Riall to reposition some of his infantry and artillery to contest the crossing. Unwilling to suffer the heavy casualties that would inevitably result if he attempted to build a bridge while under fire, Ripley held his position while sending a report back to Brown.

In response, an angry General Brown came forward, condemned Ripley for his inaction, and personally took over command, ordering the troops forward. Despite taking casualties among the work parties, the men had pushed the bridge to the midpoint of the river when a report arrived indicating that the British were abandoning their defences at the mouth of the Chippawa River and were marching north. Once this information was confirmed, the construction of the pontoon bridge was abandoned. The Second and Third Brigades were then ordered to march to rendezvous with General Winfield Scott's First Brigade, which had remained at the junction of the Chippawa and Niagara Rivers to maintain a diversionary pressure on the main British position guarding that vital bridging point. From the British perspective, this evacuation was the result of General Riall having receiving an erroneous message which claimed that, despite his precautionary redeployments, the Americans had crossed the Chippawa and were threatening to cut off his line of retreat to Queenston.

That same morning (July 8), the Incorporated Militia received orders to reinforce Riall's position. Once a detachment of the 100th Regiment arrived to take over the garrisoning of Queenston, the Incorporated Militia recommenced their advance on Chippawa. Marching a distance of nine miles under a hot and sweltering sky that increasingly threatened a repeat of the previous day's thunderstorms, the men were "expecting to see the enemy every moment."[6] Instead, they had just reached the hilltop crossroads at Lundy's Lane (some two miles short of the Chippawa) and halted for a break when supply wagons and limbered artillery appeared on the road ahead. Immediately behind them were columns of red-coated infantry, "accompanied by hundreds of women and children, besides men on foot and in vehicles,"[7] all pressing north with some speed.

Riders from the column brought new orders from General Riall that instructed the Incorporated Militia to move off the road and take up a defensive position on the hillside while the column completed its passage. Once the column had passed through, if the Americans had not appeared or attacked, the regiment was then to re-form and act as the rearguard for the duration of the march back to Queenston.

The regiment remained as ordered and then began its trek back the way it had come. Only this time they had to maintain a steady watch to their rear and flanks for any appearance by the pursuing enemy.

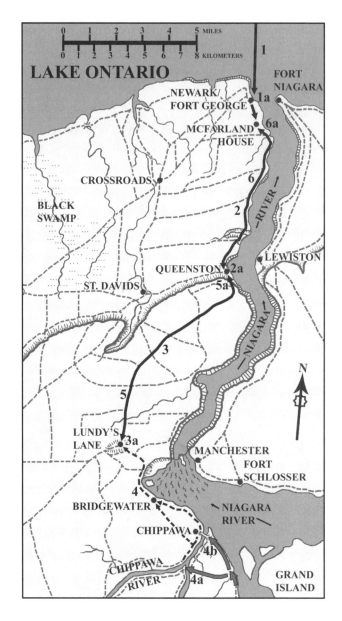

March of the Incorporated Militia to Chippawa and Back, July 6–8, 1814.

1. The Incorporated Militia arrives in boats from York (1) and disembarks at Fort George (1a) at sunset on July 6.
2. The regiment marches to Queenston (2) and encamps for the night, 10:00 p.m. (2a).
3. On the morning of July 8, the regiment is ordered to march up along the Portage Road (3) to the Lundy's Lane crossroads (3a) where it halts at around 2:00 p.m.
4. The British forces retreat from the Chippawa River (4) in the face of the American attacks at Weishoun's (4a) and the Chippawa bridge (4b).
5. After seeing the British forces pass, the Incorporated Militia retires as the rearguard of the column (5) to the Queenston Heights (5a), where it halts around 10:00 p.m.
6. The British column retreating to Newark (6); the Incorporated Militia again acts as rearguard. until it reaches the McFarland House (6a), where it halts and encamps around midnight.

Finally, around 10:00 p.m. and under a torrent of rain, the regiment reached Queenston, having marched a total of nearly eighteen miles that day. At that point:

> A short halt was made … where we got a drink of muddy sulphur water [from a stream] that crossed the road, and had served to each man and officer about half-a-pound of bread that had been brought in an open wagon, and was pretty well filled with dust and gravel, gladly eating and drinking as could be got.[8]

After a brief rest period, new orders were received to move toward Newark and Fort George. This came as something of a surprise, since the expectation was that General Riall would make a stand at the old hill-top 1812 battlefield site. Instead of being simply an open field, it had been transformed during the subsequent two years into a position of some strength. Good defensive artillery positions, blockhouses, and fortified barracks had been constructed on the site and the geographic features of the Niagara Gorge on the one flank and the escarpment on the other made this position relatively secure from any attack from either side. But instead, "during the halt at Queenston the guns were dismantled and, with the stores hauled out of a small fort built on the side of the mountain…. It had but lately been finished, and appeared sufficient to stand a siege. After the guns and stores had been removed, the block house was set on fire and destroyed, so that it could not be used by the enemy."[9]

Ordered to provide the rearguard once again, the regiment took up its assigned position behind the column and began the march. However, before reaching the river-mouth fortifications,

> we were halted at McFarland's a large deserted brick house about a mile outside the fort [Fort George] as a piquet guard, until morning, the remainder of our force passing on the fort. After placing sentries, all found a resting place on the floor of the house and ground of the orchard nearby, until daylight, from whence we could see the tents of the enemy, established on the mountain, six miles from us. After daylight we were marched [to Fort Mississauga] … and encamped within range of the fort, remaining there several days.[10]

Captain McLean also recorded his impression of this march in a subsequent letter to his father on July 12: "We arrived here about ten o'clock, having marched about eight and twenty miles dur'g the day, which was one of the warmest we have seen here this summer, and what added to the fatigues was the immense clouds of dust in which we were constantly kept by the Dragoons and Artillery."[11]

When they reached the mouth of the Niagara River, the regiment was assigned its encampment position at Fort Mississauga, where it shared the ground with a wide range of other regiments. As mentioned above, the advance guard of the American forces has appeared on the Heights at Queenston on July 9. Expecting the worst, General Riall issued orders for his forces to prepare to repel an American attack at any moment. However, the Americans remained at Queenston and established their main encampment on the heights above the village. During the days that

followed, both armies sent out patrols and pickets, resulting in a number of minor skirmishes, events that were subsequently recorded in the personal accounts of (respectively) Lieutenant Henry Ruttan and Captain Archibald McLean:

The Americans had advanced to McFarland's and placed guards and piquets, nearly surrounding us with sentries. We, of course did the same,

McFarland House was one of the few buildings on the Niagara frontier to escape wartime destruction, making it one of the oldest houses still standing along the Niagara River. Today, it is a museum run by the Niagara Parks Commission.

which brought them and our sentries within speaking distance of each other. On several occasions, attempts were made, particularly at night to capture our sentries and guards.[13]

[July 12] Since we came to this place, two hundred of our men under Col. Robinson have been out about half way to Queenston for forage, but did not meet any of the enemy, tho' they are now in possession of that place in numbers uncertain. Last night a force … advanced in order to cut off our piquets if possible, but they found them too alert and after exchanging some shots they retired. There has been no loss on our side except a Corp'l & three or four men of the kings missing, the enemy's loss is uncertain, but that they have lost a General seems to be undoubted…. We have frequent alarms here but do not expect to have anything to do till the enemy's fleet comes up — We are pretty well prepared for an attack, hav'g three months provisions in store, plenty of guns, ammunition and men, and I hope plenty of courage.[14]

UNITS AND DETACHMENTS STATIONED AT AND AROUND FORT MISSISSAUGA, JULY 10, 1814[12]	
19th Light Dragoons	1st (Royal Scots) Regiment
Provincial Light Dragoons	8th (King's) Regiment
Royal Engineers	100th Regiment
Royal Sappers and Miners	Incorporated Militia
Royal Artillery	Coloured Corps
Royal Artillery Drivers	

As confident and optimistic as this last letter appears, the reality for the British position on the Niagara was drastically different. The American invasion and occupation of the vital lines of communication radiating west and north from Fort Erie had cut off Riall's army from a major source of fresh food supplies on the southern flank of the Niagara Peninsula. No support would come from Kingston, as the American naval dominance of Lake Ontario at the time made any waterborne transportation of supplies hazardous in the extreme. Therefore, despite the desperate severity of the strategic situation and the urgent tactical need to push reinforcements into the fighting zone, General Drummond was forced to report to Sir George Prevost on July 15 that he was going to suspend any further strengthening of the British positions on the Niagara frontier:

[July 15, 1814]

I have received letters from Colonel Scott at Burlington stating his intention of moving to the Forty Mile Creek, his force at present being the 103rd Regiment, a detachment of the 19th Dragoons, about 1,000 militia and some Indians ... I have disapproved of this movement and directed him to return and retain his post at Burlington, as well as to dismiss all the too young, elderly, and inactive men of the militia ... and to keep only those of healthy and serviceable appearance as well as from this reason as it would be impossible to provision such numbers.... Although I should have wished it, I am apprehensive that I shall not have it in my power to forward any further re-enforcements to the Right Division, from the inability of the Commissariat to supply provisions, and in fact dread their failing in due supplies to those already there.[15]

Rations had already been cut the previous month and non-essential personnel and dependents of the regular regiments had been evacuated to Lower Canada to reduce the number of mouths requiring supplies, but it was still not enough. On July 13, General Drummond was forced to issue a drastic order that would, to some degree, affect every soldier on the Niagara, but most particularly the men and families of the Incorporated Militia: "General Order ... All women and children following the army above Kingston are to be immediately put upon half their usual rations until further orders and it is recommended as many as possible should be sent down to Kingston by every opportunity."[16]

Since even at full quota the women were officially entitled to only a half-ration and the children one-third, this cut now reduced their subsistence to effectively starvation levels. Some families from the eastern companies of the Incorporated Militia were left with little option but to abandon their place at Fort York and either move to Kingston, or go to their home communities in hopes of faring better there. For the families of the men from the Niagara, however, there was no such option, as many of their homes now lay in the American zone of occupation. Other than allowing themselves to be shipped off to Lower Canada, they had little choice but to eke out whatever subsistence they received and hope matters would improve soon.

Meanwhile, back at the main American encampment at Queenston, General Brown was confident that his campaign, which had so far been successful, would continue uninterrupted. Expecting Commodore Chauncey to appear with his reinforcements and a proper siege train of heavy artillery any day, Brown saw no point in prematurely risking his forces. Instead, he chose to remain at Queenston.

Looking for intelligence of his enemy's dispositions and intentions, Brown ordered General Porter to send out detachments to patrol and report back on any potential threats. As part of these detachments, General Porter chose to make use of the renegade Canadian Volunteers unit, which had been attached to his Brigade the previous month.

This action was met by undisguised hatred from the local population, who saw the return of these men, who they viewed as traitors, as the beginning of another round of pillaging, arrests, and wanton burning of their homes and crops. Within days, the Americans saw an escalation in reports of their sentries being attacked and patrols being fired on, to the point that no individual was able to leave the encampment without fear of disappearing without a trace.

Meanwhile, General Riall was deeply concerned about his strategic position and the threat that an American thrust to the shore of Lake Ontario would entirely cut off his line of retreat to

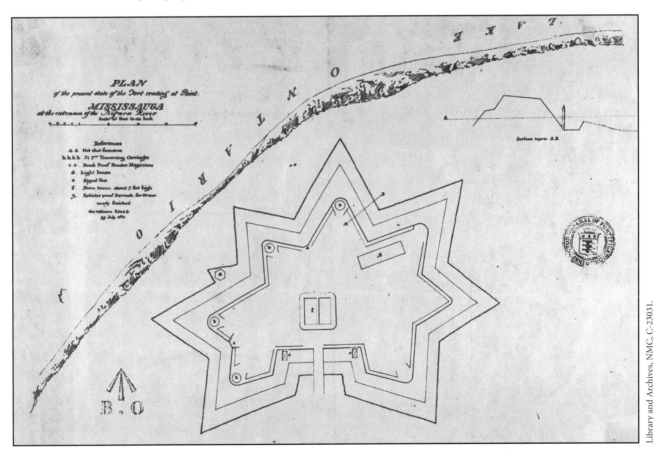

The plan of Fort Mississauga as it appeared in 1814. Local lore has it that the central blockhouse was originally constructed from bricks scavenged from the burned-out wreckage of homes in Newark following their destruction in December 1813.

the Head-of-the-Lake. Having suffered a stinging defeat after making the tactical error of having left his well-established defences at Chippawa to engage the enemy in the open, General Riall was now being overly cautious and almost appeared unwilling to go on the offensive against the Americans. Defensively, he was caught on the horns of a dilemma: On the one hand, he did not want to abandon the three vital river-mouth forts (Fort Niagara, Fort George, and Fort Mississauga) without a fight, but on the other, he could not retreat behind their defences without risking becoming trapped, the very way the Americans had the previous summer. Instead, he made the risky decision of dividing his army in the face of the enemy, and turned to General Drummond for confirmation of his action:

Following the war, the plan was to incorporate Fort Mississauga as a single bastion within a huge fortification complex to guard the mouth of the Niagara River. This reconstruction was subsequently cancelled and the land remained undeveloped. Today, the current National Historic Site of Fort Mississauga (run by Parks Canada) stands in the middle of a golf course at Niagara-on-the-Lake.

[July 12, 1814]

Sir,

The enemy still occupy the same position as they did when I sent off my last communication and are, I imagine, waiting for their fleet to furnish them with heavy ordnance for their operations against our forts. I have acquired from the officers of Artillery and Engineers their opinion upon the state of their defences and means of resistance…. If the judgement of those officers be correct, the fall of those places must be inevitable if vigorously attacked, unless the besiegers are interrupted in their operations or a diversion be made to withdraw their attention elsewhere. After mature deliberation, I have determined upon the following plan of operation, which I hope you will approve. Having left in Forts George, Missasaga, and Niagara such garrisons … necessary for their actual defence, I shall move from this towards Burlington with between 8[00] and 900 men. I have directed Colonel Scott to meet me at the 40 [Mile Creek] with the 103rd Regiment, the [embodied] militia collected at Burlington, of whom I understand there is a considerable body and the whole of the Indians that can be assembled and with this force get into the enemy's rear by the Short Hills and Lundy's Lane. I have also directed Lt. Colonel Battersby to remove from York with the Glengarry Regiment, as I conceive the protection of that place at this moment a very secondary consideration and not likely to be attacked as the enemy's whole attention seems to be engaged with the attack of our forts.[17]

The campaign on the Niagara was about to take a much more fluid turn, as both sides sought to gain both the strategic and tactical advantage for the expected showdown battle that would decide the fate of Upper Canada.

15

JOINING THE LIGHT BRIGADE

ENCAMPED AT FORT MISSISSAUGA, THE MEN OF the Incorporated Militia were initially detailed to provide fatigue parties for the strengthening of the defences at that location. They also provided picket and forage details that pushed out into the surrounding area, sometimes coming in contact with and, where occasioned, conflict with similar units from the American side. On the afternoon of July 13, however, orders came for the men to pack and prepare for an immediate and silent night march toward Burlington Heights to link up with the Glengarry Light Infantry. Leaving their campfires burning, the regiment marched throughout the night and arrived at Twelve Mile Creek around 8:00 a.m. the following morning. As well as the Glengarry Regiment awaiting their arrival, there were two pieces of good news.

The first was that Captain James Kerby had been officially promoted to the rank of major, and the second that the men of Jarvie's company, who had been taken into captivity the previous year, had been released as part of the parole agreement and were now on their way back to the regiment via Montreal and Kingston.

Riall's movement of the bulk of his force away from the Niagara River had been made not a moment too soon. On July 15, General Porter's militia brigade advanced to make a reconnaissance-in-force of Forts George and Mississauga. After receiving Porter's report, however, General Brown decided that without Chauncey's support he could not breach the British defences and that he would continue to wait for the commodore. Riall's force, meanwhile, continued its retreat to the Twenty Mile Creek and linked up with Colonel Scott's column, consisting of the 103rd Regiment and its associated embodied militia units. After receiving reports of Porter's probe toward Fort George, and seeing no comparable American advance toward his position, General Riall decided to remain at Twenty Mile Creek. Here, he established a secure base on the west side of the river, with ample communications to both his rear and southern flank. Secretly aided by loyal members of the local population then living under American occupation, he began to amass intelligence about the American dispositions and movements. Based on his subsequent assessment of the tactical situation and the forces then available to him, General Riall decided to reorganize his small army into four brigades (see sidebar).

As part of this realignment, the Incorporated Militia were assigned to the 2nd or "light" brigade. Unfortunately, this also placed them directly under the command of the Prescott companies' old nemesis, Lieutenant Colonel Pearson. Fortunately, Lieutenant

---

Brigades of the British Right Division, July 16, 1814[1]

1st Brigade (Colonel Hercules Scott)
    19th Light Dragoons (detachment)
    8th (King's) Regiment
    103rd Regiment
    Royal Artillery (three 6-pounder guns, 1 howitzer)

2nd Brigade (Lieutenant Colonel Thomas Pearson) "Light Brigade"
    19th Light Dragoons (detachment)
    Glengarry Light Infantry
    Incorporated Militia Battalion
    Royal Artillery (two 6-pounder guns)

1st Militia Brigade (Lieutenant Colonel Parry J. Parry)
    1st / 2nd / 3rd / 4th / 5th Lincoln Militia Regiments

2nd Militia Brigade (Lieutenant Colonel Christopher Hamilton)
    1st / 2nd Norfolk Militia Regiments
    2nd York Militia Regiment

Reserve (Lieutenant Colonel John Gordon)
    1st (Royal Scots) Regiment

Colonel Robinson's programme of company and regimental training at York during the previous four months seems to have paid off, since Pearson, far from issuing his usual critical assessments, issued no complaints against the regiment. Instead, he made extensive use of the Incorporated Militia in his brigade's probes and raids on the American positions during the following week.

At the larger campaign level, with the Americans continuing to show no signs of advancing on his position, General Riall began a series of redeployments of his troops that saw units advance toward the Niagara River to reoccupy strategically important positions that controlled the region's roads. By the evening of July 16, two companies of the Incorporated Militia found themselves back at Four Mile Creek, with the Americans less than two miles to their front: "Went from 20 Mile Creek with the army back to the 12 and 4 Mile Creek, very heavy rains on account of which we sheltered our men in barns and houses."[2]

For the next two days, the two companies remained in these positions, watching for American movements and sending out patrols to determine the American disposition, probe their lines for possible weak spots, harass their pickets, and make any possible opportunistic captures: "Still there [4 Mile Creek] in barns and houses drying clothes and ammunition … 800 indians passed us that day, frightful beggars."[3]

During this same interval, other companies of the regiment were dispatched to the British right flank and took up positions near the DeCou farm at Beaver Dams. In coordination with units of the embodied militia and Native allies already there, they maintained a constant harassment of the American positions and captured at least one American supply train. According to a subsequent report sent by General Riall to General Drummond on July 19, these actions prompted a strong and severe retaliation by General Porter's militia troops, who had been the principal target of the British activities:

> The troops at present occupy the position of Twelve Mile Creek having an advance of the troops at the 10 and 4 on the left, to the right extending to De Coo's and Streets Mills…. There was a good deal of skirmishing yesterday with the advance of the militia and the enemy's outposts near St. Davids, and they [the enemy] have in consequence burnt that village and several of the neighboring houses between Queenston and the Falls…. I am happy to be able to inform you that almost the whole body of militia is in arms, and seem actuated by the most determined spirit of hostility to the enemy. The Indians also are in great numbers not less, I believe, than 900, and evince the same spirit. It is very much to be regretted that it cannot be taken advantage of at the moment.[4]

Regrettably, on July 20, General Riall was forced to eat his optimistic words about the support he was receiving from his Grand River Native allies, for suddenly, and without notice, they walked away from their positions and essentially quit the war. This unexpected event was the result of these warriors having concluded a mutual non-aggression pact with their tribal brothers living on the American side of the Niagara River and fighting for the Americans. As might be expected, the simultaneous departure of these irregular troops from both the British and American armies led to some rapid recalculation of logistics and strategy on the part of both commanders.

Despite this loss, General Brown remained determined to maintain control of the Lake Ontario waterfront to secure his planned link-up with the now suspiciously overdue Chauncey. Considering Queenston to be too far away, General Brown ordered the wholesale movement of his army from Queenston to the outskirts of Newark. Here, his army began to establish a new camp and positions for gun emplacements in front of Fort George, and began making strong probes upon the British garrison there.

This American movement and subsequent attacks alarmed the British garrison commander, Lieutenant Colonel Tucker (41st Regiment), especially when he saw them begin construction of new artillery emplacements at Youngstown, directly opposite Fort George. Once these emplacements were completed, it would place his fort between two sets of fire and would inevitably lead to the loss of the position. This loss, in turn, would threaten the security of both Fort Niagara and Fort Mississauga. He, therefore, called on General Riall to bring forward his troops and engage the enemy as soon as possible.

This call for aid placed General Riall, back at Twenty Mile Creek, in an awkward position. Supporting the argument in favour of making an energetic probe of the enemy's positions were the combined facts that his forces on the Niagara had just received a reinforcement of regular troops and his embodied militia units were seemingly itching to come to grips with the enemy. While his Grand River Natives had deserted him, numbers of the Western Natives had remained and were equally vocal in their calls for action. On the other hand, Riall was well aware that his forces were still numerically inferior to that commanded by General Brown. Furthermore, having already been beaten by the Americans because he had taken the offensive too soon, Riall was in no hurry to repeat his error.

Instead, he sent an urgent appeal to General Drummond at Kingston to forward additional reinforcements to the Niagara frontier and asked for his superior's advice as to how he should best pursue the campaign. He did, however, gather additional intelligence on the enemy by sending out reconnaissance parties, which often contained detachments from the Incorporated Militia, to probe the American positions for possible weaknesses. Whether this appeal reached General Drummond is not known, for by this time the general had recognized the necessity of his taking over personal command of the army on the Niagara frontier and was already en route from Kingston to York with additional troops.

On the American side, General Brown moved his army before the forts but decided that laying siege to the British positions was beyond his means without Chauncey's heavy guns to demolish the defensive works. To better secure his movement options, he ordered his forces back to Queenston on July 22, only to find that a strong party of British regulars and embodied militia had occupied the American's former defensive positions.

Seeking to envelop and capture this enemy force by a swift movement on both flanks, the American plan of action collapsed once the two sides engaged in combat across the broken and forested landscape. Throughout the remainder of the day, as the Americans gradually pushed back the British, a confusing series of skirmishes took place between Queenston and St. Davids. Eventually, additional British troops were committed to the fight, including the Incorporated Militia, which halted the American pursuit. As a result, the American army encamped once again on the heights above Queenston village.

Chippawa, E. Walsh, artist, 1804. Looking west, up the Chippawa River. To the right is the British garrison and to the left is the hamlet of Chippawa as they appeared in 1804.

Clement Library, University of Michigan.

The following morning, Brown learned that Commodore Chauncey was NOT going to make any rendezvous. The commodore, it was revealed, had been ill and had steadfastly refused to give his subordinates permission to venture out onto the lake to challenge Yeo's blockade and link up with Brown. Given the new circumstances, Brown decided his only recourse was to retire on the Chippawa River, where he could secure his existing supply line with Buffalo, place himself in a position to manoeuvre according to the tactical situation, and prepare a new plan of campaign. To speed this movement, he also ordered his regiments to rid themselves of all non-essential encampment equipment and superfluous baggage.

By July 23, 1814, General Drummond had arrived at York and had reviewed duplicate copies of Riall's

A view of the same location today. Because of the installation of massive intake sluices during the construction of recent hydroelectric power schemes upriver (west) of this point, this lower part of the river can now sometimes flow backward to its original natural flow into the Niagara River.

latest reports sent to that post. Not knowing of the American retreat, he recognized that the new batteries at Youngstown represented a significant threat to his defences at Fort George and Fort Mississauga. He therefore determined on coming to Niagara himself to personally supervise a strong sortie from Fort Niagara to eliminate this threat and then press on to Lewiston and Fort Schlosser, thus cutting Brown's supply lines. To ensure that Brown would be unable to bring troops back across the Niagara River to counter this sortie, he sent a detailed instruction to Riall on the need to advance his light division to make a display of force toward the enemy and keep Brown's attention on the west bank of the river. Conscious of Riall's hesitancy to engage the enemy, Drummond included a set of specific directions on how Riall should place his troops should they come to battle with the Americans before he arrived to take charge:

> In order to favour [Tucker's sortie on the American positions at Youngstown and Lewiston] … and to draw the attention of the enemy from that side of the river … march to St Davids and concentrate the whole of the regular force under your command at that place, throwing the militia and Indians into the woods toward the enemy's position and the lake…. This movement may be made with perfect safety on your part, as in event of the enemy's pushing … forward to attack or interpose betwixt you and Burlington, you can always … reach Shipman's before him, that is, provided you take precautions to cause his movements to be properly watched and reported…. Should the enemy by pressing suddenly and boldly on you make an action unavoidable, you must by means of the Glengarry Light Infantry and Incorporated Militia endeavour to check his light troops until you reach an open space in which, keeping your guns in your centre and your force concentrated, your flanks secured by light troops, militia and Indians, you must depend upon the superior discipline of the troops under your command for success over an undisciplined though confident and numerous enemy.[5]

16

MARCHING INTO BATTLE

With the withdrawal of the Americans from Fort George and the Lake Ontario shoreline, Riall's communications with the river-mouth garrisons were soon re-established and secured. However, it also meant that there was now the threat of the Americans making a flanking move along the interior roads above the escarpment. To counter this possibility, General Riall sought to concentrate his forces by withdrawing his regular troops, as well as the Incorporated Militia detachments, from their advanced positions to Twelve Mile Creek, leaving men from the embodied militias in their place. He also began to prepare his army for further movement at short notice. In the Right Division order of July 23, he wrote: "The troops will be paraded in marching order opposite their respective cantonments this day at 2 o'clock. No man to be absent, the sick only excepted. No person to quit their stations for a moment until further orders. The troops will have two days provisions cooked in advance."[1]

Once General Riall received Drummond's letter on the morning of July 24, he immediately initiated the plan to advance the light brigade toward the American position at Chippawa, as recorded by Ensign Andrew Warffe (Captain Archibald McLean's 6th Company): "Still encamped at 12 Mile Creek, rec'd orders to be in readiness to march at a moments warning, heard the enemy were retreating towards Chippawa. Left the encampment at ten o'clock in the evening and marched the whole of that night, fatigued."[2]

The Incorporated Militia, in conjunction with the remainder of the light brigade, began its march

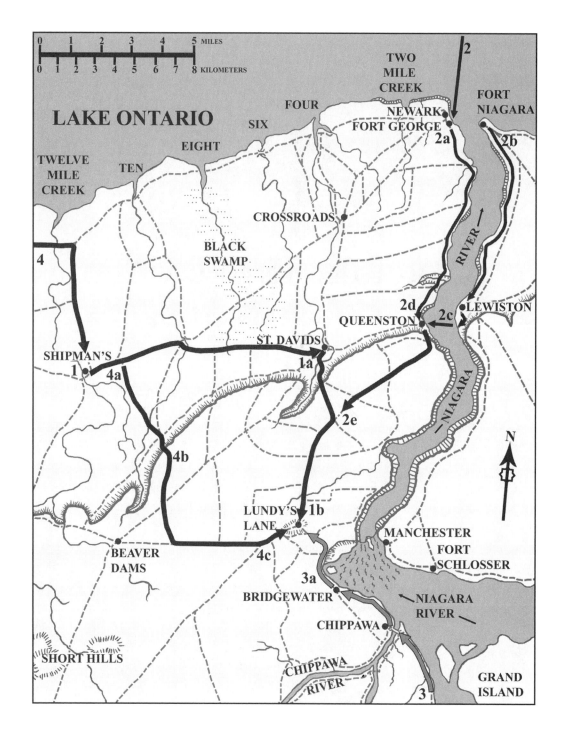

The "March" to Lundy's Lane, July 24–25, 1814.

1. The British Light Division (including the Incorporated Militia) (1) leaves Shipman's Corners around 10:00 p.m. on July 24 and march overnight, arriving at St. Davids around dawn. (1a). They then march on to the Lundy's Lane crossroads and encamp on the hilltop at around 7:00 a.m. (1b).
2. General Drummond arrives by boat from York (2) early on the morning of July 25. He orders a two-pronged advance up the Niagara River from Fort George (2a) on the British side and Fort Niagara (2b) on the American side. Upon overrunning General Brown's baggage supplies at Lewiston (2c), General Drummond crosses back to Queenston at noon. After consulting with General Riall, General Drummond orders an advance on Lundy's Lane (2e).
3. After receiving reports of a British advance on the American side of the river in mid-afternoon, General Brown orders General Scott's brigade to advance toward Lundy's Lane (3a) around 4:00 p.m.
4. Hercules Scott's column (4) marches up from the Twenty Mile Creek to Shipman's Corners and halts early on the morning of July 25 (4a). Around 1:00 p.m., and on receiving initial orders to rendezvous with Brown at Lundy's Lane, it advances toward the hill. Due to possible undocumented and unknown diversions (as these orders are first counter-manded and then revoked), the exact route of the column is conjectural (4b) up to the Beaver Dams Road. From this point, the column advances toward the Lundy's Lane hilltop (4c), arriving as the battle is already well underway at around 9:00 p.m.

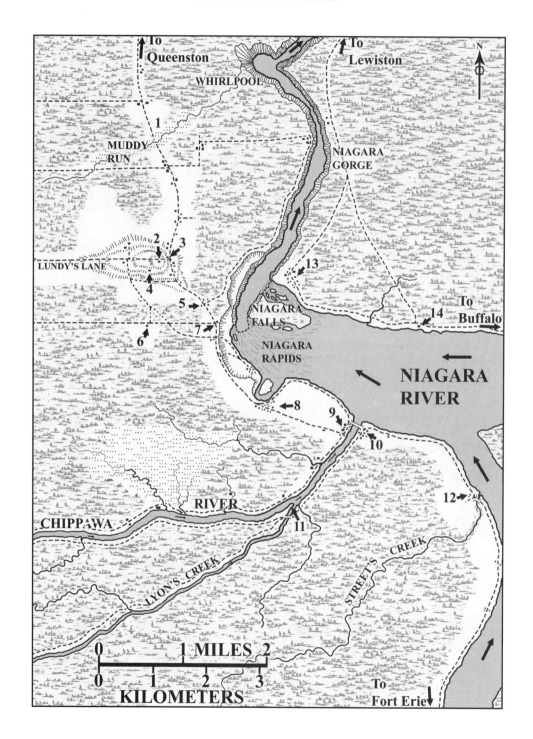

Locations Around the Great Falls of Niagara, July 25, 1814.

1. Cook's Bog or "Muddy Run"
2. The Lundy's Lane church on the hilltop
3. Johnson's Tavern at the Lundy's Lane/Portage Road crossroad
4. The Buchner House
5. Forsyth's Tavern
6. The Haggai Skinner farmstead
7. Mrs. Wilson's tavern
8. Bridgewater Mills
9. The old British fortifications at the Chippawa River
10. Chippawa Village
11. Weishoun's Point
12. Ussher's Farmstead

toward the enemy in the dead of night. Passing along the rough trackways that cut through the heavy woodland and swamps bordering the foot of the escarpment, they reached the devastated community of St. Davids around dawn. Turning south, they climbed the Niagara Escarpment and marched along the old Portage Road toward the main crossroads with Lundy's Lane, arriving around 7:00 a.m. on the bright sunny morning of the 25th. Here, they joined up with the party of John Norton's Native warriors who had also arrived during the previous night.

An hour or so later, an additional small column of troops was seen moving up from Queenston. These turned out to be detachments from the 1st Militia Brigade, which had made a march from their positions at Queenston in response to additional orders from General Riall. Among them was the 2nd York Militia Regiment, commanded by Major Titus G. Simons. This was probably the first occasion that the major had been reunited with the Incorporated Militia since the incident of the previous month, but whether any socialization between the major and his former officer comrades took place is not documented. Nonetheless, it must have elicited some comments and embarrassment for all concerned; however, the necessities of the war had to be placed first.

Once he had secured his position astride the strategically important two main trackways that controlled the north–south route between Chippawa and Queenston and the east–west route between the Great Falls and the interior road to Burlington, Pearson established a strong line of pickets to his front, then sent out scouts to locate the Americans.

Receiving word back that the enemy were encamped on the south side of the Chippawa River, Pearson allowed his men to take a well-deserved rest. As the day progressed, the troops of the enhanced light brigade either dozed, cooked, or attended to the maintenance of their equipment and weapons, all the while keeping a watchful eye to the south and their strong screen of pickets.

Back at York, General Drummond had shipped the 89th Regiment across the lake on July 24, agreeing with Riall's assessment that the town was in little danger of being attacked and that every man possible should be collected along the Niagara frontier. He then sailed aboard the schooner *Netley*, arriving at Newark the following morning. Here, he heard of Brown's retreat to Chippawa and fully approved of General Riall's countermeasure of shadowing Brown's forces with elements of the light brigade while concentrating his remaining forces at Twelve Mile Creek. Recognizing that this American retreat created an opportunity, Drummond set his earlier plan into motion by ordering a sortie from Fort Niagara to eliminate the enemy's batteries at Youngstown. Once this was achieved, and if not otherwise prevented, the sortie force was then to push on to Lewiston and Fort Schlosser.

General Drummond also ordered detachments from Fort George and Fort Mississauga to make a simultaneous move on the Canadian side of the river, supported by a small fleet of boats on the Niagara River itself. Advancing from Fort Niagara on the morning of July 25, the British quickly overran the Youngstown batteries and continued south to Lewiston, where they captured Brown's entire stockpile of baggage and tents, which had been laboriously transported across the river the day before. Satisfied with this windfall, General Drummond called off the advance on Fort Schlosser and ordered the captured goods transported back to Fort Niagara and the bulk of his remaining troops and Natives to be ferried back across the Niagara River to Queenston.

During the same period, the American troops were enjoying the fine weather by relaxing or attending to their own daily ritual of duties. By noon, however, reports from their pickets told of groups of British troops and Natives being south of the Falls at a small tavern run by a local widow, Mrs. Wilson. Not unduly concerned about this appearance of the enemy, Brown

The Great Falls of Niagara as Seen from Below Table Rock in 1801, *A.M. Hoffy, artist, (after J. Vanderlyn),* circa *1840.*

nevertheless ordered a reconnaissance through the woods west and north of the American encampment. What was more alarming were the dispatches from Colonel Philetus Swift at Lewiston, which told of a large British force rapidly advancing on that position and threatening to capture Brown's supplies and baggage. Convinced that this British advance was the main thrust of the enemy to cut off his supply line from Fort Schlosser, General Brown concluded that whatever was before him at Lundy's Lane could only be a diversionary force, deliberately being exposed to attract his attention and pin him in place while the main body took Fort Schlosser. Ironically, this was exactly what Drummond had originally planned.

Niagara Falls, F.C. Christian, artist (after G. Heriot), 1807. The Great Falls of Niagara as the advancing American troops would have seen it as they marched to Lundy's Lane past Mrs. Wilson's Tavern on the Portage Road.

By 2:00 p.m., General Brown decided to detach a portion of General Porter's Third Brigade to reinforce Fort Schlosser. He also chose to send a strong probe toward Queenston and Fort George. By doing this, Brown reasoned that since General Riall had remained on the defensive following his defeat at Chippawa (Brown was still unaware of Drummond's arrival), this probe would cause Riall to abandon his advance on the American side of the Niagara River and retire back on his forts to maintain their safety. Confident that only a part of his army would be required for this countermeasure, Brown chose Scott's brigade to undertake the advance along the Portage-Queenston Road.

General Brown directed General Winfield Scott to take his brigade north along the Portage Road and push aside any small detachments of enemy troops he came across. He was then to secure the crossroads at Lundy's Lane and, if not otherwise opposed, continue his advance toward Queenston with the intent of forcing Riall to abandon his activities on the American side of the Niagara River. Meanwhile, the remaining American brigades were to remain at Chippawa and only be alerted if Scott ran into difficulties.

Drummond's forces, meanwhile, had completed their re-crossing of the Niagara River at Queenston. With the bulk of his force back on the west side of the river, General Drummond ordered the 41st and 100th Regiments to march back to Fort George, while the remainder of the troops were to remain at Queenston. Shortly thereafter, General Riall arrived at Queenston bearing news that Pearson's force was in position at Lundy's Lane watching the Americans to the south at Chippawa. After discussing options with Riall, Drummond decided that the situation was opportune and ordered the concentration of all units at Lundy's Lane. Riall then left to rejoin Pearson at the Lundy's Lane hilltop, while Drummond was to follow with the remaining part of Lieutenant Colonel Morrison's column. Riders were also sent to order up Colonel Hercules Scott's brigade from the Twelve Mile Creek, thus placing the British in an advantageous position for a probable attack on the Americans the following day.

Unfortunately, circumstances pre-empted this orderly plan and precipitated a battle of confusion and chaos in the darkness of the approaching night.

17

THE BATTLE OF LUNDY'S LANE, JULY 25, 1814

BY THE LATE AFTERNOON OF JULY 25, THE MEN of Pearson's light brigade were preparing their evening meal when reports began to come in of an American column advancing up the road from Chippawa. Mistakenly believing this to be the entire American force, Riall decided that he was greatly outnumbered and ordered a withdrawal toward Queenston to unite with Drummond and Morrison's forces. He also dispatched a courier with orders for Hercules Scott's column to rendezvous at Queenston and not Lundy's Lane. After recalling the pickets, repacking their food and cooking implements, and limbering up their artillery, the light brigade formed a column and marched north along the Portage Road for Queenston, leaving the hilltop undefended and free for the taking.

Heading the column were the units of the embodied militias and Native warriors. Behind were the supply wagons and artillery pieces, followed by the detachments of cavalry. At the rear of the column, the Incorporated Militia and Glengarry Light Infantry were assigned the duty of rearguard, with orders to turn back if the Americans attacked and make a fighting retreat to allow the valuable guns to escape. However, after marching less than two miles and reaching the lowland swampy area officially known as Cook's Bog, or as the locals called it, Muddy Run, the light column came upon Drummond's force, marching south from Queenston.

Halting both columns, Drummond assessed Riall's report on the advancing American threat and decided that in spite of the distinct likelihood of being outnumbered, his combined force would reclaim the hill and

The lanes leading to the Lundy's Lane hilltop in the postwar period: Near Colonel Delatre's, A Road Parallel with Lundy's Lane, Niagara Falls, *E.B.B. Estcourt, artist,* circa *1838, and* Part of a Road, Second Concession Between Stamford and Lundy's Lane, *C.B.B. Estcourt, artist,* circa *1838.*

make a defensive stand. He also recognized that he would have to countermand General Riall's previous directive and ensure that Hercules Scott's column march, once again, directly to Lundy's Lane and not to Queenston.

Because of Major James Kerby's extensive and intimate knowledge of the roads and byways of the area, Drummond chose him for the vital duty of locating Hercules Scott's column and guiding it to Lundy's Lane with all speed. The general then ordered both columns to march back to the Lundy's Lane hilltop. Because several days of heavy rains had turned the ground on either side of the road into a muddy quagmire, the only practical way of returning Pearson's force to the hill was to have every unit in that column about face and march back the way they had come.

This would be a simple manoeuvre for the infantry, but for the more cumbersome and considerably heavier wagons and artillery, turning around would prove more difficult because of the soft, sodden ground on either side of the road. Determined to deny the advancing enemy the strategic advantage of holding the high ground, Drummond ordered the Glengarry Light Infantry and Incorporated Militia, who were not encumbered by the offending vehicles, to move at double-quick pace, secure the high ground, and then attempt to hold back the Americans until the remaining units could clear the obstructions and move up to extend the hilltop position.

TAKING A STAND

Running back the way they had just come, the companies composing the two regiments began to fan out, each taking their own path as they sought to get to the hilltop as quickly as possible. Engaged in a virtual steeplechase, they cut diagonally across the fences and fields before reaching the crest of the hill and forming their line-of-battle. On the left were the companies of the Incorporated Militia, positioned on the eastern slope of the hilltop between the chapel and the Portage Road crossroad. On the right, the Glengarries formed on the western slope of the hill. Shortly thereafter, the light brigade's artillery arrived and immediately unlimbered their guns at the boundary of the small cemetery that marked the crest of the hill of Lundy's Lane, precisely where they had been only a couple of hours before. Finally, to complete this initial deployment, the units of embodied militia and Natives moved across to the west side of the hill to join the Glengarries.

As successive units of Morrison's column arrived on the field, General Drummond applied the guidelines he had previously given General Riall for the disposition of his forces by forming up his regulars in a solid line, placed below the crest of the hill and directly behind the meeting point of the Glengarry Light Infantry and Incorporated Militia. He then ordered the two regiments to march outward from each other, thus creating a gap in the centre, into which he inserted his regular infantry, while keeping his colonial light troops on the flanks. As additional artillery units from Morrison's column arrived, they extended the battery on the hilltop, while a small Royal Marine Artillery Congreve rocket detachment set up their position at the main crossroads to the east of the hill, supported by the 19th Light Dragoons.

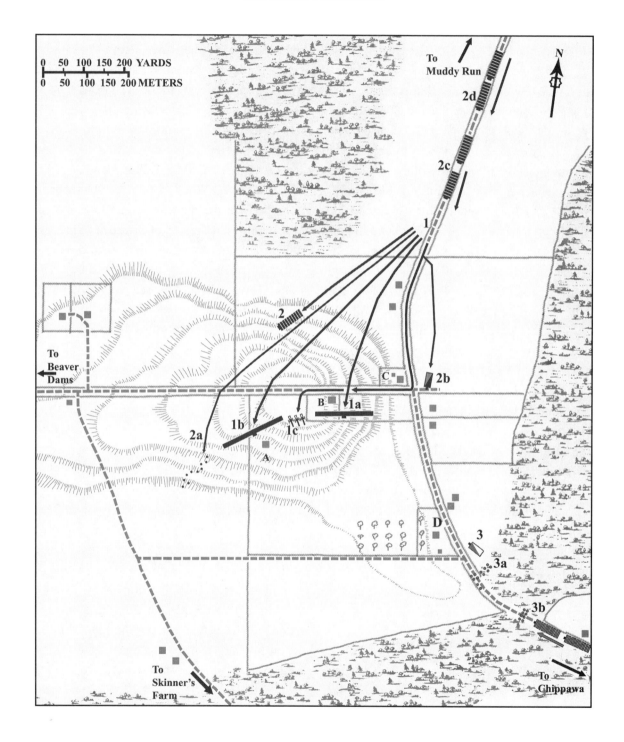

The Race for Lundy's Lane Hilltop (circa 5:30–6:30 p.m.).

A. Buchner House
B. Lundy's Lane churchyard
C. Johnson's Tavern, at the crossroads of Lundy's Lane (E–W) and Portage Road (N–S)
D. Pier's farmstead

1. Following its meeting with General Drummond's column at Muddy Run, Pearson's retiring Light Brigade (1) moves back to the Lundy's Lane hilltop at the double-quick pace. The Incorporated Militia (1a) forms its line on the left (east) side of the hill, while the Glengarry Light Infantry deploys in line to the right (west) side. The Light Brigade artillery (1c) unlimbers on the crest of the hill at the edge of the cemetery.
2. The Embodied Militias (2) and Native allies (2a) advance to take up positions on the far right (west) of the British line. The 19th Light Dragoons and militia cavalry detachment (2b) move up ahead of Drummond's still advancing column (2c, 2d) and take up a covering position at the crossroads.
3. The U.S. cavalry detachment (3) and associated infantry advanced guard (3a) remain at the south end of the open ground near to the Pier's farm. The leading element of General Winfield Scott's First Brigade (3b) advances up the Portage Road from Chippawa.

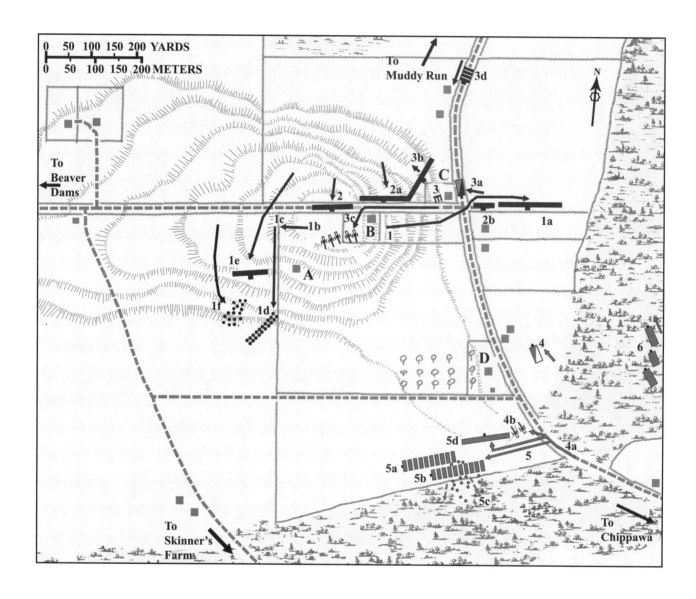

Battle of Lundy's Lane: Both Armies Make Their Initial Deployments (circa 6:30–7:00 p.m.).

A. Buchner House
B. Lundy's Lane churchyard
C. Johnson's Tavern
D. Pier's farmstead

1. The Incorporated Militia (1) moves left (east) and takes up a position as the far left of the developing British line (1a). The Glengarry Light Infantry (1b) initially mirrors this move by shifting to the right (west) (1c). It then advances (south) and extends into light infantry formation (1d). The embodied militias (1e) and Native allies (1f) also advance down the west side of the hill.
2. Additional units from General Drummond's column, composed of a detachment of the 1st (Royal Scots) (2), the 89th Regiment (2a), and a detachment of the 8th (King's), arrive on the field and take up positions in the line.
3. The Royal Marine Congreve rocket detachment (3) arrives at the crossroads and deploys in the grounds of the Forsyth Tavern. The British cavalry detachments move right (west) to occupy the crossroads (3a). Threatened by the back-blast of the rockets, the 89th Regiment (3b) retires its left wing. Additional artillery from General Drummond's column (3c) arrive and deploy on the crest of the hill. A detachment of the 41st Regiment (3d) arrives on the field as the action commences.
4. The U.S. cavalry detachment (4) advances to cover the deployment of General Winfield Scott's First Brigade (4a) to the west of the Portage Road. A battery of U.S. artillery (Towson's) (4b) unlimbers alongside the road and commences fire at the hilltop.
5. General Scott's column (5) moves left (west) to deploy into line and comes under heavy artillery fire from the hilltop. The Twenty-Second (5a) and Eleventh (5b) regiments suffer casualties and suffer a partial rout without having fired a shot. The Ninth Regiment (5d) remains relatively unscathed and deploys into line.
6. The Twenty-Fifth Regiment (6) advances through the woods in file toward the British left flank.

Surprised, but gratified to have regained the position on the hilltop without opposition, the troops looked to the south, fully expecting to see the enemy formed in the fields before them. Instead, apart from some enemy cavalry skirmishers, the anticipated formations of American infantry and artillery were only now coming into view, marching down the road from Chippawa.

This relatively late appearance by the Americans can be explained by the fact that since leaving the American encampment some hours earlier, General Winfield Scott had received several contradictory reports from his advanced pickets about the size of the British presence at Lundy's Lane. As a result, he had repeatedly halted his column to reorganize its formation according to his developing assessment of the situation. These delays had cost him the opportunity to capture the important road junction and strategic hilltop without a fight. Instead, looking toward the hilltop, having previously been assured by General Brown that only a small diversionary detachment was in the vicinity, General Scott was now confronted by an enemy line that stretched across the entire crest of the hill. Not only did the British force hold the high ground and outflank him on both sides, it also consisted of considerably more troops than he had believed could possibly be in the area. Faced with the choice of retiring his force toward the cover of the woods and calling for reinforcements, or continuing forward and engaging a strong force of the enemy in a solid defensive position, Winfield Scott, supremely confident of his own command abilities, chose to continue the advance.

Marching along the road into the open fields south of the hill, Scott's Brigade wheeled left and began to deploy into line, while the artillery positioned itself on the road. Behind them and off to the right, the Twenty-Fifth Infantry Regiment (under Colonel Jesup) had been previously detached from the advancing column to act independently on the right of the main force and use the cover of the heavy woods to the east of the hilltop in an attempt to turn the British left flank. This decision would shortly see it come into action directly against that part of the British line occupied by the Incorporated Militia.

Meanwhile, the Incorporated Militia, after having moved down the eastern slope of the hillside and past the crossroads into an open field, took up their new position. According to Lieutenant Duncan Clark of Fraser's (7th Company):

> The Incorporated Militia formed the left of the line, a wood on their left and a buckwheat field between them and another wood in their front. The 89th Regiment were on their right on the brow of the hill and detachments of the Royals, 8th, 104th and 41st Rgts formed the right of the line. The Glengarry Fencibles and militia were in a wood in advance of the British right.[1]

Similarly, Ensign John Kilborn (Captain E. Walker's 10th Company) recorded:

Our regiment was on the left of the line from the main road to the river, which was skirted by a strip of woods…. About three quarters of a mile below the Falls, the Glengarry, 85th Regiment, and detachments [from other regiments] were formed from the main road on our right, up Lundy's Lane where our artillery was posted, the ground rising in that direction.[2]

Still well out of musketry range, the initial American deployment into line was done under fire from the British artillery on the hilltop. Opening up at a range of around four hundred yards, the British guns began to pound the American force with roundshot and heavy grapeshot, inflicting significant casualties and causing parts of the column to break and head for the trees. After forming his line-of-battle, and instead of following the standard military practice of advancing it to within musket-shot range and engaging the British line directly, Winfield Scott ordered his troops to halt and had them remain in that exposed position for nearly thirty minutes under this artillery punishment, without being able to effectively fire back. At the same time, the American artillery attached to Scott's command, finding that its guns could not elevate sufficiently to fire upon the British hilltop, advanced farther along the road and prepared to fire from within the cover of a small orchard.

Seeing the enemy artillery as a tempting target of opportunity, Lieutenant Colonel Robinson ordered the Incorporated Militia to advance and engage the guns by wheeling the line forward, like a door swinging on its hinge, with the right-hand end of the line acting as the pivot flank. As they did so, however, they were fired on by the leading element of Jesup's Twenty-Fifth Regiment, who had located a pathway through the woods and reached a point where they could now fire on the front and left flank of the Incorporated Militia. Reacting to this new danger, the advanced companies swung back and concentrated their fire on the enemy infantry in the woods. For the next half-hour or more the contest between the Incorporated Militia and Twenty-Fifth became intense, as both sides sought to reload and fire as rapidly as possible. According to Lieutenant Duncan Clark:

The attack commenced on the left of the British position about 6 o'clock in the afternoon by riflemen from the opposite wood, which was returned by the Incorporated Militia under Lieutenant Colonel Robinson "and by whom" says General Drummond in his official despatch "the brunt of the action was for a considerable time sustained and whose loss has been severe." At this time Ensign Campbell and two Sergeants were killed, Lieutenant Colonel Robinson and Lieutenant Hamilton were wounded, and Captain

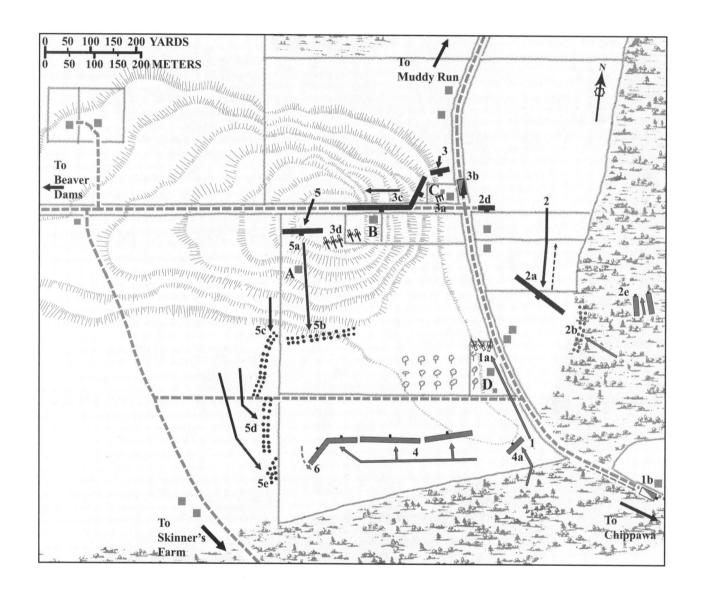

The American First Brigade Is Outflanked (circa *7:00–8:00 p.m.*).

A. Buchner House
B. Lundy's Lane churchyard
C. Johnson's Tavern
D. Pier's farmstead

1. Unable to effectively engage the British guns on the hill, Towson's artillery (1) advances to a new position on the Pier's farmstead (1a). The U.S. cavalry detachment (1b) leaves the field.
2. The Incorporated Militia (2) advances from the line in an attempt to outflank Towson's artillery (1a) but comes under fire from part of the Twenty-Fifth Regiment (2b) hiding at the treeline to the east. The remainder of the Twenty-Fifth (2c) continues to move north through the woods. Outflanked and under fire from two directions, the Incorporated Militia retires to its original position alongside the 8th (King's) Regiment.
3. The detachment of the 41st Regiment (3) arrives at the line and takes up a position behind the Congreve rockets (3a) and cavalry detachments (3b). This allows the 89th Regiment to move to the right (west) to better cover the artillery (3d).
4. General Winfield Scott's First Brigade (4) deploys into line and halts, but at too great a range to fire on the British lines. It remains here in the open for over half an hour and suffers severe casualties from the British artillery fire. Elements of the previously broken column are rallied and returned to the line (4a).
5. The 1st (Royal Scots) detachment (5) are initially moved forward (south) in line (5a) and then advance to the foot of the hill in light infantry formation (5b) to engage the American line (4) from the front. This advance is supported by a similar advance by the Glengarry Light Infantry (5c), detachments of embodied militia (5d), and Native allies (5e), who succeed in outflanking the American left flank.
6. Responding to this flanking threat, the Eleventh Regiment (6) swings back its left flank and engages the British infantry while continuing to suffer casualties from the British artillery on the hilltop.

MacDonell and Lieutenant Clark at close quarters received balls, one through the sash and the other in the cap without further damage.[3]

Similarly, Ensign Kilborn wrote:

As soon as they [the enemy infantry] came in range, although behind a rail fence, along the edge of the woods, we opened fire on them, our men standing exposed in the open field until the approaching darkness and smoke hid them from view, except what could be seen by the fire from their muskets. In this position our men falling fast around us, we stood until some time after darkness had come on; how it was on our right I could not see. Our artillery in the centre kept up a continued roar, nearly drowning the sound of musketry except at short intervals.[4]

By that point the heavy and consistent firing had used up most of the sixty rounds of ammunition each man carried in his individual cartouche box (ammunition pouch), worn at his right hip. As a result, the wagon containing the regiment's reserve supply of ammunition was brought up from the rear to replenish the men's cartouches and keep them in action. During this same period, at least one of the regiment's officers, Ensign John Kilborn (Captain Hamilton Walker's No. 10 Company), stationed on the left flank noted a new threat: "Before [it became] too dark, our line had advanced near the woods in front, and I could frequently see the enemy moving to the right, apparently for the purpose of outflanking us and getting to our rear — nor was I mistaken."[5]

Under normal circumstances, this American threat to the regiment's front and flank would have been dealt with by detaching companies to infiltrate the woods and take on the enemy at closer range, sweeping them out and securing that flank. However, placed as it was at the far end of the British line, with no additional support or reinforcements, and coupled with the double absence of its two senior field officers (Lieutenant Colonel Robinson had by this point been incapacitated by a wound that had thrown him from his horse and Major Kerby was still on detached duty to locate Hercules Scott's column), it was now up to the individual captains of the companies to deal with this developing danger. Recognizing that any detachment of manpower would open up an exploitable gap in the British line, the decision was made to have the companies on the right of the regiment remain in line, while the companies on the left would extend their ranks and take up a light infantry formation. Despite seeing his regiment suffering casualties all along its line, Lieutenant Colonel Robinson was still able to give his men some sagacious advice:

When his men were acting as Light Infantry, he [Robinson] was knocked off his horse by a ball which struck him in the forehead and came out over his ear. This would have knocked the life out of most men, but it did not knock the wit out of Billy. He was raised and placed in a blanket, his eyes still fixed on his men, who he saw were pushing on in a way to expose themselves. "Stop till I spake to the boys," said he to the men who were carrying him off the field; "Boys!" shouted he, "I have only one remark to make, and that is, that a stump or a log will stand a leaden bullet better than the best of yees, and therefore give them the honor to be your front rank men."[6]

Robinson also attempted to extract the Incorporated Militia from its now dangerously exposed position by ordering it to retire by companies back toward the hill. Accordingly, the companies on the right hand end of the line began to fall back in good order. However, in the darkness, those farther to the left were less prompt:

Some time after dark, Lieutenant McDougall [6th Company] … came to me [Ensign Kilborn, 10th Company] saying that I was too far in advance, that our men on the right had fallen back some distance and were likely to fire into us from behind. I told him what I suspected, that they [the enemy] were trying to outflank us and get in our rear. He at once proposed to extend our line towards the river, and at the same time, falling back to regain our line on the right.[7]

As the companies were in the process of making this change of position and alignment, Jesup's main force from the Twenty-Fifth Regiment completed its infiltration, charged from the wood, and poured a particularly heavy fire into the rear of the left flank of the Incorporated Militia. Caught between two sets of fire, the men on the left flank recoiled but did not break. Instead, acting on Lieutenant Colonel Robinson's last active commands on the field, they continued to wheel their line backward ninety degrees. Despite having performed this move during the course of their training at York, it still remained one of the more difficult changes of position that any regiment could be called upon to execute. Now it had to be done in the dark, in the heat of battle, and while under fire from two directions.

For the most part, the companies on the right of the regimental line completed the change with only minor disruptions. However, the companies in the centre and left were not as fortunate, and a number of men were cut off and captured, as subsequently recorded by three of the regiment's officers. In the first case, Lieutenant Duncan Clark of No. 7 Company wrote:

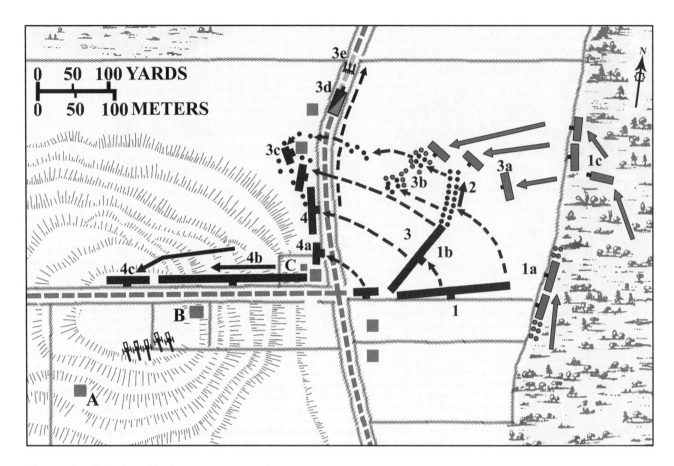

The British Left Flank Buckles (circa 7:45–8:15 p.m.).

A. Buchner House
B. Lundy's Lane churchyard
C. Johnson's Tavern

1. The Incorporated Militia (1) coming under additional flanking fire from elements of the Twenty-Fifth Regiment (1a), makes a partial wheel backward on its right to establish a new line (1b), and re-engages. The remaining companies of the Twenty-Fifth Regiment (1c) arrive at the wood line, severely threatening the British line.
2. Responding to the new threat, the Incorporated Militia extends companies on its left flank into a light infantry formation (2).
3. In the darkening twilight, the Incorporated Militia begins to make a further backward wheel on its right (3). As they do so, the Twenty-Fifth charges (3a) and captures men from several companies stationed on the left flank (3b). This disrupts that end of the line, forcing it to regroup once it reaches the Portage Road (3c). Responding to this American flanking threat, the British cavalry detachments (3d) and Congreve rocket detachment (3e) retire north along the Portage Road and leave the action.
4. The companies stationed on the right flank of the Incorporated Militia's line (4), plus the detachment of the 8th (King's) Regiment(4a), having wheeled back in good order, re-form on the west side of the Portage Road, fronting to the east. This frees the 89th Regiment (4b) to move farther to the right (west), while the detachment of the 41st (4c) moves across the hilltop to cover the open right flank of the British line.

The wood between the British left and the river was swarming with American riflemen through which a strong division passed imperceived, and about sunset appeared on the Queenston Road in the rear of the British left. Being thus placed between two foes, the Incorporated Militia, under a heavy fire, retired by companies to the hill … into which period Lieutenant McDougall [No. 6 Company] was seriously wounded, Captains McLean [No. 6 Company] and Washburn [No. 4 Company], Ensigns Kilburn [No. 10 Company] and Warffe [No. 6 Company], Quartermaster Thrower, 4 Sergeants and 30 Rank and File of the Incorporated Militia were made prisoners.[8]

In the second, Ensign Warffe of No. 6 Company recalled the fighting as, "sharp firing, hot work, The In'd M were on the left of Lundy's Lane blasing away like the devil, when a d – d scouting party of the enemy came in our rear and made prisoners of a number of us … cannot tell what happ'd after being taken prisoner."[9]

And finally, Ensign Kilborn of No. 10 Company later recorded:

While [retiring in the darkness] … I came directly on a company of Americans formed two deep, the front rank with bayonets charged and the rear rank arms presented ready to fire. I was within twenty feet of them when discovered. The officer at the head of the company demanded a surrender. I hesitated for a short time, but seeing no possibility of escape, I told the men near me to throw down their muskets. Three or four others that were much farther from them than we were attempted to escape, also Lieutenant McDougall. They were shot down and probably killed, except Lieutenant McDougall, who was reported in the General's order of the next day as being mortally wounded with six buckshot. He recovered, however and lived many years after.[10]

On reaching the Queenston Road, the regiment re-formed its line at a right angle to the main British position behind the slight cover of a line of split-rail fencing. From here, they started once again to pour volleys of fire into the approaching enemy, bringing them to a halt. After a short exchange of fire, the American's began to retire into the darkness of the night, leaving the Incorporated Militia to assess the damage to its ranks, but having successfully secured the flank and rear of the main line from further attack.

In reviewing this movement, it is not only possible to argue that it stands as a credit to the training of Lieutenant Colonel Robinson, and to the relatively short time that it had taken the officers and men to learn their catechism of regular army drill techniques and battalion field manoeuvres before being thrust into battle. It should also be noted that this successful manoeuvre by the Incorporated Militia prevented the entire British line from being "rolled up," and saved General Drummond from suffering a defeat similar to that of General Riall.

The British line now faced in two directions and those British regular troops that had been positioned directly to the right of the Incorporated Militia, namely the 8th (King's) and the 89th Regiment, were forced to swing back to maintain contact with the unit, thus creating a "corner" and leaving the crossroads of Lundy's Lane and the Queenston Road directly in front of the British position undefended. Without this protection on their flanks, the Congreve rocket detachment and its covering detachment of 19th Light Dragoons, which had been previously stationed at the crossroads, were forced to retire in the face of the American incursion.

This left Jesup's troops in control of the ground between the woods and the east side of the Queenston Road, threatening to cut off any further British reinforcements from the north and intercepting anyone who might come back from the disorganized British corner. Because of this, a number of British officers and men, including a wounded General Riall, fell into the hands of the Americans. With daylight gone, his ammunition depleted, and encumbered with a large body of prisoners, Jesup received word that General Drummond was on the Queenston Road with reinforcements and that Scott's main body had met with a severe mauling on the far side of the hill. Assessing his position as being more than a little exposed, and concerned at being cut off himself, Jesup ordered his remaining troops to break off and retire to Mrs. Wilson's Tavern with their haul of prisoners. This American retreat temporarily ended the threat to the British left flank but saw a number of men from the regiment taken into captivity, including Ensign Kilborn of the No. 10 Company:

> After I had, with five or six men, surrendered, the Lieutenant in command of the company of about sixty men, formed his men in a hollow square, placed his prisoners within it, marched us round near the river and up by the Falls in rear of their army and beyond the reach of a shot from either side, placed me under a strong guard in charge of his junior officer, and with the balance of his company returned back to the battlefield.[11]

THE FIGHT FOR THE GUNS

While Jesup's information on Drummond was wrong, the news of the mauling of Winfield Scott's forces was certainly no exaggeration. After initially exposing his men to the fire of the British artillery, and suffering the consequential heavy casualties, General Scott had finally advanced his line toward the right flank of the British line. Unfortunately for Scott, this move had been immediately countered by General Drummond, who ordered three companies of the 1st (Royal Scots) Regiment (under Captain Brereton) to move down from the crest of the hill to fire on the advancing enemy from the front. In support of this movement, detachments from the Glengarry Light Infantry (Lieutenant Colonel Battersby), the 2nd York Embodied Militia (Major T.G. Simons), and the Natives (Captain J. Norton), far from retiring, swung even farther forward in an arc and succeeded in outflanking the Americans.

The combined fire of these infantry units brought the Americans to a complete halt once again and a firefight of volleys ensued between the opposing lines. From the hilltop, the British artillery continued to pound the exposed Americans at an even better and more deadly range than before. Caught in this crossfire, Scott's already depleted brigade was being torn to shreds. Inevitably, the casualties being inflicted on the First Brigade, and the fact that significant portions of the line had run out of ammunition, brought the situation to the point where even its most aggressive officers began to recommend an immediate withdrawal under the cover of darkness.

The opportunity was now there for General Drummond to advance and sweep the remnants of the First Brigade from the field, but with the onset of darkness and dense smoke from the sustained volleys, visibility had been reduced to a matter of a few yards. Certain that additional American support was immediately behind Scott's depleted line and unable to see anything of their strengths or dispositions, Drummond chose to remain on the defensive. Concerned that his now widely dispersed forces would be rendered vulnerable in the darkness, he sought to concentrate his units. He ordered the recall of the regiments on the right flank, and also repositioned the detachments of the 89th, 1st (Royal Scots), and 8th (King's) Regiments on the left flank. To further strengthen his position, the General ordered the removal of a number of companies from the Incorporated Militia to fill gaps at the left, centre, and right of his new line.

Back at Chippawa, General Brown heard the sounds of heavy gunfire coming from the north, and, upon receiving Winfield Scott's initial report, ordered General Ripley to advance his brigade. General Porter was directed to assemble his militia force on the north bank of the Chippawa and await orders. However, while marching toward Lundy's Lane with Ripley's brigade, Brown received a further report from Scott, calling for immediate reinforcements. In response, he sent orders to General Porter to bring forward his Third Brigade, as well as any other units that could be formed from those troops still in camp.

Arriving on the battlefield after darkness had already fallen, Brown dispatched runners to locate General Scott and obtain a report of the situation. After hearing of the mauling suffered by the First Brigade, Brown ordered Ripley to advance his brigade and form nearer to the hill, where its volleys could be

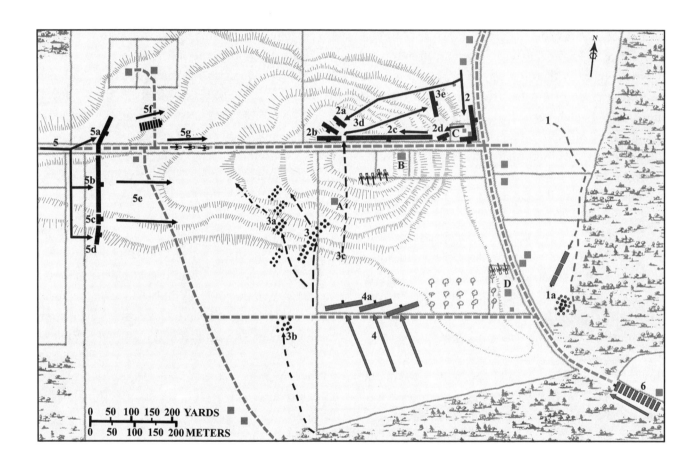

Both Armies Redeploy and Receive Reinforcements (circa 8:00–8:45 p.m.).

A.   Buchner House
B.   Lundy's Lane churchyard
C.   Johnson's Tavern
D.   Pier's farmstead

1.   The U.S. Twenty-Fifth Regiment (1) withdraws east to the treeline and then retires (south) with its prisoners (1a).
2.   In the aftermath of the American flanking attack, General Drummond reorganizes his line. Most of the companies from the Incorporated Militia (2) are moved right (south) to secure the crossroads at right angles to the remainder of the British line. Two companies are detached (2a) and transferred to the right flank to support the 41st detachment (2b), the 89th Regiment (2c) and 8th (King's) detachment (2d) both move right (west) to secure the line of Lundy's Lane and the hilltop.
3.   The British right flank is recalled. In response, the Glengarry Light Infantry (3), embodied militias, and Natives (3b) withdraw northwest toward Lundy's Lane. The detachment of the 1st (Royal Scots) (3c) withdraws north to behind the main British line and re-forms into line (3d) before being ordered to move across the hill to support the British left flank (3e).
4.   With the British withdrawing, the American First Brigade (4) initially advances and then again halts (4a), suffering additional losses from the British artillery on the hilltop.
5.   The British reinforcement column commanded by Colonel Hercules Scott and guided by Major Kerby (Incorporated Militia) arrives on the battlefield from the west (5). The leading elements of the column's regiments (composed of the right flank of the 103rd (5a), the 1st (Royal Scots) (5b), the grenadier company of the 103rd (5c), and flank companies of the 104th (5d)) form line across and to the south of Lundy's Lane before advancing toward the hill (5e). The left flank of the 103rd Regiment (5f) advances separately toward the British line on the hill, while three artillery pieces (5g) move directly on the hilltop.
6.   The leading elements of General Ripley's 2nd Brigade (6) approach the battlefield from Chippawa, marching north along the Portage Road.

more effective on the enemy, as well as drawing fire away from Scott's shattered line. He also sent his aide, Major McCree, to reconnoitre the British positions, since it was obvious that the primary threat of the British guns had to be eliminated as soon as possible.

On the crest of the hill, the previous accuracy and effectiveness of the British artillery had steadily been degraded by darkness, and any firing done from this point onward was random at best. Furthermore, the infantry units that had been engaging Winfield Scott's brigade were reporting that they were running out of ammunition. Inexplicably unable to access the reserve ammunition, General Drummond was forced to make the difficult decision to strip his remaining embodied militias (being held in reserve on the British right) of their ammunition, effectively rendering them useless for further participation in the battle.*

Fortunately for Drummond, Major Kerby had succeeded in locating Colonel Hercules Scott's column and had successfully guided it to the battlefield. These exhausted troops now marched up Lundy's Lane from the west. Despite having just made a forced march of nearly twenty miles, the first of these units (the 103rd and 104th Regiments) were immediately pressed into combat, extending the British line to the west. Their accompanying guns (three 6-pounders) ascended the hill at the same time and began to unlimber alongside the already established battery. Having completed his assigned duty, Major Kerby left the column to locate and rejoin his regiment.

Unfortunately, having recalled his right wing, General Drummond failed to notify the new arrivals of the expected return of these troops to their front. In the darkness, the arriving regiments mistook the retiring formations of Glengarries and York Militia for Americans making an attack, and opened fire on their hapless comrades, causing numerous casualties. Included in these casualties was Major Simons, who was forced to leave the field to seek medical treatment. More significantly, General Drummond failed to establish any covering screen of light troops on the slope in front of and below his battery of guns. Because of this omission, the artillery were left exposed to attack and the only force available for their defence came from the gun crews and some detached companies of the 89th Regiment stationed behind the battery on the reverse (north) slope of the hill.

On the open ground, to the south of the hill, the American Second Brigade advanced to the foot of the slope, with the Twenty-First (including a company from each of the Seventeenth and Nineteenth Regiments) (Colonel Miller) on the left and the Twenty-Third (Colonel McFarland) on the right of the Portage Road. Ripley then ordered his two

---

* N.B. Due to the onset of darkness restricting visibility and the lack of any international standardized time settings, subsequent "eye-witness" accounts of the battle give sequences of events or times that are disjointed and sometimes contradictory, especially when comparing American and British/Canadian versions of the battle. Consequently, compiling a coherent version of events becomes more and more difficult to achieve as the battle progresses. The following is the author's interpretation, which may not necessarily coincide with other authors' accounts. In addition, once the companies of the Incorporated Militia were split up — except in certain identifiable instances — no coherent documentation exists as to which company was where and did what throughout the remaining course of the action. As a result, to follow the participation of the regiment, it is necessary to trace the wider scope of the battle and recognize that the Incorporated Militia was simply "in there, somewhere."

regimental commanders to attack the British battery. For this assault, Colonel Miller's regiment was instructed to move directly uphill toward the guns. At the same time, Colonel McFarland's column would advance along the road, under Ripley's personal supervision, before wheeling left into line and assaulting the artillery position from the flank.

Meanwhile, off to the American left flank, General Brown discovered that a strong body of British troops lay immediately to the west of the British guns. This consisted of Captain Brereton's 1st (Royal Scots) Regiment, two companies from the Incorporated Militia (Captain Fraser, Captain MacDonell) and the light company of the 41st Regiment (Captain Glew). Concerned that this force could advance and outflank the American assault on the guns, Brown crossed to the American centre and halted Miller's troops. After discussing the situation with Colonel Miller, however,

Brown relented and Miller's troops moved forward once again. Silently advancing up the slope under the cover of the darkness, Miller began to hear the sounds of heavy firing coming from both his right and left flanks.

The noise from the right was caused by the Twenty-Third Regiment, which had run into a wall of fire from the left flank of the 89th Regiment and the remainder of the companies of the Incorporated Militia. Together, these units quickly routed the Twenty-Third, killing Colonel McFarland and most of the leading company in his column. The firing from the left was the British firing on a detachment of the First Regiment under Lieutenant Colonel Nicholas. Although this regiment had only just arrived on the Niagara frontier, was not officially incorporated into the Second Brigade, and had neither orders nor information of what lay ahead,

Lundy's Lane hilltop as it looks today, viewed from the direction of attack taken by Colonel James Miller's forces. The original chapel was located at the far end of the small path on the right side of the image, while the bulk of the British guns occupied the high ground, directly in front of the modern church.

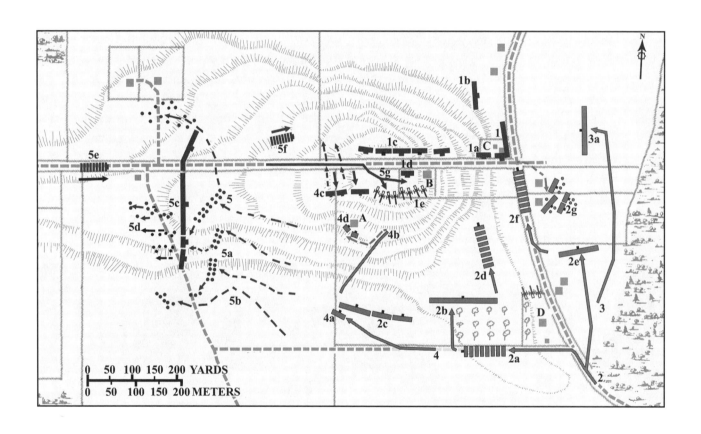

Ripley's 2nd Brigade Advances on the Hill and the British Suffer Friendly Fire (circa 8:45–9:15 p.m.).

A. Buchner House
B. Lundy's Lane churchyard
C. Johnson's Tavern
D. Pier's farmstead

1. The Incorporated Militia (1) secures the crossroads, supported on the right by the detachment of the 8th (King's) (1a) and on the left rear by the Royal Scots (1b). On the hilltop, companies of the main body of the 89th (1c) are dispersed to cover more ground, while a detachment (1d) is moved forward to support the guns (1e).
2. General Ripley's 2nd Brigade (2), accompanied by General Brown, enters the field. The Twenty-First Regiment moves left (west) in column (2a), passing the Pier's farm before advancing (north) and forming line (2b) on the right of Winfield Scott's severely mauled First Brigade (2c). Considered to be too far from the hill, the Twenty-First then re-forms column and advances toward the hill (2d) to attack the guns. At the same time, the Twenty-Third Regiment initially forms line (2e) on the east of the Portage Road. It then re-forms its column and advances to attack the crossroads (2f). Upon having the head of the column killed by fire from the Incorporated Militia and 8th (King's) at the crossroads, the Twenty-Third Regiment breaks and retreats behind some nearby farm buildings and begins to re-form (2g).
3   The Twenty-Fifth Regiment (3), having deposited its prisoners and looking to support the 2nd Brigade's attack, re-enters the field and advances toward the crossroads (3a).
4. The detachment of the U.S. First Regiment (4) arrives on the battlefield without instructions and looking to join Ripley's 2nd Brigade. The First initially moves across to General Winfield Scott's First Brigade position (4a) and obtains directions. It then marches toward the hill (4b) but comes under fire from the British artillery and the detachments of 41st and Incorporated Militia (4c) who have advanced to counter this threat to the guns. Under this fire, the First retreats behind the Buchner farm buildings, where they begin to re-form (4d).
5. On the far west of the field, the retiring units (Glengarry Light Infantry (5), embodied militias (5a), and Native allies (5b)) are mistakenly fired on by Hercules Scott's line (5c) and suffer casualties. Routed, the three disordered units pass through and around Hercules Scott's line and move north to the rear of the British positions (5d). The last unit of Hercules Scott's column, the 8th Regiment (5e), arrives on the field and is placed in reserve. The detached left flank of the 103rd (5f) advances toward the hill and the column's artillery arrive at the hilltop and begin to unlimber (5g).

Nicholas had brought his men onto the battlefield to join the fight. Having wandered around the battlefield in the darkness in search of Ripley's brigade, Nicholas's small force was heading toward the hilltop when he suddenly realized he was almost on top of the British lines:

> The fire of a division of the Royal Scott's under Captain Brereton, two companies of the Incorporated Militia under Captains Fraser and McDonell and 41st Flank Companies under Captain Glew opened upon them with effect and threw them in some confusion but they soon ralleyed and firmly stood their ground for a time, till the well directed and destructive fire of the British compelled them to fall back with a heavy loss.[12]

Recognizing that to remain in place or advance would be suicidal, Lieutenant Colonel Nicholas ordered his force to retreat and take cover behind a white farmhouse on the lower slopes of the south-west side of the hill. These two separate and uncoordinated movements, while achieving little beyond mounting the American casualty roll, did distract the British gunners on the hilltop, as well as the troops on either side. This diversion of attention, and General Drummond's prior failure to establish a covering screen of troops, allowed Colonel Miller's troops to creep up through the undefended centre and position themselves behind the cover of a fence and bushes lining the boundary of the small graveyard. From there, they delivered a devastating volley into the crowd of artillerymen, who were fully occupied with attending to their guns.

Most of the men in the British battery were either killed or wounded by this fire, while the teams of horses, which had just hauled up the additional guns, were either killed or stampeded through the lines of the British right flank, disordering that formation and preventing it from mounting a counterattack. Charging forward, the Twenty-First Regiment attacked and soon overwhelmed the surviving gun crews, capturing around forty men, who were quickly secured inside the church building.

Located directly behind the artillery position on the crest, the covering detachment of the 89th Regiment was initially caught off guard by the American attack and suffered several injuries when the artillery horses stampeded. However, the detachment rallied, and were soon joined by General Drummond, who ordered an immediate counterattack to regain the vital guns.

As they marched forward, the 89th detachment fired into the milling mass of dark shapes vaguely discernible among the cannon, only to be met by an increasing volume of fire as the Americans reacted and formed their own line. Outnumbered and unable to drive off the enemy, the British detachment was forced to retreat, but soon returned with reinforcements that included additional companies of the 89th, 1st (Royal Scots), 41st Regiment, and Incorporated Militia.

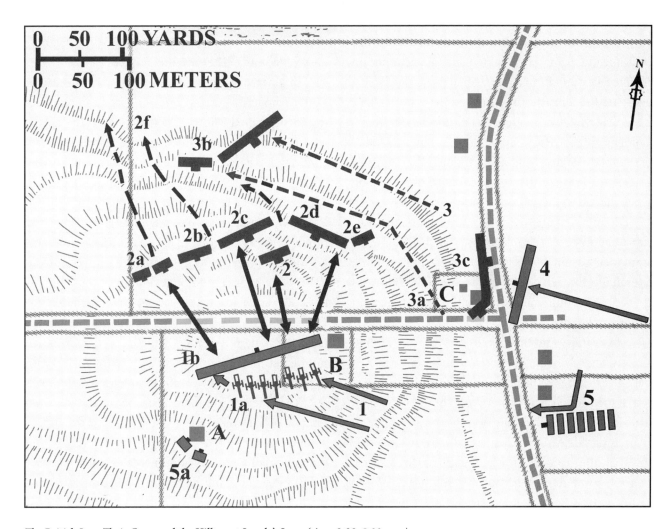

The British Lose Their Guns and the Hilltop at Lundy's Lane (circa *9:00–9:30 p.m.*).

A. Buchner House   B. Lundy's Lane churchyard   C. Johnson's Tavern

1. The Twenty-First Regiment (1) advance, attack, and overrun the British artillery position (1a) on the hilltop and begin to form into line (1b).
2. The advanced detachment of the 89th (2) counterattacks, but is driven off. It returns with reinforcements (Incorporated Militia) (2a), 41st (2b), and detached companies of the 89th (2c, 2d, 2e). In a series of counterattacks, the British are unable to break the American position and eventually retire toward the northwest of the hill (2f).
3. The detachment of 1st (Royal Scots) (3) and 8th (King's) (3a) are withdrawn from the left flank to support the British counterattacks on the guns (3b), leaving the Incorporated Militia (3c) alone at the crossroads.
4. The Twenty-Fifth Regiment (4) advances in darkness, arrives at the crossroads, and engages the Incorporated Militia in heavy, close-quarter volley action.
5. Under orders from General Brown, the re-formed Twenty-Third Regiment (5) moves round and begins its march to join the Twenty-First on the hilltop. The detachment of the First (5a) remain behind the Buchner farmstead building.

Twice more, the two lines clashed and the carnage continued. During this fight, General Drummond received a wound from a musket ball that lodged in his neck and that only narrowly missed the commander's main artery, while Lieutenant Duncan Clark (No. 7 Company) recorded: "Captain and Ensign McDonell of the Incorporated Militia and Captain Brereton and Lieutenant Fraser of the Royal Scotts ... were among the wounded in this action."[13]

Despite making repeated assaults, the British-Canadian force was unable to dislodge the Americans from their advantageous position on the high ground. Eventually, the defenders were forced to withdraw to the foot of the hill, leaving their entire artillery park in American hands.

Meanwhile, on the south side of the hilltop, shortly after leaving Miller's force, General Brown had heard the sound of firing from the previously mentioned action between the Incorporated Militia and the American Twenty-Third Regiment. Hastening forward, Brown eventually located the lines of the Twenty-Third attempting to re-form behind some buildings to the southeast of the Lundy's Lane-Portage Road crossroads. Upon hearing the sound of combat on the hilltop, General Brown concluded that Miller's efforts had been successful and ordered Ripley to cease his planned flanking attack. Instead, Ripley was to move back around to the left and ascend the hill, following Miller's route, to support the Twenty-First. Brown then pressed forward along the road, intending to reconnoitre toward Lundy's Lane. As he did so, he nearly ran directly into a fierce firefight that erupted immediately before him when someone in the darkness yelled out, "They are the Yankees."[14]

This warning call possibly came from Major Kerby, who had located the now isolated companies of the Incorporated Militia still stationed on the northwest side of the road junction, and had taken over command. The cause of the alarm was not Brown's party, however, but Jesup's Twenty-Fifth Regiment, which was once again trying to outflank the British left. According to Brown's eyewitness testimony, "The moment the British officer gave Major Jesup notice of having discovered him, Jesup ordered his command to fire. The lines could not have been more than four rods [22 yards] apart. The slaughter was dreadful."[15]

Although heavily outnumbered and separated from the remainder of the British line, the Canadian militiamen stood their ground and traded volleys with the enemy, forcing it to retire once again. However, once the renewed sounds of firing began coming from directly behind their line at the hilltop (as the British counterattacks on the guns began), Kerby recognized that his small force was in immediate danger of being surrounded. Looking to extricate his unit from this predicament, he retired his command north, along the Portage Road, before swinging west. After renewing contact with the left of the main British line, he took up a new defensive position on the north side of the hill, facing northeast. Except for this thin screen of men from the Incorporated Militia, the way was now open for Jesup to swing around the east side of the hill and engage the main British force from the rear.

Since the darkness prevented Jesup from knowing what forces lay before him, he was uncertain of

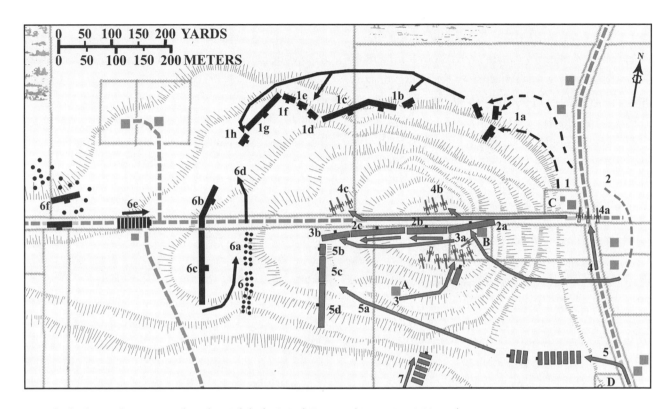

Porter's Third Brigade Arrives and Deploys While the British Regroup (circa 9:30–10:00 p.m.).

A. Buchner House   B. Lundy's Lane churchyard   C. Johnson's Tavern

1. Following the fight at the crossroads, the Incorporated Militia (1) withdraws to the north side of the hill, establishing a new position to cover that flank (1a). They are subsequently ordered west to join in the preparations for the British counterattack on the hill and are dispersed in detachments (det.) along the line, thus: det. Incorporated Militia (1b), 89th (1c), det. 8th (King's) (1d), det. Incorporated Militia (1e), det.1st (Royal Scots)(1f), left flank 103rd (1g), det. Incorporated Militia (1h).

2. Withdrawing from the fight at the crossroads, the Twenty-Fifth (2) is ordered by General Brown to move to the hilltop, where it forms on the right of the American line as it is repositioning (2a). The remaining U.S. regiments, Twenty-Third (2b) and Twenty-First (2c), move to their left (west) and establish a new line on the south side of Lundy's Lane.

3. The re-formed detachment from the First Regiment (3) moves up to the hilltop and is initially placed behind the right flank of the American line (3a). It is then moved over to the left flank (3b) where it extends the American line to the west.

4. Three U.S. artillery batteries (4) are brought up from the rear. Biddle's Battery (4a) is emplaced at the crossroads, while Towson's (4b) and Richie's (4c) move up and are unlimbered on the north side of the hill in front of the infantry line.

5. The U.S. Third Brigade (Porter's militia) (5) enters the field in column and advances to the far left flank of the American line (5a). Here, it forms a line at right angles to Lundy's Lane fronting to the west: Canadian Volunteers (5b), New York State militias (5c), Pennsylvania State militias (5d).

6. On the British right, the Flank Companies 104th (6) and Grenadier Company 103rd (6a) are initially posted as a skirmish line in front of the British right line (right flank 103rd (6b), and 1st (Royal Scots)), but are then directed to march to join the assembly of units at the north side of the hill (6d). The 8th (6e), in reserve, advances to support the British line, while the Glengarry Light Infantry, embodied militias, and Natives (6f) remain out of action at the edge of the field.

7. Winfield Scott's consolidated remnants of the First Brigade (7) are ordered up to support the American position on the hill.

how best to proceed. The opportunity passed, however, when General Brown arrived and informed Jesup that his force was required on the hilltop in support of Miller and Ripley. In his own words, he "abandoned his position, moved back and joined General Ripley on the heights, by whom he was posted with his command on the right of the line which was then forming."[16] Once again, the Incorporated Militia had foiled an American flanking movement.

COUNTERATTACK

On top of the hill, the desperate fight to hold onto the guns had cost Miller's command dearly and he urgently needed reinforcements. Fearing another British counterattack, Miller ordered the removal of the captured artillery pieces down the American side of the hill. Shortly thereafter, the First and Twenty-Third Regiments arrived, extending the American line from the churchyard on the east, across the crest of the hill toward Skinners Lane in the west.

When General Ripley arrived at the hilltop, he took over command and decided that the captured artillery could be better used as part of the new line of defence. Thus, he countermanded Miller's removal order, and sent orders for the American artillery batteries to move up onto the hilltop.

Once there, the American artillery was posted directly in front of the infantry. With these pieces in place, further inspection of the captured British artillery revealed that the essential hand tools required to load and fire the guns had either broken during the initial fight, or were entirely missing. Without these tools, the captured guns were unworkable, and Ripley ordered them removed to the American camp. Before the removal could occur, however, General Brown and his staff arrived, and the general dismissed Ripley's order, stating that "there were matters of more importance to attend to at that moment."[17]

By this time, Porter's reduced brigade of around three hundred men had also arrived and was immediately directed by Brown to form their line at right angles to the First Regiment, facing due west toward Skinners Lane. Certain that the British would not let the loss of their guns go unchallenged and that a new counterattack was imminent, Ripley urged caution. Brown, however, was confident that the enemy was fleeing from the field. To prove his point, he personally rode in front of his own lines, only to find that he "could no longer doubt that a more extensive line than he had before seen during the engagement was near and rapidly advancing on us."[18]

In a show of extreme daring, Brown's aide, Captain Ambrose Spencer, sought to confirm the identity of the approaching force, and, "without a remark, put spurs to his horse and rode directly up to the advancing lines then turning toward the enemy's right enquired in a firm and strong voice, 'What Regiment is that?' And was as promptly answered, 'The Royal Scotts, Sir.'"[19] In response, General Brown and Captain Spencer "threw themselves in the rear of [the] troops without loss of time."[20]

Confirmation of this incident and information about subsequent events comes from the reminiscences of Lieutenant Henry Ruttan of Captain Edward Walker's No. 5 Company:

At this time, about 9 o'clock at night there was as if by common consent, a general cessation of firing. Although there was a moon, it was yet as dark as to prevent distinguishing our men from those of the Enemy. We could plainly see [the silhouette on the hilltop of] a line forming in our front and hear every order given. General Drummond, who was immediately behind my company called for an officer and 20 men to advance and ascertain whether we had a friend or foe in front. At this particular juncture of time I saw a mounted officer in front of our line but about a company distant on my right and heard him ask in a bold and commanding way "What regiment is this?" The answer was "Scott's Royals Sir" He replied "Very Well, stand you fast Scottish Royals" and disappeared toward the enemy's line.

A good deal of confusion ensued upon the call of General Drummond from the superabundance of our men volunteering for the service. However, being of the opinion that one or two men would execute this order better than twenty, I took Corporal Ferguson, who happened to be next to me and quietly advanced under a cover of a fence and lying trees until I could discover long tailed coats turned up with white. I could not distinguish blue from scarlet cloth but heard the words "Forward, March" words never so combined with us and "Halt" and other indications, which convinced us that those in front of us were enemies.

Immediately after I turned to retire my steps, a field piece was "Let Off" from the [American] line when their firing at once became general. I fell in with a number of our men, some of whom never lived to return to our lines. Providence however, protected the Corporal and me thus far, but I had but just taken my place in the ranks when I was shot through the right shoulder. I scarcely felt the shock, but was conscious that something unusual was the matter as I was involuntarily brought up on both feet (we were all on one knee) and turned quite around. I had gone but a few steps to the rear when I remembered nothing more until about 2 o'clock the next morning when I found myself lying on my back on the floor of a room being examined by a surgeon who promised me "Done For."[21]

Ensign John Lampman (Jarvie's No. 2 Company) later recorded:

> During this part of the battle, the British noted a commotion to their front and Lampman was given permission to reconnoitre. He went around the flank of his regiment and concealed himself under the shadow of some trees directly in front of the British line. Soon a cavalcade rode up and halted directly before him. They held a brief conversation and they challenged the army before them, hidden in the darkness of the night…. The night was generally cloudy but as the challenge was being given the moon came out for a moment and he (Lampman) believed it was the Commander of the US Army. The British reply was a furious fire along the whole line and which the enemy made equally furious and sustained fire. Lampman hurried back to his position in the ranks and as he was jumping a fence he had his trousers knee shot through and one of his epaulettes shot off.[22]

Not having these reports, General Drummond had no accurate intelligence of what he was facing on the hilltop. However, deciding he could not afford to wait any longer, he ordered the entire line to advance. Obeying the order, the composite line of British and Canadian troops moved up the slope, maintaining a disciplined and "profound silence"[23] as they approached the equally silent and determined line of American troops.

Beginning on the far right of the American position, the two forces began firing into each other. Positioned in front of their line, the American artillery may have been able to get off a single round of canister (short-range artillery) ammunition into the British formations, but no more, since the subsequent British musket volleys cut down the gun crews, almost to a man. For the next twenty minutes, the two lines of infantry stood almost toe-to-toe and hammered each other with devastating volley fire. At these close quarters, commands being given by one side's officers were clearly audible to the men of the opposing line. As they were both speaking English, and the commands so similar, they were occasionally mistakenly obeyed, adding to the confusion of the already deadly situation. Unable to breach the American line, the British eventually fell back to the bottom of the hill, leaving behind them a line of dead and wounded to mark their farthest advance. Once at the foot of the slope, the surviving officers and NCOs immediately began the difficult process of collecting their scattered forces out of the darkness to comply with General Drummond's order to mount another frontal assault.

Certain the British would return, General Ripley ordered Porter's brigade to swing forward and extend

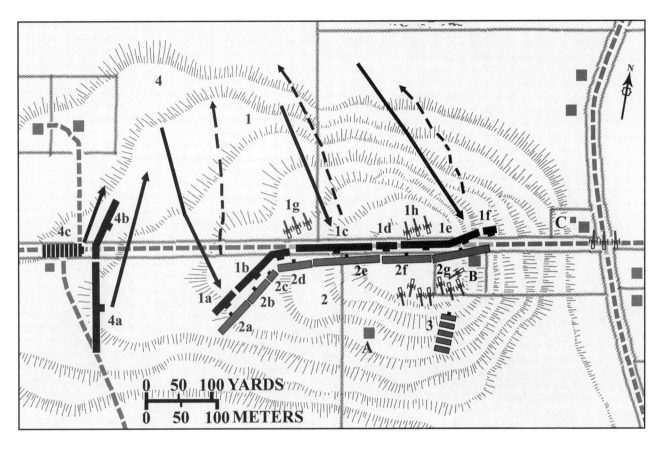

The 1st British Counterattack for the Guns (circa 10:00–10:30 p.m.).

A. Buchner House
B. Lundy's Lane churchyard
C. Johnson's Tavern

1. The Composite British line (1), composed of: det. Incorporated Militia (1a), Grenadier Company 103rd/Flank Company 104th/det. 41st (1b), det. Incorporated Militia (1c), det. 8th (King's) (1d), 89th (1e), det. Incorporated Militia (1f), advance to attack the hilltop. The line overruns the American hilltop artillery (1g, 1h) before opening fire on the main American line at close range.

2. The American line (2) composed of: Pennsylvania State militias (2a), New York State militias (2b), Canadian Volunteers (2c), First (2d), Twenty-First (2e), Twenty-Third (2f), and Twenty-Fifth (2g) engages the British line and after considerable heavy fighting at point-blank range beats off the first British counterattack for the guns.

3. Winfield Scott's consolidated 1st Brigade (3) is positioned at the foot of the hill as a reserve.

4. Retreating to the foot of the slope at the northwest corner of the hill, the British (4) begin to regroup for a second counterattack. To support this, General Drummond orders the units on the right flank: 1st (Royal Scots) (4a), left flank 103rd (4b), 8th (King's) (4c), to move up in close support.

the American line westward, facing to the north. He also pressed General Brown to bring up the remains of Winfield Scott's brigade to bolster the depleted American position. The remnants of Scott's three regiments, which had been consolidated into a single force, were moved into a new position behind the American right flank. At the same time, the British appeared out of the darkness and the duel of musketry began once more. According to some accounts, this round of fighting lasted for up to half an hour and was even more desperate than the first, as sections of the lines converged, resulting in hand-to-hand combat.

According to one officer of the Incorporated Militia (Lieutenant Clark, No. 7 Company), the attacking line was composed of

the 89th Regiment and divisions of the 8th Regiment ... three companies of the Incorporated Militia under Captains Walker, Kerr and Rapelje, stationed in the centre and a party of Royals, 103rd, 104th and 41st Flank companies stationed on the

A postwar impression of the height of the battle of Lundy's Lane. While inaccurate in details, it is evocative of the atmosphere of the conflict. W. Strickland, artist and engraver, not dated. The artwork was first published in the Portfolio, Naval and Military Chronicle of the United States.

Library and Archives Canada, C-4071.

right. At the same time, a division of [at least two companies from] the Incorporated Militia on the right under Captain Fraser, supported by Lieutenant Clark and Burritt wheeled on its left and made a charge under the direction of Lt. Colonel Pearson with such effect that the enemy was thrown back in great disorder and with loss.[24]

The renewed British attack began to tell on the American units. On the left, the charge by Pearson's force caused parts of Porter's militia to waver and break, forcing the First Regiment to swing backward to cover the gap until Porter's militia officers could re-form their men. In the centre, the Twenty-First and Twenty-Third Regiments had wide gaps blown in their line, again causing some men to edge back and break ranks. Finally, on the right flank, Jesup's corps was taking a heavy pounding but remained in position. Behind this wavering line, Winfield Scott decided that he could save the day if he led his men in a strong counterattack on the British line.

Without ensuring that the regiments in the American front line were made aware of his plan, General Scott marched his depleted First Brigade north across Lundy's Lane, heading for the British line. Almost immediately, the head of his column came under heavy fire from the line of British and Canadian troops ahead, and was effectively wiped out. Seeking to avoid this devastating fire, the remainder of the column veered left, which caused it to march west, directly along Lundy's Lane, where they were trapped between the two opposing lines!

In the confusion of the darkness, and unaware of who was before them, the American line blasted the First Brigade's column. With no option but to press on in an attempt to escape this gauntlet of fire, Winfield Scott's corps was systematically raked with repeated, point-blank fire from the two opposing lines. This double blow was too much for the men in the column and they broke, fleeing west along Lundy's Lane until they passed the left flank of the American line. Once there, they were able to work their way behind the American position, where, to their credit, they began to re-form their companies once again. Across the hilltop, the firing and hand-to-hand combat continued unabated, until eventually the British units, unable to break the American position and running out of ammunition, were again forced to withdraw.

At the foot of the hill, Drummond's force was in desperately poor shape, for the cumulative efforts of a day's march to the field of action, followed by nearly four hours of almost continuous battle, had exhausted the troops. Despite his wound and the two previous failures, Drummond decided to risk one more attempt at recapturing the hilltop and his artillery. Reforming his troops in composite units and establishing a ragged line, Drummond's dogged British and Canadian veterans — for no one could claim there were novices in the British line by this time — marched up the slope once more toward the waiting Americans.

According to Jesup, on the right of the American line, this third assault "was now more obstinate than in any of the previous attacks of the enemy — for

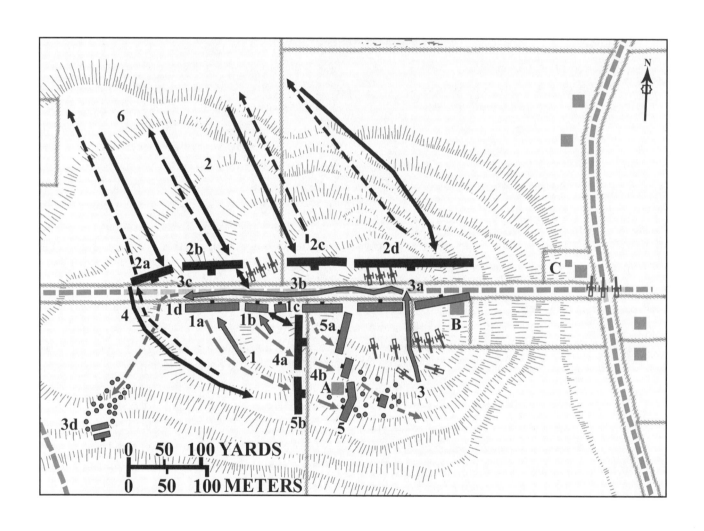

The 2nd British Counterattack for the Guns (circa 11:00–11:40 p.m.).

A.   Buchner House   B.   Lundy's Lane churchyard

1.   General Porter's Third Brigade (1), consisting of: Pennsylvania State militias, (1a) New York State militias (1b), and Canadian Volunteers (1c), swing forward to extend the American line (1d).
2.   The British Composite line (2), composed of: det. Incorporated Militia (2a), det. 1st (Royal Scots) / Flank Companies 104th / Grenadier Company 103rd / 41st (2b), det. Incorporated Militia, det. 8th (King's) (2c), 89th (2d), makes a second counterattack on the hilltop, exchanging fire with the American line across the width of Lundy's Lane.
3.   General Winfield Scott decides to use his consolidated brigade (3) to break through the British left flank. Passing through the American line (3a), his column is hit by heavy British fire and veers left (west) (3b). His column then runs the gauntlet of fire from both lines until it passes the left flank of the American line (3c), where it passes back and begins to re-form (3d) near Skinners Lane.
4.   Under heavy pressure from the right flank of the British attack (4) (2a, 2b), Porter's brigade (4a) (1a, 1b, 1c) begins to crumble (4b).
5.   The entire American left flank is forced back (5) and only stabilizes with difficulty after the detachment from the First Regiment (5a) swings back, securing the corner, halting the British advance at a new line (5b).
6.   The second British counterattack fails to break the American line and retires to the northwest of the hill (6).

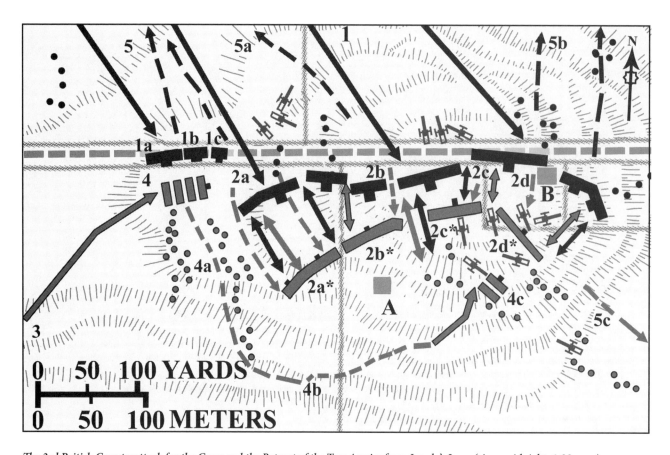

The 3rd British Counterattack for the Guns and the Retreat of the Two Armies from Lundy's Lane (circa midnight–1:30 a.m.).

A. Buchner House   B. Lundy's Lane churchyard

1. The re-formed British line made up of composite and ad-hoc companies (whose component elements and positions are not documented) advances on the American line. An identified division, composed of Incorporated Militia (1a) and some unidentified regular detachments (1b, 1c), take up a kneeling position behind a fence and hedge that lines Lundy's Lane to secure the British flank.

2. The composite American line – det. Nineteenth, New York State militias, Pennsylvania State militias, Canadian Volunteers, det. First (2a), Twenty-First (2b), Twenty-Third (2c), Twenty-Fifth (2d) –advances and takes up its previous positions along Lundy's Lane. Under the British attack the American line is forced back to a new position: 2a* 2b* 2c* 2d*. In heavy hand-to hand fighting, the hillside becomes a melee of individual battles between enemy units.

3. Looking to attack the British right flank, General Winfield Scott orders the reorganized remnants of his First Brigade (3) to advance, but fails to spot the kneeling British units (1a, 1b, 1c).

4. The Incorporated Militia (1a) and regulars (1b, 1c) fire into Scott's column (4) at point-blank range, causing it to waver and then break (4a). After retreating, it is rallied and reorganizes yet again (4b). It is then brought up to the hilltop as the fighting ends and is posted as a reserve on the American right flank (4c).

5. Unable to capitalize on their attack and recapture the guns, British units begin to independently withdraw in various states of discipline and order (5, 5a, 5b) to positions five hundred yards to the north of the hill, where they remain for the night. The Americans remain on the hill for about an hour before withdrawing to Chippawa (5c), leaving behind most of the artillery pieces from both sides.

half an hour, the blaze of the muskets of the two lines mixed."[25] But despite suffering heavy casualties, especially amongst the officer corps, the American right flank held firm until the British left flank was forced, yet again, to withdraw.

Similarly, on the left of the American line, the British force advanced, having to step on or clamber over the bodies on the ground in a final attempt to come to grips with the Americans. As the combatants began to trade volleys, Winfield Scott once again attempted to make his mark by ordering his partially re-formed remnant of a brigade to advance out from the relative security of Skinners Lane and attack the advancing British right flank. Unfortunately for him, in the darkness and smoke, he failed to note that a line of Incorporated Militia and regulars were positioned on his left, hidden behind a line of bushes and fencing that bordered Lundy's Lane. According to Lieutenant Duncan Clark, the British and Canadian troops "kneeled sufficiently low to prevent being seen by the enemy; and when [the Americans came] within a few paces of the British line, a signal was given to fire."[26]

Despite suffering heavy casualties from the point-blank volleys, parts of the American formation began to return fire, and "both sides were soon engaged in a conflict obstinate beyond description, disorder and dispute was the consequence."[27] Elsewhere in the American formation, General Scott attempted to respond to this additional disaster by ordering, "Battalion, left wheel into line, quick march."[28]

By this point, however, the limits of the First Brigade had been reached and, according to a contemporary American account, "perceiving that his word of command ... was no longer heeded by his wearied and almost heart-broken ranks, he [Winfield Scott] exclaimed in a voice of thunder, 'Then you may all go to Hell,'"[29] whereupon Scott rode away from his men and disappeared into the darkness. Abandoned by their leader in the face of the enemy, and unable to stand the fire from the British and Canadians, the First Brigade column broke and was scattered.

As Winfield Scott's few remaining men fled past to the rear, General Porter's militia troops, supported by a detachment of regulars from the Nineteenth Regiment (previously attached to the Twenty-First), took up the brunt of the fighting on the American left flank and traded volleys with the advancing British line. During this exchange, General Brown, who had been following Scott's column, was severely wounded and had to withdraw from the action. After a sustained effort, the British units on this flank were unable to break through and, possibly fearing a further attack by an unseen American column, also withdrew for the last time.

At the centre of the third British attack, the assault by Drummond's troops had driven the American line back into the midst of the scattered artillery positions on top of the hill. This was followed by savage hand-to-hand combat as both sides desperately sought to possess these valuable prizes. The attack almost succeeded, but the inability of the two flank attacks to break through the American line left the centre unsupported, and there were no reserves available at the foot of the hill that could be pushed forward to swing the balance. Eventually, the British centre was also forced to break off and retire, leaving behind the guns they had come so close to regaining.

As he withdrew from the field, General Brown looked for General Winfield Scott to whom he hoped to pass over the command of the army. However, he was informed that the general had already preceded him in leaving the field after being wounded. This left Brown with no alternative but to relinquish command to General Ripley, and he sent orders to Ripley that the army should retire from the hill and return to camp.

Unfortunately, this message took some time to reach its intended recipient. Unaware of the departure of both Brown and Scott, General Ripley had maintained his line of defence on the south face of the hill while he awaited further orders. When he received Brown's notification that he had been placed in charge of the army but that he was being ordered to retire his command to the American camp, he was placed in a difficult situation. He could either disobey a direct order and remain in control of the hill, with a diminished force, low on ammunition, and under threat of further attack by an enemy of unknown strength, or he could obey and abandon the ground so desperately fought over for the past few hours. After assembling a council of officers, Ripley found that only General Porter was adamant of the need to retain the ground, while the remainder felt that they could not survive another attack and that withdrawal was essential and in accordance with General Brown's specific commands. While still undecided, Ripley was informed that most of the American artillery had already been withdrawn from in front of the American position. This news swung the balance, and General Ripley gave the order for the American army to quietly withdraw to their encampment at the Chippawa River, much to the disgust of General Porter.

On the British side of the hill, the troops were, if anything, even more exhausted and thirsty than their American counterparts. Most of them had been on the move since sunrise. Furthermore, after three devastating assaults on the hilltop, the failure to recapture the guns had demoralized the troops to such an extent that there was no question of there being a fourth attempt. General Drummond was also faced with the fact that during the third assault, the Americans had been able to undertake a counterattack with a column of troops. Admittedly this had been beaten off, but it left the question as to what additional reserves the Americans had available for a further attack, for there were none in the British force to stop them.

Fully expecting the battle to continue with an American advance from the hilltop either within the next hour or as soon as daylight returned, General Drummond, wounded as he was, retained command and ordered the majority of his surviving troops to withdraw some five hundred yards north and re-form. According to Lieutenant Duncan Clark, "the enemy had in the majesty of his pride disappeared from Lundy's Lane when the writer of this sketch looked at his watch, which told him by the light of the moon that it was 11 o'clock."[30] For the remainder of the night, the hilltop of Lundy's Lane became relatively unoccupied by the two armies, except for the wounded and the dead. It fell, therefore, to the initiative of individual British commanders to move their men forward and establish a picket line to warn of any American advance, while other detachments went in search of missing or wounded comrades. It was also time to assess the tally of killed and wounded from the regimental rolls.

The first roll call for the Incorporated Militia was made during the course of that night, as soon as the separate companies had been reunited after the fighting ended. The total casualties at this point were assessed at:

Killed: 1 Ensign, 2 Sergeants, 14 Rank and File

Wounded: 1 Lieutenant Colonel, 3 Captains, 3 Lieutenants, 1 Ensign, 3 Sergeants, 32 Rank and File

Known Prisoner: 1 Captain, 1 Ensign, 1 Quartermaster, 14 Rank and File

Missing: 3 Sergeants, 72 Rank and File[31]

Since the action had only ended shortly before, and some men were still wandering the battlefield or tending to the wounded, the number of missing referenced to here appears huge. Unfortunately, in later histories of the battle, it is this figure that is quoted as the official losses attributed to the Incorporated Militia for this action.

In the subsequent light of day, however, once the wanderers had returned and the field had been scoured, the balance of numbers altered somewhat:

Killed: 1 Ensign (John Campbell, 7th Company), 3 Sergeants, 13 Rank and File

Wounded: 1 Lieutenant Colonel (William J. Robinson — dangerously), 3 Captains: (John McDonell, 9th Company — dangerously), (Thomas Fraser, 7th Company — severely), (Daniel Washburn, 4th Company — severely), 3 Lieutenants (Daniel McDougall, 6th Company — dangerously), (Henry Ruttan, 5th Company — severely), (James Hamilton, 1st Company — slightly), 1 Ensign (John McDonell, 9th Company — dangerously), 3 Sergeants, 33 Rank and File

Known Prisoner: 2 Captains: (Daniel Washburn, 4th Company), (Archibald McLean, 6th Company), 2 Ensigns (Andrew Warffe, 6th Company), (John Kilborn, 10th Company), 1 Quartermaster (George Thrower, Staff), 1 Quartermaster Sergeant, 2 Sergeants, 29 Rank and File.[32]

While not quite so devastating as the previous list had made things appear, it was still a serious loss of manpower from a relatively small unit, and an indication both of the ferocity of the action and the important role the Incorporated Militia had within it.

The Lundy's Lane battlefield monument and crypt is located in the hilltop cemetery. This mausoleum is the final resting place for the remains of soldiers from both sides, which became unearthed during the two centuries that followed the war.

18

THE MORNING AFTER

As daylight returned and visibility increased on the morning of July 26, 1814, the intensity of the night's carnage became apparent to the British pickets. Everywhere one looked, the crest of the hill was covered with lines of bodies, marking where the opposing regimental formations had stood, fought, and died, sometimes within feet of each other.

Expecting the Americans to rejoin the action, General Drummond formed his troops at dawn and advanced toward the hill, reoccupying it unopposed. Even more pleasing was the discovery that, not only had most of the captured British artillery been found scattered across the hillside, but two American pieces were also lying abandoned and ready for use. After advancing pickets to report on any American movements,

Drummond directed his troops to spread out across the fields and find the wounded who had survived the night to remove them for treatment at Fort George.

There was also the less pleasant but necessary duty of collecting the bodies of the dead for burial. Initially, they interred the dead of both sides in long trenches, but the large numbers of casualties soon made it apparent that this work would take far longer than anticipated. Concerned that the Americans would return to rejoin the fight, and partially due to a rumour, later determined to be false, that the Americans had cremated the bodies of the British and Canadian dead after Chippawa, a difficult and subsequently controversial decision was made to bury only those bodies identified as British and Canadian and cremate those identified as American. Although an unfortunate necessity of war, this decision was later used by the American press as grounds to cite the inhumanity and bestiality of the British soldiery. In his later account, Lieutenant Clark recorded his impression of this event:

> The British troops were now in possession of the battlefield, the remainder of the night and the whole of the next day was employed in burying their own dead and burning those of the enemy which were collected and piled up on the hill in three heaps, sometimes upwards of 30 lifeless bodies, each with layers of dried oak rails, the torch was applied and the whole reduced to ashes.[1]

Similarly, Ensign Lampman's memories contained another aspect of this event that typifies the well-documented black humour of survivors of battles:

> As Lampman and another officer were strolling in view of the burning pyre, they came across a dead enemy soldier. One of them said that the man should be in the fire because he was fat and would burn well. Just then a musket, which had been thrown into the fire, went off and the bullet struck at the officer's feet, showering them with sand. They agreed that when the dead Yankees began to shoot, it was time for them to retreat, and they retreated.[2]

Later that morning, and as expected, an American force did appear on the Portage Road, marching up from their position at the Chippawa River. The British troops formed their line-of-battle and prepared to recommence the fighting. The Americans, however, merely made a show of announcing their presence and gave no indication of having any inclination to fight by soon withdrawing toward Chippawa, leaving the British masters of the field.

From the other side of the field, the Americans could see that the British were once more firmly in control of the Lundy's Lane hilltop and seemingly well-prepared to renew the conflict. Under these circumstances, Ripley and his subordinates agreed that it would be imprudent to attempt another frontal attack on the hilltop in broad daylight. Instead, the principal topic of discussion became that, in light of the previous night's losses, what should the next move for the American forces be? The obvious choice was to continue to garrison the mouth of the Chippawa River and await the next move by the British. However, such was the concern over the numbers of irreplaceable casualties, as well as the potential movement of Drummond's force around the American flank, that a split in opinion developed among the senior commanders. In the end, a small majority of the officers came down in favour of making a retreat to the vicinity of Fort Erie.

General Ripley, on the other hand, went one step further and proposed evacuating the army back across the Niagara River to Buffalo. However, when General Porter and most of the other officers vehemently opposed this move (which they argued could only be interpreted as an open admission of defeat), Ripley backed down and agreed to move back to Fort Erie and then decide what should be done next. Ordering the burning of the small community of Bridgewater Mills at the Falls, Ripley went to notify General Brown of the decision to cease offensive actions by the army. Furious at this turn of events, but too badly wounded to take back command, Brown dismissed Ripley by stating, "Sir, you will do as you please,"[3] before allowing himself to be shipped out for medical attention at Buffalo.

Once the order to break camp and prepare to march was given, additional difficulties arose because many of the wagons, previously used to transport supplies and ammunition, were now filled with wounded men. Without the means to carry off these supplies, an order was issued to burn or dump into the river anything that could not be removed, to prevent it from falling into the hands of the British. Around three in the afternoon, the American army began its retreat to Fort Erie. Fortunately, the personal diaries of two officers of the Incorporated Militia who had been captured during the previous night's battle remain to document their experiences as they entered captivity for what was to be the remainder of the war.

According to Ensign Kilborne:

I was … taken with my men under guard to their encampment beyond the Chippawa bridge, put in a tent alone, sentry being posted at each end, and my men put in another tent with like guard … we were taken from our tents to the main road where we fell in with all our officers and men that had been made prisoners, viz, about fifty men and eighteen officers…. We were all marched a distance above Chippawa, and put in a large Durham boat, and, surrounded by a strong guard, rowed across the Niagara River, and landed at a place called Slusher, a short distance above the Falls. After leaving the boat we were encompassed by a strong guard, where we remained until daylight. Early in the morning, we were taken (that is, the officers only as the privates were not taken across) in charge of a new guard and marched to Buffalo, which we reached early in the evening, and were kept that night in a large unfurnished house, used as a hotel…. The next day, we were visited by the commanding officer at Buffalo. They had paroles made out, by which we promised to go to Greenbush, and report to the commanding officer there. These being signed by all, the guard was withdrawn and we were no longer close prisoners.[4]

While Ensign Warffe later recorded in his journal:

26 July … being prisoner, they marched us to Fort Slusher and from their to Bufalow, where we remained that night under guard.

27 July … got parolled at Buffalow and proceeded to Batavia in wagons.[5]

After learning that the enemy was retiring toward Fort Erie, General Drummond had the opportunity to press forward and actively harass the retreating Americans, or, at the very least, advance to secure the Chippawa crossing. However, as he was suffering from his wound (the musket ball was still lodged in his neck) and concerned about his own battlefield casualties, Drummond ordered that only Norton's Natives and detachments of light troops (including Captain Fraser's and Captain Rapelje's companies) were to advance on Chippawa. The remainder of his diminished force was to retire to Queenston to regroup and await reinforcements, which were due to arrive a few days later in the form of the DeWatteville Regiment.

Finding that the Americans had destroyed the bridge across the Chippawa, the British advance force encamped, and early the next morning crossed to the south bank of the river. Led by a party of John Norton's Native warriors, the advance guard marched past the mounds marking the graves of those who had fallen at the battle of Chippawa. Shortly thereafter, they met emissaries from the Americans who asked for an exchange of prisoners — a request that was subsequently refused.

For the three days that followed, the men of the Incorporated Militia remained in the area of the Chippawa River, where, in addition to performing duties as pickets and scouting parties, they worked alongside the regular troops in the reconstruction of the bridge. It was to Norton's warriors that the job of sustaining the pressure on the Americans fell, and they maintained an aggressive roaming presence in the area as far south as the old ferry wharf opposite Black Rock. There they seized some of the American supply boats and continued reporting on the entrenchment work happening within the American encampment at Fort Erie, until the first units of the main British force finally approached on August 1.

19

THE SIEGE OF FORT ERIE

CLOSING THE CIRCLE

After being resupplied and reinforced, General Drummond's army finally advanced toward Fort Erie on July 30. Delayed at each creek by the necessity of repairing the bridges that the Americans had destroyed as they retreated, it was not until August 1 that the British army approached Fort Erie. Occupying the ferry dock opposite Black Rock, the British advanced force engaged the American line of pickets and forced them to retreat, leaving the area under British control.

Although the men from the Incorporated Militia are listed in the surviving duty rosters as having served in the advance guard of the army during this move (the regimental roll records two sergeants killed in action and two other men wounded on this date), no additional official British or Canadian account of this action is known to exist. There is, however, the view of an American officer who faced this incursion:

At a distance of a couple of hundred yards, the fort was surrounded by a dense forest, which on the river shelf a mile or more below was bounded by some fields extending some distance back from the river. Soon after our arrival at the fort it fell to my lot … to be stationed in the edge of this wood near the river and looking into the fields with a guard of 50 men, one third of which were stationed or extended in line reaching on our left toward the next guard. In the morning early, two small detachments of the enemy were seen by several of our men to enter the wood of two different points at a distance from our station and suspecting that their intention was to cut off the guard, I sent a message to the officer of the day stationed in the fort and requesting reinforcement. He came down and told me to assemble the sentries and if they [the enemy] proved too strong, we must retreat under the cover of the fort.

Shortly after, several shots from the sentries put us on our guard, when a sudden rush was made upon us by a party of the enemy in front, upon which we fired and received a volley in return, which struck down several of the guard and just at the same moment discovering that the other party was nearly in our rear and being outnumbered at least three to one, our escape depended upon a hasty retreat to the river and up the shore which we effected with the loss of half the guard.[1]

Although the American position at Fort Erie was now cut off from its main ferry dock to Black Rock, it did not prevent the garrison from obtaining supplies and reinforcements directly from Buffalo, under the protective artillery cover from vessels of their Lake Erie squadron and the shore batteries at Black Rock.

Recognizing that if he could cut the American supply line he could avoid a long drawn-out siege, General Drummond issued orders for a cross-river sortie, with the primary goal of destroying any supplies and boats that could be found and a secondary goal of locating and freeing any British prisoners of war taken during the previous weeks. Unfortunately, the sortie's commanding officer, Lieutenant Colonel Tucker (41st Regiment) made no effort to ensure the secrecy of his preparations. As a result, the Americans soon became aware of the operation and laid a trap, which inflicted heavy casualties on the attacking British units.

Thwarted in his hopes to quickly finish off the campaign, General Drummond recognized that his only recourse was to initiate a formal siege of the fort and attempt to batter it with sufficient artillery fire to ensure a successful infantry assault. Establishing his main encampment within a dense wood about two miles away from the fort, he ordered his engineers to begin their first line of entrenchments closer to the fort and near the riverbank. But the inexperience of the engineering officers led them to select a location that was more than a thousand yards from the American defences. This was well beyond any effective range for the artillery at the general's disposal, handicapping the attackers from the outset.

As part of this initial siege work, and throughout the following days, the Glengarry Light Infantry and Incorporated Militia regiments were consistently paired up for duty as the advance guard for the army. In this role, they were assigned the task of pushing back the American pickets and then maintaining a round-the-clock picket guard of their own in defence of the lengthening siege lines.

While watching the Americans continue their feverish efforts to expand their defences, General Drummond was frustrated by the knowledge that his own forces were working on their fortifications with a woefully inadequate supply of shovels, picks, and other essential tools. Nor could he simply order up additional stocks of these items from York or Kingston, since Chauncey's fleet had arrived off the mouth of the Niagara River on August 4, trapping three British supply boats and establishing a blockade on the river-mouth forts.

During the ensuing week, General Drummond was also to find that the exposed riverbank position chosen for the artillery battery left it vulnerable to gunfire from both the American vessels offshore and the batteries at Black Rock. Consequently, he was forced to suspend building the main battery in favour of constructing additional flanking earthworks and defensive structures. By August 9, the main battery and its flanking emplacements were almost complete. By the 11th, the battery's guns were installed and set to open fire on the fort.

Throughout this period, the Americans steadily escalated their artillery fire from the fort and ships, while making increasingly aggressive sorties in an attempt to slow construction and throw the British on the defensive. These repeated American incursions led to a number of fierce confrontations in the dense woodland in front of the British positions. As a principal part of the British advanced picket guard, this meant that detachments of the Incorporated Militia regularly saw combat with the enemy at close quarters, engagements resulted in a lengthening of the regiment's casualty rolls.

By August 12, the British battery of three 24-pounder guns, a 24-pounder carronade, and an 8-inch mortar were ready to begin their artillery bombardment of the American defences. As a result of this threat, the Americans made their largest sortie yet, which, while ultimately unsuccessful, did inflict the following additional casualties upon the already reduced ranks of the Incorporated Militia: killed, Captain Edward Walker; wounded, Major James Kerby, one sergeant, and five privates.

In reporting on the action to General Prevost on August 12, General Drummond not only recounted the events, but officially mentioned the regiment in dispatches. This was no mean feat, as it represented an official military distinction and mark of approval usually reserved for units or individuals whose actions did not qualify for a medal or other honour, but warranted recognition:

> I cannot forbear of taking this occasion of expression to your Excellency my most marked approbation of the uniform exemplary good conduct of

the ... Incorporated Militia ... under Major Kerby. Of the services ... I regret to say that I have this day been deprived by two wounds, which I trust will prove slight ... [the regiment] have constantly been in close contact with the enemy's outposts and riflemen during the severe service of the last fortnight; their steadfastness and gallantry, as well as their superiority as Light troops have on every occasion been conspicuous.[2]

Acknowledging that the Incorporated Militia was now an experienced and competent combat unit that had also lost its second senior officer to battlefield action in less than a month, General Drummond needed to ensure that his appointment of a new commander would maintain the regiment's effectiveness. As the Incorporated Militia had constantly and successfully served alongside the Glengarry Light Infantry since it had arrived on the Niagara frontier, it was probably no great surprise when Captain James FitzGibbon of the Glengarry Light Infantry, the commander of the Beaver Dams victory, was appointed to take over the role of commanding officer until further notice.

Following the repulse of the American sortie on August 12, and secure behind their picket screen, the British Artillery sought to create a breach in the American fortifications at Fort Erie that could then be assaulted by the infantry. But, at a range of over a thousand yards, the firing only served to compact the earth defences into a denser mass, while the solid stonework masonry of the original fort simply caused the cannonballs to bounce off. Nor could the single gun facing the lake adequately deal with the three American vessels that could move in at will and attack the British positions. Without the option of moving his battery, General Drummond approved a daring nighttime sortie to capture or destroy the vessels while they were at anchor.

Since his assault force was comprised of some seventy sailors and marines and six large bateaux, General Drummond recognized that any attempt to make the attack from the mouth of the Niagara River would undoubtedly alert the enemy at the fort, as well as the nearby vessels. Instead, he decided to make the move from another direction entirely. Because of their intimate knowledge of the immediate area, a detachment of the Incorporated Militia under Captain Rapelje was given an immediate and urgent assignment to march downriver to Frenchman's Creek and haul the required six bateaux from the water. They were then expected to drag the cumbersome and heavy vessels, mounted on sleds, through eight miles of dense forest and swampland before finally launching the boats into Lake Erie, well beyond the sight of the Americans. Furthermore, this task was to be done before dawn the following day!

After an arduous and difficult passage, the boats and their crews were safely delivered to the assigned beach on the lake around midnight. The sailors and marines climbed aboard, leaving the men of the militia to march back to camp for what most hoped would be an uninterrupted rest.

Under cover of darkness, the boats were quietly rowed down the lake and, after a brief fight, the British force successfully captured two of the three American vessels. These prizes (the *Somers* and the *Ohio*) were then sailed into the Niagara River and moored at the British depot on the Chippawa River. For their part in this action, Captain Rapelje and twenty men were later officially listed as being entitled to a portion of the prize money granted to the participants in the capture.

Encouraged by this display of daring, General Drummond looked for a similar effort from his ground troops and ordered a night assault on the fort as soon as the artillery had done sufficient damage to the American defences. Unfortunately, he badly underestimated what level of damage would be required to ensure a successful assault or how long it would take to achieve this effect with the guns at his disposal. After only two days of active firing, he ignored the cautionary advice of his more experienced subordinates for a longer preparatory fire, and scheduled the assault for the night of August 14–15.

Why he made this decision to attack in the face of the obvious ineffectiveness of the artillery bombardment is debatable, but perhaps one reason may be attributed to his continued difficulty of maintaining his supply lines and feeding his men. This problem was principally the result of American warships continuing to control the Lake Ontario shipping lanes and thus effectively throttling Drummond's supply lines. This left the general in a contradictory position. On the one hand, he had a dominant control of the entire Niagara Peninsula while his enemy's army was firmly on the defensive and bottled up in a narrow enclave. On the other hand, because of Chauncey's flotilla, he was in such desperate straits as to stockpiles of food and ammunition that he had to consider retreating and abandoning the siege. In a strongly worded letter to General Prevost, dated August 14, General Drummond clarified his difficulties:

The naval ascendancy possessed by the enemy on Lake Ontario enables him to perform in two days what our troops going from Kingston to reinforce the Right Division require from sixteen to twenty of severe marching to accomplish. Their men arrive fresh, whilst ours are fatigued and with an exhausted equipment. The route from Kingston to the Niagara frontier exceeds two hundred and fifty miles and passes in several places through a tract of country impracticable for the conveyance of extensive supplies.[3]

He also hinted that his decision to make an immediate attack on the fort would solve his supply difficulties once the enemy was routed and their supplies captured: "By our exertions, the Right Division will be placed beyond the apprehension of any material want before the period fixed by Sir James Yeo for taking to the lake with his augmented fleet

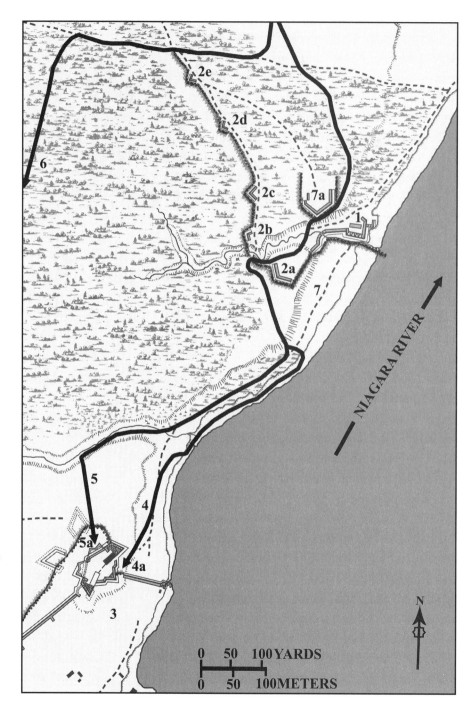

Fort Erie and the British Siege Lines, August 15–16, 1814.

1. British Artillery Battery No. 1 (1)
2. British picket line emplacements. (2a, 2b, 2c, 2d, 2e)
3. The American encampment at Fort Erie (3)
4. The British left column, (4) attacks the line between the fort and the Douglass Battery (4a)
5. The British Centre column (5) attacks the northwest face of the fort (5a)
6. The British right column (6), marches around the American positions during the course of the day to attack Snake Hill
7. The British reserve, (7, 7a) including the Incorporated Militia

and until [then] … will be used to prevent the enemy from making a serious impression on the Upper Province by defeating it."[4]

Because both the Glengarry Light Infantry and Incorporated Militia had seen almost continuous active service on the front lines for nearly two weeks, General Drummond drew up his plan of assault, leaving both regiments in reserve. Why he chose to do this is not documented, but it is possible that as a regular army officer, and with the examples of the campaign sieges and assaults in the Spanish Peninsula fresh in his mind, he might well have decided that the two units, skilled as they were for light infantry work in the woods, were less suitable for a direct assault on a defensive fortification. Whatever the reason, after having served as pickets during a day of steady rain, the men of the Incorporated Militia took up their night's assigned positions at the various picket posts along the perimeter of the British siege lines. From here they watched as the various columns of troops marched out from camp to their assault positions. This was a piece of fortune that some, at that moment, might have perceived as depriving them of the final laurels of victory; in fact, it probably saved their lives.

A Deadly Assault

Having decided to assault Fort Erie, General Drummond hoped to repeat his previous success of capturing Fort Niagara by again choosing to attack at night. However, he failed to consider the fact that conditions for this attack were far different from those he had previously faced. First and foremost, the attack was fully expected by the American garrison. Their defences were well-manned, with pickets on the alert during a warm summer's night instead of huddling indoors during the bitter cold of a December winter. Second, Drummond's plan required three separate columns (designated the right, centre and left columns) to make coordinated attacks from three separate directions, in the middle of the night, with no communication between the columns and without artillery support or covering fire. Third, while his advance on Fort Niagara had been made with the soldiers' muskets unloaded, he now ordered the complete removal of the flints from the muskets, thus making them impossible to fire until those flints were replaced.

A subsequent objection from several officers persuaded Drummond to rescind this last requirement for the two columns approaching the fort from the north. But the order for the column to attack Snake Hill was kept, a decision that had fatal consequences once the attack began. In hindsight, the cumulative effect of these difficulties and handicaps has been used to claim that the assault was doomed before it had even begun. Nevertheless, the determined efforts of the troops undertaking the assault were such that, despite horrendous losses, they nearly carried it off.

As the British right column, assigned to attack the Snake Hill defences, approached its target, the American pickets fired. Alerted to the presence of the enemy by this firing, the main line of troops at Snake Hill and no less than six artillery pieces opened up on the British column with a devastating fire at point-blank range. Caught in a lethal crossfire and unable to return fire until they had refitted their flints, the attackers continued to press forward and threw up their ladders, only to find that they were too short to reach the enemy parapet from the outside of the ditch.

Nevertheless, for over fifteen minutes the British troops attempted to break through the American line by using only bayonets, hatchets, and bare hands, until they were eventually forced back into the darkness. They then attempted to outflank the defences and enter the American camp by wading up to their chests in the strong current and cold water of Lake Erie. However, a reserve of American troops had been stationed at this location to prevent just such an occurrence and most of the men in the water were slaughtered or captured before they could reach

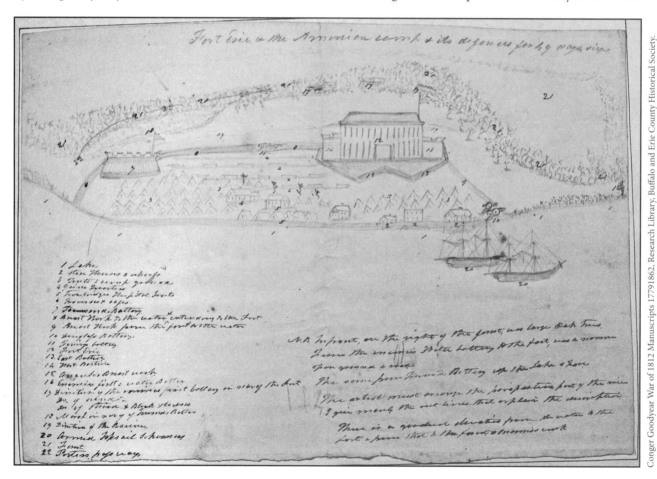

This black and white pencil and ink sketch (artist unknown) is a contemporary view of the American positions at Fort Erie during the siege. Mss. BOO-1 A.

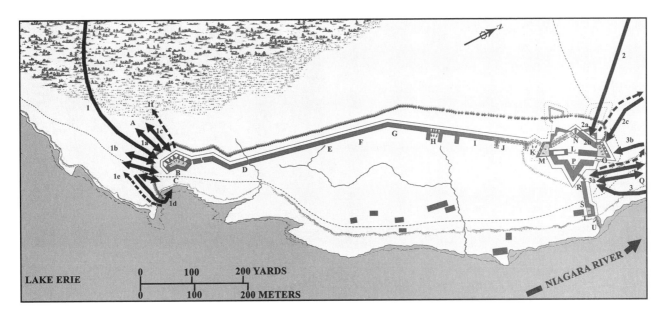

The British Assault and American Positions Around Fort Erie, August 15–16, 1814.

A. Snake Hill picket (20 other ranks)
B. Snake Hill Battery, 6 x 6-pounders, (100)
C. Twenty-first Infantry (475)
D. Seventeenth/Nineteenth Infantry (64)
E. Twenty-third Infantry (350)
F. First/Fourth Rifle Regiment (350)
G. New York State/Pennsylvania State militias (500)
H. Biddle's Battery, 2 x 12-pounders, 1 x Howitzer (40)
I. Eleventh Infantry (250)
J. Twenty-second Infantry (275)
K. Fontaine's Battery, 2 x 6-pounders (30)

L. Nineteenth Infantry (130)
M. Southeast bastion, 1 x 18-pounder, 1 x 12-pounder (25)
N. Western redan gun, 1 x 18-pounder (10)
O. Northeast bastion, 2 x 12-pounders, 1 x 24-pounder, 1 x 6-pounder, (30)
P. Eastern Ravalin gun, 1 x 12-pounder (10)
Q. Douglas Battery picket (20)
R. Ninth Infantry (175)
S. New York State/Pennsylvania State militias (120)
T. Douglas Battery, 1 x 18-pounder, 1 x 6-pounder, (50)
U. New York State Militia Dragoons (100)

1. The right column's attack on Snake Hill. The right column (1) is detected by the American Pickets (A). Charging forward, the initial assault fails and is repulsed. Repeated additional assaults are made at additional points (1a, 1b, 1c,) but are also repulsed, with heavy losses. The British attempt to outflank the defences by wading into the lake (1d) but are slaughtered by the American troops stationed on the shore (C) The attack collapses and the survivors withdraw in disorder (1e, 1f).

2. The centre column's attack on the fort's northwest picket line. The centre column (2) attacks the northwest picket line and breaks through (2a), only to find the ditch and earthwork wall hidden behind it, and the wall lined with American troops (2b). Caught in a "killing-zone," and after repeated failed assaults, the centre column moves left and joins in the assault on the demi-bastion (2c).

3. The left column's attack on the Douglas Battery line. The left column (3) is detected by the American picket (Q) and makes a series of failed assaults on the abbatis gap (3a) in the Douglas line of defences. Repulsed at this point, most of the left column move right to attack the demi-bastion (3b).

dry ground. Overall, no less than five successive assaults were made, but the solid line of entrenchments and barricades, backed by the continuous fire of untouched infantry and artillery, eventually proved too much for the attackers. Retreating in confusion and disorder, the survivors blundered into the remainder of the formations at the rear of the column, precipitating a cascade retreat by the entire body toward the woods. The British assault on this flank had now collapsed before the other attacks had even begun. As a result, instead of being held in place, the Americans were able to reinforce their units at the other end of the fort once the other British columns made their assaults.

On the other side of the American positions, the British left column approached a now fully alerted line of defences that ran from the fort to the lake, and was similarly blasted at short range by artillery and musket fire. Despite making several charges, the column also failed to breach the American lines. Unable to penetrate the enemy defences at the location originally planned, part of the troops spread out and commenced a firefight with the Americans to hold them in place, while others moved to their right. Here, they met up with the centre column, which had also suffered heavy casualties in a repeated series of failed attempts to storm their assigned position before moving to their left. Together, the combined force pressed forward and succeeded in reaching the walls of the fort's northern demi-bastion. Hacking apart the abattis (a field fortification) barricade and wooden palisades in the ditch, the British troops clambered up scaling ladders and cut their way into the demi-bastion.

The ditch and northern demi-bastion of Fort Erie as it looks today, viewed from the perspective of the attacking British centre column.

In response, a portion of American defenders blockaded themselves in the fort's northern "Mess House" and began firing down from the building's upper windows into the courtyard and parts of the bastion they overlooked. The remaining troops, reinforced from regiments stationed outside the fort and Snake Hill, established a strong line of fire across the fort's small interior courtyard. Despite repeated attempts and charges into this confined area, the British were unable to break through the American cordon, while the Americans equally failed to evict their enemy.

According to at least one report, this stalemate of attack and counterattack, across a space of only twenty yards, lasted for up to an hour. That is, until an ammunition magazine, located under the artillery platform in the demi-bastion, exploded. The resulting blast created a massive detonation and fireball that hurled masonry, rocks, planking, cannons, and bodies into the air. The explosion's concussion wave, concentrated by the surrounding structures, knocked everyone off their feet, both inside the fort and in the ditch outside. Deafened by the explosion and with heads reeling from the concussion, the surviving British attackers in the ditch were bombarded with the airborne debris, which caused more casualties and sealed the fate of the attack.

The interior courtyard of Fort Erie today, looking from the western-gun platform toward the northern demi-bastion. Most of the fighting inside the fort took place within this small area.

Over four hundred casualties were inflicted on the exposed British troops while the fort's structure protected most of the Americans from the deadly blast. In fact, only one American soldier is officially recorded as having been directly killed by debris from the explosion. Although how many, in the confined space of the courtyard and mess house, suffered blast concussions, sonic damage to their hearing, or other invisible internal injuries, was never documented.

Seeing his troops retreating in confusion, and fearing an immediate counterattack from the Americans, General Drummond instructed the few surviving officers to re-form any rank and file they could, without regard to regimental affiliation, while the reserve were moved forward to cover the retreat.

From the perspective of the men of the Incorporated Militia, the distant flashes and periodic concussions of battle would have signalled action taking place, but not any indication of how the attack was progressing. However, the longer it continued, the less optimistic the prospects of an easy victory became. Once the massive explosion of the magazine occurred, however, the blast's concussion would have been felt as a strong tremor under their feet and the fireball would have illuminated the sky.

Ordered forward to cover the subsequent retreat, the men of the Incorporated Militia and Glengarries passed through a steady stream of dazed, battered, burned, and bloodied British survivors. The Canadian regiments formed a strong light infantry screen and deterred the Americans from making an immediate counterattack, thus allowing the remnants of the regiments that had made up the two attacking columns targeting the fort to retreat unmolested. Due to the darkness and the uncertainty of American intentions, however, little could be done to search the zone of explosion debris for injured survivors, although the cries of the wounded could clearly be heard. Eventually, ordered to retire by companies, the screen moved back, collecting any survivors that they came across and assisting them back to the British lines.

STALEMATE

At daybreak, under a pall of rain, the carnage of the night was revealed. At the fort, the Americans immediately began repairing the destroyed defences to counter the possibility of a follow-up attack by the British. However, the British were in no state to make any kind of offensive and were fully occupied in simply recovering as many of their scattered troops as possible. Looking to replace his severe losses, General Drummond sent off urgent calls for reinforcements to be forwarded from the forts at the other end of the peninsula, Burlington Heights, and York.

Seeking to regain the initiative, Drummond openly recognized the failure of the British artillery batteries to be effective because of their extreme distance from the fort. To correct this error, he ordered his troops to begin construction of both an extension of the British siege lines toward the enemy and a new battery at half the existing distance from the enemy's defences. Once again, he called upon the experienced and, at this point still relatively intact, regiments of the Glengarries and Incorporated Militia to provide picket screens and covering patrols against a renewed series of marauding American sorties.

At a wider logistical level, the general was also faced with the fact that his gambit to ease his supply problems had failed. He knew that unless he received some immediate assistance and supplies from Sir James Yeo's fleet, his army would be starving by the end of the month. Yeo's navy, however, remained firmly docked at Kingston, prompting Drummond to appeal to Prevost on August 18:

I trust Your Excellency will impress on the Commodore's mind that the Right Division, after its misfortune on the 15th inst. Depends almost entirely on his prompt and vigorous exertions for its relief, nay perhaps even for its safety. How widely different the glorious prospects which were in view on the day preceding that deplorable catastrophe! I have directed Mr. Couche at all risques to forward to York some flour in bateaux, but still its safe arrival cannot be calculated upon with certainty.[5]

On August 27, Quartermaster General Robinson in Montreal noted the acuteness of these problems within the Right Division in his own report to Sir George Prevost:

Deputy Commissary General Couche has endeavoured by every means to forward supplies to the head of Lake Ontario … but as the exertions of the enemy have been more successful than ours in building ships sufficient to command the navigation of the lake, that resource is for the moment, cut off and only bateaux can be employed…. This feeble means of transport will never effect the forming of a sufficient depot at York, Burlington Heights and Niagara and unless the Commissariat can be aided to a great extent by the Royal Navy, the most disastrous consequences must ensue; which no efforts or arrangements of mine can avert.... Your Excellency is aware that the road between Kingston and Niagara is not practicable for loaded wagons; therefore land carriage is out of the question and the most ample assistance from the Royal Navy will be imperiously demanded as the only means of supporting the Right Division of the Army.[6]

Even Prevost, writing the same day to Lord Bathurst in England, stressed the seriousness of the issue:

The vacillating communications I have received from Sir James Yeo ... all hopes of seeing our squadron on Lake Ontario before the first week in October have vanished. The most pressing and important service to be performed by the Commodore ... is the conveyance of fresh troops, with a large proportion of provisions and supplies of every description to York and the Niagara frontier, before the navigation closes , and to bring from those places to Kingston the exhausted Corps, the disabled and the sick who can endure transport. The resources of the upper Province being exhausted, a large supply of provisions of every nature must be thrown into it before the navigation of the St. Lawrence and Lake Ontario becomes impracticable.[7]

In the British camp, the men of the Incorporated Militia were in exactly the same predicament as those in every other regiment, and suffered the shortages of food accordingly. However, they also had one additional concern that the other units did not — their families at York. Since the ration allotment to families had been halved on July 13, these dependents had been surviving on near-starvation allotments of food. Without the essential means of sustaining themselves, the incidences of sickness involving the near 150 women and children had risen alarmingly. Having received letters and messages of ever-increasing distress from their loved ones, the men became increasingly concerned, and, in a few cases, individuals went AWOL in an attempt to return to York to care for their families. Although forced to convene courts martial for the recaptured offenders, the regimental commander, Lieutenant Colonel FitzGibbon, may well have been sympathetic to the men's plight. Nonetheless, he and his panel of officers imposed sentences of imprisonment for up to four months in the cells at Fort Niagara, thus placing the Niagara River as a significant physical barrier between the men and their families to prevent them from reoffending.

In an attempt to respond to this particularly difficult situation, FitzGibbon sent a strong representation to General Drummond to make the case for some relief of the dire needs of the regiment's families. Considering the grave state of affairs regarding supplies for the army as a whole, it would not have been unreasonable to see this plea rejected. However, a week later, on August 25, Lieutenant Colonel Pearson received an extraordinary letter from Lieutenant Colonel Harvey, deputy adjutant general to General Drummond. The terms of this communication, while addressing the issue at hand, also provide clear evidence that the undocumented services performed by the officers and men of this colonial militia regiment during the previous weeks of campaigning, were of such a high degree as to impress a general of the regular British army and cause him to change his mind on a vital issue affecting his whole command:

Sir,

In consequence of the exemplary good conduct of the soldiers of the Incorporated Militia and the particular circumstances in which the wives and children are placed, the Lieutenant General commanding and President had been pleased to rescind the regulation which the state of the public stores had induced his Honor to make regarding their rations, and directions have accordingly been sent to the Commissariat Department at York to issue the usual rations to the families of the Incorporated Militia till further orders. In communicating this indulgence to the men of the Incorporated Militia, Lieutenant General Drummond requests that the motives which have influenced him in granting it may be fully explained to them, and he cannot doubt of its producing a due effect.[8]

With this assurance in hand, the attention of the regiment once again focused on the war effort and the continuation of the siege at Fort Erie. Active picket duties during the construction of the second battery had caused additional casualties, and by the time the monthly roll call was submitted on August 24, a significant number of men were listed as being sick or wounded and recovering at Fort George. These included: one major, one lieutenant, three ensigns, one sergeant major, five sergeants, and seventy rank and file.[9] No details about the exact date of each man's injury are given and thus the list could represent actions from August 2 onward. However, as a significant number of these men were from the same company (Captain Fraser's No.7), it is not unreasonable to infer the action of the 12th as the likely date for at least some of these casualties.

Life in the camp now took on a repetitive form as the round of picket duties and fatigues to work upon the extended defences continued. Little detail exists in the official records to document this period. However, in his postwar recollections, the surgeon, William "Tiger" Dunlop, referred to his life in the "camp" as well as making comparisons between the regular British soldiers, the Incorporated Militia, and the troops of the "foreign" DeWatteville regiment:

The leaguer before Fort Erie had always been called the "Camp" and I certainly expected that, like other camps, it would have been provided with tents; but in this I was mistaken. It was rather a bivouac than a camp, the troops sheltering themselves under some branches of trees that only collected the scattered drops of rain and sent them down in a stream on the heads of the inhabitants, and as it rained incessantly for two months, neither clothes nor bedding could be kept dry.... I may here remark what has always struck me as a great deficiency in the military education of the soldiers of the British Army — they are too much taken care of by their officers, and never taught to take care of themselves.... The result ... is that you make men mere children. When the soldier leaves his clean comfortable barracks in England and is put into the field, where he has few or none of the accommodations he had at home, he is utterly helpless when a new state of things arises.... All this was most fully illustrated before Fort Erie. The line might nearly as well have slept in the open air. The Incorporated Militia, on the contrary, erected shanties, far superior, in warmth, tightness and comfort, to any canvas tent. The DeWatteville's regiment ... though they ... could not equal the Canadian Militia in woodcraft, greatly exceeded them in gastronomic lore; and thus, while our Regular fellows had no better shift than to frizzle their rations of salt provisions on the ends of their ramrods, these being practical botanists sent out one soldier from each mess, who gathered a haversack full of wild pot herbs, with which and a little flour their ration was converted into a capital kettle of soup.[10]

By the end of August, the No. 2 Battery was completed and the thick belt of trees that had been left standing in front of the position to provide protection for the workers was felled. However, once the trees were cleared, it was realized that the position had been constructed behind a low rise in the ground that was not noticeable while the trees were still standing.

Unfortunately, the higher ground in front of the battery blocked any direct firing on the fort! Frustrated at the ineptitude shown by his engineering "experts" in creating a worthless battery position, Drummond's only solution was to start all over again and construct a third battery, farther to the right of the previous two and within five hundred yards of the fort. Carefully sited to ensure it could be used once completed, this new work represented a serious threat to the Americans, since it would fire directly into their main encampment at lethally close range. Between September 4 and September 6, the men of the Incorporated Militia once again found themselves on the front line, this time acting as pickets and bearing the brunt of American sorties and attempts to disrupt the ongoing construction. Once the battery was completed, several pieces of artillery from batteries 1 and 2 were laboriously transferred, but no firing began — the result of General Drummond having to cope with a number of severe issues. His concerns included a severe shortage of artillery ammunition and powder; continued food shortages; reports that American troops were massing at Buffalo, Fort Schlosser, and Lewiston, and threatening Drummond's supply lines at Chippawa and Queenston; and unusually cold temperatures and incessant rainstorms that had swept the region during the previous month and had turned the ground into a quagmire of semi-frozen mud.

So severe had this latter situation become that one contemporary witness compared the British encampment to a virtual lake, dotted with islands made up of sodden tents and leaky brushwood huts. Fires were almost impossible to keep going, preventing the troops from warming themselves, drying out their clothes and bedding, or properly cooking what little food had being issued. Not surprisingly, the incidence of sickness increased dramatically as the bad weather continued. However, General Drummond knew that abandoning the siege and retiring on the Chippawa or the river-mouth forts would expose his force to attack while on the march over roads reduced to deep quagmires of mud. As well, the prevailing ground conditions would make the movement of the heavy artillery pieces by the few available draft animals far more difficult. After weighing these factors against the threat of attack, Drummond decided to maintain his main position opposite Fort Erie for a short while longer.

Within Fort Erie, General Brown decided to eliminate the threat of the new battery by making an all-out sortie against the British lines. Because he knew the British were using a three-division system of rotation for the troops being stationed at the front line (i.e. one brigade on duty, a second in reserve at the camp nearly two miles to the rear, and the third off-duty and engaged in various duties and fatigues), Brown believed he could overwhelm the enemy position if his force could approach undetected, attack and destroy the batteries and guns, then withdraw before the British reinforcements could arrive.

To ensure a successful mission, Brown kept his plan secret from most of his senior officers until the night before the offensive. He also made use of diversions to cover his main attack by leaking information that he was planning an assault on the British camp from Black Rock. To support this, he ordered the militia stationed there to parade openly along the riverbank, where they could be seen and reported on prior to the actual event. Once the attack began, if the British reacted by sending their reserves forward and abandoning their camp, the militias were then to seize the opportunity to cross the river and attack the British rear.

During the next two days (September 15–16), General Brown dramatically increased the rate of firing from his own batteries. Under the cover of this bombardment and the ongoing rainstorms, work parties were sent out into the dense woods to cut a series of pathways from the fort to positions flanking the British lines. The intent was to provide a hidden route to allow the attack to be made with the maximum of surprise. What Brown did not know was that General Drummond had finally given the order for lifting the siege and withdrawing the army to Chippawa. During the night of September 16–17, several of the British guns were withdrawn from their positions, while the rest were scheduled for removal the following day, but had not been attended to when the American attack took place.

Within the British encampment, the Incorporated Militia had continued to perform their rotation of picket duty and fatigues as the weather deteriorated and life became increasingly miserable in the mud and rain. Despite this, when on September 10 the official period of attached duties for the men from the embodied militias expired, only about one-third chose to exercise their option to quit the corps, while the remainder extended their term for an additional two months. As well, Lieutenant Humberstone and his small unit of former parolees had finally rejoined the

Muster Rolls, Incorporated Militia, September 1814[11]	
Fort Erie: (Fit)	**Fort George: (Sick and Wounded)**
3 Staff	
2 Captains	1 Major
5 Lieutenants	1 Lieutenant
4 Ensigns	3 Ensigns
14 Sergeants	5 Sergeants
10 Drummers	70 Rank and File
173 Rank and File	
	York: (Garrison
Fort Erie:	**Detachment, Sick and**
(Sick and Wounded)	**Wounded)**
1 Captain	2 Captains
1 Ensign	5 Lieutenants
2 Sergeants	1 Sergeant
27 Rank and File	16 Rank and File

regiment. Despite being relatively few in number, these men were immediately put into service, since by this time the regimental strength had been severely diminished by the combination of casualties and illness.

Under these circumstances, the regiments probably welcomed the news that the army was about to break camp and retire to the Chippawa River. Unfortunately, the subsequent American surprise attack was to change the mood considerably.

According to the rotation of regiments, the Incorporated Militia should have been at the front line on September 16, during the period when the American work parties were in the process of cutting down trees and clearing dense bush around the British right flank to create the pathway described above. As a result, they would have been only a matter of a hundred yards or less away from any properly placed picket posts and should have been clearly audible. However, instead of being assigned the duty they had almost continuously performed throughout the course of the siege, the men of the Incorporated Militia had now been assigned the menial task of collecting and removing stocks of ammunition and other supplies from the blockhouses and batteries in preparation for their transportation to Chippawa. Instead, these picket duties had been assigned to detachments of regular troops.

As had been the case for most of the previous weeks, the weather was heavily overcast, cold, blustery, and rainy, effectively deadening sounds made by the American working parties. However, there are also later reports of sentries being found spending more time sheltering from the weather than attending to their duty on this day. There is no evidence to say that the course of subsequent events might have changed had the men of the Incorporated Militia been given that vital duty on September 16, but given their recognized superiority as woodsmen, it may have made all the difference.

The next day (September 17) the regiment was on the part of the rotation that saw them stationed within the encampment and acting as camp guard. Reports of American troop movements on the other side of the Niagara River at Black Rock had caused a heightened state of alert to be issued for the riverside pickets, but otherwise the preparations for the abandonment of the Erie encampment continued — until the sounds of firing erupted from the direction of the front lines.

SORTIE

Attacking in two separate columns, the first American force swept around the right flank of the British line and rushed the British No. 3 Battery position from the rear. According to General Brown's later official account, this initial attack was portrayed as being totally overwhelming and virtually without loss on the part of the Americans. However, reports subsequently written by his subordinates, General Porter and Colonel Miller, indicate that the assault was far from being an instant success. By their accounts, the British pickets fired on the flanking column of Americans, alerting the line and commencing a defence that only got stronger as time passed. As a result, the second American column attacked an alerted enemy, still in possession of its defences.

Nevertheless, the British line was breached and after heavy hand-to-hand combat, the Americans succeeded in capturing Batteries 2 and 3 and set about destroying everything they could. According to Brown's stated goals, the attack had achieved its prime objectives and could have been concluded without the attackers having suffered any significant losses. Instead, the Americans pushed their luck too far by pressing on toward Battery No.1, only to face fierce opposition from the troops manning the battery as they looked for reinforcements to come to their aid.

In the British camp, General Drummond's two subordinate brigade commanders had immediately reacted to the sounds of firing by calling out the brigade being held in reserve (1st Brigade), as well as part of the 3rd Brigade and several parties of Natives.

General DeWatteville then led his force forward at a run, while General Richard Stovin remained at the camp with the remainder of the 3rd Brigade, including the Incorporated Militia, to maintain a watch on the riverbank in case the supposed attack from Black Rock materialized. Once they reached the crossroads that connected the main road from the camp to the various battery positions, the British relief column divided, with General Drummond leading one force down the path leading to Battery No. 3, while General DeWatteville led the other toward Battery No.1.

Arriving at the field, DeWatteville saw that the Americans had already captured most of the line of entrenchments and batteries and that any delay in forming his troops would be fatal. Without waiting to form his men from a column into a line-of-battle, he led his troops forward in a bayonet charge. After severe hand-to-hand combat, the Americans at Battery No.1 began to give ground and retired toward Battery No. 2.

At the other end of the British positions, Drummond's column reached Battery No. 3 and likewise made an immediate attack, evicting the Americans from the battery. The British then began firing upon the Americans milling about in the area between the two batteries. Caught between two sets of fire, the American assault now became a retreat that became more hectic and disorganized as time passed. Seeking to press his advantage, General Drummond sent back orders that unless the American threat from the Black Rock was proving a significant danger, General Stovin should bring the remainder of the troops at the British camp as quickly as possible to assist in the routing of the retreating enemy.

Upon receiving these orders, and considering the threat as having passed, General Stovin withdrew all but some small detachments of the Incorporated Militia and moved toward the front lines with all speed. However, they failed to arrive before the American force had retreated beyond the British entrenchments.

In the aftermath of this major engagement that had seen most of the other British regiments suffer serious losses, the Incorporated Militia remained relatively intact. As a result, General Drummond assigned them the duties of re-establishing the picket lines, searching for and collecting wounded casualties of both armies, ferreting out any remaining American stragglers, and escorting prisoners to the rear.

In reviewing the previous day's events, it is possible that the detachment that had been posted at the riverbank felt they had missed out on the "action." In fact, their contribution was not as negligible as they might have supposed, for in his subsequent postwar recollections, surgeon Dunlop referred to this aspect of the day's action:

> The party [of American Militia] sent down the right bank of the Niagara to take us in the rear, on arriving at the place where it was determined they should cross, saw a body of troops … on the bank, and supposing their plan was betrayed, desisted from the attempt … had even a small force landed, they must have taken our baggage, ammunition and field guns

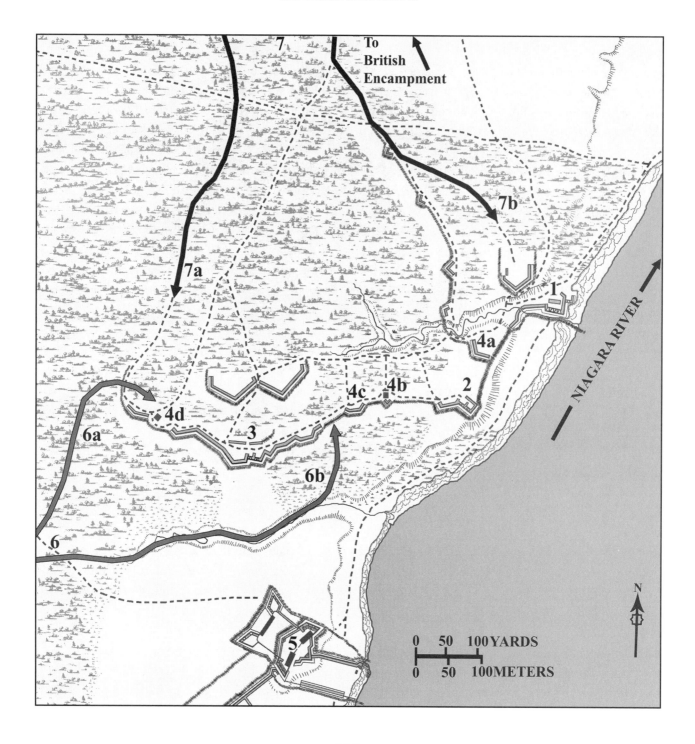

To
British
Encampment

7

7b

7a

1

4a

NIAGARA RIVER

4c 4b

2

6a

4d

3

6b

6

5

N

| 0 | 50 | 100 | YARDS |

| 0 | 50 | 100 | METERS |

The British Siege Lines and Fort Erie Defences at the Time of the American Sortie, September 17, 1814.

1. British Artillery Battery No. 1 (1)
2. British Artillery Battery No. 2 (2)
3. British Artillery Battery No. 3 (3)
4. British picket line emplacements and blockhouses (4a, 4b, 4c, 4d)
5. Fort Erie (5)
6. The American columns advance under the cover of rainstorms (6) and then divide to attack the British line. The "left" column by swinging around the end of the British line to attack the No. 3 Battery (6a), the "right" column by infiltrating the woods between the No. 3 Battery (3) and the picket posts (4c).
7. The British forces at their encampment advance to make a counter attack (7). After dividing his force, General Drummond leads one column (7a) toward the No. 3 Battery, while General DeWatteville leads the other (7b) toward Battery No.1.

(for the camp was deserted except by the few guards that were mounted more for show than use) and had they attacked us in rear, must have thrown us into inextricable confusion.[12]

The memorial cairn to the fallen of the siege of Fort Erie is located immediately outside the walls of the northern demi-bastion of Fort Erie, on the spot where the massive explosion of the night of August 15–16, 1814, inflicted such heavy casualties on the attacking British columns.

At the end of the day, the British had regained possession of the entire line of the entrenchments, but the casualties resulting from the action had been extremely heavy, especially in terms of those regiments involved in the initial American assault. In addition, the damage wrought by the Americans had rendered the No. 2 and No. 3 Batteries unusable and the cannon within inoperative. But these points were glossed over in Drummond's report in favour of emphasizing his army's poor living conditions and supply situation.

Having already decided to retire his force to the Chippawa, General Drummond was now, ironically, forced to remain at Erie until sufficient repairs had been made to the artillery carriages to allow them to be removed along with the small remaining stocks of ammunition and food. This was completed by September 20, and the following day Drummond issued orders for the evacuation of the camp, but without destroying their encampment or otherwise alerting the Americans.

Once again, the Incorporated Militia was assigned the duty of providing the picket guard while the entrenchments were cleared and the retreat from Fort Erie begun. The last unit to leave the siege lines, the regiment was to suffer one final casualty, as later recorded by its commanding officer, James FitzGibbon:

I certify that on the 21st Sept. 1814, when the piquets of the Right Division of the Army were returning from the batteries before Fort Erie, about nine o'clock in the evening, they were fired upon by one of our piquets in reserve, who mistook them for the enemy — A soldier of the Incorporated Militia named John McGrath was in consequence, wounded in the thigh, of which wound he died in a few days after. I was near him when the unfortunate accident happened and saw him carried off.[13]

Marching back toward the Chippawa River under yet another downpour of chilling rain, the Incorporated Militia was about to enter into its final phase of service on the Niagara frontier in 1814.

20

STRENGTHENING THE CHIPPAWA LINE

As the regiment marched north, away from Fort Erie and toward their new assigned positions at the Chippawa River defensive lines, they followed the road that ran along the bank of the Niagara River. In doing so, they were exposed to the visible consequences of the effects of two years of war upon this previously peaceful and productive region. Virtually all of the buildings they passed had either been gutted by fire or abandoned and most of the fields had reverted to weeds. Only a few farmsteads remained where settlers were attempting to grow crops to feed themselves and to provide a cash crop, if sold to the army commissariat.

These families were now caught up in the British retreat at the time when what little had grown could be harvested. Ordered to retreat with the army, they desperately sought to salvage something before being forced out of their homes. Since many of these people were the neighbours of the men from the Niagara companies, their plight was particularly felt by the men in the regiment. Many of the men of the rear-guard, without any senior commanders nearby and with no sign of an American pursuit, broke ranks, under the "blind eye" of their officers, to assist the farmers to harvest the ripe grain. After a few hours' labour, they rejoined the retreat.

Once General Drummond had the main portion of the army secure on the north bank of the Chippawa River, he called a halt to the retreat. He then established his advanced forces in a series of positions that extended from Frenchman's Creek back to the Chippawa River. This defensive formation had two

---

DISPOSITION OF BRITISH TROOPS,
NIAGARA FRONTIER, SEPTEMBER 23, 1814[1]

Frenchman's Creek (Advance): 19th Light Dragoons

Palmer's: Glengarry Light Infantry, Incorporated Militia and Western Natives, "with one company [Glengarry Light Infantry] advanced to Andrew Miller's to support the cavalry."

Black Creek: 97th Regiment, 2 x 6-pounder guns

Street's Grove: 1st (Royal Scots) Regiment, 1 x 6-pounder gun, Rocket Troop, Royal Marine Artillery (detachment)

Advance Headquarters (Major General DeWatteville) "at Gander's, 1 mile below Black Creek."

Chippewa: 6th Regiment, 2 x 24-pounder guns, 1 x 6-pounder gun, 1 x howitzer

Lundy's Lane to Queenston: 82nd, 89th, 104th Regiment (Flank Companies)

Fort George, Fort Mississauga, Fort Niagara: 8th (King's), 41st, DeWatteville Regiment

Burlington Heights: 103rd Regiment

Main Headquarters (Lieutenant General Drummond): "at Forsyth's, near the Falls."

---

main advantages. First, if the Americans advanced and attacked, they would be detected much earlier by the leading pickets at Frenchman's Creek, thus allowing additional time for the warning to arrive at Chippawa. Second, as each successive defensive post engaged the enemy and then retired, the British defensive force would grow and be better able to slow down the enemy's rate of advance until the main body of troop concentrations at Chippawa could be brought into action. This redeployment also had the advantage of allowing Drummond to place forces at the vulnerable river crossing points between Queenston and Lake Ontario; he had received reports indicating that General George Izard was advancing on the frontier from Sackets Harbor with Chauncey's fleet in support.

On September 22, American scouts found the British siege lines at Fort Erie deserted. Looking to re-establish contact with the enemy, they moved north in a slow and cautious advance until they located the British rearguard at Frenchman's Creek. Curiously, although the British were now retreating, General Brown made no effort to initiate a pursuit or to attack the British positions. Instead, he decided to wait for the arrival of General Izard from Sackets Harbor with more than 4,000 additional troops before commencing a joint operation that would pin the British between the two American armies.

Meanwhile, although his forces were relatively well-positioned, General Drummond was deeply concerned about the continued viability of maintaining his army on the frontier. Foremost among his worries was his almost completely exhausted local stockpiles of food. Nor was there any sign of any relief supplies coming from Kingston aboard Commodore Yeo's squadron. This was despite having applied every pressure himself, backed by the efforts of Sir George Prevost, who had travelled up from Montreal to Kingston to see Yeo and personally elicit his co-operation. With Yeo remaining firm in his refusal to challenge the blockade of the Americans, General Drummond was left with no choice but to cut the army's rations once again and requisition all of the available crops and cattle within the region.

Having obviously heard about the activities of the men of the Incorporated Militia in assisting the farmers during the retreat, he decided to officially recognize this activity and make it a formal duty for the benefit of his army:

[September 24]

The Lieutenant General approves of the men of the Incorporated Militia being employed in giving assistance to the farmers in threshing out their grain and in otherwise being made useful under the direction of the Commissariat in securing the produce of the country for the use of the Army.[2]

During an all too brief period of good weather, the regiments and detachments stationed south of the Chippawa took advantage of the temporary respite in action and better weather to undertake cleaning and repairs on their clothing and accoutrements. In addition, there were the required duties of pickets and guards, fatigue duties, and the occasional minor engagement of enemy pickets who advanced too close to be permitted to continue without being warned off by a shot or two over their heads.

No such respite was available to the men of the Incorporated Militia, however, since in addition to their picket duties, the additional assigned duties of farm work were necessarily done at a rapid pace to ensure the maximum yield while the temporary "Indian Summer" held. Every available man was involved at the nearby farms to harvest and thresh the grain crops, and in the case of Lieutenant William Jarvis, it allowed him to finally rejoin the regiment; having been previously kept as part of the small detachment left at York in July. After something of a meandering journey to join his unit, he recorded his activities and other thoughts to his parents in a letter dated September 28, 1814:

Willowby [Willoughby] Dear Parents … I arrived here on Sunday and had a very pleasant passage. We left York about 12 o'clock, arrived at the 40 Mile Creek at 11 at night. Breakfasted there, left there about 10, arrived about a mile and half the other side of Nia'ra Falls at 8 o'clock [p.m.]. Left there at 7, [a.m.] arrived at Fort George at 12 o'clock A.M. [noon].

Left therefore this place at 5 [p.m.], arrived at Field's at 7 o'clock [p.m.] Left there at 6 o'clock [a.m.], breakfasted at Major Kerby's and arrived here at 5 o'clock [p.m.] on Sunday … we are going to York as soon as we have done threshing wheat. Mr. Nair of the Kings was taken and wounded in the skirmish the other day. Stigin of the DeWattevilles was wounded in the head, Lapier severely wounded; they lost a great many officers. George Jarvis was taken but made his escape. Miss Lawe was married on the 21st to an officer of the Navy. I believe the Devil has got into all the girls…. Major Kerby is appointed Assistant Adjutant General…. Will you tell Mrs. Thom I delivered all the stores to Mrs. Kerby, except the black silk handkerchief for W. Kerr, which I sent to him by a Sergeant of the Glengarry's.[3]

By early October, the brief respite of action was about to come to an end for Drummond's army, and the threat of a second American army arriving on the Niagara frontier had become a reality. Emboldened by this advancing support, General Brown pushed his own forces forward from Fort Erie, forcing the advanced units of the British defences, including the Incorporated Militia, to gradually fall back. As General Drummond had planned, once each defensive position retreated north, it concentrated the British body of troops at Chippawa. Unfortunately, it also created a serious overcrowding of the available shelter and accommodation at the positions along the north bank of the Chippawa River.

General Drummond commented on this and other points in his report to General Prevost:

[October 2]

This arrangement will very much diminish the comfort which the troops experience in their present cantonments, but it is a necessary precaution. Through the exertions of the parties of the Incorporated Militia employed on that duty, the greatest part of the grain in the possession of the farmers in front of the Chippawa has been threshed out and the produce generally withdrawn for the use of the Army…. The inhabitants themselves had driven their cattle behind the Black Creek on the first movement of the troops.[4]

By October 5, General Drummond was in an increasingly difficult position. His total disposable defensive force was composed of around four thousand exhausted and near-starved regular, militia, and Native troops. To the south, General Brown was slowly advancing north with more than five thousand troops from Fort Erie, while on the other side of the river, General Izard had arrived from Sackets Harbor with an additional four thousand troops.

He was now faced with three alternate threats. First, Izard's army could cross the Niagara somewhere below the Niagara Gorge, cut off his retreat, and attack him from the rear in co-operation with Brown from the south. Second, it could move up the Niagara River on the American side and then cross over from Fort Schlosser and make an immediate flanking attack in co-operation with Brown. And third, it could move south to unite with Brown's army and in the process create an army that outnumbered his own more than two to one in any full frontal attack.

Faced with these risks, General Drummond ordered the withdrawal of most of his advanced forces to the north side of the Chippawa River, leaving only a reduced screen of light troops on the south bank. He also sought to improve the defences of the Chippawa River crossing by ordering that a new "tete-de-pont" earthwork be constructed at the south end of the bridge. Once again, he gave this duty to the Incorporated Militia. While working on this project, Lieutenant Jarvis found time to write another missive to his parents, revealing some interesting pieces of information:

8 October, Streets Grove

My Dear Parents … The Americans have advanced, it is said as far as Palmers, the other side of Black Creek with 4,000 men. 4,000 men are encamped under the mountain at Lewiston under the command of General Izzard; it is supposed they will cross … at Lewiston and attack us from the rear … I have not received a line from anyone of the family since I left home. I suppose out of sight, out of mind. We have just received an order to be in readiness to march at a moment's warning. We are struck off part of our rations as there is but five days rations left for the whole army. Don't mention this again, if you do you will get me in a scrape. We had the promise of going to York after we had finished threshing wheat, instead of that, after we had finished that lot, they set us cutting down the trees this side of the Chippawa Creek. I suppose after we have finished that they will set us at something else. I suppose we shall only see York when we return from Greenbush [the U.S. prisoner of war camp] Sir James Yeo has been kind enough to offer to bring up a puncheon of spirits and a pipe of wine in the fleet for every regiment in the Right Division; if he would bring up 2 or 3,000 men it would be much better … General De Watteville and the Brigade major passed this [place] early this morning with a field piece on the way to Chippawa. I suppose we shall follow him soon.[5]

Fortunately for the British, Lieutenant Jarvis's concern about Izard's immediate intentions proved false, and by the morning of October 9, the bulk of the contending armies of General Drummond and General Izard were facing each other across the rapids above the Falls of Niagara, while General Brown's force was preparing to advance south from Frenchman's Creek. A major battle now seemed inevitable. But, unfortunately for the American plan, there were only sufficient boats available at Cayuga Creek to transport a quarter of the total number of troops at a time. Unwilling to risk having his force caught and attacked while divided, Izard again changed his plans. He decided to march to Buffalo and cross in relative safety, but was delayed by having to rebuild the bridge to cross the Tonawanto (Tonawanda) Creek. So it was not until October 11 that the last of his force was on the Canadian side of the river at Fort Erie and could march north to link up with Brown's army and take over command of operations.

As a countermeasure to these series of American army movements, General Drummond had redeployed his troops to be able to react to the several possible routes of an enemy attack. As part of these precautions, detachments of the Incorporated Militia were pushed inland, along the banks of the Chippawa River and Lyon's Creek to report on possible flanking movements by the Americans. He also directed the remainder of the troops of the regiment to speedily complete their work at the tete-de-pont, then immediately march inland to the junction of Lyon's Creek and the Chippawa River. Here, they were to participate in another rush job to construct an earthwork and blockhouse on the spit of land marking the confluence of the two waterways. As far as General Drummond was concerned, this new emplacement was particularly important as a means of preventing the Americans from using this position to construct a bridge and outflank the British defensive lines, as they had nearly succeeded in doing in July.

In sending his regular report to Sir George Prevost, General Drummond outlined his status on October 10:

The following changes have been made in the distribution of the troops … the advance posts are still in front of the Black Creek, the bridge over which has been destroyed and from which I thought it prudent to withdraw the troops and guns, with the exception of a detachment of 50 men of the Glengarry Light Infantry; the remainder of that regiment is stationed at Street's Grove; the 6th Regiment at Chippawa, with the Incorporated Militia at Wisehoun's on the forks of the Lyons and Chippawa; about a mile above the mouth of the latter, and on which a field work is now constructing…. The right of the position is further watched by small parties of Incorporated militia and dragoons extending as high as Brown's bridge, sixteen miles up the Chippawa and to Cook's Mills, ten miles up Lyons Creek. It is my intention also to throw the Indians over this river, and, unless assailed in my centre by the forces under General Izard, I do not apprehend it being possible for the enemy to force it and to turn the position at Chippawa.... The 97th, 82nd and Royals [1st Regiment] are cantoned from Bridgewater to Stamford. They can be concentrated at or near the Chippawa in two hours time. A force consisting of the 89th and 100th Regiments, flank companies, 104th, one troop, 19th Dragoons, with two

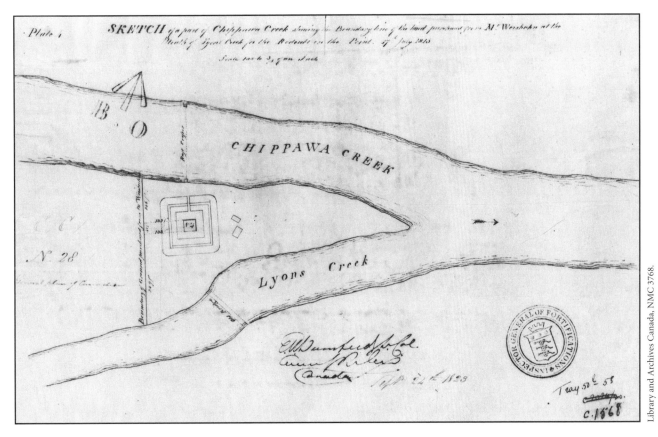

The 1814 plans for the construction of a fortification at Weishoun's Point, located at the junction of the Chippawa River and Lyon's Creek. The men of the Incorporated Militia were principal builders of this position.

six-pounders, under Lt. Colonel Lord Tweedale, occupies Queenston; the remaining corps, viz: 8th, 41st, and DeWattevilles are in the Forts.[6]

Delayed once again by the destruction of the bridges crossing the various creeks, the combined American army finally reached the Chippawa south bank on October 15, only to find that the new fortification at the south end of the bridge had been completed by a round-the-clock work effort on the part of the Incorporated Militia and was occupied by regular troops and artillery.

Disconcerted by the strength of the Chippawa defences, Izard and Brown decided not to make a direct attack. Instead, after seeing their artillery bombardment prove ineffectual, they retired to Street's Creek and established their camp on the same ground originally occupied by Brown's army in July.

The next day (October 16) Izard repeated Brown's July tactics by sending scouts upstream to locate crossing points that would allow him to cross and outflank the British positions. Drummond, however, had anticipated this probe and effectively blocked the Americans at every point with his screen of pickets from the Incorporated Militia, cavalry, and associated Native allies.

That same day, Izard received word that Chauncey and his entire fleet had quit the lake for the season and had retired on Sackets Harbor, with no intention of emerging again that year. With the elimination of this strategic advantage and Yeo now free to bring his squadron out onto Lake Ontario, Izard fully expected Drummond to receive substantial reinforcements within days, instead of weeks.

Convinced that any further attempts to continue the campaign as originally intended would result in failure and possible disaster, Izard made one final attempt to outflank the Chippawa line. For this mission, he sent a strong force of infantry and artillery six miles inland from the Niagara to Cook's Mills on Lyon's Creek. In response, General Drummond sent detachments of his own to monitor the situation. The two sides encountered each other at the mill site on October 19. After a short and inconclusive engagement, which did nothing but add to the list of casualties on both sides and destroy some grain supplies, both forces withdrew to their respective encampments claiming victory.

General Izard, by this time, had come to the conclusion that it would be in the best interest of the army to cease operations for the year. The combined armies would instead move back and establish winter quarters at Fort Erie and Buffalo, before beginning to make plans for next year's campaign. Izard also had serious concerns about the security of Sackets Harbor and decided to detach General Brown and a sizable part of the army back to that location to support its defences.

General Drummond soon became aware of Izard's retreat and pushed forward the detachments of cavalry, Incorporated Militia, and Natives to locate and shadow the enemy. So suddenly had this American movement taken place that when a party of men from the Incorporated Militia reached the site of the American camp at Street's Creek, they saw two boats already being rowed across the Niagara River from Fort Schlosser. Hiding in the undergrowth, they allowed the vessels to approach the shore before springing their trap. After a brief struggle, one of the heavily laden boats was captured, while the other was rowed desperately by the crew back to the American side. On being questioned, the captured crew revealed that they had been ordered over to Fort Schlosser only that morning to collect food from the depot, and that they had no inkling of the American intention to retreat. As a result, desperately needed "fresh meat, bread, and spirits, for at least a brigade,"[7] fell into the welcoming arms of the Canadian soldiers.

General Drummond also received more good news. A fleet of vessels had been sighted on Lake Ontario and identified as Yeo's squadron. Considering the repeated calls Drummond had made on Yeo to bring up as many reinforcements and vitally needed supplies as possible, he fully expected that his pleas were about to be answered. However, once the fleet arrived, Drummond found to his dismay that Yeo had only provided space for five hundred men of the 90th Regiment, while the rest were being forced to march to the frontier along almost impassable roads. If this was not bad enough, Yeo had also refused to load more than a token amount of supplies aboard his warships, since he still considered his "mission" to be separate from that of the army and was unwilling to subordinate himself and his fleet to anything less than the defeat of Chauncey's warships.

To say that Drummond was infuriated by this attitude would be a gross understatement. Nor was Prevost far behind, as can be seen in his letter to Earl Bathurst in England, dated October 18: "Thus instead of that zealous, prompt, and cheerful co-operation so essential to the movement and very existence of His Majesty's troops on this widely extended frontier, every demand for the transport either of men or of stores is considered as hampering the powers of the fleet and endangering its safety."[8]

Back at Fort Erie, General Izard initially considered maintaining a strong garrison at the fort, while ordering the remaining bulk of his force to cross to Black Rock and Buffalo. However, he soon realized that the oncoming winter weather could isolate this garrison from any practical support for days at a time and leave it vulnerable to attack. He, therefore, decided to abandon the Canadian side of the river entirely and ordered the destruction of the encampment and fortifications at Fort Erie. On October 25, the evacuation of the American army from Fort Erie began with an around-the-clock shuttle service of boats.

Although bad weather frequently interrupted the work, the retreat to the American side of the river continued without interference from the nearby British pickets (including detachments of the Incorporated Militia) until the last of their regimental forces, guns, and ammunition were removed. Finally, on November 5, 1814, the rearguard ignited the fuses on numerous demolition charges placed throughout the fort and ran for the boats waiting to ferry them to the American side of the river.

With this final threat removed, General Drummond ordered his troops to enter winter quarters, while he passed over command on the Niagara to Major General Stovin and sailed to Kingston with Yeo's fleet. Once there, he continued to press Yeo to send his vessels back up the lake with more of the supplies needed to feed the army throughout the forthcoming winter.

But despite the fact that there was no enemy fleet to threaten his squadron, and quite aware of the desperate conditions that were affecting the entire military and civilian population at the other end of the lake, Yeo remained obdurate and uncooperative. Eventually, the deteriorating sailing conditions made the point moot, and the full onset of winter suspended any further lake traffic until spring. As a result, the all but devastated Niagara region and the rest of western Upper Canada was effectively left to fend for itself in the face of an increasingly harsh winter.

PART VI:

RESPITE AND RECOVERY

21

WINTER QUARTERS AND A NEW YEAR'S RESOLUTION

LEAVING A COMPANY-STRONG DETACHMENT OF the Incorporated Militia, two artillery pieces, and a detachment from the 19th Light Dragoons at the Fort Erie ferry dock to maintain a secure watch on the Americans across the river, General Stovin took on the arduous job of finding sufficient surviving buildings within the Niagara frontier to accommodate the troops of his new command before the winter set in. Most of his regular regiments were soon assigned quarters in the newly rebuilt barracks at Fort George, Fort Mississauga, and Queenston. Once these locations were filled, the remaining regular regiments on the frontier were provided with all the available tools to begin repairs and reconstruction of the buildings in which they were located. The Incorporated Militia were also assigned quarters. However, unlike their regular counterparts, their new headquarters was at Butler's Barracks, a series of partially derelict and battle-damaged sets of storehouses that in some cases dated back over forty years to the American Revolutionary period.

Without tools or supplies to make proper repairs, the men of the regiment were forced to make the best of their new living quarters and shift for themselves. Although they were no longer considered to be on active duty in the field, the married men learned that their families were not permitted to join them. For some, this offhand treatment by the military authorities for whom they had fought and sacrificed proved to be more than they were willing to accept after their previous active service, and a rash of desertions occurred. Similarly frustrated, the remaining men of the embodied militia (who had volunteered for active service and upon the expiration of their term remained with the regiment), now took up their option and they, too, left the corps to return home.

The regiment also lost the services of the two regular officers that had led it since the companies had been unified in March. In the case of Lieutenant Colonel FitzGibbon, he was recalled to serve with the Glengarry Light Infantry when it was transferred to York. The other, Lieutenant Colonel Robinson of the 8th (King's) Regiment, was ordered to rejoin his regiment when it was transferred to Lower Canada. To replace the two officers, Colonel J.G. Tucker (41st Regiment) was appointed the Incorporated Militia's new colonel on November 5, 1814.

This news was not considered good at the regimental level, since Colonel Tucker's unofficial nickname was "Brigadier Shindy," a colloquial term that implied the subject was a quarrelsome individual with a reputation for causing trouble if he failed to get his own way. It is also possible to infer from the events that were to follow that this appointment was made as a sign of General Drummond's displeasure at Tucker for his failure to capture the American positions at Black Rock in August, thus forcing Drummond to undertake the costly siege at Fort Erie.

It would appear that this antipathy was mutual.

To understand this conclusion, it is necessary to look behind the surface of the appointment and consider the nature of field promotions of this kind, the personalities concerned, and some previous events that might have had a bearing on the case.

When a regular officer was given the command of a militia unit he would be given a temporary promotion to a senior rank ("breveted") to confirm

A view of the road leading into Newark, with Butler's Barracks on the right and Fort Niagara visible in the distance (centre) beyond the Niagara River, detail from the larger painting, Butler's Barracks, *J.P. Cockburn, artist, 1829.*

his authority. This had happened to both Captain Robinson and Captain FitzGibbon, both of whom became breveted to lieutenant colonels. Furthermore, although these kinds of promotions were officially considered to be temporary, they also carried with them a cachet of official approval. Consequently, unless the officer in question had failed dismally in the application of his new duties, it in most cases resulted in a permanent promotion once the officer returned to his original regiment.

In the case of Colonel Tucker, however, an entirely different set of conditions applied.

Tucker was already a colonel in the regular army, with obvious aspirations for further promotion. However, he had also incurred the displeasure of General Drummond and earned a "black mark" against his record for his failure at Fort Erie. These deficiencies included his inadequate efforts to maintain the secrecy of his preparations, his failure to capture an important enemy position, and his subsequent refusal to take any responsibility for the failure by categorizing and slandering his men as cowards. To be a colonel posted as a replacement for a breveted captain in these circumstances — with a depleted militia force, at a time when it was going into winter quarters — and to do it without any promotion in rank or other sign of recognition, could only be interpreted as a slight upon his honour and very clearly carried with it the impression of official disapproval to anyone with an understanding of the system.

It should, therefore, come as no surprise that there is no reference to the colonel actually taking up his duties with the regiment on the Niagara frontier during the next two months. Nor is there any known order issued in his name or with his signature on it. Instead, Colonel Tucker remained at York throughout November and then went on to Montreal in early December. Here, he is recorded as meeting with senior aides to General Prevost, following which he returned to York with a warrant in his pocket appointing him to the command of that garrison.

Without any active commanding officer, the responsibility for the well-being of the Incorporated Militia fell, once again, upon its senior ranking officer, Major Kerby. Still recovering from the wound suffered on August 12, he had previously requested permission to resign his commission, or at least receive a leave of absence. Now, instead, he was applying the old maxim of "beg, borrow, or steal" to see the men of the regiment more suitably provisioned.

To begin with, he sent work parties out to scavenge materials from the burned-out buildings in Newark and make repairs to the regimental barracks. He also "acquired" a number of tents, although he recognized these would not serve as comfortable shelter once winter began in earnest. Next, he made sure that a fair proportion of the supplies of food now arriving from Kingston found its way into the cooking pots of the men's messes, as well as sending out hunting and fishing parties to supplement the larder. There was also the outstanding issue of obtaining replacement clothing, most especially shoes, for items that had been lost, damaged, or worn out during the season's campaign. And, finally, despite the difficult terms of service to the Crown, there were significant arrears of pay owing to the men.

Two of the restored buildings that constitute Butler's Barracks today, a Parks Canada Historic Site at Niagara-on-the-Lake. Recent government cutbacks in staff and funding have limited public access to these buildings. Photo taken in 2011.

Taking these latter two issues in hand, Major Kerby wrote a strongly worded letter expressing the difficulties the unit was experiencing. However, instead of sending it through the normal chain of official communications, he sent it directly to General Drummond at Kingston. By the time the official response of the general arrived nearly a month later, most of the difficulties outlined in Kerby's letter had been solved by his own initiatives. As well, the regiment had been transferred back to the garrison at York, where they were reunited with their families and quite comfortably ensconced in one of the new sets of barracks located inside the rebuilt Fort York. Nonetheless, it is obvious that Kerby's letter had ruffled a few official feathers, as the tone of the December 17 reply from Lieutenant Colonel Foster clearly indicates:

> In reply to your letter of this instant, which by direction of his Honor the President I have handed to Lt. Colonel Nichol, Quarter Master General. I have the honour to acquaint you that the necessaries and supplies you require therein are to be forwarded to you without delay. It is a matter of concern to Lt. General Drummond that it should have been supposed for a moment that the Battalion of Incorporated Militia had been neglected in any way but the most trivial instance … and he is somewhat surprised that you should have been led to express yourself to that effect. It is not for his Honor to explain the reasons of necessary warrants on the estate of the Paymaster not having been hitherto issued; suffice it to say that they are not issued to this day. From a supply of funds however, I expect that they will issue from the President's office forthwith. You may depend on my making due enquiries on the subject.
>
> His Honor has been pleased to direct the purchase, at a very heavy expense, of two pairs of bugles, the only number which could be procured at Montreal. They will be forwarded to you as soon as received here…. You will be pleased to transmit to me a return of such officers and men as have been desirous of obtaining leave of absence, to what place and on what account — In the first instance, however, I have much pleasure in signifying to you that the president has been pleased to grant leave of absence to proceed to the Lower Province on their private affairs to Captain H. Walker, and to Lieutenant D. McDonell — to the 1st of February next each — With regard to your own leave of absence, his has commanded me to assure you that he will have the

very great pleasure in acquiescing in your respect as soon as another Field Officer is appointed to the command of the Corps, vice Colonel Tucker, who is about to be appointed to the permanent command at York, and cannot consequently continue in command of the Incorporated Militia. Major Glew of the 41st Regiment, an excellent and experienced officer of the most conciliatory manners has been offered the situation. His Honor cannot possibly think of accepting your resignation, who have hitherto experienced his best opinion.[1]

Interestingly, while the above letter, referring to Major Joseph B. Glew's offer, was dated December 17, the letter addressed to the major was not entered in the official letterbook until December 28:

Sir,

As the command of the Battalion of Incorporated Militia will shortly become vacant by the appointment of Colonel Tucker to the permanent command of York, I have received the instruction of his Honor the President and Lieutenant General commanding to offer to your acceptance the

succession to Colonel Tucker. You will of course be gazetted to the Provincial rank of Lieutenant Colonel and be entitled to the same pay and allowances as Lieutenant Colonel Robinson had.

Lt. Colonel Foster[2]

During this period, another regular officer, Lieutenant Francis Miles of the 89th Regiment, joined the regiment as its regimental adjutant. To conclude the record of this year, it is perhaps appropriate to note that the regiment received a belated Christmas present on December 31, when Major Kerby posted the following order that had just arrived at the regiment's headquarters:

Dear Sir,

On the subject of Furloughs or leaves of absence to the excellent fellows, the Serjeants and Rank and File of the Incorporated Militia under your command. I am apprehensive I was silent in my last communication not from intention, however, but from the hurry of business. Permit me therefore now to say that His Honor the President has been friendly and considerably pleased to authorize you or the Commanding officer for the time being, to grant furloughs to the Battalion in the proportion of one man to every ten effective in the Corps and for the space of one month each man. On whose return to the Headquarters of the Regiment individually a similar proportion is to have a similar indulgence and for the like period.[3]

With the approval for leave, despite the coldness of the season and difficulties of winter travel, no less than one major, two captains, five lieutenants, and one ensign took an immediate furlough. Similarly, an allotment of three sergeants, one drummer, and forty-one rank and file also appears as "Absent with Leave" on the regimental rolls for January.

For the remainder, duties continued as normal at Fort York, with daily parades and drills taking place on the parade ground, except when winter storms or extreme cold made it too dangerous. The detachments of men were frequently assigned to perform duties within the fort's administrative and supply departments, including the Commissariat Department, the Engineers Department, the Marine Department, and the Quarter Master General's Department. Finally, they also served as guards at the Gibraltar Point, Yonge Street, and Don River blockhouses.

For General Drummond, the past season's service of the Incorporated Militia had impressed him to the point that he now swung his entire support and influence to establishing the unit on a more regular and permanent footing. He also sought to ensure that it could attract a sufficient number of new recruits to replace its earlier casualties and allow for the establishment of full-strength companies. To this end, on January 9, 1815, warrants were issued for the payment of substantial bounties to any man recruited to join the Incorporated Militia. The following day, this news was forwarded to the regiment's headquarters:

As the President has been anxious to complete the establishment of the Incorporated Militia, he has directed a Bounty of Ten Pounds to be paid each recruit in future to be enlisted. Two Pounds to be paid at the time of enlistment. Six on joining the Headquarters of the Battalion, and the remaining two to be laid out in necessaries unless the recruit be provided with a sufficiency of those articles when it is to be instantly paid in money. Two Pounds is also to be paid to the recruiting Officer for each recruit approved at Headquarters of the Regiment. One Pound of which, at least and as much more as he pleases he is to divide amongst the party under his command. It is to be hoped that the officers will exert themselves to fill up the Corps as speedily as possible, for without suitable increase to its numbers it will be totally out of the question to promote officers to the vacant companies etc.

Lt. Colonel Foster[4]

General Drummond also took it upon himself to press the case for the Incorporated Militia with his superiors. In his report to General Prevost on January 12, his reference relating to the confirmation of Major Glew as the commanding officer for the regiment was fairly succinct: "I request your approval of the appointment of Major Glew vice Tucker to the position … as it is essentially necessary that that most useful Corps, the Battalion of Incorporated Militia of this Province should be commanded by an officer who can devote his whole time to that duty."[5]

On the other hand, his letter of January 18, sent directly to Earl Bathurst in England, was far more effusive and contains significant details about his future intentions and expectations for the regiment and the province:

My Lord,

In consequence of the very meritorious conduct of the Battalion of Incorporated Militia of this Province, from the time they were first embodied, and particularly from the great gallantry and good conduct evidenced by them on every occasion during the late campaign, but especially in the arduous and trying conflict in which they were engaged on the 25th of July last, where their bravery and steadiness, under the hottest fire, contributed not a little to the glorious result of the action. I have now induced with the view of increasing the numbers of that most serviceable body of men to offer an increase of bounty to that originally provided by the Legislature, a measure in which I have not the smallest doubt of receiving the full concurrence of both branches at the approaching session which is to be opened on the 1st of next month. With this increased inducement to enlist, I am sanguine in my expectations that the effective numbers of this valuable Corps will shortly be augmented to six hundred.

Their loss in both Officers and men during the last campaign has been severe indeed, but the respectable bounty of ten Pounds, which it will be in my power, thro' the well known liberality of the House of Assembly, to pay out to such as are inclined to enlist in the Corps, will gain many recruits, not only from the inhabitants of this country, from which materials alone the regiment has hitherto been formed, but likewise from the vast number of men discharged on account of the expiration of their period of service from Regular corps and who have declined altogether remaining therein.

The retention of such a military force, which would otherwise in all probability return immediately to Europe, Your Lordship will doubtless consider a most desirable object, but one of still greater importance points itself out, as the natural result of that close intermixture, which must, during the continuance of this war with America, take place between soldiers thus obtained for this Corps, and those who have been procured from the youth of the country. This acquaintance and connection will be the means of inducing such men at the close of the present war to settle in Upper Canada and thus an increase will be obtained to the population in the province of a body of settlers who inherit feelings of loyalty and military valor which will operate as a barrier against the contagion of American sentiments, introduced, as Your Lordship well knows, by many of the inhabitants who at different times have intruded themselves from the neighbouring states.

The regiment of Incorporated Militia has, from its being particularly adapted for that service, been chiefly employed as a Light Corps and as such very frequently engaged with the enemy's riflemen in the woods. Here the natural expertness in the use of the gun and the axe in clearing their way, throwing up breastworks of timber etc. for which the inhabitants of Upper Canada are so remarkable, was certainly productive of the most beneficial service. But this Corps labours under a very material disadvantage from being clothed in red, which rendered them too frequently a marked object.

To obviate in future this impediment to their success against the enemy, I beg leave therefore to request four hundred suits of rifle clothing, complete with the same number of appointments, to be sent out early in the spring for this Corps. As also twenty bugles. I likewise from a conviction that the Regiment merits every encouragement, further beg leave to recommend that Your Lordship will procure for them two stand of Colours, with the gracious permission of His Royal Highness the Prince Regent, that they may bear the word NIAGARA on them and on their appointments as an honourable testimony of their gallantry and meritorious conduct throughout the whole of the arduous operations on that frontier.[6]

General Drummond added one other element to his message that would have seen yet another change in command had it come into effect:

As nothing can contribute so much to the good formation and discipline of a young Provincial Corps as having a few officers of experience of the Line attached to it. Particularly the Field Officers and Staff, thro' whose exertions, where well selected a Corps is principally brought to a state of perfection. I have it in mind to appoint, with Provincial rank for the present, Major Foster to act as Lieutenant Colonel of the Incorporated Militia and Captain Glew of the 41st as their Major.[7]

In the end, these changes and expansions were not to come to pass. Margin notes, written on the back of the original document by Earl Bathurst, tell the actual story: "As far as that dispatch related to the military arrangements for the future defence of the Province, it is unnecessary to enter into details, the ratification of the Treaty of Peace having superseded the necessity of increasing the Colonial military force."[8]

22

THE FINAL PARADE

UNAWARE OF THE OFFICIAL END OF THE WAR, the military authorities on both sides were actively engaged in making plans for the spring campaign in 1815. The Americans were contemplating an attack up the Champlain Valley toward Montreal, while the British, freed from their war against Napoleon after his military defeat and abdication the previous year, had used the opportunity to build up their regular forces in the Canadas. With these resources in place, they planned to use Kingston and the Niagara as the focus for a major offensive that would take the war into American territory. For this reason, Prevost finally allowed substantial quantities of additional supplies and reinforcements to be sent to Upper Canada.

With these resources available for the upcoming campaign season, the repair of existing fortifications and the construction of new defences and accommodation for the troops and supplies took top priority in the mind of General Drummond. While work on the development of fortifications continued across Upper Canada, it was particularly concentrated in the Niagara region. Fort Mississauga was completed, Fort George was repaired, and additional barracks and blockhouses were constructed at Chippawa, Queenston and at Turkey Point on Lake Erie.

Nor was the Incorporated Militia left out of these developments and plans. Although Drummond's proposal to convert the regiment to a green-coated light infantry regiment could not be put into effect until a response from England arrived, the expansion of recruitment and the supplying of new redcoats and other associated clothing and accoutrements could be pressed forward.

In the Upper Canada Legislature, General Drummond made his proposed amendment to the *Militia Act* on February 4, 1815, and included a personal appeal to the members of the House in the body of his speech:

> It is with peculiar pleasure that I have assented in his Majesty's name to the bill affecting the Incorporated Militia of this Province, who after having been honoured with the most substantial marks of your approbation [and the end of the war] will be enabled to retire to their domestic avocations, animated with a consciousness of having in the day of trial, proved that they deserved the gratitude and applause of their country.[1]

Drummond also followed up on his earlier communication to Earl Bathurst with a subsequent endorsement on February 20 for the enhancement of the Incorporated Militia to a level that implied the prospect of it becoming the founding core of a future permanent military armed force in Upper Canada:

> According to my expectation, a bill is at present in advanced process through the House of Assembly for placing at my disposal the sum of nine thousand Pounds for the purpose of procuring recruits for the Battalion of Incorporated Militia in this Province and likewise a further sum of one thousand Pounds to provide for the purchase of Colours for the Regiment and of furniture necessary for the Officer's Mess, the well regulated establishment of which is to be looked on as a step highly necessary to the respectability of the Corps. This liberal appropriation will afford Your Lordship a convincing proof that in my former letter I have not laid too much in favour of this young Corps and will likewise give to your Lordship a clear view of the estimation in which it deservedly stands in the opinion of all ranks in the Province. The presentation of Colours to this Regiment will therefore both by the representatives of the people and the Corps itself, be most gratefully received as a flattering testimony of the approbation of His Majesties Government at home of their uniform good conduct and gallantry.[2]

At the regimental level, plans and activities being designed to prepare for a new round of campaigning in the spring were pushed ahead. Since the new round of recruitment was yet to begin, additional men of the embodied militia were again drafted in to fill out the ranks. This time, however, no rotating or voluntary system was to be applied. Instead, entire companies were to be attached for training, starting with the Kent County Militia:

> [Regimental Orders, February 25, 1815]
>
> In consequence of the General Order of the 24th instant, Captain McGregor's company of Loyal Kent Volunteers will be attached to and taken on the strength of the Battalion of Incorporated Militia. The Quartermaster will issue clothing and necessaries and such appointments as he has in his possession to Captain McGregor, who is referred to the regimental Order of the 14th instant where he will see a list of the articles that is required for each man. Captain McGregor's company will fall in on the left of the Battalion at all parades.[3]

In taking up his new command, Lieutenant Colonel Glew was pleased to see that, apart from the furloughed Major Kerby, all of his other company officers had returned and were at their posts. Wasting no time, Glew undertook to replace the combat casualties by promoting individuals from the ranks according to recommendations made by their officers. Experienced NCOs were transferred among companies to create a balance within the existing company lists. Glew also undertook to raise the level of military discipline and duty in both the men and officers of the regiment by instituting additional company drills and adherence to regimental regulations, all backed by detailed inspections and regimental orders such as that issued on March 4:

> Notwithstanding the repeated orders that have been issued and so often repeated respecting the regulating of the men's messing, the Commanding Officer is sorry to find that out of the ten companies, Captain Walker's is the only one who has obeyed the orders. The officers are particularly required to pay the strictest attention to the most essential part of their duty by immediately re-establishing the messes of the companies.[4]

Buckling down to conform to the new higher standards, the men of the regiment were cheered a day earlier when on March 3, a complete set of new uniforms and accoutrements arrived at the post. General

Drummond had come through in style, providing them with regimental coats faced with the amended regulation dark-blue cuffs and collar. It is also likely that while the regiment might have received a number of the newer style British army "Belgic"-type shako caps in the June 1814 shipment, this time everyone would have received one, creating for the first and last time a full regimental parade with a truly uniform appearance. The regimental orders of March 3 stated: "The companies will appear in their new clothing on Sunday [6th] and will continue to wear it until further notice…. The Great Coats to be worn on Guard and in very bad weather."[5]

This "regularization" of the regiment continued a few days later (March 6) when an additional order was posted:

> The acting Quartermaster will issue a white jacket for every effective Non-Commissioned Officer and Private to the Officers commanding companies immediately after morning parade tomorrow, which will in future be worn in all parades. The new clothing is only to be [worn] on Sundays until further orders.[6]

According to the reminiscences of Lieutenant Henry Ruttan, this final period was remembered as follows:

Later in December following, I had sufficiently recovered to join my regiment at York … which had retired into winter quarters…. The war spirit having now being fairly aroused, the Legislature in session 1814 and 1815, voted the supplies necessary to fill up the Incorporated Regiment to 800 men, a service of plate and pension of £ 20/-/- per annum for the wounded or for the widows of the felled as well as an address to His Majesty for an allowance of 100 acres of land for each militia man, whether belonging to this regiment or Flank Companies of the Sedentary Militia. But alas! As the best concocted schemes of men and mice often fail, so in this case. In March 1815, the unwelcome (to our men) news of peace made havoc of our hope and expectations. The Legislature being then in session and acting upon the suggestion of the military authorities voted us six months pay each and we were reduced![7]

On March 8, all the plans and activity to promote the development of the Incorporated Militia came to an abrupt halt when news reached the garrison at York that the war between Great Britain and the United States of America had officially ended. With this message, the courier also brought a series of orders that terminated any future construction work on all but a select few military emplacements deemed essential for the defence of the country. In a like measure, the orders stipulated that all non-essential military expenditures were to cease and any outstanding accounts were to be settled. Finally, the orders stipulated that all of the currently active detachments of Upper Canada militias were to be released from duty according to a posted schedule and all uniforms and arms then in their possession were to be handed in for storage.

In the case of the Incorporated Militia, the news was officially posted on March 10, 1815:

Militia General Order,

1st: The General Staff, Battalion of Incorporated, Company of Artillery, Company of Loyal Kent Volunteers, and all other Incorporated and Embodied Militia will be permitted to return to their homes on the 24th instant, from which day all pay and garrison, field and other allowances to them will cease; with the exception of the Battalion of Incorporated Militia, to whom one month's pay … free of deductions, an account of rations will be paid to take them to their respective districts.

2nd: The arms, accoutrements and extra clothing of this Battalion will be delivered into store at this post, and the different books and papers will be deposited in the office of the Adjutant General of Militia.

3rd: Regular discharges will be granted to such Non-Commissioned Officers and Privates to show that those who have remained steady to their engagements may be distinguished from those who have basely deserted their Corps and their Country's cause.

4th: His Honor the President cannot dismiss that truly deserving Corps, the Battalion of Incorporated Militia, without expressing his warmest approbation of their bravery, steadiness and uniform good conduct on all occasions as his strongest instance of which he had already made application for Colours to be granted them by His Majesty's Government: upon which and upon their appointments his Honor likewise has humbly solicited the Royal permission that the word "*NIAGARA*" might be borne in testimony of His Royal Highness the Prince Regent's generous consideration of their merits.

5th: It is with peculiar satisfaction that His Honor has to announce to the Incorporated Militia that so high a sense is entertained of their conduct by the Provincial Legislature, who with most grateful liberality have bestowed among other donations a gratuity of six months pay to the whole Corps.

By Command of his Honor the President.[8]

Three days later, a formal recognition of the service of the battalion was authorized when a substantial detachment was ordered to parade for the inspection of General Drummond and the members of the Legislative Assembly. The requisite regimental order, issued on March 13, read, in part, "A guard of Honour, consisting of one Captain, three Subalterns, five Sergeants and one hundred Rank and File will assemble at the House of Assembly tomorrow at one o'clock. For the above duty, Captain Kerr, Lieutenant Ruttan, Lieutenant Hamilton and Ensign Kerby."[9]

Following this final acknowledgement of this official duty, the remainder of the term of the men's enlistment was taken up in fulfilling garrison duties and preparing to disband the regiment by returning all of the uniforms and equipment they had just received, and receiving a suit of civilian clothes, which would a century later be known as a "demob suit." There was also the matter of outstanding balances owing for services rendered as the regimental books had to balance before being submitted, as noted in the regimental order of March 15:

Officers commanding companies will give in tomorrow to the Quartermaster, nominal lists of their companies present that are entitled to draw trousers and a pair of shoes each. The Quartermaster will issue to each effective Non-Commissioned Officer and Drummer and Private present materials for making one pair of trousers each. And one pair of shoes as regimental clothing and for which no charge will be made.[10]

Finally, on March 20, the time came for the final official regimental order to be posted for the attention of the officers and men of the Incorporated Militia:

The Battalion will parade tomorrow morning at 7 o'clock, no man to be absent, sick in hospital excepted. The Captain of the Day and an officer per company to attend. The regiment will be marched up to the ordinance store and will deposit their arms, accoutrements and ammunition… The Quartermaster will take into store at 6 o'clock in the morning of the 24th instant the bedding and barrack utensils by company.

The battalion will parade for muster at 10 o'clock in the morning… after which they will be marched to the quarters of the officers paying them and will receive one months pay up to the 24th March and one months pay to the 24th April without any deductions for rations [it] being a gratuity from His Honor the Lieutenant General Drummond, in order to enable the men to proceed to their respective homes. The commanding officer is sorry the 6 months pay voted by the House of Assembly cannot be paid for some time as it must come through the Paymaster General of Militia… Acquaintance rolls will be given in as soon as possible after the 25th instant, the officers will take care that the men sign the receipts on the back of the discharge and witnessed by a third person, after which the discharges will be delivered to the men.[11]

Thus it was that on the afternoon of March 24, 1815, a total of one major, seven captains, eleven lieutenants, nine ensigns, twenty-nine sergeants, ten drummers/buglers, and 263 rank and file — or, more accurately,

INCORPORATED MILITIA, ACQUITTANCE PAYROLL ACCOUNT, MARCH 24, 1815		
Pay Scale	Daily	Sum Total (2 Months Pay) £ / s / d
Lieutenant Colonel	17/-	51/17/-
Major	16/-	48/16/-
Captain	10/6	32/-/6
Lieutenant	6/6	19/16/6
Ensign	5/3	16/-/3
Paymaster	10 -	30/10/-
Adjutant	10/-	30/10/-
Surgeon	7/6	22/17/6
Quartermaster	6/6	19/16/6
Sergeant Major	2/-	6/2/-
Quartermaster Sgt.	2/-	6/2/-
Paymaster Sgt.	1/6	4/11/6
Sergeant	1/4	3/16/6
Corporal	10d	2/10/10
Drummer	7 ¾d	1/19/4 ¾
Private	6d	1/10/6

330 civilians and their associated wives and children — found themselves walking out the gate at Fort York. Their departure was accompanied by with a hearty "well-done," a pat on the back, a pocketful of cash, but, apart from the official offer of places in boats travelling toward their home locations, they had nowhere to sleep, no supplied food or drink, and only the clothes they stood up in (unless they had a personal wardrobe). No official or personal documentation exists to detail

the days that followed. It would be reasonable, however, to surmise that as gentlemen, the officers would have been quickly made the guests of members of the local community while they made arrangements for their transport. However, the rank and file, unless their former officers made arrangements for them, were left to their own devices.

Thus ends the official service of the Volunteer Battalion of Incorporated Militia of Upper Canada, but not the story.

23

POSTWAR AFTERMATH

DESPITE THE OFFICIAL DISBANDING OF THE regiment and the dispersal of the body of the troops, there were some significant administrative details still needing to be cleared out. To begin with, there was the matter of two captains, two ensigns, one quartermaster, two sergeants, and twenty-seven rank and file now in the process of returning home after being held as prisoners of war. Upon their eventual arrival back in Upper Canada, they too were officially disbanded. However, bureaucracy being what it ever has been, these men found themselves in an administrative "grey" area and unable to claim their due clothing allowance, back pay, and bonus without appropriate authorization from the higher chain of command.

Fortunately, the approval came through by the end of April and the men were to receive their due pay. The provincial authorities also voted through the financial measures required for the six months' pay and allowances to the men of the regiment:

> To the officers, non-commissioned officers, and privates of the incorporated militia, six months' pay, £4,594 15s 2d. To the officers and non-commissioned officers of the line attached to the incorporated militia, the full pay of their respective ranks in the said corps, £1,000…. To the Speaker of the House of Assembly, to purchase a sword to be presented to Colonel Robinson, late of the incorporated militia, 100 guineas.[1]

There was also the issue of pensions due for wounded veterans of the militia. During the six months following the disbandment of the regiment, many of those who had suffered injury, as well as the widows of those who were killed, submitted their petitions for consideration by the established regional medical boards. Despite this prompt address, unlike the quick attention to the issue of the six months' pay, the government's response was plodding and divisive. The process required multiple hearings, requests for affidavits, proofs and reports that delayed many awards for over a decade, by which time a significant number of individuals were already dead. (See Appendix G for additional details regarding sickness and disability.)

At another level of recognition of the services of the Incorporated Militia, it had been mentioned upon several occasions that it was the intention of higher command to propose the official issuance of a pair of regimental "colours." This was no mean award, especially as it was additionally proposed to have the colours carry the battle honour "Niagara."

To understand just how important this accolade was for the official acknowledgement of the regiment's service, it must be understood that within the regular British army, regimental colours held an almost reverential place of honour and renown. They were officially blessed and showcased at all official events and parades. Once on the battlefield, the colours were placed at the centre of the regimental line, where they served a vital role as a fixed point for dressing the regimental formation and a highly visible rallying point in the smoke and confusion of battle. As such, they were protected at all costs by a select cadre of veteran "colour sergeants." Their loss to an enemy would be considered a disgrace to the regiment as a whole. Victory in battle or significant actions were commemorated by the official (and highly selective) awarding of a "battle honour," whereby the name of the battle would be affixed to the colours for all to see.

Despite the ending of the regiment's official status, the wheels of bureaucracy, once started, were difficult to stop. As a result, after more than six years of peace, the militia general orders for April 12, 1822, read:

> The Lieutenant Governor has much satisfaction in announcing to the Militia of the province that the Colours have been received which His Majesty had been graciously pleased to command should be prepared for the late Incorporated Battalion and which in commemoration of the services rendered by the Corps on that frontier are inscribed with the word "Niagara." As the Officers and Soldiers who composed the late Incorporated Battalion are now serving in the different County regiments throughout the Province, the Colours will be lodged in the Government House until the formation of a similar Corps shall require them being brought into the field…. A Guard of Honour consisting of 100 Rank and File … will be formed in front

of the centre [of the line] to receive the Colours as the representative of the Militia of the province, and will escort them to Government House … it is suggested … to employ on the Guard of Honor such Officers and soldiers of the respective Regiments as may have belonged to the late Incorporated battalion.[2]

On April 23, 1822 (St. George's Day), the formal parade for this presentation was held. As the general orders had stipulated, standing proudly in the company lines were one hundred veterans of the Incorporated Militia. Furthermore, they were led by their old commanding officer, Lieutenant Colonel James FitzGibbon.

The colours were subsequently stored as directed until 1837, when rebellion broke out and the legislation covering the Incorporated Militia was revived. This time four full battalions were raised and served in different locales during the course of the uprising. During this period, the colours were taken out and paraded, but are not recorded as seeing action in the minor skirmishes that characterized this period of internal political conflict. Following the 1837 rebellion, the colours passed through various official hands until they were eventually deposited in the National War Museum collection in Ottawa, where they remain today, hidden away in a storage area and unavailable to those who wish to view them.

Beyond the military purview, there was also the issue of an association of Upper Canada residents who, under the grandiose title of the Loyal and Patriotic Society of Upper Canada, had been providing charitable support for Upper Canada militiamen and their families during the course of the war. With the war ended, their Committee for the Distribution of Medals put out a request for commanding officers of the various corps of militia to submit the names of men who had distinguished themselves during the course of the war and were therefore deserving of a medal that the society had commissioned. Upon receipt of this request, Lieutenant Glew replied, recommending the entire regimental roll as being eminently qualified for the award.

To say that the committee was shocked by this answer would be an understatement. They urgently wrote back to Glew, indicating that, while they understood his response, they could not possibly issue a medal to every man of the regiment, as it exceeded the total number of medals that had been produced:

> The committee also consider with respect to those of the inhabitants of this Province who in the Corps of Incorporated Militia have devoted their services entirely to its defences during the war and have acquired in such warm terms the approbation of the Commander of the Forces, that in gratitude to their voluntary assistance rendered our case it is but fair to consider their entering into that Corps as a result

of a patriotic sense of duty, and that every individual of the Incorporated Militia who has conducted himself during his service so as to incur no reproach should be considered as having given sufficient proof of extraordinary fidelity in defence of this Province to entitle him to a mark in some way (by the gift of a medal if it were possible) of the honourable notice of the Society.[3]

But despite having lengthy lists of eligible candidates, none of the medals were ever officially awarded. Furthermore, after two decades of increasing public scandal over the non-issuance of the medals and questions related to associated funds, it is generally believed that all but three of the originals were deliberately destroyed in 1840.

On another matter, as veterans of the war and gentlemen, the corps of officers of the Incorporated Militia believed they were entitled to the same privileges and rights of receiving a pension allowance (half-pay) that was generally awarded to demobilized regular officers. Furthermore, the fact that this

The "Upper Canada Preserved" medal was produced, but never officially issued, by the Loyal and Patriotic Society of Upper Canada in 1814. Originally created as a limited edition of sixty gold and 550 silver medals, most were deliberately destroyed in 1840. From Benson J. Lossing's 1868 work, Pictorial Field Book of the War of 1812.

allowance had also been extended to officers serving in several of the Canadian fencible regiments, as well as the Voltigeur Militia Regiment in Lower Canada, made their request seem even more reasonable.

The initial submission for half-pay was made in March 1816 to General Drummond's successor, Francis Gore, who rejected the appeal outright. After a period of five years and the replacement of Gore with Sir Peregrine Maitland as lieutenant-governor of Upper Canada, not to mention the election of several officers of the regiment to official governmental posts as legislative assemblymen, a new application was submitted in March 1821, and was soon after referred to a special parliamentary committee. Supporting the submission, the Upper Canada Legislature forwarded the petition to London. This included a letter of support from Sir Peregrine that read, in part: "altho' I cannot from personal knowledge speak of the services of the respective Corps, I believe that it will be found upon record that those of the Battalion of Upper Canada were most respectable and such as to entitle them at least to equal consideration with the Canadian Voltigeurs."[4]

Unfortunately, this plea was also rejected.

After revising their tactics, the officers of the corps redrafted their submission and obtained additional letters of endorsement from several regular officers with whom they had either served alongside or under. This included Colonel John Harvey, the former deputy adjutant general, who wrote:

> In point of fact, the Incorporated Militia Battalion of Upper Canada had

more frequently and trying occasions on which to display its gallantry and devotion in line with His Majesty's forces than the nature and accidents of war afforded to any Corps whose services were confined chiefly to the Lower Province and I can truly add that these occasions were not neglected.[5]

With this support in hand, they scheduled a meeting with Maitland. As the former senior officer and the leading proponent of the issue, Colonel James Kerby headed the delegation and persuaded the lieutenant-governor to approve the petition's resubmission. The new petition passed through the House with ease and was forwarded to London with a strong endorsement from that body:

> The operations of the enemy during the late war with the United States being directed throughout almost exclusively against Upper Canada, the Corps of Voltigeurs had not an equal opportunity of service in the face of the enemy, while the Battalion of Incorporated Militia, as will appear to His Majesty by the honourable testimony of the General Officers in command, formed a very effective part of an army that were engaged in constant operations against a

superior force and shared with such fidelity the dangers of active service that their casualties in killed and wounded were not less in proportion than those of the Regiments of the Line with whom they were brigaded.[6]

However, while he maintained an official position of supporting the petition, Maitland also submitted a separate private correspondence to his superiors that sought to undermine it. In his letter, Maitland questioned the constitutional variance between the terms of service applicable to the Voltigeurs and Incorporated Militia, and warned of the costly precedent such an award could establish if adopted.

Latching on to Maitland's points, Earl Bathurst denied the petition, but added that if the Upper Canada Legislature wished to pay the pension out of their own funds, he would have no objection. Obviously, the Legislature did *not* wish to do so. As a final attempt at achieving what they perceived as a justified claim, the colonial government authorized a high-powered delegation to travel to England to take the matter directly and personally to the British government. For this duty, the legislature sent Attorney General John Beverly Robinson, supported by someone who had intimate and personal knowledge of the issue, the chief justice of Upper Canada and member of the legislature, Archibald George McLean, the former captain of the regiment's No. 6 Company.

Armed with a brief packed with legal summaries and letters of support, the duo made the parliamentary rounds, drumming up support and influence for the regiment's claim. Fortunately, they had one "ace" that they played — a letter written by Sir Gordon Drummond, who had succeeded Sir George Prevost to the senior post of governor after the disgraced Prevost was recalled to England for his mishandling of the war in late 1814. In his letter, Sir Gordon clearly invalidated the British government's excuses, leaving them little room to further evade the issue:

> As I had myself many opportunities of observing in the course of a long and arduous campaign, the gallantry and good conduct of this Corps (whose long list of killed and wounded is a sufficient record of their merit in the field). I am the more disposed strongly to urge their claims for a reward at least equal to that which his Majesty's Government were pleased to confer on the Voltigeurs of Lower Canada, to which Battalion it was in every respect (except the name) similar.[7]

Even with this evidence and support, the British government procrastinated and sidetracked the matter with bureaucratic red tape for another four years, until eventually the following notice was forwarded to Archibald McLean from Downing Street, dated January 18, 1826:

Sir,

I am directed by Lord Bathurst to acquaint you that the Lords Commissioners of the Treasury, having under their consideration Sir P. Maitland's dispatch with an address from the Legislative Assembly of Upper Canada, praying that half pay be granted to the Incorporated Militia of Upper Canada for their services during the late war with the United States. Their Lordships have been pleased to authorise the Secretary at War, under the special circumstances of the case, to place the Officers of this Battalion of Incorporated Militia upon the list of half-pay and to make provision for the same in the estimate to be submitted to Parliament in the ensuing year.[8]

As a final topic for consideration in looking at the postwar story of the regiment, there is the matter of the land grants that were originally promised at the time of the regiment being raised in 1813. At the end of the war, the authorities initially seemed prepared to act promptly on General Sheaffe's original commitment to award grants of Crown land to all veterans of the war, which he outlined in an order issued in 1813:

Each soldier to receive 100 acres of land; officers entitled, in the first instance, to 200; to receive provisions for themselves and families for one year … implements of husbandry and tools to be supplied in sufficient quantities, and other comforts, according to necessity, to cultivate the land. The land thus taken cannot be sold until after three years of cultivation.[9]

In reality, the system of allocation fell into an abyss of official delays and procrastination that did not last mere years, but rather decades. So protracted were some of these delays that when the official governmental commission finally began to process and award grants of land, the best tracts had long since gone to preferred "insiders" and political cronies. Consequently, in many instances, all that was left were plots totally unsuitable for agriculture or in such remote and uninhabitable locations that they were all but useless. Even where a tract may have proven suitable, due to the inordinate delays many veterans were now at an age where they were no longer physically capable of undertaking the backbreaking task of clearing the virgin forest in accordance with the government-imposed timetable to assure continued permanent ownership.

As a result, many claimants were forced to accept the payment of government scrip (money) at substantially discounted rates, which in no way matched the prospective value of their awarded land.

Nor were those who accepted the tracts and then attempted to resell them better off. Unscrupulous land speculators, often holding official positions within the government commission itself, bought up these properties at massive discounts, amassing significant fortunes upon their subsequent resale at a full market value.

Having documented the story of the regiment, it is appropriate to examine the question of what happened to the men of the Incorporated Militia after the war ended, However, with over nine hundred names on the rolls and more than thirty categories of information for each man, it is not possible to include this massive volume of information within this work. Furthermore, compiling the service records of each man, as well as his individual personal data, has proved to be a Herculean task that is still ongoing. In the long term, it is to be hoped that this sizable collection of information will become available for the use of researchers and genealogists in a future publication or as an internet database. In the meantime, the subsequent careers of a few of the most notable personalities from the regiment are included in Appendix A.

As to the remainder, suffice it to say that many other men of the regiment also saw their duty to their developing colony as one in which they were intimately involved. References to names drawn from the regimental rolls repeatedly appear in the accounts of the foundation and maintenance of early Ontario settlements and their town councils etc., not to mention the histories of numerous church, social, educational, and charitable organizations across the province.

Interestingly, at the time of the outbreak of rebellion in 1837, the provincial legislature in Upper Canada resurrected the Incorporated Militia regimental system for the duration of the emergency. As well as seeing many of the former officers playing significant roles in the events of the next two years, a substantial number of men rejoined the ranks to serve again for the preservation of "Crown and Country."

Ironically, studies of the documentation related to this period indicate that in more than a few cases at the outset of the emergency, the military authorities and Commissariat Department were forced to make use of whatever supplies were in immediate storage for the official issuance of uniforms, weapons, and accoutrements to the incoming rank and file. As a result, in 1837, the veterans of the War of 1812–1815 found themselves donning the same set of uniforms and picking up the same muskets that they had handed in back in March 1815! Apparently, nothing much had changed when it came to dealing with the parsimonious military Commissariat Department or their civil government masters.

From today's perspective, it is an unfortunate fact that the service, actions, and contributions of the regiment during the course of the war were soon relegated to the status of footnotes or appendices within the numerous biographical accounts and community histories published during the later part of the nineteenth century. By the mid twentieth century, books published about the war either mistakenly lumped the Incorporated Militia in with the part-time embodied Upper Canada militia or omitted it altogether.

Today, as events commemorating the bicentennial of the War of 1812–1815 are taking place, it is time to set the record straight and tell the story of this short-lived regiment, the Volunteer Battalion of Incorporated Militia of Upper Canada.

It is also only just that credit and honour is paid to those who served with the regiment. This includes the officers and non-commissioned officers of the British regular army who were seconded for duty with the Incorporated Militia between 1813 and 1815; the officers, non-commissioned officers, and rank and file of the Incorporated Militia, who left the security of their homes to defend their country when it was threatened with invasion; and the families of the men, who either remained behind and maintained the homes and farms so their husbands and fathers would have something to "come home to," or left the security of their communities to go "on campaign," suffering and sacrificing alongside their menfolk.

APPENDIX A:

THE CAREERS OF SELECTED INDIVIDUALS FROM THE INCORPORATED MILITIA OF UPPER CANADA

1. James Kerby (1785–1854) (twenty-seven years old in 1812), Captain, No. 1 Company, Major (1814)

In the pre-war years, James Kerby had engaged in a forwarding/shipping business with Robert Grant. This business and its warehouses, located near Fort Erie, were destroyed during the siege. However, following the war, the business was re-established and for a time prospered.

Prior to joining the Incorporated Militia, he had served as both the adjutant in the 2nd Lincoln Militia and commander of an artillery detachment in the shelling of the *Caledonia* and *Detroit* (October 9, 1812). He also commanded an artillery unit in the Frenchman's Creek action (November 29, 1812). On December 2, 1812, while engaged in firing on the American batteries at Black Rock, his 24-pound cannon ruptured, severely wounding Kerby in the right hand and arm. He also sustained wounds at Lundy's Lane and Fort Erie.

1817: Justice of the peace for Bertie Township, Lincoln County.
1822: Major, 2nd Lincoln Militia.
1823: Lieutenant colonel, 2nd Lincoln Militia (honorary colonel and regimental commanding officer).

1826: Town warden, township postmaster, Bertie Township, Welland County.
1831: Appointed to the Provincial Legislative Council.
1834: Appointed customs collector, Fort Erie.
1837: Authorized to raise the Queen's Niagara Fencibles as a special military unit to counter rebel incursions.
1838: Appointed senior officer of militia for the Niagara region.
1846: Commanding officer, Welland Militia Regiment. Committee member of the Brock's monument project for Queenston Heights.

2. Archibald McLean (1791–1865) (twenty-one years old in 1812), Captain, No. 6 Company

A law student when war broke out, McLean served in the 3rd York Militia. Prior to serving in the Incorporated Militia, he saw action at the taking of Detroit (August 6, 1812), Queenston Heights (October 13, 1812), and York (April 27, 1814). He was taken prisoner at Lundy's Lane (July 25, 1814). Upon his return, he was offered a commission in the regular British army, but declined in favour of resuming his law studies.

1820–34: Served as a Member of the Upper Canada House of Assembly (MLA) for Stormont.
1834–36: Elected MLA for Cornwall.
1836: Elected Speaker of the House.
1837: Colonel of the York Militia. Commanded the left wing of the Crown line in the action against the rebels at Montgomery's Tavern. Appointed judge (King's Bench).
1850: Appointed judge (Court of Common Pleas).
1856: Appointed senior judge (Queen's Bench).
1862: Appointed chief justice (Queen's Bench).
1863: Appointed senior presiding judge (Court of Error and Appeal); president of the St. Andrews Society.

3. Jonas Jones (1791–1848) (twenty-one years old in 1812), Captain (1813–14)

A student-at-law at the time war broke out, Jones had previously served in the 1st Leeds Militia. He previously saw action at Ogdensburg (February 22, 1813). Following the war, he returned to his studies and came to the bar in 1815. In later life, he became one of the leading breeders of purebred horses and cattle in eastern Ontario.

1816–28: Served as MLA for Grenville.
1818: Appointed to serve on the joint Parliamentary committee for the improvement of the St. Lawrence River canal system. Appointed public notary for the Johnstown District.
1822: Appointed trustee to the Johnstown Board of Education. Appointed judge (Bathurst District and Surrogate Court). Appointed colonel of 3rd Leeds Militia.
1824: Appointed judge, Johnstown District (present-day United Counties of Leeds and Grenville).
1833: Elected president of the Brockville Board of Police.
1834–37: Elected MLA for Brockville.
1837: Appointed judge (King's Bench). Saw action in the 1837 rebellion at Montgomery's Tavern.
1839–40: Elected Speaker of the Upper Canada Legislative Council.

4. William Morris (1786–1858) (twenty-six years old in 1812), Lieutenant, Regimental Adjutant (1813–14)

Proprietor of a mercantile store in Elizabethtown (Brockville) prior to the war, Morris served in the 1st Leeds Militia. He saw action at Ogdensburg (February 22, 1813).

1818: Appointed justice of the peace for Perth.
1819–36: Served as MLA for Carleton County and later Lanark County.
1822: Lieutenant colonel, 2nd Regiment, Carleton Militia.
1836: Appointed to the Legislative Council.
1837: Appointed senior colonel for Lanark County.
1841: Founding trustee and principal advocate for Queen's College, Kingston.
1841: Appointed to the Legislative Council for the United Canadas.
1844: Appointed receiver general for the United Canadas.
1846–47: President of the Executive Council for the United Canadas.

5. Henry Ruttan (1792–1871) (twenty years old in 1812), Lieutenant, No. 5 Company

Proprietor of a mercantile store in Grafton, Ruttan returned to his business following the war. He was a recognized technological innovator and inventor of several heating and cooling technologies later adopted for use in buildings and railway carriages.

1820–24: Served as MLA for Northumberland.
1827: Appointed sheriff of the Newcastle District.
1836–41: Re-elected as MLA for Northumberland.
1837–38: Elected Speaker of the Upper Canada Legislature.
1846: Colonel of the Northumberland Militia.
1849: Appointed sheriff of the United Counties of Northumberland and Durham.

6. Henry Burritt (1791–1872) (twenty-one years old in 1812), Lieutenant, No. 10 and No. 2 Companies

A farmer and landowner, he is best known as the founder of the Burritt's Rapids community on the Rideau Canal.

1818: Major in 3rd Grenville Militia.
1828: Appointed justice of the peace for the Johnstown District.
1830–40: Lieutenant colonel, Grenville Militia.
1839–41: Served as MLA for Grenville.

7. Henry (Heinrich) Davy (1768–1832) (forty-four years old in 1812), Captain (1813–14)

Veteran of the Revolutionary War and a United Empire Loyalist, he served as a captain in the Addington Militia in

1812. Postwar he became a major landowner and farmer in the Earnstown and Camden area.

8. John Kilborn (1794–1886) (eighteen years old in 1812), Ensign, No. 7 and No. 10 Companies.

A store clerk at Elizabethtown at the outbreak of war, he served with the flank company of Leeds Militia, and saw action at Ogdensburg (February 22, 1813). He acted as quartermaster to Fraser's company in 1813. Following the war, Kilborn returned to the mercantile trade at Unionville (inland from Elizabethtown) and was employed as a forwarding agent by the Commissariat Department, responsible for the settlement of new immigrants to Perth County. Later in life he relocated to Newboro (south of Smith's Falls) where he established a hotel on the banks of the Rideau Canal that is still operating to this day.

1818: Ensign in 1st Leeds Militia.
1828–30: Served as MLA for Perth County.
1830: Captain in 4th Leeds Militia.
1831: Appointed justice of the peace.
1837–38: Served with his regiment during the Rebellion crisis.
1841: Major, 2nd Leeds Militia.
1846: Lieutenant colonel, 8th Leeds Militia.
1848: Appointed judge (Queen's Bench).
1852: Postmaster, Brockville.
1853–55: Associate judge of assize, Brockville District.

APPENDIX B:

UNIFORMS AND CLOTHING

In the case of the Incorporated Militia, its uniforms, weapons, accoutrements, camp equipage, and rations, as well as its training, would have conformed to the British military standards and systems of the day. Once fully outfitted and practised in the various elements of the "Manual and Platoon" exercises, the men would have been virtually indistinguishable from the British regular troops alongside whom they served. As a result, while the references included in the main text were selected because of their direct connection to the story of the Incorporated Militia, some of those included in the following appendices, while not overtly referring to the regiment, would have been fully applicable to their situation.

ORDERS PERTAINING TO UNIFORMS AND CLOTHING

December 24, 1811, Regulations for Officers of Infantry:

To wear a cap of a pattern similar to that established for the Line…. A Regimental coat similar to the Private men's, but with lapels to button over the breast and body…. A grey cloth Greatcoat corresponding in colour with that established for the Line, with a stand up collar and a cape to protect the shoulders and regimental buttons…. The Officers are to wear grey pantaloons or overalls with short boots and gaiters such as the Private men's.[1]

Similarly, the General Orders of March 12, 1812, stated: "All units on service abroad to be supplied with pantaloons and gaiters according to regulation instead of breeches and leggings as worn by the troops at home."[2]

With war looming in 1812, the military authorities, under Sir George Prevost, attempted to forward stockpiles of uniforms, accoutrements, and weapons for the use of the Upper Canada militias. However, when it came to uniforms, there was a combined problem of local military supply shortages and delays in shipments arriving from England. As a result, it became necessary to use old and worn-out regular army regimental coats as an interim, ready-to-wear substitute until new made-up replacement uniforms arrived. In the event of continued difficulties in procuring these items, it was decided that whatever was available in the way of fabrics, fittings, and accessories would be shipped out instead, with the intent that these would subsequently be turned into uniforms at the regimental level in Upper Canada:

On May 21, 1812, the order to ship these materials to Upper Canada was issued:

Cloth*: White, 717 yards; Red, 2418 yards; Yellow, 200 yards; Grey, 90 yards.

Linings: Cotton, 4,173 yards; Baize, 2000 yards; Serge, 250 yards.

Coat Buttons: Large, 40,080; Small 6,612

Felt Caps with cockades and brass plates, 1,606

Leather Caps (Light Infantry), 34

Looping for hats, 2,000 yards

Shoes, 124 pairs

Haversacks (Linen), 500

Knapsacks, 500

Thread, 20 pounds; Needles, 1,500; Thimbles, 300.[3]

(*"Cloth" is the term used in original lists to describe the dense woollen material used in the making of regimental clothing. Today, this kind of material is often referred to as heavy coating or Melton wool.)

On July 15, 1812, the following "Regulations for Clothing — Great Coats" was issued:

Each soldier of regiments of infantry shall be furnished at the public expense in the first instance with a Great Coat … Great Coats for Sergeants are to be furnished without cuffs and collars; these articles (which are to correspond with the facings of the regiment) shall be added to the coats at the Headquarters of the respective regiments; and the necessary expense thereof, not exceeding one shilling and seven pence for each coat will be defrayed by the Commissary in Chief…. The cuffs and collars are to be made of Army coat cloth…. Chevrons on the right sleeves may be added at the regiments to the Great Coats of Sergeants and Corporals; but the expense thereof is, as usual, to be defrayed by the Corps or the individual themselves.[4]

These greatcoats were made according to official government specifications, as revealed in a supplier's contractual document from November:

One Greatcoat to be made for every 3½ yards of Kersey. Sleeves of the Sergeant's coats are to be made to the full length so that the facing may be put on at the end thereof, as recommended by the Inspector of army clothing … 1 coat in every 31 to be made to be of size No. 4 [Extra Large], the remaining 30 coats to be in equal proportion of sizes 1, 2, and 3 … To be delivered at the rate of from 15,000 to 20,000 monthly.[5]

In August 1812, a new regulation arrived at Quebec, notifying the regiments stationed in British North America that a new design of regimental cap (known commonly as the "Belgic" style shako) had been approved for use by the army. However, not wishing to waste those "Stovepipe" caps already in service, a term of grace was provided for the official changeover: "Regiments which have been supplied with caps of the old pattern are to be permitted to wear them until the expiration of the period [two years] of which they have been furnished."[6]

In reality, however, the difficulties inherent to the supply chain meant that, for the most part, these caps were not seen in Upper Canada until the beginning of the campaign season of 1814. In fact, it is documented that at least one regular regiment was still wearing its stovepipe shako when it fought at Waterloo in 1815.

By October 1812, it was recognized that the sending of materials to Upper Canada to be made into uniforms had been a failure. Significant quantities of supplies had been "lost," either to enemy interception while being transported up the St. Lawrence River or to the more clandestine disappearance of items from the supply boats and depots along the way. As a result, the remaining stocks of materiel were woefully insufficient to clothe all of the militia serving in Upper Canada. Nor would additional replacement supplies be forthcoming from England, as the approaching winter would soon close down the shipping season.

Lieutenant Colonel Robert Nichol, the Upper Canada quartermaster general, was ordered to proceed to Montreal to purchase clothing and necessaries for the Upper Canada militias directly from local Lower Canada manufacturers: "[Lieutenant Colonel] Nichol will represent to the Commissary General that the cloth received for the clothing of the militia will not clothe more than 1,000 or 1,200 men and to know whether cloth for 4,000 more could be forwarded."[7]

A total of over £7,000 was budgeted for the purchase of:

Shoes and Beef Shoes	£1,000
Watch Coats (Greatcoats)	£1,000
Trousers (Grey Cloth)	£2,000
Flannel Shirts	£1,100
Stockings (1,200 pairs @ 3/4 per pair)	£200
Blankets (1,500 pairs)	£1,800/-/-[8]

When complete, the supplies were to be directed as follows: 5/12 to Kingston, 1/12 to the Western Districts, and 6/12 to the Niagara and York Districts.[9] These funds produced a flurry of purchases that were sent up to Upper Canada as soon as transportation could be arranged.

On December 22, 1812, an order was issued for the manufacturig of:

2,000 jackets, "well lined with kersey flannel or strong linen"

2,000 pairs of "Gunmouth" trousers

2,000 hats or caps (with brass plates)

2,000 pairs of leather shoes

2,000 knapsacks

2,000 haversacks

and 200 canteens and straps[10]

However, as the proper red cloth was known to be in short supply, Lieutenant Colonel Nichol was given some leeway in his spending: "As his Honor is aware of the difficulty in procuring cloth of any particular colour … use your discretion in the selection of the cloth best adopted for service, keeping in view of the comfort of the men and giving scarlet the preference for the jackets."[11]

As predicted, the required quantity of red wool cloth was not available, leading to the following communication and official change in regulations, dated January 1, 1813:

Major Freer will have made known to you the preparations which are making for the comfortable clothing of your militia. I regret that the total want of scarlet cloth has compelled me to consent to green being made use of for the purpose. When the militia are clothed and paid [it is for you to] establish … a system of discipline which may render that force very efficient against an American

Army.[12] (Sir George Prevost to Major General Sheaffe)

By January 2, 1813, the revised Upper Canada militia uniform regulations were issued. In part, they included a green "Regimental Coat" with red cuffs and collar, these being defined as "Facings". Plain white "Lace" (woollen twill tape applied to the uniform as decoration) set in a single-spaced, square-ended pattern. Blue cloth "Gunmouth" trousers. A felt "Regulation Cap" (A "Stovepipe" cylindrical black-felt shako with a leather peak, woollen tufted plume, and brass plate or bugle badge affixed to the centre-front of the cap.) The covering letter also stipulated: "The jackets to be well lined with Kersey flannel or strong linen … and it will be satisfactory to you to be informed that measures have been adopted for complying with that requisition and there is reason to believe that the several articles will be in readiness to be forwarded to you at the period stated at the opening of the navigation in the spring."[13]

The green uniform described above was issued to the Upper Canada militias in the spring of 1813 and remained in use as their primary uniform until later in the year, when supplies of red coats became available. The green coats were then officially withdrawn and put into stores. However, in practice, they remained a uniform issued at times of need, as in the case of the drafts of embodied militias attached to the Incorporated Militia in 1814.

Other references to the types of materials issued to the men of the Incorporated Militia (Captain Jarvie's company at York) included:

[April 16, 1813] 15 yards of white cotton for collars and wristbands for 24 flannel shirts, made up with part of the flannel drawn from the Government at 2/6 per yard (£1/17/6); 6 oz thread at 1/3 per ounce (7/6)[14]

[April 18, 1813] 6 yards of fine grey cloth for gaiters at 11/3 per yard (£3/7/6); 2 gross of plated buttons at 11/3 per gross (£1/2/6); ¼ pound of thread at 10/- per pound (2/6)[15]

[May 22, 1813] 2 pieces of strong white cotton for shirts, at £2/-/- per 22 yard piece (£4/-/-); Thread and needles for making shirts; 21 yards of grey cloth for trousers, 5/- per yard (£5/5/-); Brown Holland thread and buttons as trimmings for trousers[16]

Losses were also recorded, as seen in a list of items lost by the 1st Battalion, 49th Regiment, at the American capture of Fort George on May 25, 1813:

1½ yards, Officer's superfine scarlet cloth, at £1/4/- per yard. (£4/4/-)

6 yards, Officer's superfine green cloth, at £1/17/3 per yard. (£11/4/-)

13 yards, double-milled Cassimere (Cashmere), at 16/6 per yard. (£10/12/4)

1¼ yards, Officer's grey cloth (for trousers), at £1/5/- per yard. (£2/6/8)

26 yards, Patent Nett (for officer's sashes), at 14/- per yard. (£18/4/-)

4 Officers Epaulettes, at £3/14/7½d. (£14/18/6)

22 pairs, Private's Black cloth leggings, at 6/3 per pair. (£6/17/6)

50¾ yards, Black cloth (for Private's leggings), at 8/2 per yard. (£20/14/5½d)[17]

Since each soldier was responsible for the maintenance of his uniform and equipment according to a schedule of depreciation established by the army, replacing damaged or lost items prior to an official resupply could prove expensive to an individual's pocket:

A July 1813 assessment of the "Values of Clothing and Accoutrements" was listed as:

Gaiters (Sergeant's) per pair	2/6
Gaiters (Private's) per pair	2/3
Stocks and Clasps	1/9
Stocks only	1/3
Clasps only	7½d
Trousers (Sergeant's) per pair	11/1
Trousers (Private's) per pair	10/-
Caps (Sergeant's)	10/-
Caps (Private's)	7/2
Forage Caps	2/9
Gloves, per pair	9d
Waistcoats (Sergeant's)	8/10
Waistcoats (Private's)	4/6
Canteens	3/4
Haversacks	1/8
Shoes	6/8
Shirts (Linen)	5/6
Half Stockings, per pair	10d
Knapsacks	12/-
Straps for Greatcoat	1/3
Camp Colours	2/6[18]

In comparison, the soldiers' daily pay scale (net) was as follows:

Lieutenant Colonel	17/-
Major	16/-
Captain	10/6
Lieutenant	6/6
Ensign	5/3
Paymaster	10/-
Adjutant	8/6
Surgeon	11/4
Quartermaster	6/6
Sergeant Major	2/-
Quartermaster Sgt.	2/-
Paymaster Sgt.	1/6
Sergeant	1/10
Corporal	10d
Drummer	7 ¾d
Private	6d[19]

During the summer of 1813, new supplies arrived from England and were ordered forwarded into Upper Canada for issuance to the troops. These included: 4,000 pairs of blue trousers; 4,080 flannel waistcoats, 4,080 white cloth "Forage" waistcoats; 6,000 pairs of "half-stockings"; 4,017 forage caps; 4,000 linen shirts; 1,879 pairs of "half-gaiters"; 4,005 knapsacks; 5,000 canteens and straps; and 1,500 greatcoats.[20]

This was followed by a subsidiary order for the preparation of a shipment in early July, to: "outfit 3 Staff Sergeants, 16 Sergeants, 12 Drummers, [and] 580 Privates of the Incorporated Militia." Each man receiving a regulation cap and plume; a red coat with dark green facings; a pair of grey trousers; a cloth forage cap; a pair of gaiters; a linen shirt; a flannel shirt; two pairs of stockings; one pair of shoes; a knapsack; a leather neck stock with brass clasps; a flannel or cloth waistcoat with sleeves.[21]

Unfortunately for the militias in Upper Canada, the regiments in Lower Canada had first access to the supplies coming from England. As a result, when the June shipment arrived, the Lower Canada militias "acquired" most of the uniforms that fitted their men and only forwarded the smallest and largest sizes to the Upper Canada militias. This shortfall prompted complaints from the commanders of the Upper Canada militia units that were parading their men in uniforms that were little better than rags.

There was also the question of who would pay for the cost of making the few uniforms that had arrived into ones that would fit the men. On September 3, 1813, Lieutenant Colonel Freer wrote to General Sheaffe outlining Sir George Prevost's decision on the matter: "with respect to the expenses of fitting the clothing which has been supplied to the Embodied Militia, the Commander of the Forces is pleased to authorize that 2/6 currency be allowed for the alteration of each suit."[22]

During that same summer, the British raid on Black Rock on July 11 also netted a significant amount of vital supplies, including the following materials previously captured by the Americans at their taking of Fort George and Fort Erie: five casks of clothing, 396 felt shakos, and eight sides of leather.[23]

Finally, in September, the long-awaited additional supplies of clothing arrived at the Quebec docks from England. Only a portion of this supply actually arrived in Upper Canada, however. This included: 17,000 flannel shirts valued at 5/- each (of which 10,800 are recorded as being sent to Upper Canada); 8,595 pairs of trousers at 10/- per pair (8,595 pairs) 40,000 pairs of shoes at 6/- per

pair, (30,305 pairs). The list also included an annotation offering to send one other interesting item: "There are 10,000 pairs of milled serge drawers [woolen underwear] remaining in stores."[24]

As mentioned in the main text, the American successes at the Battles of Lake Erie and Moravianstown threw the British entirely on the defensive, and in the October retreat on the Niagara frontier, huge quantities of valuable supplies were abandoned or destroyed. Under the category of clothing, the losses included 9 regimental jackets; 161 pairs of grey cloth trousers; 12 pairs of white cotton duck (lightweight canvas) trousers; 9 pairs of shoes; and 960 waistcoats.[25]

By the end of November, the main storage warehouse in Kingston recorded having on hand: 230 green cloth jackets; 602 bucket caps (possibly the obsolete early stovepipe-style shakos, made entirely of leather); 600 pairs of shoes; 50 pairs of "moccasans"; 604 knapsacks; 100 canteens; and 6 flannel jackets.[26]

Having 230 green regimental coats in storage at this late point in the year would suggest that the later red coats had already been issued in replacement, allowing the green coats to be taken out of active use. It is interesting to note that this number of green coats remain unchanged in a subsequent list, dated February 5, 1814.

Also around this time, Sir George Prevost was looking toward the new campaign season and made his needs known to Earl Bathurst in England on January 9, 1814:

> The period having arrived when it becomes necessary that arrangements should be made for providing clothing to meet the wants of the … militia at the opening of the ensuing campaign, I find that the remains of the last year at present in the Commissariat stores will be sufficient to answer the demands, excepting the [following] articles: 10,000 pairs, grey cloth gunmouth trousers; 10,000 pairs, grey cloth half-gaiters; 10,000 pairs, worsted stockings; 10,000 pairs, flannel drawers; 10,000 flannel waistcoats with sleeves.[27]

With the arrival of the red-faced green uniforms in June 1814 (as mentioned in the main text), and the order to alter the facings to blue, the only reference indicating that work was done to this effect comes in a letter sent from the Kingston Commissariat to Lieutenant Colonel Robinson, dated June 16, 1814: "Colonel Nichol has purchased blue cloth for facings, he also purchased on bespeck, 50 Sergeants sashes…. There are plenty of shirts, shoes, half stockings, etc. here. You can get nine very good swords for drummers from here."[28]

At this point, documentation begins to dry up as the unit prepared to go on campaign; however, two additional orders are of note, detailing supplies provided to the men and their expected appearance:

July 2, 1814 — Supplies issued to the Incorporated Militia, York: 282 pairs of shoes, at 6/8 per pair; 483 shirts at 3/9 each.[29]

July 4, 1814 — Regimental Order, York:

"The men are forbidden to wear their blue trousers except on duty or parade."[30]

During the course of the active campaigning during the summer of 1814 and winter of 1814–15, there are no references related to clothing supplies being issued to the Incorporated Militia, beyond those that appear in the main text, until January 25, 1815. At that point, some testimony appears in a court martial of four men from Captain Kerr's No. 8 Company who were identified as all being "regimentally dressed, with caps uncovered and wings on their coats."[31] This would indicate all were fully outfitted with their uniforms, the uncovered cap suggests the use of the Belgic variety of shako, while wings confirm other indications and references that Captain Kerr's company had distinctions appropriate to a light company uniform.

To conclude the clothing references, at the time of the disbanding of the regiment, the commissariat stores at York recorded every item handed in by the men before being discharged. Since the lists for seven of the ten companies have survived, they provide a valuable insight into the load of official equipment each man was expected to carry. However, the lists do not include the additional volume and weight created by any personal items, food supplies, water in the canteen, and ammunition in the cartridge box:

ARMS, ACCOUTREMENTS, AND NECESSARIES DEPOSITED IN THE COMMISSARIAT STORES AT YORK UPON THE DISBANDING OF THE INCORPORATED MILITIA, MARCH 24, 1815[32]

	Kerby's Company	Washburn's Company	McClean's Company	Fraser's Company	Kerr's Company	McDonell's Company	Walker's Company
Other Ranks, Present*	12	27	23	29	29	32	26
Arms	11	26	23	22	28	31	29
Bayonets	11	25	21	23	27	31	25
Breast Plate	11	25	22	26	28	31	26
Scabbards	11	25	22	27	28	31	25
Slings	11	26	5	21	26	31	12
Bayonet Belts	11	25	22	22	27	31	26
Cartridge Box Belts	11	26	22	22	27	31	25
Cartridge Boxes	11	26	22	22	27	31	25
Regimental Coats	12	27	23	29	27	30	23
Waistcoats	2	15	6	17	3	32	13
Trousers(pairs)	12	47	42	46	42	47	24
Great Coats	6	16	23	20	14	23	24
Regimental Caps	12	27	23	29	28	29	26
Shirts	26	74	55	83	93	90	71
Shoes (pairs)	26	61	46	42	60	54	51
Stockings (pairs)	39	66	62	52	57	53	71
Gaiters (pairs)	12	41	23	30	37	36	31
Stocks and Clasps	13	24	23	29	30	32	26
Mittens (pairs)	8	23	23	24	28	27	21
Scissors	0	5	5	9	2	9	1
Combs	0	7	7	9	7	10	6
Razors	9	34	22	16	24	23	15
Shaving Boxes	8	6	21	11	21	16	12
Blackball	0	8	21	8	25	10	1
Brushes	13	48	23	29	37	55	51
Turnkeys and Worms	12	6	2	11	15	16	13
Prickers and Brushes	0	7	2	6	15	12	5
Coat Slings	1	9	1	9	21	11	11
Canteens	2	11	2	15	21	18	11
Haversacks	5	16	1	10	16	18	10
Blankets	12	24	23	24	24	27	12
Knapsacks	12	23	23	28	29	29	26

*Including Sergeant and Drummer

APPENDIX C:

WEAPONS AND ACCOUTREMENTS

DURING THE WAR OF 1812–15, WHILE THE VARIOUS FORCES used a wide variety of weapons, the primary firearm supplied to the British army regulars and Canadian militia infantry was the Land Pattern Musket, commonly referred to as the "Brown Bess." In numerous lists from the War of 1812, it is also referred to as the "English musket," to differentiate it from the smaller-calibre "French musket" of captured French or American origin. Several variants of the Bess are documented as being used during the war. However, the "India pattern" was the standard infantry musket of the day and was the variety most frequently distributed and used in Upper Canada between 1812 and 1815. Some of the specifications of the India pattern musket include: weight, 10 pounds; overall length, 55 inches; barrel length: 39 inches; calibre of barrel bore, 3/4 inch.

Each musket was supplied with a triangular-shaped bayonet that fitted over the end of the muzzle, converting the musket into a bladed weapon. Unfortunately, the blade interfered with the quick reloading of the musket. The bayonet was carried at the left buttock in a protective metal-capped leather scabbard, suspended on a wide leather shoulder belt. Specifications of the bayonet include: weight, 24 ounces; overall length, 21½ inches; length of blade, 17 inches.

Ready-to-fire ammunition for the musket was generally carried in a heavy leather cartridge box, worn directly above the right buttock and suspended on a wide leather shoulder belt. As in the case of the musket, there were several variants of the cartridge box used during the course of the war, which could carry from twenty-nine to sixty rounds. Internally, they held either hollowed-out wooden "blocks" or tin compartments for the cartridges that could be removed in time of emergency to allow additional rounds to be carried. A variety of supplementary magazine boxes, sometimes referred to as "belly boxes" could also be carried. These ranged from a simple homemade block of wood, drilled out to hold cartridges and covered by a flap of leather, to officially issued versions made from leather with an internal wooden block, a tin box covered with painted leather, or a painted tin "magazine" designed to attach to either a separate belt or the leather shoulder belt.

Specifics: calibre of musket ball, .69 to .71; weight of musket ball, 1 1/10 to 1 1/4 ounces; cartridge powder content, 90 to 120 grains; weight of a full sixty-round cartridge box, 6 pounds.

An example of the variety of weapons available prior to the outset of the war can be seen in a listing of weapons and accoutrements stored at the armouries at Quebec City and in various depots in Upper Canada:

October 28, 1811, Quebec City

Muskets (with Bayonets):

"English" (Brown Bess), 3,245 serviceable, 542 needing repair

"Black" (Naval), 653 serviceable, 3 needing repair, 17 unserviceable

Carbines (with Bayonets): 1,094 serviceable, 4 needing repair, 1 unserviceable

Bayonet Scabbards: (Musket) 4,759; (Carbine) 1,092

Rifles: 95 serviceable

Pistols: "Long" (Cavalry) 485 pairs; "Short" (Infantry) 98

Swords: Broadswords 430; Brass Mounted (Sergeant's) 204; Black (Naval) 722

Sword Scabbards: 973

Cartridge Boxes for muskets: (leather) 2,066; (tin) 1,900

Cartridge Boxes for carbines: (leather) 748

Belts for Bayonets and Cartridge Boxes (pairs): 4,059

Slings: (Cartridge Pouch) 4,000; (Musket) 3,188; (Carbine) 200

Prepared cartridges: (Musket) 1,589,500; (Carbine) 36,240; (Pistol) 23,470; (Buckshot) 570

Flints: (Musket) 292,200; (Carbine) 100,024; (Pistol) 26,825[1]

November 1, 1811

Kingston: "English" Muskets: 1,000; Cartridges: 60,000; Flints: 6,000

York: "French" Muskets: 2,329; Cartridges: 13,140: Flints: 14,106

Fort George: "English" Muskets: 1,029; Cartridges: 60,000; Flints: 6,000

Amherstburg: "English" Muskets: 500; Cartridges: 30,000; Flints: 3,000

"The French muskets to be removed from Amherstburg, Fort George and Kingston to York, to make the above number and the ammunition sent to York is calculated for the French arms."[2]

There was also the problem of ensuring that issued arms and equipment could be identified if lost. To this end, the general order of January 16, 1812 read: "To avoid losses of equipment and accoutrements, every article is to have marked on it the number or appellation of the Battalion or Regiment to which it may belong, as well as the number or letter of the troop or company. The marks are to be carefully placed on the inside of the belts, pouches and slings."[3]

In April 1812, a shipment of six thousand "Stand of Arms" (muskets, bayonets, bayonet scabbards, and cartridge boxes) destined for the Upper Canada Militia was lost when the transport ship *Cambo* sank in a gale while sailing from Bermuda to Quebec. In response, Sir George Prevost ordered 1,000 Stand of Arms transferred from Halifax, while a replacement 5,000 muskets and bayonets were ordered from England.[4]

Following the American declaration of war and the immediate threat of invasion, although comparatively a small-scale concern in comparison to the events occurring in Europe, Britain ordered 10,000 India pattern muskets "with steel rammers and bayonets."[5]

The capture of a substantial amount of American weaponry and accoutrements at Detroit and Queenston also provided a vital short-term supply of equipment for the use of the Upper Canada Militia until the expected supply of weapons arrived from England.

A partial inventory (August 16, 1812) of American items captured at Detroit listed the following: 2,500 muskets; 2,500 bayonets; 2,500 ammunition boxes with belts; 500 rifles; 39,000 flints; 80,000 musket cartridges; 10 cwt, musket balls; 1 ton buckshot.[6]

Similarly, some items captured at Queenston on October 13 included: 435 muskets; 380 bayonets; 141 scabbards for bayonets; 245 ammunition boxes and belts; 80 ammunition boxes without belts; 2,810 musket cartridges (with ball and buckshot); 3,140 musket cartridges (with buckshot only).[7]

Unfortunately, when the shipment referred to above arrived from England at Quebec in November, it was found that the associated accoutrements were not included, forcing the Ordnance Department to improvise: "The ten thousand Stand of Arms recently arrived from England having been received without any accoutrements whatever, you will immediately take measures for providing by contract or otherwise, five thousand sets of black pouch accoutrements."[8] (Military secretary to Richard Flemming, ordnance storekeeper, Quebec, November 5, 1812.)

As a result of these supply delays, the Upper Canada Militia continued to be supplied with French muskets well into the following year. This complicated the manufacturing and distribution of ammunition because the smaller-calibre French Charleville, or its American copy, the Springfield, could not fire the larger Bess musket balls. Consequently, it was vital to keep track of what type of muskets each militia regiment was using. A general order issued at Fort George, October 29, 1812, stated: "Where there are two companies of Militia with mixed English and French weapons, they will exchange such that 1 company has all English muskets and the other French, in order to avoid mistakes in the distribution of ammunition."[9]

Similarly, on November 9: "State of muskets held by the 1st Lincoln Militia: the two Flank companies have English muskets and ammunition, the rest American and French."[10]

And on February 2, 1813, muskets and accoutrements held by the 1st Lincoln Militia were listed as follows:

Captain Law's Company:

28 muskets, "all French except 1"

28 cartridge boxes, "12 of which are belly boxes without belts"

28 bayonets, "half of which do not fit well"

28 scabbards, "16 of which have no belts"

Captain McClellan's Company:

34 muskets, "all French"

34 cartridge boxes, "11 of which are belly boxes without straps"[11]

Further evidence of the state of the muskets and accoutrements in the possession of the Upper Canada militias appears in a letter written by Lieutenant Colonel Neil McLean (father of Captain Archibald McLean of the Incorporated Militia) to the adjutant general of militia on June 5, 1813:

Sir, here you will receive the return of the Stormont Regiment of Militia and also the return of arms and accoutrements and ammunition in our possession. By the latter you will perceive that we are greatly deficient in serviceable arms and that a great proportion of the arms and accoutrements are unfit for service.

To account for this it is necessary to observe that a considerable part of them have been in possession of the militia … for nearly thirty years and were slightly repaired … last summer and that the remaining part were in use by the different Corps serving in these Provinces for probably fifty years, and consequently soon became unserviceable … [having been] drag'd about the country by militiamen who cannot be always under the eyes of their Officers and Non Comm'd Officers and whose want of experience and variety of occupations does not admit of their taking … care of them.[12]

As the year progressed, the American successes at York and Fort George resulted in severe losses to the British stocks of weapons. However, successes at Stoney Creek, the Forty Mile Creek, and the raids on Fort Schlosser and Black Rock netted vital supplies of weaponry and associated equipment. These included, for the Fort Schlosser raid (July 5): 53 French muskets; 6 English muskets; 26 bayonets; and 2½ kegs of musket ball cartridges.[13]

The Black Rock raid (July 11) garnered: 60 English muskets; 118 French muskets; 38 English bayonets; 35 French bayonets; 32 scabbards; 45 leather belts; 62 cartridge boxes; and 6 kegs of ammunition.[14]

In September 1813, the list of stocks of muskets held at Kingston included: English, bright (bare polished metal barrels), 2,379; English, black (naval issue), 120; French, bright (French "Charleville" muskets sent from Europe), 27; and American, bright (U.S. "Springfield" copies of the French Charleville), 101.[15]

At the capture of Fort Niagara in December 1813, a huge collection of items was either captured or recovered. In the subsequent official report, the weapons from this haul were described as including: "Arms, about 4,000 stand, with capital accoutrements to the same amount. An immense quantity of musquet ammunition."[16]

By the summer of 1814, some of the companies of the Incorporated Militia were fairly well supplied with weapons and accoutrements. For others, however, significant shortages still remained, as shown by an inventory of items in the hands of some of the companies of the regiment at the beginning of June.

ARMS AND ACCOUTREMENTS IN POSSESSION OF THE INCORPORATED MILITIA, JUNE 1814[17]

Company	1	2	3	4	5	7
Rank and File Present	25	37	33	38	42	43
Muskets	24	23	22	16	11	15
Pouches	24	23	22	16	11	13
Bayonets	24	23	22	16	11	15
Pouch Belts	24	23	22	16	11	13
Side Belts	24	23	22	16	11	15
Slings	24	22	22	15	11	15

Fortunately, by the time the unit left for the Niagara these deficiencies had been eliminated. From this point, because of the active campaigning during the summer of 1814, no additional references are known to exist until the disbandment of the unit, when the previously documented company acquittance lists were compiled. However, in the postwar period (August 25, 1820), a list of militia arms in store at Kingston provides an indication that, in addition to the regulation whitened "buff" belting, black belts were issued for militia use during the course of the war:

403 Light Infantry muskets (New Land pattern)

3,978 India pattern muskets

Bayonet Belts:

1,614 black leather "Volunteer side" belts

1,962 buff leather Infantry shoulder belts

42 buff leather Artillery shoulder belts

Sword Belts:

12 black leather Drummer belts

25 buff leather Artillery Private's belts

Pouches:

4,980 black leather Infantry "regular pattern"

41 buff leather Artillery Private's "with slings"

Slings:

568 black leather "Volunteer infantry musket slings"

875 black leather "Volunteer infantry pouch slings"

1,200 buff leather "Infantry musket slings"

46 buff leather "Artillery musket slings"[18]

APPENDIX D:

LIVING IN BARRACKS AND ON CAMPAIGN

As soldiers, the men of the Incorporated Militia were subject to the necessity of living at various garrisons or in the field while on campaign. Their degree of comfort could vary greatly according to the availability and condition of the barracks where they were posted, or the age and condition of the tents and other field equipment supplied to them. As well, many dependent families accompanied their men, creating a veritable mobile community that lived at the various depots and campsites during the course of the war. The following selected references illustrate the nature and availability of some of these accommodations and encampment supplies.

Prior to the war (October 4, 1811), the tents being held in the military stores at Quebec City were described as: "all of the old [square] form and have been in store ever since the American war, but are nevertheless in such a state of preservation, that on an emergency they might be found serviceable, tho' I should doubt their lasting for any time."[1]

Stocks on this list included: 101 officer's wall tents and flys; 2 provision tents; 1,053 "square" private's tents with poles (2 x 7 feet, 1 x 9 feet); 1,059 "Bell at Arms" tents (for musket storage); 69 casks of tent pins; 94 bags of mallets; 5,760 canteens; 1,090 camp kettles; 33½ bales of haversacks (in bales of 100).[2]

By January 19, 1813, this stockpile had been altered to: 24 officer's wall tents and flys; 3 provision tents; 769 "Square" private's tents; 164 "Flanders" tents (bell tents); 1,385 blankets; 3,958 canteens and straps; 915 camp kettles (old pattern); 280 "Flanders" camp kettles; 4,926 haversacks.[3]

In Upper Canada, the volume of tentage stored at Fort George on March 3, 1813, was listed as: 1 laboratory tent, 1; 14 circular tents ("Flanders"); 14 poles for circular tents; and 1 officer's marquee.[4]

Finally, the lists for the stores at Kingston on May 4 recorded holding: 27 "Flanders" tents; 178 "Square" private's tents; 2 "Bell at Arms" tents; 3 officer's marquees; 570 tent poles; 2,800 tent pins; 220 mallets; 995 canteens; 79 camp kettles; and 635 haversacks.[5]

Other associated references to this topic include:

May 25, 1813 — Regulation for camp equipment applying to two corps of 500 men, plus regimental staff

Flanders tents ("new pattern with poles and pins"): 90

Officer's tents ("old pattern with poles and pins"): 59

Private's tents ("old, square pattern with poles and pins"): 40

Bell at arms tents ("old pattern with poles and pins"): 4[6]

June 18, 1813 — Equipment and supplies ordered to be shipped to Upper Canada

Flanders Tents: 520

Flanders Poles: 520

Marquees (complete): 5

Wooden Tent Pins: 20,000

Mallets: 1,500

Blankets: 5,350

Flanders kettles with cradles: 200

Haversacks: 1,085[7]

July 11, 1813 — Part of the supplies captured during the British raid on Black Rock

2 large bales of blankets (200)

70 loose blankets[8]

Camp equipage lost or destroyed in the retreat of October 1813

2 officer's fly tents

86 private's tents

4 Flanders tents

"The Private's tents destroyed were of the old square pattern, calculated to contain 5 men each."[9]

Supplies ordered for shipment to Upper Canada by the Barracks Department to cover expected requirements in 1814

Rugs, green, knotted: 18,000

Woollen blankets, 6 feet by 7 feet 6 inches: 40,000

"Russian" sheeting, 6 feet by 7 feet 6 inches: 36,000 pairs

Osnaburg [Oznaburg] palliasses [straw-filled mattresses], 6 feet x 7 feet 6 inches: 18,000

Osnaburg bolsters (pillows), 1 foot 6 inches x 4 feet 6 inches: 18,000

Candles, moulded, 4 candles to the pound, 200 candles per box: 30,000 pounds

Candles, moulded, 6 candles to the pound, 300 candles per box: 50,000 pounds

Candles, dipped, 6 candles to the pound, 300 candles per box: 70,000 pounds[10]

July 28, 1814 — Camp equipment in stores at Quebec

Flanders tents: 6

Flanders poles: 6

Blankets: 28

Camp kettles (tin): 99

Flanders kettles: 2,246

Canteens: 2,738[11]

July 29, 1814 — Camp equipment in stores at Montreal

Flanders tents: 0

Flanders poles: 316

Square private's tents: 322

Square private's poles "ridge and standing": 265

Hospital marquees: 6

Hospital marquee poles: 7 sets

Bell at arms tents: 61

Bell at arms poles: 50

Canteens (wood): 1,703[12]

December 10, 1814 — "The barrack bedding in quarters is to consist in winter of a palliasse, bolster, rug, and two blankets for each double berth, these articles are on no account whatever to be removed from the barracks and are to be held in trust by the Corps."[13]

APPENDIX E:

FOOD AND DRINK:
OFFICIAL MILITARY RATIONS

Prior to the war, the official issuance of rations to the troops is referenced as:

March 19, 1812 — Scale of rations in garrison

Per man, per day:

Flour: 1 pound

Pork: 9 1/7 ounces

Peas: 3/7 pint

Rice: 1 1/7 ounces

Butter: 6/7 ounce ("or substitute an additional 1 3/7 ounces Pork")[1]

March 19, 1812 — Circular regarding the wives of regiments

1. Rations to be issued to the women and children of regular regiments:
   In Garrison, 12 women and attached children per troop or company.
   In the Field, 6 women and attached children per troop or company.

2. Royal Veterans battalions to be victulled to the full number of women and attached children with the regiment.

3. Widows and orphans of officers and soldiers to be victulled until they can obtain a passage home.

4. No women or children except the wives and children of the NCOs or Privates to be entitled to rations except as above.

5. Women's rations to be 1/2 that of a man's. Children's rations to be 1/3 that of a man's.[2]

With the outbreak of war, the threat or actual capture of supply convoys in transit between Montreal and Upper Canada along the St. Lawrence River caused significant problems of maintaining a steady supply of food for the armies in the field. On the other hand, attacks on the American supply bases netted significant amounts of vital supplies, including *matériel* previously captured by the Americans in their raids.

July 5, 1813 — Part of the supplies captured during the raid on Fort Schlosser

20 barrels of salt

17 casks of tobacco

8 barrels of pork

1 barrel of whisky[3]

July 11, 1813 — Part of the supplies captured during the British raid on Black Rock

123 barrels of salt

46 barrels of whisky

11 barrels of flour

1 barrel of molasses

1 barrel of jam[4]

As the campaign continued and the avalability of steady supplies of rations became increasingly variable (as the control of the St. Lawrence and lake Ontario repeatedly changed hands), so too did the associated regulations and issuances.

July 15, 1813 — Scale of rations in garrison

Per man:

Flour or Biscuit: 1 pound daily

Rum: ½ pint daily

Beef: 2 pounds on Tuesday and Saturday

Pork: 1 pound on Sunday and Thursday

Peas: ½ pint on Sunday, Wednesday, Thursday, and Friday

Oatmeal: 3/14 pint

Sugar: ½ ounce on Monday, Wednesday, and Friday

Butter or Sugar: 2 ounces on Monday, Wednesday, and Friday

Cheese or Rice or Cocoa: 2 ounces on Monday, Wednesday, and Friday

Vinegar: 4 pints on Monday, Wednesday, and Friday

"Where circumstances will not admit of provisions at the necessary supplies, the substitution is to be made according to the table above … one pound of fresh beef is equal to one pound salt beef and one pound and half of fresh beef is equal to one pound of pork."[5]

August 13, 1813 — General Orders, Prescott

"The field rations for the troops is in future to consist of the following quantities: Vis, daily 1 ½ lbs of flour or biscuits, 10 ½ ounces salt pork or 1 lb fresh or salt beef.… Much inconvenience has arisen in the service of the Commissariat Dept in consequence of general Officers in command of Divisions of the army having taken upon themselves to make alteration in addition to the rations established by the King for the troops serving in North American provinces. His Excellency the Commander of the Forces has been pleased to direct that in future, no change or alteration to that allowance be made without his positive consent being obtained, except in very extraordinary occurrence when the necessity of the service will be stated for consideration."[6]

October 9, 1813 — Supplies lost or destroyed in the retreat from the Niagara to Burlington

Biscuit: 6,230 pounds

Flour: 1,130 pounds

Beef (fresh): 570 pounds

Pork (salted): 77 barrels

Salt: 10 barrels

Whisky: 5 casks

Cattle on the hoof: 13[7]

January 20, 1814 — Scale of rations — Per man, per day

Treasury Scale: (rations issued when in garrison)

Flour or Biscuit: 1 pound

Pork: 10 4/7 ounces (or) Fresh or Salt Beef: 1 pound

Peas: 3/7 pint

Rice: 1 1/7 ounces

Salt (only with fresh beef): ½ ounce

Field Scale: (rations issued while in the field and on the march)

Flour or biscuit: 1½ pounds

Pork: 10 ½ ounces (or) Fresh or salt beef: 1 pound

Salt (only with fresh beef): ½ ounce[8]

August 13, 1814 — Provisions remaining on the Niagara frontier

Flour: 1,298 barrels (254,420 pounds)

Pork: 565 barrels (117,568 pounds)

Salt beef: 353 barrels (73,568 pounds)

Rice: 3,515 pounds

Salt: 200 ½ barrels

Rum: 4,358 gallons

Vinegar: 319 gallons[9]

The above quantities were deemed as only being sufficient to supply the army on the Niagara frontier for the following durations:

Flour (at 9 pounds per week per man): 33 days

Pork: 30 days

Beef: 12 days[10]

October 6, 1814 — District General Order, Niagara Falls

"Until the arrival of the squadron, the following change will be made in the rations issued to the troops of the Right Division to commence on the 8th October, inclusive: 1 pound of beef, one pound fresh beef or pork and 1/7 ounces salt pork, 3/7 of a pint of pease per man … no rice being in store, the value of it to be paid in money at the rate of 6/- per lb, Halifax."[11]

December 1814 — Prices paid by the Upper Canada Commissariat Department

"when delivered to the Commissariat … at Burlington"

Fresh Pork: £3/2/6 per 100 pounds

Salt Pork: £7/10/- per barrel (200 pounds net), "for which the

Government will furnish ½ bushel of salt"

Beef: £2/10/- per animal on the hoof

Flour: £3/10/- per barrel

Peas: 10/- per bushel

Wheat: 12/6 per bushel

Indian corn: 10/- per bushel

Potatoes: 5/- per bushel

Oats: 5/- per bushel

Buckwheat: 5/- per bushel (delivered at any mill in the district)[12]

January 1815 — Prices paid for food supplies by the Upper Canada Commissariat Department

Salt pork: £8/-/- per barrel

Beef: £2/10/- per 100 pounds

Flour: £2/-/- per Cwt (hundredweight, 112 pounds)

Wheat Flour: £3/10/- per barrel

Peas: 10/- per bushel

Oats: 7/6 per bushel

Rice: 6d per pound[13]

Non-Regulation Food Supplies

In addition to the official rations, there was the option, if the individual had the wherewithal, to purchase supplementary rations from civilian retailers, or where a unit was stationed at a garrison for a particularly long period, to obtain food from hunting, fishing, and growing vegetables and herbs in regimental gardens that surrounded most of the forts. In a publication titled *A Statistical Account of Upper Canada*, produced by Robert Gourlay in 1817, he made the following reference to foodstuffs available in Upper Canada prior to the war.

> Wheat is the staple of the province … [while] other grains, such as rye, maize (here called corn), pease, barley, oats, buck-wheat, etc. are successfully cultivated…. The principal fruit of Upper Canada is the apple. The various species of this most useful of fruits grow in all the districts; but most plentifully around Niagara…. Peaches flourish at Niagara … cherries, plums, pears, and currants succeed … [while] Elder, wild cherries, plums, thorns, gooseberries, blackberries, raspberries, grapes, and many other bushes, shrubs, and vines abound…. Strawberries grow freely in the meadow, and are cultivated with success in gardens. The gardens produce, in abundance, melons, cucumbers, squashes, and all the esculent vegetables that are planted in them.[14]

This work also listed a variety of animal sources available as food sources within Upper Canada. These included: "cow; sheep; goat; chicken; oxen; bison (in western regions); moose; black bear; deer; beaver; porcupine; duck; goose; wild turkey; pheasant; sturgeon (75 to 100 pounds); salmon (10 to 20 pounds); pike (3 to 10 pounds); pickerel; trout; bass."[15]

Additional information may also be drawn from adverts placed in various Upper Canada newspapers during this period.

February 1808 — Plant seeds for sale, *York Gazette*: Red Onion; White Onion; Breen marrow-fat peas; Blood Beet (Beetroot); Early Cabbage; Winter Cabbage; Savoy Cabbage; Scarcity; Lettuce; Cucumber; Early Cucumber; Long Cucumber; Turnip; Sage; Carrots; Parsnip; Radish; French Turnip; Summer Squash; Watermelon; Musk Melon; Early Beans; Cranberry Beans; Early

Purple Beans; Asparagus; Celery; Parsley; Pepper Grass; Burnet; Saffron; Carraway; Pink.

May 29, 1812 — Goods for sale, *Kingston Gazette*: tea (hyson and green); coffee; chocolate; vinegar; loaf sugar (white refined sugar in conical blocks); muscovado sugar (modern-day "raw" brown sugar in loose crystalline form); spirits; wine; brandy; "schrub" (shrub: a blended combination of fruit and alcohol); mustard; nutmeg; almonds; pepper; allspice; ginger; smoking tobacco; chewing tobacco.

July 24, 1813 — Goods for sale, *Kingston Gazette*: rum; schrub; peppermint cordial; Teneriffe wine; lime juice; bottled porter beer; tea (green and hyson); sugar (loaf and muscovado); raisins (muscatel and cask); currants; mustard; barley; pepper; allspice; ginger.

February 7, 1814 — Goods for sale, *Kingston Gazette*: tea; coffee; pepper; allspice; nutmeg; almonds; raisins; mustard; sugar (lump and muscovado); lime juice; rum; brandy; Best Holland gin; whisky; schrub; peppermint cordial; port wine; Teneriffe wine.

July 29, 1814 — Goods for sale, *Kingston Gazette*: tea (hyson and hyson skin); sugar (loaf and muscovado); coffee; chocolate; raisins; cinnamon; cloves; allspice; ginger; almonds; mustard; saltpetre; Jamaica spirits; brandy; schrub; peppermint cordial; Madeira wine (best, and low priced); Teneriffe wine (low priced); port wine; Spanish wine.

September 16, 1814 — Goods for sale, *Kingston Gazette*: 300 pounds pineapple cheese; 300 pounds Double Glouster [Gloucester] cheese; 300 pounds Berkley cheese; 9 kegs pickled tongues; best port wine (in barrels and quarter casks); Old Vidonia wine (in barrels and quarter casks); Congal wine (in barrels and quarter casks); Jamaica spirits; white wine vinegar; schrub; tea (hyson and hyson skin); peppermint cordial; sugar (loaf and muscovado); coffee; chocolate; tobacco (pigtail, plug, and ladies twist).

Beyond their availability, there was also the matter of how much these items would cost. For this comparison, the following three references provide an interesting answer:

November 2, 1812 — (per 4 ounces): common tea: 4/-; fine tea: £1/4/-; butter: 1/ -; sugar: 2/ -.[16]

November 1, 1814 — Prices for supplies at Kingston: meat (per pound), 1/3 to 2/-; butter (per pound), 4/-; milk (per quart), 1/-; sugar (per pound), 3/6.[18]

PRICES FOR SUPPLIES AT QUEBEC CITY
DURING THE COURSE OF 1813[17]

(Silver exchange rate: 5/- = $1:00 Halifax currency)

January 1813	December 1813	
Wheat (per bushel)	12/- to 12/6	None for sale
Oats (per bushel)	3/-	4/- to 4/6
Barley (per bushel)	None for sale	8/- to 10/-
Pease (per bushel)	8/6 to 9/-	None for sale
Rice (per Cwt.)	None for sale	None for sale
Flour (per barrel)	[blank]	[blank]
Superfine:	None for sale	None for sale
Fine: ($ Halifax)	$18:00 to $20:00	None for sale
Common:	$15:00	$22:00
Oatmeal	None for sale	None for sale
Butter	None for sale	None for sale
Biscuit (per barrel)	None for sale	None for sale
Muscovado Sugar (per Cwt = 112 lbs)	£2/10/-	£4/-/-
Molasses (per gallon)	2/9	None for sale
Coffee (per lb.)	10d	1/3 (=15d)
Vinegar (per gallon)	3/6 to 4/-	2/6 to 4/-
Madeira Wine (per pipe = 144 gallons)	£60/-/- to £90/-/-	£100/-/- to £150/-/-
Port Wine (per pipe)	£50/-/- to £80/-/-	£70/-/- to £90/-/-

APPENDIX F:

CLOTHING THE REGIMENTAL WOMEN AND CHILDREN

As referenced in the main text, the number of women and children following the regiment during its existence varied according to location and circumstance. However, no evidence has appeared to document that any of the ladies of the officers lived with the regiment, but instead seemed to have remained at home. It would appear that only those women married to the "other ranks" journeyed to York in February 1814. There, they and their children would have been billeted in the same barracks as the men, as separate or private accommodations for families were not considered necessary by the army.

In these cramped and noisy conditions, the only privacy any woman could expect would be in the form of a blanket or curtain pinned up around the legs of a lower berth of a double occupancy bunk bed, while the children would be squeezed into a corner or on the floor under the beds.

While the women and children of the regiment were provided with rations, they received no such allowance for clothing or personal items. Instead, it was up to the woman to either survive on her husband's pay, using anything that came to hand in the way of old uniforms and worn out shirts, etc., or earn some money to provide additional food and clothing for herself and the children. Officially, this could be done by acting as housekeepers for the officers, or as laundresses and seamstresses to the military departments and men of the regiment. However, obtaining and reselling items to make a profit was not unknown, although in every case these activities were tightly controlled and regulated by the military authorities:

October 18, 1812 — Garrison Orders, York

"Any woman who presumes to bring liquor into the garrison will be turned out of barracks and deprived of her rations. The sentry at the gate will examine every soldier's wife that comes in and prevent her bringing in any liquor."[1]

March 1813 — Bedclothes and Barrack supplies, Washing Rates, York

Sheets, (washed once a month) 3d per pair

Palliases, (washed once a quarter) 3d each

Blankets and Rugs, (washed once a year) 3d each[2]

March 1814 — Bedclothes and Barrack supplies, Washing/Repair Rates

Palliases, washing: 6d each   (making repairs 6d)

Bolsters, 2d each   (1d)

Sheets, 7½d per pair   (6d)

Blankets, 6d each   (4d)

Rugs, 8d each   (6d)[3]

May 26, 1814 — Regimental Orders

"The women will charge two pence halfpenny for washing each shirt for the men, any woman refusing to work for the above sum will be struck off rations."[4]

Making the assumption that a woman could accumulate some money, there was then the issue of finding suitable and affordable items. New, ready-made clothes were available, but were extremely expensive, while a thriving second- or third-hand clothing market supplied older finished pieces at more reasonable prices. Many women, however, took it upon themselves to make their family's clothes or adapt and refurbish older clothing. As a result, there was a widespread market for lengths of material and sewing supplies.

As in the case of ready-made clothing, there was a wide range of items available on the civilian market, but unfortunately the prices were such that, for the most part, they were out of reach of the common soldier's wife's pocket. In view of these financial limitations, many of the items listed below, although taken from advertisements of the time and therefore indicating what was available, should not all be construed as affordable to the family of an average rank and file soldier or even an NCO's wife, but rather are more likely applicable to an officer's family at home:

May 29, 1812 — *Kingston Gazette*: Cotton (India); Cotton (Printed); Cambrick (Linen or Cotton); Muslin (Leno or Book); Shambray; Velvet (Silk or Cotton); Lutestring (Black); Corduroy; Thicksett; Fustian; York Stripe; Nankeen (blue or yellow); Bombazette; Sheeting (Russian); Handkerchiefs (Bandana, Cotton, or Silk); Sewing Silks.

March 9, 1813 — *Kingston Gazette*: Broadcloth (Superfine, Fine, or Low priced); Bath coatings; Cassimeres; Flannel (green, red, blue, or white); Scotch Sheeting; Osnaburghs; Cotton (Striped, Check, India, Bengal Striped, or Sheeting); Linen; Nankeen (blue, or coloured); Jean (black or blue); Stockinett; Bombazette (black or green); Calico (Printed); Ginghams; Muslin (Seeded or Leno); Spot Swanskin; Baize (red); Velvet (Pelice, or twilled); Cambric (Embossed or Dimity); Silk; Corduroy; Fastnett; Larsnett; Lutestring and embossed ribbon; Toillenet (Ribbed, or Fancy vesting).

October 23, 1813 — *Kingston Gazette*: Calico (Superfine, Common, or Furniture); Cotton (Shirting, India, Gingham; Cotton (white, check, striped, or Bengal striped); Gingham; Cambric (Cotton); Toillenette (Vesting); Broadcloth, Superfine (blue, scarlet, grey, or black); Broadcloth, Second (olive, black, grey, dark mixed); Broadcloth, Low priced (blue or grey); Bath Coating; Fearnoughts (Double-milled); Cassimeres (black, white, dark mixed, drab, flesh-coloured); Jackinetts; Brunswick Cord (drab); Velveteen and Thicksett (black, olive); Velvet (Pelice); Flannel (Pelice); Flannel (red, white, yellow, or blue); Muslin (Book, Spring'd); Cambric (black, white, or coloured); Chambrays (Silk, black); Satin; Bedticking; Dimity; Linen; Bombazette (black); Sheeting (Russian).

July 29, 1814 — *Kingston Gazette*: Broadcloth, Best Superfine (blue, black, or grey); Cassimere, Double milled (blue, black, or grey); Flannel (white, red, or yellow); Cotton (striped, white, blue, check, Shirting, Bedticking, Diaper); Velveteens (black, blue); Cambric (black, white, or coloured); Calico, Superfine (dressed and undressed); Calico, Low priced; Linen, (bedticking or Irish);

Stockinett; Tartan Plaid; Dimity; Durants; Calimanicoes; Lawn; Chambrays (silk); Silk veils (black, white); Gimps, Superfine (grey); Sarcenet (sage-coloured, slate-coloured, grey, or blue); Lutestring (India, black); Blacknett; Muslin (scarlet, black); Muslin (Plain and figured Jaconette); Muslinette; Cambric (Linen); Bombazette (black, coloured); Bombazine; White Marselles and Fancy Vesting; Russian Duck; Jeans (white, coloured); Nankeen (coloured); Crepe (black).

✤ ✤ ✤

The British authorities also made a particular show of providing gifts to the Native allies to ensure and maintain their loyalty. It is also documented that the Natives frequently traded these gifts back to the white settlers in exchange for more desired articles. As a result, it is possible to infer that some of the following materials may have come into the possession of the soldiers' families.

Price list for Native goods distributed in 1812:

Blankets,

1 point (per pair): 7/-

1½ point (per pair): 8/-

2 point (per pair): 9/6

2½ point (per pair): 13/-

3 point (per pair): 17/6

Caddie (per piece of 40 yards): 2/9 (blue, brown, grey, green)

Calico (18 yards): £1/8/6 (2 colour), £1/14/6 (3 colour)

Callimanico (30 yards): £1/7/3

Cloth (15 yards): 10/- (green, blue, black, scarlet)

Cotton (15 yards): 2/- (striped)

Cambric (30 yards): £1/10/-

Coating (Bath) (30 yards): 5/6

Flannel (30 yards): 1/3 (white), ¼½d (green, yellow)

Linen (Irish) (per yard): 2/-

Osnaburg (144 yards): 8d

Rateen (per yard): 4/1 (green), 5/6 (blue, grey), 7/6 (scarlet)

Serge (40 yards): 2/- (embossed)

Sheeting (30 yards): £5/5/- (Russian), £7/-/- (Scotch)

Strouds (30 yards): £4/12/6 (blue), £9/1/- (black)

Thread (per pound): 2/7 (sewing), 5/- (stitching), 3/6 (worsted)[5]

Native goods distributed in 1814:

Blankets (1 point to 3 point): 12,500

Broadcloth (scarlet, blue, green, black): 100 yards

Buttons: 100 Gross

Coating (blue, grey, brown, white): 50 pieces

Caddie (blue, grey, brown, purple): 150 pieces

Calico: 1,500 yards

Flannel: 200 pieces

Linen (Irish): 1,000 yards

Melton (wool) (blue, green, brown, purple): 250 yards

Needles (sewing): 10,000

Rateen (blue, brown, green, grey, white): 150 yards

Ribbon (crimson, green, blue, purple): 1,600 yards

Serge (Embossed): 300 yards

Sheeting (Russian): 100 yards
   (Scotch): 120 yards

Strouds (blue, black): 1,300 yards[6]

APPENDIX G:

Sickness and Disability

Without the resources or knowledge of present-day medical capabilities — the absence of modern qualified medical personnel, and in some cases even an understanding of the value of nutrition, cleanliness, and hygiene — what today would be considered minor sicknesses were life-threatening illnesses in 1812. Even without the complication of wartime-campaign living and the threat of being wounded, injured, or killed, the poor and unbalanced diets of most of the populace, coupled with the physical toll of living and working in a frontier environment, inflicted significant strain and wear upon the human body.

Under these circumstances, and in comparison to modern standards, daily life in 1812 prematurely aged the body, leading to an increase in arthritic conditions, hernias, and deteriorated vision and hearing, not to mention the rotting of teeth. For the military, these circumstances were taken into consideration at the recruitment stage of an individual's military service, theoretically weeding out those unsuited or incapable of undertaking the rigours of campaign life.

However, there were certain conditions that could develop at relatively short notice, resulting in a man's dismissal from the regiment. One obvious category would be the development of a hernia or "rupture" that would prevent the man from carrying his equipment or performing heavy manual labour or fatigues. Another would be the case where an individual's dental decay progressed to the point that insufficient teeth remained intact in the upper and lower jaw to be able to grasp and tear open the heavy-duty paper of the musket cartridge, thus making the individual unable to properly load the musket. This condition was termed being "worn out" and in reviewing the records was a common cause of dismissal from the regiment.

Likewise, combat injuries were obvious reasons for dismissal or resignation from the corps. In the case of several of the officers of the regiment, however, otherwise debilitating or disfiguring wounds, incurred prior to or during their term in the regiment, did not prevent them from serving until the end of the war. Unfortunately, details of less serious or temporary medical conditions and remedies are not recorded in the available official records. As a result, the details listed below can only give a small degree of enlightenment of this fascinating topic.

June 24 to December 24, 1813 — Sick list for the militia detachments at Kingston

Incorporated Militia: 130 Other Ranks

Embodied Militia: 390 Other Ranks

Total: 520 Other Ranks

Cynachi Perotiel: 4 cases
Diarhoia (Diarrhea): 160 cases
Dysinteria (Dysentery): 165 cases
Dispepsia (Dyspepsia): 42 cases
Debility: 46 cases
Febus com contin: 83 cases
Typhus (Typhoid): 3 cases
Intermittens: 12 cases
Pneumonia: 24 cases
Putulis (Pustules): 7 cases
Rhumatismas (Rheumatism): 15 cases
Icterus: 14 cases
Epitaxis: 1 case
Hemouroids (Hemorrhoids): 4 cases
Lucs Veneria (Varicose Veins): 5 cases
Gononhoea (Gonorrhea): 2 cases
Hernia: 3 cases
Herpes: 2 cases
Burns: 1 case
Tumor Sestisis (Cystisis): 1 case
Lame: 37 cases[1]

April–October, 1814 — Men deemed unfit for further service and discharged

Name	Born (Age, 1814)	Company	Cause of Discharge
Richard Griffith	Not known	1	Unfit for Service
John Reilly	Not known	1	Unfit for Service
Joseph Millard	1783 (31)	1	Ruptured
Patrick Bern	1763 (51)	2	Unfit for Service
George Chase	1783 (31)	2	Fractured Leg
John Cameron	1750 (64)	2	Unfit for Service
Thomas Armsworth	1764 (50)	2	Unfit for Service
Jacob Axley	1886 (28)	2	Old Ulsers
James O'Hara	1767 (47)	2	Old Wound
William Huntington	Not known	2	Unfit for Service
Daniel McKay	1754 (60)	3	Worn Out
Thomas Whitticker	1762 (52)	3	Worn Out
William Burke	1781 (33)	4	Old Ulsers
Alexander Green	1778 (36)	5	Epilepsy
William Eyke	Not known	6	Unfit for Service
David Jones	Not known	6	Unfit for Service
Francis Legro	1796 (18)	7	Scalded Head
Jacob Mills	1773 (41)	7	Lame Right Arm
Michael Boleau	1759 (55)	7	Ruptured
Paul Millott	1765 (49)	7	Unfit for Service
Duncan Valud	1764 (50)	7	Unfit for Service
Christopher Apple	1774 (40)	7	Unfit for Service
Henry Lovell	Not known	8	Unfit for Service
Donald McPhee	1759 (55)	9	Worn Out
Daniel Baxter	1751 (63)	9	Worn Out
John Richardson	1759 (56)	9	Worn Out
Norbar Dupee	Not known	9	Unfit for Service
William Sheffield	1768 (46)	9	Ruptured
Anthony Jarvie	Not known	10	Unfit for Service
John Grant	1796 (18)	10	Ruptured
William Morrison	1768 (46)	10	Unfit for Service
Ewen Mc Donell	Not known	10	Unfit for Service
Baptiste Boudria	1759 (55)	Davey	Unfit for Service
Peter Charles	1775 (39)	Davey	Unfit for Service

✠ ✠ ✠

In the aftermath of the war, boards of pension were established to determine the nature and extent of the wounds and disabilities suffered by those men who were injured while in the service of the Crown. The following are examples of cases from these files, relating to the Incorporated Militia:

Titus G. Simons (Major): Lundy's Lane (July 25, 1814). Wounded while serving with the 2nd York Militia. Right arm disabled from being hit in the right arm and breast by an iron case shot. The wound being dressed on the field by Robert Kerr, the senior surgeon to the Indian Department.

James Kerby (Major): Fort Erie (December 2, 1812). Injured while serving with the 2nd Lincoln Militia. Right hand injured and partially disabled when the cannon he was serving exploded. Fort Erie (August 12, 1814). Wounded by two musket balls, one in the right shoulder and one in the right hip.

William Jarvie (Captain): York (April 27, 1813). Wounded in the thigh and had his right hand disabled from being hit by a musket ball through the right wrist. Lay for two days and nights in the woods after being wounded without medical attention.

Thomas Fraser (Captain): Lundy's Lane (July 25, 1814). Wounded in the right arm by a musket ball that passed through the triceps muscle.

John McDonell (Captain): Lundy's Lane (July 25, 1814). Right arm amputated after being hit by a musket ball.

William Jarvis (Lieutenant): York (April 27, 1813). Lost the sight of an eye by the explosion of the magazine in the Western battery.

Daniel MacDougal (Lieutenant): Lundy's Lane (July 25, 1814). Multiple musket ball wounds in the body and arm. Wounded in the thorax by a musket ball causing post-war complications resulting in severe restriction of breathing.

George Ryerson (Lieutenant): Frenchman's Creek (November 21, 1812) while serving with the 1st Lincoln Militia. Wounded by a musket ball that shattered his lower jaw, carrying off part of the jawbone, all of his front teeth, and a section of his tongue.

Alexander Rose (Lieutenant): Prescott (July 26, 1813). Fractured his leg and injured his back by a fall during the construction of the blockhouse at Fort Wellington.

Henry Ruttan (Lieutenant): Lundy's Lane (July 25, 1814). Wounded by a musket ball below the right shoulder that passed clean through from front to rear.

John Bertrand (Bugler/Drummer): Niagara frontier (October 8, 1814). Right arm amputated following an accident that occurred during the retreat from Fort Erie to Chippawa.

John Bryant (Private): Fort Erie (October 12, 1814) Disabled in action at Fort Erie. No additional details.

George Chase (Private): Cedars, Lower Canada (June 7, 1814) Injured by accident while escorting prisoners of war to Montreal.

William Chisholm (Sergeant): Lundy's Lane (July 25, 1814). Wounded by a musket ball. No additional details.

John Conell (Private): Lundy's Lane (July 25, 1814). Right leg amputated after being wounded by a musket ball.

William Empey (Private): Grass River (March 1, 1814). Suffered severe frostbite to his toes and feet while on a raid against the Americans at Grass River.

Richard Hull (Private): Fort Erie (October 12, 1814). Disabled in action at Fort Erie. No additional details.

Joseph Long (Private): Crossroads (September 19, 1813). Wounded by the accidental discharge of a musket.

William Mattimore (Private): Lundy's Lane (July 25, 1814). Wounded by a musket ball that entered the left leg below the knee, breaking the fibula. The ball was deflected and exited at the inferior (inside) part of the thigh. Also wounded by five pieces of buckshot in the left ankle.

John Seeley (Private): Lundy's Lane (July 25, 1814). Left arm amputated after being wounded by a musket ball.

Jacob Snyder (Private): Lundy's Lane (July 25, 1814). Wounded by a musket ball that passed through the left hand and waist, another musket ball that broke the right shoulder, and a third that passed through the skull behind the left ear that caused post-war migraines and impairment of his senses during severe changes in weather (air pressure).

APPENDIX H:

CRIME AND PUNISHMENT

I N ADDITION TO THE EXAMPLES REFERRED TO IN THE MAIN text, there are a number of other cases of misdemeanours and crimes recorded in the regimental records. For the most part these refer to incidents of insolence or disrespect to a senior officer, temporary absenteeism, or occasionally attempts to desert, all of which received fairly standardized sentences, selected examples of which are included below. However, there are also a few instances of other, more unusual crimes that are illuminating as an illustration of life within the regiment.

SELECTED COURTS MARTIAL RECORDS FOR THE INCORPORATED MILITIA, 1814–1815

Date/Location	Prisoner(s)	Charge	Plea	Sentence
March 26, 1814, Fort York	Private William McDonell Private Adam VanWinkin Private Peter Huffman	AWOL AWOL AWOL	Guilty Guilty Guilty	Confined in Cells for 15 days on bread and water. To be marched for 5 mornings at the regimental parade with their coats turned inside out and a log chained to their legs.
March 26, 1814, Fort York	Private Andrew Lasher	Insolence and Unsoldierlike conduct.	Guilty	Confined in Cells for 15 days on bread and water.

April 12, 1814, Fort York	Private Andrew Althouse	AWOL	Guilty	Confined in the regimental guardroom for 7 days. To be led by the company drummer through the lines of the regiment with his coat turned inside out and a rope around his neck. His crime to be printed on a card in large letters and attached to his back.
April 12, 1814, Fort York	Private John Jackson	Attempting to desert while drunk	Guilty	As per Private Althouse.
April 12, 1814, Fort York	Private John Dunn	Insolence and disobedience of orders.	Not Guilty	Confined in the regimental guardroom for 7 days on bread and water. To attend all drills and to be marched for 2 hours each day outside the guardroom wearing a 20 lb pack. To be marched on the parades in the same manner as Privates Althouse and Jackson.
April 12, 1814, Fort York	Private Christian Avichouser	Asleep at his picket post.	Not Guilty	Confined in the regimental guardroom for 20 days on bread and water. To attend all drills and to be marched for 2 hours each day outside the guardroom wearing a 20 lb backpack.
April 27, 1814, Fort York	Private Frederick Lampman Private John Lounsbury Private Richard Hull	Desertion Desertion Desertion	Guilty Guilty Guilty	To be confined in the regimental guardroom for 8 days on bread and water. To appear each day on the regimental parade with coats turned inside out, carrying a backpack filled with stones. To be drilled for an hour and a half each day wearing the pack. On the 8th day to be marched in front of the battalion with their coats turned inside out and a label attached to their back with the word "deserter" on it. The drummer to play the "Rogues March." Following which the men to rejoin their companies.

May 4, 1814, Fort York	Private David Fralick	Neglect of duty on Picket and Insolent language to the Corporal of the Guard.	Guilty	To wear a 24 lb roundshot chained to the leg for three days, except when at drill. To work at weeding on the regimental parade ground for 4 hours each day and otherwise to be confined in the regimental guardroom.
May 16, 1814, Fort York	Private Isaac Fitchell, Private Jacob Ham, Private Hiram Yonge	Drunk while on duty at the Don River guardhouse on May 14.	All three pled Guilty	Confined to the regimental cells on bread and water for 25 days.
May 21, 1814, Fort York	Private Henry Ouderkirk	AWOL from a working party from May 15 to May 21.	Guilty	Found Guilty. To do 4 months of fatigues (without extra pay) with a 24 lb roundshot chained to his leg. To be confined in the regimental cells each night.
May 26, 1814, Fort York	Corporal John Mills	Use of improper language at the Union Hotel in York.	Not Guilty	Found Guilty. Reduced in rank to a Private. To do 10 days of fatigues (without extra pay) with a 24 lb roundshot chained to the leg. To be confined in the regimental cells each night.
June 6, 1814, Fort York	Private Abraham Montross	AWOL from April 10, 1814, until brought back as a prisoner on June 3.	Guilty	To do 4 months of hard labour (without extra pay) with a 24 lb roundshot chained to his leg.
June 6, 1814, Fort York	Private Simon McIntire	Found asleep on guard duty.	Not Guilty	Found Guilty. To carry a 3-stone (48 lb) weight of sand for two weeks and to be kept marching in front of the regimental guardhouse from sunrise to sunset except when at drill. (This sentence was subsequently quashed by Lt. Colonel Robinson).
June 17, 1814, Fort York	Private William Graham	Attempted desertion. Improper conduct and insolence to a senior officer.	Not Guilty	Acquitted of attempted desertion. Found Guilty of the other charges. To be confined for 4 days in the regimental cells and to be put on a bread and water ration for 20 days.

August 30, 1814, Fort Erie Encampment	Corporal Benjamin Markle	Use of improper language and improper conduct on August 29	Not Guilty	Found Guilty. Reduced to the rank of Private.
September 26, 1814, Palmer's Farm on the Niagara River	Private Peter Morin, Private Enias Langolie (also listed as Ignace Langolier)	Desertion from the encampment at Fort Erie on September 5, 1814 until recaptured.	Guilty Guilty	To be confined at Fort Niagara on hard labour for 4 months (without extra pay or any ration of liquor) with a 24 lb roundshot chained to their legs.
September 26, 1814, Palmer's	Private James Grant	Unsoldierlike conduct on September 23. (*1)	Not Guilty	Found Guilty. To pay a £5/-/- fine or to be confined at Fort Niagara for 3 months.
September 26, 1814, Palmer's	Private Duncan Grant	Disobedience of orders in refusing to go on guard duty. Use of abusive language. Threatening senior officers.	Not Guilty	Found Guilty. To pay a £5/-/- fine or to be confined at Fort Niagara for 3 months.
October 13, 1814, Chippawa River	Private Samuel Harris, Private Joseph Amarable	Desertion at York on June 29, 1814 until brought back a prisoner.	Guilty Guilty	To be confined at Fort Niagara on hard labour for an indefinite period (without extra pay or allowances) with a 24 lb roundshot chained to their legs.
October 13, 1814, Chippawa River	Drummer David Burns	AWOL from the camp at Fort Erie until recaptured at Chippawa.	Guilty	To be confined at Fort Niagara on hard labour for 3 months (without extra pay or allowances).
October 31, 1814, Butler's Barracks	Private William Bullis	Disobedience of orders on October 28 in refusing to go on guard duty. (*2)	Not Guilty	Found Guilty. To pay a 15/- fine or to be confined at Fort Niagara for 30 days.

October 31, 1814, Butler's Barracks	Private Joseph Robillard	Dereliction of duty in allowing Private Samuel Harris to escape while being held a prisoner in his tent at York on June 29, 1814.	Not Guilty	Found Guilty. To pay a £1/-/- fine or to be confined at Fort Niagara for 30 days.
October 31, 1814, Butler's Barracks	Private Jacob Fennor (also listed as Jacob Ferrier)	AWOL from October 9, 1814 until recaptured on October 28. (*3)	Not Guilty	Found Guilty. To be confined in Fort Niagara for 2 months.
November 30, 1814, Fort George	Private Asa Kimner	AWOL from May 1814. (*4)	Not Guilty	Found Guilty. To pay a £1/-/- fine or to be confined at Fort Niagara for 1 month. This sentence subsequently commuted to House Arrest for the same period.
November 30, 1814, Fort George	Private Edward Logan	Unsoldierlike conduct on November 21, 1814, being found drunk on guard duty with his canteen two-third's full of rum.	Not Guilty	Found Guilty. To be marched continuously for 2 hours each day for 4 days in front of the barracks. His coat to be turned inside out and with a label pinned to the back reading "For unsoldierlike conduct."
December 23, 1814, Fort York	Corporal Duncan McCrimmon	Unsoldierlike conduct during the march from Fort George to York. (*5)	Not Guilty	Found guilty. Reduced to a Private.
December 23, 1814, Fort York	Private John Mills	Unsoldierlike conduct on December 6, 1814 in refusing to work when ordered on fatigues. (*6)	Not Guilty	Found Guilty. To be confined in the regimental cells for 2 weeks. Due to previous good behaviour the court recommended clemency and the charge was subsequently commuted to time served.
December 23, 1814, Fort York	Private Duncan VanAlstine	Insolence and disobedience of orders from Sergeant Bigelow.	Not Guilty	Found Guilty. To be confined in the regimental cells for 1 month.

December 31, 1814, Fort York	Private Baptiste Ladrea (also listed as Baptist Ladrue, Ladree, Ladraw, Ladray, Ladreu, Ladrial, Ladrie)	Unsoldierlike conduct. Fighting while drunk and using abusive language to Lieutenant Fraser.	Not Guilty	Found Not Guilty of using abusive language. Found Guilty of unsoldierlike conduct. To pay a 10/- fine or to be confined in the regimental cells for 1 week on bread and water.
January 18, 1815, Fort York	Sergeant Daniel McGuire	Contravening orders regarding the purchase of necessaries from a soldier of the 89th Regiment. (*7)	Not Guilty	Found Not Guilty.
January 18, 1815, Fort York	Private John Butler	AWOL from February 1814 until brought back a prisoner.	Guilty	Considered to have already served his punishment awaiting trial and returned to duty.
January 25, 1815, Fort York	1. Private John Fralick 2. Private James Grant 3. Private Francis Boucher (*8) 4. Private Duncan Grant	AWOL after the tattoo. Committing violence to a soldier of the 89th Regiment and his wife. (*9)	All four pled Not Guilty	1. Found Guilty of violence. 2. To be put on a bread and water ration for 10 days. 3. Found Not Guilty of violence. Found Guilty of being AWOL after tattoo. To do 4 additional guard duties. 4. Found Not Guilty on all Counts.
January 27, 1815, Fort York	Private Asa Jones	AWOL from April 10, 1814 until brought back a prisoner on January 2, 1815.	Guilty	To be confined at Fort Niagara on hard labour for 2 months (without extra pay or any ration of liquor).
January 27, 1815, Fort York	Private Benjamin Gokea (*10)	AWOL from barracks after tattoo. Theft of $7:00 from Private Legro's trunk.	Not Guilty	Found Guilty on both Counts. To be marched in front of the regimental parade every morning for 6 days wearing a label pinned to his back marked "Thief". To have $7:00 stopped from his pay and paid to Private Legro.

January 27, 1815, Fort York	Private Thomas Abelman	Unsoldierlike conduct while acting as barrack orderly in allowing a party to be conducted in the men's mess. Disrespect to an officer.	Not Guilty	Found Guilty on both Counts. To be publicly reprimanded on the regimental parade and returned to duty.
February 23, 1815, Fort York	Sergeant Alexander Fraser	Drunk while on duty.	Guilty	Suspended from Rank and pay until March 24, 1815.
February 23, 1815, Fort York	Private Charles Seney	Found with necessaries (1 pair of shoes and 2 pairs of socks) that were not his.	Guilty	Found Guilty. To pay a £1/-/- fine or to be confined in the regimental cells in solitary confinement for 15 days.

(*1) Refused to go on guard duty and when pushed by Sergeant Francis Baucher to get him moving, drew his bayonet and struck the sergeant across the face with the weapon.

(*2) Refused to go on guard duty as it was raining and he had only just returned from illness at the hospital.

(*3) Went AWOL from Chippawa while en route to the hospital at Fort George. Claimed in his defence he had simply returned to his home nearby because he was sick and had intended to return but was taken the day before having done so.

(*4) Failed to return to the regiment after being released from parole. Claimed in his defence that he was wounded and made a prisoner of war at the Battle of Fort George on May 23, 1813. When exchanged he was lame and unable to rejoin the regiment and was given permission by Ensign Simons to remain at home until recovered.

(*5) Ensign John Fraser stated that during the march of the regiment from Fort George to York in early December, the prisoner was instructed by Captain Thomas Fraser to go thirty rods in front of the regiment with an advanced party of men. Instead he went six to seven miles further with a few of the men, allowing the remainder to straggle as they wished. In his defence, McCrimmon claimed he was not aware he was in charge of the party, that some of the men were lame and could not keep up, forcing him to hire a sleigh to rejoin the regiment.

(*6) Accused that he stated that he would go as ordered but would be damned if he would work. Claimed in his defence that he was drunk.

(*7) A yellow flannel shirt, value 1/-.

(*8) Also listed as Bushie, Bucher, Bushee, Busher, Bushy, Busheai, Bouchir, Bushey, and Bushay.

(*9) Evidence given that the four men accosted the couple, grabbing the wife and striking the soldier. According to one male witness, one individual then pushed the wife to the ground and "farted" in her face. According to the wife's testimony they "spat" in her face.

(*10) Also listed as Gochee, Gokew, Gokey, Goroke, Gothier, Gotier, Gautier, and Gorokie.

Notes

1: The Road to War

1. Library and Archives Canada (hereafter referred to as LAC), British Military and Naval Records, RG8-I, Vol. 688a, 40.
2. *Ibid.*, RG8-I, Vol. 688a, 169.

2: The Opening Round, June–October 1812

1. LAC, British Military and Naval Records, Freer Papers, RG8-1, Vol. 1705, 3; and Ernest Cruikshank, *The Documentary History of the Campaigns upon the Niagara Frontier, 1812–1814, Vol. 3* (Welland, ON: Tribune Press, 1896–1908), 63.
2. Alexander Clark Casselman, *Richardson's War of 1812* (Toronto: Historical Publishing Program, 1902), 15.
3. LAC, Duncan Clark Papers, Vol. 3, 66–67, MG19.A39, Vol. 3, 66–67.
4. *Ibid.*
5. *Ibid.*
6. Casselman, *Richardson's War of 1812*, 104–06.
7. Cruikshank, *The Documentary History of the Campaigns upon the Niagara Frontier, 1812–1814, Vol. 4*, 246.

3: Forming the Incorporated Militia

1. LAC, Pre-Confederation Records, RG9.IB1, Vol. 2.
2. *Ibid.*
3. *Ibid.*
4. *Ibid.*
5. *Ibid.*
6. LAC, British Colonial Office, original correspondence, Canada, MG11.CO42, Vol. 695, 76.
7. *Ibid.*, MG11.CO42, Vol. 354, 52.
8. LAC, British Military and Naval Records, RG8-I, Vol. 695, 76.
9. *Ibid.*, Vol. 703, 82.

6: The Niagara Division

1. Cruikshank, *The Documentary History of the Campaigns upon the Niagara Frontier, 1812–1814, Vol. 3*, 294. Letter from General Vincent to Major Simons.
2. Government of the United States, "Causes of the Failure of the Army on the Northern Frontier," Report to the House of Representatives, February 2, 1814, 13th Congress, 2nd Session, Military Affairs, 447. Colonel Burn to Major General Dearborn (extract, Letter No. 2).

3. *Ibid.*, 457. General Lewis to Secretary of War Armstrong.
4. *Ibid.*
5. Detroit Public Library Archives, Kirby Papers.
6. Matilda Ridout Edgar, *Ten Years in Upper Canada in Peace and War, 1805-1815: Being the Ridout Letters, with Annotations by Matilda Edgar: also an Appendix of the Narrative of the Captivity Among the Shawnese Indians in 1788, of Thos. Ridout, Afterwards Surveyor-General of Upper Canada, and a Vocabulary, Compiled by Him of the Shawnese Language* (Toronto: William Briggs, 1890), 204.
7. Cruikshank, *The Documentary History of the Campaigns upon the Niagara Frontier, 1812–1814, Vol. 6*, 234.
8. *Ibid., Vol. 6*, 207–08.
9. Matilda Ridout Edgar, *Ten Years of Upper Canada in War and Peace, 1805–1815*, 185–86.
10. *Ibid.*
11. J. Armstrong, *Notices of the War of 1812, Vol. I* (New York: Wiley & Putnam, 1840), 198–200.
12. Niagara Historical Society Papers, No. 11, 36.
13. LAC, British Military and Naval Records, 1757–1903, RG8-1, Vol. 1, 181, 219.
14. *Ibid.*

7: The Kingston Division: Soldier, Builder, or Sailor?
1. LAC, British Military Records, RG5.A1, Vol. 17, 7302.
2. *Ibid.*, RG8-I, Vol. 1203 ½ R, 93.
3. *Ibid.*
4. LAC, British Military Records, 1757–1903, RG8-I, Vol. 1203 ½ R, 68.
5. LAC, Duncan Clark Papers, MG19.A39, Vol. 3, 166.
6. *Ibid.*
7. *Ibid.*

8: The Prescott Division
1. LAC, Duncan Clark Papers, MG19.A39, Vol. 3, 29.
2. *Ibid.*, MG19.A39, Vol. 3, 35.
3. *Ibid.*, MG19.A39, Vol. 3, 37.
4. *Ibid.*, MG19.A39, Vol. 3, 43.
5. *Ibid.*, MG19.A39, Vol. 3, 44.
6. *Ibid.*
7. *Ibid.*, MG19.A39, Vol. 3, 73.
8. *Ibid.*, MG19.A39, Vol. 3, 75.

9. *Ibid.*, MG19.A39, Vol. 3, 49.
10. LAC, Pre-Confederation Records, Military, RG9.IB7, Vol. 7.
11. LAC, Civil Secretary's Office, Upper Canada Sundries, 1791–1867, RG5.A1, Vol. 17, 7335–337.
12. LAC, Duncan Clark Papers, MG19.A39, Vol. 3, 52.
13. *Ibid.*, MG19.A39, Vol. 3, 86.
14. *Ibid.*, MG19.A39, Vol. 3, 60.
15. *Ibid.*, MG19.A39, Vol. 3, 94.
16. *Ibid.*, MG19.A39, Vol. 3, 95.
17. *Ibid.*
18. *Ibid.*, MG19.A39. Vol. 3, 104.
19. *Ibid.*, MG19.A39. Vol. 3, 108.
20. Transactions of the Royal Society of Canada, Sec. II, Series III, Vol. X, 193.
21. LAC, Duncan Clark Papers, MG19.A39, Vol. 3, 108.
22. *Ibid.*, MG19.A39, Vol. 3, 123.
23. Lt. Colonel Noah Freer, H.Q. Montreal, to Lt. Colonel Pearson, Prescott, October 20, 1813. *Ibid.*, MG19.A39, Vol. 3, 204.
24. Regimental orders, September 29, 1813. *Ibid.*, MG19.A39, Vol. 3, 124.
25. *Ibid.*, MG19.A39, Vol. 3, 125.
26. *Ibid.*, MG19.A39, Vol. 3, 137.
27. *Ibid.*, MG19.A39, Vol. 3, 129.
28. LAC, Pre-Confederation Records, Military, RG9.IB1, Vol. 2.
29. LAC, Duncan Clark Papers, MG19.A39, Vol. 3, 129.
30. *Ibid.*, MG19.A39, Vol. 3, 137.
31. LAC, Duncan Clark Papers, MG19.A39, Vol. 3, 139.
32. John Kilborn, "Accounts of the War of 1812," in T.W.H. Leavitt, *History of Leeds and Grenville Counties from 1749 to 1879* (Brockville:1879), 36.
33. LAC, Duncan Clark Papers, MG19.A39, Vol. 3, 142.
34. *Ibid.*, MG19.A39, Vol. 3, 144.
35. *Ibid.*, MG19.A39, Vol. 3, 153.
36. *Ibid.*, MG19.A39, Vol. 3, 176.
37. LAC, Pre-Confederation Records, Military, RG9.IB1, Vol. 2.
38. LAC, Duncan Clark Papers, MG19.A39, Vol. 3, 169.
39. *Ibid.*, MG19.A39, Vol. 3, 1764.
40. LAC, British Military and Naval Records, 1757–1903, RG8, Vol. 681, 35.
41. F.B. Hough, *A History of St. Lawrence and Franklin Counties* (Albany, NY: Hough, Little & Co., 1853), 55.

42. *Ibid.*

43. LAC, Duncan Clark Papers, MG19.A39, Vol. 3, 187.

44. *Ibid.*, MG19.A39, Vol. 3, 190.

45. *Ibid.*, MG19.A39, Vol. 3, 191.

46. *Ibid.*, MG19.A39, Vol. 3, 192.

47. *Ibid.*

48. LAC, Pre-Confederation Records, Military, RG9.IB7, Vol. 7.

49. *Ibid.*

9: United We Stand on Guard

1. LAC, British Military and Naval Records, 1757–1903, RG8, Vol. 1222, 14.

2. Archives Ontario, Ontario Government Records. Microfilm B91, Chapter 17.

3. Cruikshank, *The Documentary History of the Campaigns upon the Niagara Frontier, 1812–1814, Vol. 9,* 190.

4. LAC, British Colonial Office, Original Correspondence, Canada, MG11.CO42, Vol. 355, 18.

5. LAC, Civil Secretary's Office, Upper Canada Sundries, 1791–1867, RG5.A1, Vol. 19, 1812.

6. LAC, Duncan Clark Papers, MG19.A39, 236; LAC, Pre-Confederation Records, Military, RG9.IB7, Vol. 3; and LAC, British Military and Naval Records, 1757–1903, RG8, Vol. 1708.

7. W. Dunlop, *Tiger Dunlop's Upper Canada.* (Ottawa: Carleton University Press, 1967), 71–72.

8. LAC, Pre-Confederation Records, Military, RG9.IB7, Vol. 3.

9. LAC, Duncan Clark Papers, MG19.A39, Vol. 3, 199.

10. *Ibid.*, MG19.A39, Vol. 3, 200.

11. LAC, Pre-Confederation Records, Military, RG9.IB1, Vol. 3.

12. LAC, Duncan Clark Papers, MG19.A39, Vol. 3, 203.

13. *Ibid.*, MG19.A39, Vol. 3, 201.

14. Cruikshank, *The Documentary History of the Campaigns upon the Niagara Frontier, 1812–1814, Vol. 9,* 190.

15. LAC, British Military and Naval Records, 1757–1903, RG8, Vol. 1222, 60.

16. LAC, Pre-Confederation Records, Military, RG9.IB1, Vol. 3.

17. LAC, British Military and Naval Records, 1757–1903, RG8-I, Vol. 1222, 77.

18. *Ibid.*

19. *Ibid.*, RG8, Vol. 100, 100.

20. LAC, Pre-Confederation Records, Military, RG9.IB7, Vol. 3.

10: The Calm Before the Storm, April–June 1814

1. LAC, Duncan Clark Papers, MG19.A39, Vol. 3, 209.

2. LAC, Pre-Confederation Records, Military, RG9.IB1, Vol. 4.

3. LAC, Duncan Clark Papers, MG19.A39, Vol. 3, 203.

4. LAC, Pre-Confederation Records, Military, RG9.IB1.Vol. 3.

5. *Ibid.*

6. LAC, British Military and Naval Records, 1757–1903, RG8, Vol. 1222, 121.

7. *Ibid.*, RG8, Vol. 1223, 24.

8. LAC, Duncan Clark Papers, MG19.A39, Vol. 3, 230.

9. *Ibid.*, MG19.A39, Vol. 3, 237.

10. *Ibid.*, MG19.A39, Vol. 3, 238.

11. LAC, Pre Confederation Records, Military, RG9.IB1, Vol. 5.

11: Preparing for Action

1. Cruikshank, *The Documentary History of the Campaigns upon the Niagara Frontier, Vol. 1,* 28–30.

2. LAC, Pre-Confederation Records, Military, RG9.IB3, Vol. 2, 120.

3. LAC, British Military and Naval Records, 1757–1903, RG8-I, Vol. 100, 152.

4. LAC, Pre-Confederation Records, Military, RG9.IB1, Vol. 3.

5. LAC, British Military and Naval Records, 1757–1903, RG8-I, Vol. 100, 162.

12: The Affair of the Mess Dinner

1. LAC, Pre-Confederation Records, Military, RG9.IB1, Vol. 3.

2. *Ibid.*, RG9.IB1, Vol. 3.

3. *Ibid.*, RG9.IB3, Vol. 3.

4. *Ibid.*

5. *Ibid.*, RG9.IB1, Vol. 3.

6. *Ibid.*, RG9.IB1, Vol. 3.

7. *Ibid.*

8. Robert I. Warner, "Memoirs of Capt. John Lampman and His Wife Mary Secord," *Welland County Historical Society, Papers and Records,* Vol. 3 (1927), 126–31.

13: The Invasion Begins

1. Winfield Scott, *Memoirs of Lieut. General Scott* (Sheldon & Co., 1869), 129.

2. W.C.H. Wood, Select British Documents of the War of 1812, Vol. 3 (Toronto: Champlain Society, 1920), 115–16; see also

Cruikshank, *The Documentary History of the Campaigns upon the Niagara Frontier, 1812–1814, Vol. 1,* 32.

14: The King Commands and We Obey: Over the Hills and Far Away

1. LAC, Duncan Clark Papers, Garrison Order, July 3, 1814, MG19.A39, Vol. 3, 254.
2. Warffe Diary, July 6, 1814, Burton Historical Library, Detroit, Michigan.
3. Archives Ontario, Henry Ruttan Papers, MS74.R5.
4. Warffe Diary, July 6, 1814.
5. *Ibid.*, July 8, 1814.
6. *Ibid.*
7. Archives Ontario, Henry Ruttan Papers, MS74.R5.
8. *Ibid.*
9. *Ibid.*
10. *Ibid.*
11. LAC, Archibald McLean's Papers, MG24.13, Vol. 9.
12. LAC, Pre-Confederation Records, Military, RG9.IB7, Vol. 4.
13. Archives Ontario, Henry Ruttan Papers, MS74.R5.
14. LAC, Archibald McLean Papers, MG24.I3, Vol. 9.
15. LAC, British Military and Naval Records, 1757–1903, RG8-I, Drummond Letterbook, 170.
16. LAC, Duncan Clark Papers, MG19.A39, Vol. 3, 261.
17. LAC, British Military and Naval Records, 1757–1903, RG8-I, Vol. 387, 46.

15: Joining the Light Brigade

1. LAC, Duncan Clark Papers, MG19.A39, Vol. 3, 259.
2. Warffe Diary, July 16, 1814, Burton Historical Library, Detroit, Michigan.
3. *Ibid.*, July 18, 1814.
4. Cruickshank, *The Documentary History of the Campaigns upon the Niagara Frontier, 1812–1814, Vol. 1,* 72.
5. Warffe Diary, July 20, 1814.
6. LAC, British Military and Naval Records, 1757–1903, RG8-I, Vol. 684, 169.

16: Marching into Battle

1. LAC, Duncan Clark Papers, MG19.A39, Vol. 3, 263.
2. Warffe Diary, July 24, 1814.

17: The Battle of Lundy's Lane, July 25, 1814

1. LAC, Duncan Clark Papers, MG19.A39, File 1.
2. John Kilborn, "Accounts of the War of 1812," in T.W.H. Leavitt, *A History of Leeds and Grenville Counties from 1749 to 1879* (Brockville: 1879), 70.
3. LAC, Duncan Clark Papers, MG19.A39, File 1.
4. Leavitt, *History of Leeds and Grenville Counties,* 70.
5. *Ibid.*
6. William "Tiger" Dunlop, *Recollections of the American War* (Ottawa: Carleton University Press, 1967), 72.
7. Leavitt, *History of Leeds and Grenville,* 70.
8. LAC, Duncan Clark Papers, MG19.A39, File 1.
9. Warffe Diary, July 25, 1814.
10. T.W.H. Leavitt, *History of Leeds and Grenville Counties,* 70.
11. *Ibid.*
12. Lieutenant Clark, No. 7 Company. LAC, Duncan Clark Papers, MG19.A69, File 1.
13. *Ibid.*
14. Jacob Brown, "Memoranda of Occurrences and Some Important Facts Attending the Campaign on the Niagara," original hand-written manuscript held in William R. Perkins Library, Duke University, North Carolina. Copy in author's collection.
15. *Ibid.*
16. Thomas Jesup, "Memoir of the Campaign on the Niagara," original hand-written manuscript, unknown provenance. Copy in author's collection.
17. E.A. Ripley, *Facts Relative to the Campaign on the Niagara in 1814* (Boston, MA: Patriot Office, 1815), 13.
18. Brown, "Memoranda of Occurrences," 20.
19. *Ibid.*
20. *Ibid.*
21. Henry Ruttan, *Reminiscences of the Hon. Henry Ruttan: Loyalist Narratives from Upper Canada,* Toronto: Champlain Society, 1946, 310.
22. LAC, Pre-Confederation Records, Military, Lampman, RG9. IB1, Vol. 3.
23. Brown, "Memoranda of Occurrences," 22.
24. LAC, Duncan Clark Papers, MG19.A69, File 1.
25. Jesup, "Memoir of the Campaign on the Niagara."
26. Lieutenant Clark, No. 7 Company. LAC, Duncan Clark Papers, MG19.A69, File 1.

27. *Ibid.*

28. David B. Douglass, "An Original Narrative of the Niagara Campaign in 1814," *The Historical Magazine,* Vol. II, Third Series (1873), 17. Published by the Buffalo and Erie Historical Society.

29. Brown, "Memoranda of Occurrences," 20.

30. LAC, Duncan Clark Papers, MG19.A69, File 1.

31. LAC, British Military and Naval Records, 1757–1903, RG8-I, Vol. 1219, 265.

32. LAC, Pre-Confederation Records, Military, RG9.IB7, Vol. 1, July 27, 1814.

18: The Morning After

1. LAC, Duncan Clark Papers, MG19.A69, File 1.

2. LAC, Pre-Confederation Records, Military, Lampman, RG9. IB1, Vol. 3.

3. Brown, "Memoranda of Occurrences," 25.

4. T.W.H. Leavitt, *A History of Leeds and Grenville Counties from 1749 to 1879,* 71.

5. Warffe Diary, July 26, 1814.

19: The Siege of Fort Erie

1. Lilly Library, Indiana University, Bloomington Indiana. Letter from J. Hindeman to an unnamed individual. Partial photocopy of an original handwritten manuscript. Photocopy in author's collection.

2. LAC, British Military and Naval Records, 1757–1903, RG8-I, Vol. 85, 76.

3. *Ibid.*, RG8-I, Vol. 1219, 270.

4. *Ibid.*

5. LAC, British Military and Naval Records, 1757–1903, Drummond Letterbook, RG8-I, 182.

6. LAC, British Military and Naval Records, 1757–1903, RG8-I, Vol. 1219, 277.

7. *Ibid.*, Vol. 1219, 273.

8. LAC, Duncan Clark Papers, MG19.A39, Vol. 3, 277.

9. LAC, Pre-Confederation Records, Military, RG9.IB1, Vol. 3, 204.

10. Dunlop, *Recollections of the American War,* 60–61.

11. LAC, Pre-Confederation Records, Military, RG9.IB7, Vol. 3.

12. Dunlop, *Recollections of the American War,* 62.

13. LAC, Pre-Confederation Records, Military, RG9.IB4, Vol. 1.

20: Strengthening the Chippawa Line

1. LAC, British Military and Naval Records, 1757–1903, RG8-I, Vol. 685, 168.

2. *Ibid.*, Vol. 685, 288.

3. Women's Canadian Historical Society of Toronto Papers, Jarvis Papers, Transaction No. 5, 1902, 8.

4. LAC, British Military and Naval Records, 1757–1903, RG8-I, Vol. 686, 1.

5. Women's Canadian Historical Society, Jarvis Papers.

6. LAC, British Military and Naval Records, 1757–1903, RG8, Vol. 686, 13.

7. LAC, British Colonial Office, Original Correspondence, Canada, Drummond to Prevost, October 18, 1814, MG11. CO42, Vol. 355, 169.

8. LAC, British Military and Naval Records, 1757–1903, RG8-I, Vol. 1219, 3078.

21: Winter Quarters and a New Year's Resolution

1. LAC, British Military and Naval Records, 1757–1903, RG8-I, Vol. 703E, 68–72.

2. *Ibid.*, RG8-I, Vol. 703E, 81.

3. *Ibid.*, RG8-I, Vol. 703E, 86.

4. *Ibid.*, RG8-I, Vol. 703E, 97.

5. *Ibid.*, RG8-I, Vol. 704, 6.

6. LAC, British Colonial Office, Original Correspondence, Canada, MG11.CO42, Vol. 356, 6.

7. *Ibid.*

8. *Ibid.*

22: The Final Parade

1. LAC, British Colonial Office, Original Correspondence, Canada, MG11.CO42, Vol. 356, 33.

2. *Ibid.*, MG11.CO42, Vol. 356, 13.

3. LAC, Duncan Clark Papers, MG19.A39, Vol. 3, 309.

4. *Ibid.*, MG19.A39, Vol. 3, 313.

5. *Ibid.*, MG19.A39, Vol. 3, 312.

6. *Ibid.*, MG19.A39, Vol. 3, 313.

7. Ruttan, *Reminiscences of the Hon. Henry Ruttan,* 318.

8. LAC, Duncan Clark Papers, MG19.A39, Vol. 3, 322.

9. *Ibid.*

10. LAC, Duncan Clark Papers, MG19.A39, Vol. 3, 318.

11. *Ibid.*, MG19.A39, Vol. 3, 321.

12. LAC, Pre-Confederation Records, Military, RG9.B7, Vol. 34, 470.

23: Postwar Aftermath

1. *Illustrated Historical Atlas of the Counties of Frontenac, Lennox, and Addington* (Toronto: J.H. Meachan & Co., 1878), 9.
2. LAC, Duncan Clark Papers, MG19.A39, File 3, P326; and Women's Canadian Historical Society of Toronto, Jarvis Papers, 19–20.
3. Archives Ontario, Strachan Papers, MS 35, 1.
4. Ernest Cruikshank, "A Memoir of Colonel the Honourable James Kerby," *Welland County Historical Society, Papers and Records,* No. 4 (1931) 17–37.
5. *Ibid.*
6. *Ibid.*
7. *Ibid.*
8. LAC, Duncan Clark Papers, MG19.A39, Vol. 3, 329.
9. *Illustrated Historical Atlas of Frontenac, Lennox, and Addington Counties,* 9.

Appendix B: Uniforms and Clothing

1. LAC, British Military and Naval Records, 1757–1903, RG8-I, Vol. 30, 130–32.
2. *Ibid.,* RG8-I, Vol. 1172.
3. *Ibid.,* RG8-I, Vol. 1218, 250–52.
4. *Ibid.,* RG8-I, Vol. 116, 304.
5. LAC, Commissariat Department, Miscellaneous Records, 1809–1814, MG13.WO62, Vol. 44.
6. LAC, British Military and Naval Records, 1757–1903, RG8-I, Vol. 1168, 225.
7. *Ibid.,* RG8-I, Vol. 668B, 99.
8. *Ibid.*
9. *Ibid.*
10. *Ibid.,* RG8-I, Vol. 1220, 73.
11. *Ibid.* Military Secretary's Office to Lieutenant Colonel Nichol, December 22, 1812.
12. *Ibid.,* RG8-I, Vol. 1220, 83.
13. *Ibid.*
14. LAC, Pre-Confederation Records, Military, RG9.IB7, Vol. 34.
15. *Ibid.*

16. *Ibid.*
17. LAC, British Military and Naval Records, 1757–1903, RG8-I, Vol. 1227, 11.
18. LAC, Pre-Confederation Records, Military, RG9.IB7, Vol. 1203½ M, 57.
19. *Ibid.,* RG9.IB7, Vol. 2.
20. LAC, British Military and Naval Records, 1757–1903, RG8-I, Vol. 1220, 404.
21. *Ibid.,* RG8-I, Vol. 1221, 71.
22. *Ibid.,* RG8-I, Vol. 1221, 41.
23. *Ibid.,* RG8-I, Vol. 1219, 84; and RG8-I, Vol. 679, 230.
24. *Ibid.,* RG8-I, Vol. 118, 70.
25. *Ibid.,* RG8-I, Vol. 681, 227.
26. LAC, Pre-Confederation Records, Military, RG9.IB7, Vol. 1.
27. LAC, British Military and Naval Records, 1757–1903, RG8-I, Vol. 1219, 181.
28. LAC, Pre-Confederation Records, Military, RG9.IB1, Vol. 3.
29. Toronto Historical Board, Fort York Garrison Account Books.
30. LAC, Duncan Clark Papers, MG19/A39, Vol. 3, 255.
31. LAC, Pre-Confederation Records, Military, RG9/IB1, Vol. 4.
32. *Ibid.,* RG9.IB7, Vol. 2.

Appendix C: Weapons and Accoutrements

1. LAC, British Military and Naval Records, 1757–1903, RG8-I, Vol. 1218, 43.
2. *Ibid.,* RG8-I, Vol. 1218, 47.
3. *Ibid.,* RG8-I, Vol. 1172A.
4. *Ibid.,* RG8-I, Vol. 1218, 311.
5. *Ibid.,* RG8-I, Vol. 386, 75.
6. *Ibid.,* RG8-I, Vol. 1219, 8.
7. *Ibid.,* RG8-I, Vol. 1219, 169.
8. *Ibid.,* RG8-I, Vol. 1212, 416.
9. *Ibid.,* RG8-I, Vol. 1203½A, 58.
10. *Ibid.,* RG8-I, Vol. 1701, 215.
11. *Ibid.,* RG8-I, Vol. 1701, 230.
12. LAC, Archibald McLean Papers, MG24.I3, Vol. 9.
13. LAC, British Military and Naval Records, 1757–1903, RG8-I, Vol. 679, 187; and Cruikshank, *The Documentary History of the Campaigns upon the Niagara Frontier, 1812–1814, Vol.* 6, 111, 122.
14. LAC, British Military and Naval Records, RG8-I, Vol. 1219, 84; and RG8-I, Vol. 679, 230.

15. *Ibid.*, RG8-I, Vol. 387, 107A.

16. *Ibid.*, RG8-I, Vol. 681, 269.

17. LAC, Pre-Confederation Records, Military, RG9.IB7, Vol. 3, 364–65.

18. LAC, British Military and Naval Records, 1757–1903, RG8-I, Vol. 706, 120.

Appendix D: Living in Barracks and on Campaign

1. LAC, British Military and Naval Records, 1757–1903, RG8-I, Vol. 1218, 26.

2. *Ibid.*

3. LAC, British Military and Naval Records, 1757–1903, RG8-I, Vol. 1707, 152.

4. *Ibid.*, RG8-1, Vol. 387, 345.

5. LAC, Civil Secretary's Office, Upper Canada Sundries, 1791–1867, RG5.A1, Vol. 17, 7294.

6. LAC, British Military and Naval Records, 1757–1903, RG8-I, Vol. 7, 7329.

7. *Ibid.*, RG8-I, Vol. 1220, 404.

8. *Ibid.*, RG8, Vol. 1219, 84; and RG8, Vol. 679, 230.

9. *Ibid.*, RG8, Vol. 681, 227.

10. *Ibid.*, RG8, Vol. 118, 15.

11. *Ibid.*, RG8, Vol. 118, 89.

12. *Ibid.*

13. *Ibid.*

Appendix E: Food and Drink: Official Military Rations

1. LAC, British Military and Naval Records, 1757–1903, RG8-I, Vol. 1168, 112.

2. *Ibid.*, RG8, Vol. 1168, 105.

3. *Ibid.*, RG8, Vol. 679, 187; and Cruikshank, *The Documentary History of the Campaigns upon the Niagara Frontier, 1812–1814, Vol. 6*, 111–22.

4. *Ibid.*, RG8-I, Vol. 1219, 84; and *Ibid.*, RG8, Vol. 679, 230.

5. LAC, Duncan Clark Papers, MG19.A39, Vol. 3, 98.

6. *Ibid.*, MG19.A39, Vol. 3, 115.

7. LAC, British Military and Naval Records, 1757–1903, RG8-I, Vol. 681, 227.

8. *Ibid.*, RG8-I, Vol. 1172A, 43–44.

9. *Ibid.*, RG8-I, Vol. 118, 140.

10. *Ibid.*

11. LAC, Duncan Clark Papers, MG19.A39, Vol. 3, 281.

12. LAC, British Military and Naval Records, 1757–1903, RG8-I, Vol. 119, 161.

13. Toronto Historical Board, Fort York Garrison Account Books, Book No. 4.

14. Robert Gourlay, *A Statistical Account of Upper Canada* (London: Simkin and Marshall, 1822), 154–55. Two volumes. Reprinted by the Social Science Research Council of Canada (Toronto: S.R. Publishers Ltd. Johnson Reprint Corp., 1966).

15. *Ibid.*

16. Archives Ontario, Rapelje Papers, MU2099.

17. LAC, Upper Canada Records, 1764–1836, Miscellaneous MG11.Q Series, Vol. 1, 82.

18. LAC, British Military and Naval Records, 1757–1903, RG8-I. WO57, Vol. 15.

Appendix F: Clothing the Regimental Women and Children

1. LAC, British Military and Naval Records, 1757–1903, RG8-I, Vol. 1203, 23.

2. *Ibid.*, RG8-I, Vol. 1706, 3.

3. *Ibid.*

4. LAC, Duncan Clark Papers, MG19.A39, Vol. 3, 230.

5. LAC, British Colonial Office, Original Correspondence, Canada, MG11.CO42, Vol. 351, 22.

6. *Ibid.*, MG11.CO42, Vol. 355, 14.

Appendix G: Sickness and Disability

1. LAC, Pre-Confederation Records, Military, RG9.IB7, Vol. 1.

2. *Ibid.*, and LAC, Duncan Clark Papers, MG19.A39, Vol. 3, 202.

Appendix H: Crime and Punishment

1. LAC, Pre-Confederation Records, Military, RG9.IB4, Vol. 3, 4.

2. LAC, Pre-Confederation Records, Military, RG9.IB1, Vol. 2.

GLOSSARY

Abatis (Abattis): A linear fieldwork obstacle created by piling up felled trees and limbs into a "wall," with the sharpened branches pointing toward the exterior of the position or towards the enemy — the period version of barbed wire.

Ammunition limber: The combination of a large locker used to contain artillery ammunition and a two-wheeled wagon, usually hitched between a team of horses and the artillery piece being served.

Bastion: A multi-sided fieldwork or fortification, usually in the shape of an elongated diamond, projecting from the main wall of a larger fortification to provide enfilade fire on an enemy force.

Battalion company: The body of troops usually forming eight of the ten companies that composed a standard regiment of the British army of the time. These companies were usually located at the centre of a regimental line and fired in unison (volleys) in battle.

Congreve rocket: A form of artillery, each rocket being composed of a long pole (usually over six feet) with a large propellant charge and an explosive warhead attached to the top (similar in appearance to a modern fireworks rocket only much bigger). These rockets, fired individually, produced a vicious back blast from the propellant, and were deadly wherever they landed — the problem being they were also notorious for their wild and varied trajectories.

Demi-bastion: A fieldwork or fortification consisting of a single point and flanking sides attached directly to the adjacent main line of fortifications.

Enfilade firing: Firing on an enemy from the side or flank as opposed to frontal or direct fire.

Fencible militia soldiers (fencibles): The body of men comprising the regiments of colonial full-time troops, listed under the authority of and paid by the British army.

Flank company: The body of elite troops composed of the combined force of a regiment's grenadier and light companies. Usually detached from their regiment for additional/remote duties as advance or rear guards.

Grenadier company: The body of troops that formed an elite unit of trained men within a regiment. These troops could not only perform as battalion troops in line but also act as "shock" troops in an assault. They were usually placed on the right flank of a regimental line and were made up of the taller and heftier individuals, skilled in both volley and independent musketry fire.

Hot shot: Solid iron shot (cannonballs) heated in a furnace before being fired, most often used to ignite fires in wooden buildings or flammable parts of fortifications.

Light company: The body of troops that formed an elite unit of trained men within a regiment. These troops could not only perform as battalion troops in line but also disperse into an extended formation and act as skirmishers, advance guards, and so on. Usually placed on the left flank of a regimental line, they were made up of the more agile and active individuals, skilled in both volley and independent musketry fire.

Other ranks: The body of men of a regiment carrying any rank below that of officer. Usually referring to the cumulative total of sergeants, corporals, and privates, with the occasional exception to include drummers, buglers, and other supernumerary ranks.

Picket(s): A single man or body of men sent or placed in advance of a body of troops, fortification, or important location, and used as a security guard and early-warning of the approaching enemy force.

Prison hulks: Condemned or unseaworthy vessels whose rotting hulls were stripped of their sailing rigging and used as floating prisons.

Prize money: A cash settlement awarded to troops involved in an action resulting in the capture of enemy goods, supplies, or valuables. These items would be assigned a value or sold off and the soldiers would be given a varying proportion of the total according to rank.

Rank and file: The body of men of a regiment making up the line of troops on parade or in battle (usually only including the privates and corporals), the ranks standing shoulder to shoulder, the files one behind the other in a two-deep line formation.

Redan (battery): A fieldwork fortification composed of two lines of earthworks joined at a point to create the shape of a wide *V*, usually used to protect one or more artillery pieces or the front of a strategic location such as a fort's gate.

Regular soldiers (regulars): The body of men comprising the regiments of the full-time British army.

Spike (a gun): The act of disabling an artillery piece by hammering a nail or other similar object into the small touch hole (ignition/firing tube), usually located on the top/back of the cannon's barrel.

Tete-de-pont: An earthwork or fieldwork of varying form and size, dependent on the circumstances of its construction. These works were constructed to guard and protect the end of a bridge from enemy attack and to act as a last line of defence in case of retreat. They were meant to delay the enemy while the bridge was being prepared for destruction, hopefully, once the rearguard had retired.

SELECTED BIBLIOGRAPHY

PRIMARY SOURCES

ARCHIVAL

1. Library and Archives of Canada
   Manuscript Groups (MG)
   - MG10A: U.S. Department of State, War of 1812 Records.
   - MG11(CO42): British Colonial Office, Original Correspondence, Canada.
   - MG11(CO47): Upper Canada Records, 1764–1836, Miscellaneous.
   - MG13 (WO62): Commissariat Dept, Miscellaneous Records 1809–1814.
   - MG19/A39: Duncan Clark Papers.
   - MG24/A9: Sir George Prevost Papers.
   - MG24/A11: Sir George Murray Papers.
   - MG24/A41: Sir Gordon Drummond Letterbook 1813–1815.
   - MG24/G17: Joseph Baker Notebook.
   Research Groups (RG)
   - RG5-A1: Civil Secretary's Office, Upper Canada Sundries, 1791–1867.
   - RG8-I: British Military and Naval Records, 1757–1903.
   - RG9-I: Pre-Confederation Records, Military.
   - RG10: Indian Department Records.
   - RG19/E5A: Department of Finance, War of 1812, Losses Board.

2. Archives Ontario
   - MS35/1: Strachan Papers.
   - MS74/R5: Merritt Papers.
   - MS501: Thorburn Papers.
   - MS58: Band Papers.
   - MS500: Street Papers.
   - MS502/B Series: Nelles Papers.
   - MU572: Duncan Clark Papers.
   - MU2099: A.A. Rapelje Papers.
   - MS519: Joel Stone Papers.
   - MS74.R5: Henry Ruttan Papers.
   - MU2036: Military Records, 1813.
   - Microfilm B91/Reel 1: Table of Statutes, Upper Canada Legislature, 1792–1840.

3. Metro Toronto Reference Library
Hagerman, C.: Journal of Christopher Hagerman.
MacDonell, G.: MacDonell Papers.
Prevost Papers, 7 Vols., S108, Cub 7.

4. Detroit Public Library Archives
Kirby, J.: James Kirby Papers.

5. Burton Historical Library (Detroit IL)
Warffe, A.: Diary of Ensign Warffe.

6. William R. Perkins Library, Duke University (Durham NC)
Brown, J., "Memoranda of Occurrences and Some Important Facts Attending the Campaign on the Niagara." Unpublished manuscript.

7. Lilly Library, Indiana University (Bloomington, ID)
Hindman, J., "Report on the Action at Lundy's Lane." Unpublished manuscript.

8. Toronto Historical Board
Fort York Garrison Account Books, 1814–1815.

9. Buffalo and Erie County Historical Society Archives, A. Conger Goodyear War of 1812 Manuscripts, 1779-1862, Mss. BOO-11.

10. Author's Collection
Jesup, T., "Memoir of the Campaign on the Niagara." Handwritten unpublished manuscript. Author has photocopy, source not known.

SECONDARY SOURCES

EARLY SECONDARY PUBLICATIONS

Armstrong, J. *Notices of the War of 1812*. New York: Wiley & Putnam, 1840.

Boyd, J.P. *Documents and Facts Relative to Military Events During the Late War*. Privately published, 1816.

Brackenridge, Henry. M. *History of the Late War Between the United States and Great Britain*. Cushing & Jewett, 1817.

Cannon, R. *Historical Record of the Eighth or the King's Regiment of Foot*. London, UK: 1844.

_____. *Historical Record of the 1st or Royal Regiment of Foot*. London: 1847.

Chapin, C. *Chapin's Review of Armstrong's Notices of the War of 1812*. Black Rock, UC: privately published, 1836.

Davis, Paris M. *An Authentick History of the Late War Between the United States and Great Britain*. Ithica, NY: Mack & Andrus, 1829.

_____. *The Four Principal Battles of the Late War Between the United States and Great Britain*. Harrisburg, NY: Jacob Baab, 1832.

Douglass, D.B. "The Attack on Fort Erie." *The Portfolio, Naval and Military Chronicle of the United States*, 4th Series, Vol. 1 (February 1816).

Government of the United States. "Causes of the Failure of the Army on the Northern Frontier." Report to the House of Representatives, February 2, 1814, 13th Congress, 2nd Session, Military Affairs.

Gray. C. *Microcosm, or a Picturesque Delineation of the Arts, Agriculture, Manufactures, &c. of Great Britain in a Series of Above a Thousand Groups of Small Figures for the Embellishment of Landscapes: Comprising the Most Interesting Subjects in Rural and Domestic Scenery, in External and Internal Navigation, in Country Sports and Employments, in the Arts of War and Peace. The Whole Accurately Drawn from Nature and Aquatinted by J. Hill to Which Are Added, Explanations of the Plates, and Essays Relating to Their Various Subjects, by C. Gray. Dedicated, by Permission, to the Right Honourable Countess of Hardwicke*. London: William Miller and John C. Nattes, 1808.

Hitsman, J.M. *History of the American War of Eighteen Hundred and Twelve*. Philadelphia, PA: W. McCarty, 1816.

James, W. *A Full and Correct Account of the Military Occurrences of the Late War Between Great Britain and the United States of America*. London: William James, 1818.

Johnson, Frederick H. *A Guide for Every Visitor to Niagara Falls*. Niagara Falls: self-published, 1852.

Lossing, Benson. *Pictorial Field Book of the War of 1812*. New York: Harper and Brothers, 1868.

McCarty, W. *History of the American War of 1812*. Philadelphia, PA: William McCarty & Davis, 1817.

Merritt, William Hamilton. *Journal of Events: Principally on the Detroit & Niagara Frontiers During the War of 1812*. St. Catharines, CW: Canada West Historical Society, 1863.

Morgan, J.C. *The Emigrant's Guide, With Recollections of Upper and Lower Canada During the Late War Between the United States of America and Great Britain*. London: Longman, Hurst, Rees, Orme & Brown, 1824.

O'Connor, T. *An Impartial and Correct History of the War Between the United States of America and Great Britain*. Belfast: Joseph Smyth, 1816. Reprint of the John Low edition, New York, 1815.

Perkins, S. *A History of the Political and Military Events of the Late War Between the United States and Great Britain*. New Haven, CN: S. Converse, 1825.

Porter, R.K. *Military Instructions: Including Each Particular Motion of the Manual and Platoon Exercise; Elucidated with Very Minute Drawings by Mr. R.K. Porter; And Dedicated with Permission to Lieutenant General The Earl of Harrington. By David Roberts, Lieutenant and Acting Adjutant of the First Regiment of Foot Guards*. London: Printed for T. Egerton, at the Military Library, near Whitehall, 1798.

"Proceedings and Debates of the House of Representatives of the United States." 12th Congress, 1st Session (1812). U.S. Government Records.

Ripley, E.A. *Facts Relative to the Campaign on the Niagara in 1814*. Boston: self-published, 1815.

Scott, Winfield. *Memoirs of Lieut. General Scott*. Sheldon & Co., 1864.

Sturtevant, I. "Barbarities of the Enemy Exposed in a Report of the Committee of the House of Representatives of the United States." Self-published in Worcester, Massachusetts, 1814.

Thomson, J.L. *Historical Sketches of the Late War Between the United States and Great Britain*. Philadelphia, PA: Thomas Delsilver, 1816.

Van Rensselaer, Solomon. *A Narrative of the Affair at Queenston in the War of 1812*.

New York: Leavitt, Lord & Co., 1836.

Wilkinson, J. *Diagrams and Plans Illustrative of the Principal Battles of the War of 1812*. Philadelphia: self-published, 1815.

LATER SECONDARY PUBLICATIONS

Buell, W. "Military Movements in Eastern Ontario During the War of 1812." *Ontario Historical Society, Papers and Records*, Vol. 10 (1913) and Vol. 17 (1919).

Carnochan, Janet. "Reminiscences of Niagara and St. David's." Niagara Historical Society, Paper No. 20 (1911).

Cruickshank, Ernest. "The Battle of Fort George." Niagara Historical Society, Paper No. 12, (1912). Reprint by Niagara Historical Society, 1990.

_____. "The Blockade of Fort George." Niagara Historical Society, Paper No. 3, 1898.

_____. "Campaigns of 1812–1814." Niagara Historical Society, Paper No. 9, 1902.

_____. "Documents Relating to the Invasion of the Niagara Peninsula by the U.S. Army." Niagara Historical Society, Paper No. 33, 1921.

_____. "Letters of 1812 from the Dominion Archives." Niagara Historical Society, Paper No. 23, 1913.

_____. "A Memoir of Colonel the Honourable James Kerby, His Life in Letters." Welland County Historical Society, Papers and Records, No. 4, 1931.

_____. "The Siege of Fort Erie." Welland, ON: Tribune Office, 1905. Booklet published by the Lundy's Lane Historical Society of Niagara Falls.

Currie, Hon. James G. "The Battle of Queenston Heights." Niagara Historical Society, Paper No. 4, 1898.

"Documents Relating to the Invasion of the Niagara Peninsula by the United States Army, Commanded by General Jacob Brown in July and August, 1814." Niagara Historical Society, Paper No. 33 (1920).

Douglass, David B. "An Original Narrative of the Niagara Campaign in 1814." *The Historical Magazine.* Vol. II, Third Series (1873). Published by the Buffalo & Erie County Historical Society.

"Family History and Reminiscences of Early Settlers and Recollections of the War of 1812." Niagara Historical Society, Paper No. 28, 1915.

"Historic Houses." Niagara Historical Society, Paper No. 5, 1899.

Kilborn, John, "Accounts of the War of 1812." In Thaddeus W.H. Leavitt. *History of Leeds and Grenville Counties from 1749 to 1879.* Brockville, ON: Recorder Press, 1879.

"Reminiscences of Arthur Galloway." Cornell University Library, Ithaca, NY. New York State Historical Monographs, Historical Literature Collection, Anonymous collection, *circa* 1850.

"Reminiscences of Niagara." Niagara Historical Society, Paper No. 11, 1904.

Severence, F.H., ed. "The War of 1812 on the Niagara Frontier." Buffalo Historical Society Publications, Vol. 29 (1927).

Warner, Robert I. "Memoirs of Capt. John Lampman and His Wife Mary Secord" *Welland County Historical Society, Papers and Records.* Vol. 3 (1927), 126–34.

Wright, Ross Pier, "The Burning of Dover." Unpublished manuscript, 1948.

BOOKS

Adams, Henry. *History of the United States of America During the Administrations of Madison.* New York: Library of America, 1986. Reprint of original 1891 volumes.

Auchinleck, George. *A History of the War Between Great Britain and the United States of America During the Years 1812, 1813 & 1814.* Toronto: Thomas Maclear, 1853. Reprint by Arms & Armour Press and Pendragon House, 1972.

Babcock, Louis L. *The Siege of Fort Erie.* Buffalo, NY: Peter Paul Book Co., 1899.

_____. *The War of 1812 on the Niagara Frontier, Volume 29.* Buffalo, NY: Buffalo Historical Society Publications, 1927.

Benn, Carl. *The Iroquois in the War of 1812.* Toronto: University of Toronto Press, 1998.

Bingham, Robert. W. *The Cradle of the Queen City: A History of Buffalo to the Incorporation of the City, Volume 31.* Buffalo, NY: Buffalo Historical Society Publications, 1931.

Bowler, R. Arthur, ed. *Essays on the War of 1812 and Its Legacy.* Youngstown, NY: Old Fort Niagara Association, 1991.

Brant, Irving, *The Fourth President: A Life of James Madison.* Indianapolis & New York: The Bobbs Merrill Company, 1970.

Casselman, Alexander C., ed. *Richardson's War of 1812*. Toronto: Historical Publishing Co., 1902. Facsimile edition by Coles Publishing Co., Toronto, 1974.

"Contest for the Command of Lake Ontario in 1812 & 1813." Transactions of the Royal Society of Canada, SEC II, Series III, Vol. X.

Cruikshank, Ernest. *The Documentary History of the Campaigns upon the Niagara Frontier in 1812–1814*. Welland, ON: Tribune Press, 1896–1908. 9 volumes.

Dunlop, William. *Tiger Dunlop's Upper Canada*. Ottawa: Carleton University Press, 1967.

Edgar, Matilda Ridout. *Ten Years of Upper Canada in Peace and War, 1805–1815; Being the Ridout Letters, with Annotations by Matilda Edgar; Also an Appendix of the Narrative of the Captivity Among the Shawnese Indians in 1788, of Thos. Ridout, Afterwards Surveyor-General of Upper Canada, and a Vocabulary, Compiled by Him of the Shawnese Language*. Toronto: William Biggs, 1890.

FitzGibbon, Mary A. *A Veteran of the War of 1812: The Life of James FitzGibbon*. Toronto: William Briggs, 1894.

Gayler, Hugh J., ed. *Niagara's Changing Landscapes*. Ottawa: Carleton University Press, 1994.

Gilleland, J.C. *History of the Late War Between the United States and Great Britain*. Baltimore, MD: Schaeffer & Maund, 1817.

Gourlay, Robert. *Statistical Account of Upper Canada Compiled with a View to a Grand System of Emigration*. London: Simpkin and Marshall, 1822. 2 Volumes. Republished by the Social Science Research Council of Canada, S.R. Publishers Ltd., Johnson Reprint Corp. 1966.

Graves, Donald E. *Field of Glory, The Battle of Crysler's Farm, 1813*. Toronto: Robin Brass Studio. 1999.

_____. *Fix Bayonets! A Royal Welch Fusilier at War 1796–1815*. Montreal: Robin Brass Studio, 2006.

_____. *Where Right and Glory Lead! The Battle of Lundy's Lane, 1814*. Toronto: Robin Brass Studio, 1997.

Hitsman, J. Mackay. *The Incredible War of 1812: A Military History*. Toronto: Robin Brass Studio, 1999. Revised edition, updated by Donald Graves.

Hough, Franklin B. *A History of St. Lawrence and Franklin Counties, New York*. Albany, NY: Little & Co., 1853.

Illustrated Historical Atlas of Norfolk County. Toronto: H. Belden & Co., 1877.

Illustrated Historical Atlas of the Counties of Frontenac, Lennox and Addington. Toronto: J.H. Meachan & Co., 1878.

Illustrated Historical Atlas of the Counties of Hastings & Prince Edward. Toronto: H. Belden & Co., 1878.

Illustrated Historical Atlas of the Counties of Lincoln and Welland. Toronto: H.R. Page, 1876.

Illustrated Historical Atlas of the Counties of Northumberland and Durham. Toronto: H. Belden & Co., 1877.

Illustrated Historical Atlas of the Counties of Stormont, Dundas & Glengarry. Toronto: Belden & Co. Toronto, 1879.

Irving, L.H. *Officers of the British Forces in Canada during the War of 1812*. Toronto: Canadian Military Institute, 1908.

Jarvis Papers. Women's Canadian Historical Society of Toronto Papers and Transactions, Transaction No. 5 (1902), 3–9.

Klinck, Carl F. *Journal of Major John Norton*. Toronto: Champlain Society of Canada, 1970. Publication No. 46.

Mackay, J. *The Incredible War of 1812*. Toronto: University of Toronto, 1965.

Malcomson, Robert. *A Very Brilliant Affair: The Battle of Queenston Heights, 1812*. Toronto, Robin Brass Studio, 2003.

_____. *Lords of the Lake: The Naval War on Lake Ontario, 1812–1814*. Toronto: Robin Brass Studio, 1998.

Ruttan, Henry. *Reminiscences of the Hon. Henry Ruttan: Loyalist Narratives from Upper Canada*. Toronto: Champlain Society, 1946.

Stagg, J.C.A. *Mr. Madison's War: Politics, Diplomacy, and Warfare in the Early American Republic 1783–1830*. Princeton, NJ: Princeton University Press, 1983.

Stanley, George F.G. *The War of 1812: Land Operations*. Toronto: Macmillan of Canada and the Canadian War Museum 1983.

Whitehorne, Joseph. *While Washington Burned: The Battle for Fort Erie 1814*. Baltimore, MA: The Nautical and Aviation Publishing Company of America Inc., 1992.

Wood, William C.H. *Select British Documents of the War of 1812*. Toronto: Champlain Society of Canada, 1920. 3 volumes.

INDEX

OF RELATED INTEREST

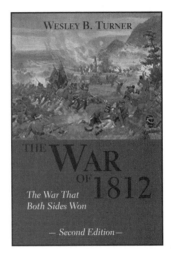

The War of 1812
*The War That Both
Sides Won 2nd Edition*
Wesley B. Turner
9781550023367
$16.99

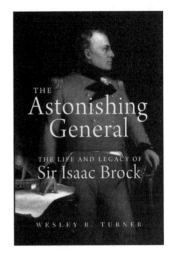

**The Astonishing
General**
*The Life and Legacy of
Sir Isaac Brock*
Wesley B. Turner
9781554887774
$35.00

Tragedy and farce, bravery and cowardice, intelligence and foolishness, sense and nonsense — all these contradictions and more have characterized the War of 1812. The real significance of the series of skirmishes that collectively made up the war between 1812 and 1814 is the enormous impact they have had on Canadian and American views of themselves and of each other. An expanded and updated edition, this investigation of the war for North America unveils new research and archaeological discoveries.

One of the most enduring legacies of the War of 1812 was the creation of heroes and heroines. The earliest of those heroic individuals was Isaac Brock. It's striking how a British general whose military role in that two-and-a-half-year war lasted less than five months became the best known hero, and one revered far and wide.

Available at your favourite bookseller.

DUNDURN
www.dundurn.com

What did you think of this book?
Visit www.dundurn.com for reviews, videos, updates, and more!

Marquis Book Printing Inc.

Québec, Canada
2012